BEYOND CAGES

For all the diversity of views within the animal protection movement, there is a surprising consensus about the need for more severe criminal justice interventions against animal abusers. More prosecutions and longer sentences, it is argued, will advance the status of animals in law and society. Breaking from this mold, Justin Marceau demonstrates that a focus on "carceral animal law" puts the animal rights movement at odds with other social justice movements, and reflects an indefensible support for a system that is inextricably linked to oppression. Animal protection efforts need to move beyond cages and toward systemic solutions if the movement hopes to be true to its own defining ethos of increased empathy and resistance to social oppression. Providing new insights into how the lessons of criminal justice reform should be imported into the animal abuse context, Beyond Cages is a valuable contribution to the literature on animal welfare and animal rights law.

Justin Marceau is a Professor of Law at the University of Denver, Sturm College of Law. His research and teaching focus on criminal law, civil rights and animal protection. He is the is the inaugural chair of the Scholars Committee for the Brooks Institute for Animal Rights Law and Policy, and the 2018 chair of the Animal Law Section of the American Association of Law Schools (AALS).

Beyond Cages

ANIMAL LAW AND CRIMINAL PUNISHMENT

JUSTIN MARCEAU
University of Denver

CAMBRIDGE
UNIVERSITY PRESS

CAMBRIDGE
UNIVERSITY PRESS

University Printing House, Cambridge CB2 8BS, United Kingdom

One Liberty Plaza, 20th Floor, New York, NY 10006, USA

477 Williamstown Road, Port Melbourne, VIC 3207, Australia

314–321, 3rd Floor, Plot 3, Splendor Forum, Jasola District Centre,
New Delhi – 110025, India

79 Anson Road, #06–04/06, Singapore 079906

Cambridge University Press is part of the University of Cambridge.

It furthers the University's mission by disseminating knowledge in the pursuit of
education, learning, and research at the highest international levels of excellence.

www.cambridge.org
Information on this title: www.cambridge.org/9781108417556
DOI: 10.1017/9781108277877

First published 2019

A catalogue record for this publication is available from the British Library.

Library of Congress Cataloging-in-Publication Data
NAMES: Marceau, Justin, author.
TITLE: Beyond cages: animal law and criminal punishment / Justin Marceau,
University of Denver.
DESCRIPTION: Oxford [UK]; New York, NY : Cambridge University Press, 2019.
IDENTIFIERS: LCCN 2018038856 | ISBN 9781108417556 (hardback)
SUBJECTS: LCSH: Animal welfare – Law and legislation – United States. | Animals – Law
and legislation – United States. | Animal welfare – United States. | Punishment – United
States. | BISAC: POLITICAL SCIENCE / Political Freedom & Security / Human Rights.
CLASSIFICATION: LCC KF3841 .M37 2019 | DDC 345.7301/87–dc23
LC record available at https://lccn.loc.gov/2018038856

ISBN 978-1-108-41755-6 Hardback
ISBN 978-1-108-40545-4 Paperback

Contents

Introduction   *page* 1

1   Setting the Stage: How Incarcerating Humans Became a Salient
    Feature of Efforts to Protect Non-Humans   12

    1.1   A Passion for Punishment – A Primer on Criminal Punishment in
          Animal Law   12
    1.2   The Historical Lack of Options   18
    1.3   The Criminal Law As Cudgel in Shaping Public Morals   22

2   Putting Carceral Animal Law in Context: An Overview of the Mass
    Criminalization Problem in the United States   25

    2.1   The Incarceration Epidemic   27
    2.2   Hardships Flowing from Convictions Beyond Incarceration   30
    2.3   Race and Mass Criminalization   39

3   A Descriptive Account of the Carceral Animal Law System   44

    3.1   Widespread Support for Carceral Animal law   44
    3.2   The Rhetoric of Incarceration: Courthouse Advocacy and Public
          Relations Campaigns   49
    3.3   The Substantive Law of Incarceration: More Crimes and
          Increased Sentences   53
    3.4   Structural or Procedural Reforms in the Service of Increased
          Incarceration   63

4   General Critiques of the Carceral Turn in Animal Protection   97

    4.1   The Legislative Cost of Felony Cruelty Laws: The Correlation
          Between Passing Felony Laws and Exempting Agricultural Cruelty   98
    4.2   Incarceration As Ineffectual in Securing Civil Rights: Lessons from
          Tough-on-Crime Policies   110

4.3   Animal Abuse Registries Are Harmful to Animal Protection Efforts   126
4.4   The Principle of Disinterested or Neutral Prosecutors and Animal
      Cruelty Prosecutions   135

5   Race, Mass Criminalization, and Animal Law   151
5.1   Animal Protection Is Perceived As a "White Thing" and That Is
      Relevant to Crime and Punishment   156
5.2   Specific Issues of Race in the Enforcement of Animal Cruelty
      Laws   166

6   Animal Protection and the "Link" Between Animal Abuse and
      Human Violence   193
6.1   An Overview of the Link As a Justification and Explanation for
      Carceral Policies   194
6.2   Overview of the Link Research in the Social Sciences   205
6.3   Critique of the Link As the Talisman and Shibboleth of Carceral
      Animal Law   227
6.4   Prison Is Not the Answer: The Link Data Does Not Support a
      Carceral Solution   236
6.5   Treatment As Opposed to Incarceration?   244
6.6   Final Thoughts on the Link: Critiquing the Link As Entrenching
      the Human/Animal Divide   248

7   Anticipating Challenges to the Critique of Carceral Animal Law   251
7.1   The Absence of Alternatives   252
7.2   The Power of Criminal Law in Shaping Norms and Mainstream
      Support for Prosecutions   258
7.3   Revenge or Retribution and Animal Protection   264
7.4   Why Do Animal Crimes Have to Be the Proverbial Guinea Pig
      for Sentencing Reform?   266
7.5   Incapacitation As the Last-Best Defense of Carceral Animal Law   270

8   Conclusion: Toward a New Research and Advocacy Agenda for
      Animal Protection   273

Index   284

Introduction

All movements seem to start out with a relatively narrow focus, which then widens in response to the recognition of the interconnectedness of oppression.

Sistah Vegan, afterword[1]

The animal protection movement is living out an untenable paradox: motivated by a vision of progressive social reform, while relying on regressive social policy. The animal protection movement's enthusiasm for criminal punishment echoes in some surprising quarters. In his Inaugural Address, President Trump described rampant crime as an "American carnage" that threatened the well-being and safety of all Americans. Attorney General Sessions has also "repeatedly hawked a nationwide crime wave," and claimed that the very "safety of the American people [is] at risk"[2] as a justification for more aggressive sentencing and charging practices. Sessions issued a memo in May 2017 instructing that federal prosecutors are prohibited, in the absence of explicit permission, from pursuing anything other than the "most serious" charges possible in each case.[3] The Brennan Center and numerous civil rights organizations have criticized as anathema to social justice this approach to criminal justice that stokes public fears in order to justify ever harsher criminal regimes. Tough-on-crime polices are a self-fulfilling prophecy because, as one scholar has noted, they are "an experiment that cannot fail – if crime goes down, prisons gain the credit; but if it goes up, we clearly need more of the same

---

[1] Pattrice Jones, *Afterword* to SISTAH VEGAN: BLACK FEMALE VEGANS SPEAK ON FOOD, IDENTITY, HEALTH, AND SOCIETY 187, 188 (A. Breeze Harper ed., 2010). For an even more recent and equally compelling set of observations about the animal protection movement's race and class problems *see* APH KO & SYL KO, APHRO-ISM: ESSAYS ON POP CULTURE, FEMINISM, AND BLACK VEGANISM FROM TWO SISTERS (2017).

[2] The Editorial Board, Opinion, *Donald Trump and the Undoing of Justice Reform*, N.Y. TIMES (Feb. 17, 2018), www.nytimes.com/2018/02/17/opinion/sunday/donald-trump-and-the-undoing-of-justice-reform .html.

[3] Memorandum from the Office of the Attorney General to All Federal Prosecutors: Department Charging and Sentencing Policy (May 10, 2017), www.justice.gov/opa/press-release/file/965896 /download.

medicine whatever the cost."[4] Moreover, tough-on-crime policies are oppressive, discriminatory on racial and class lines, unproven as tools of crime reduction, and strikingly lacking in empathy. Yet this same carceral logic – appealing to mainstream persons by exaggerating the risks of crime and the benefits of incarceration – permeates the thinking of activists, organizations, and commentators in the animal protection movement.

Animal protection groups champion the elimination of systemic violence, and yet it is not uncommon for animal advocates to label the dismissal of criminal charges or short prison sentences in the realm of animal abuse as among the most urgent problems facing the animal protection movement. Leaders of the movement have made clear that carceral animal law[5] polices are a critical strategic priority. The longstanding motto of one leading organization is fairly representative as a motto for the entire disparate movement, "Abuse an animal – Go to Jail!" In 2018, light sentences or leniency in the application of the criminal law are not just regarded as unfortunate, they are characterized by the leaders of the animal protection movement as, to quote a 2018 fundraising email, "injustices of the highest degree."[6] As another letter to donors explained, with "your support [we can help] . . . lock up animal abusers – and keep both people and animals safe."[7] This book argues that a substantial tempering of the animal protection movement's enthusiasm for criminal punishment is overdue. Perhaps it is possible to move *beyond cages* and toward more systemic solutions. This book is a specific critique of carceral strategies pursued in the name of improving the lives and status of animals; it is also a more

---

[4] David Downes, *The Macho Penal Economy: Mass Incarceration in the United States–A European Perspective*, in MASS IMPRISONMENT: SOCIAL CAUSES AND CONSEQUENCES 51, 57 (David Garland ed., 2001). On the other hand, "[a]ny system of criminal justice that purports to deter this behavior must seek to make it socially unacceptable for any person of any age to engage in animal cruelty." Margit Livingston, *Desecrating the Ark: Animal Abuse and the Law's Role in Prevention*, 87 IOWA L. REV. 1, 60–61 (2001).

[5] Carceral animal law is the notion that increased policing, prosecution, and imprisonment are necessarily a central aspect of ensuring greater status for animals within the legal system. The phrase "carceral animal law" was inspired by commentators who have critiqued what they called carceral feminism. *See generally* Aziza Ahmed, *Trafficked? AIDS, Criminal Law and the Politics of Measurement*, 70 U. MIAMI L. REV. 96, 108–09 (2015); Elizabeth Bernstein, *Carceral Politics as Gender Justice? The "Traffic in Women" and Neoliberal Circuits of Crime, Sex, and Rights*, 41 THEORY SOC'Y 233, 235 (2012) (documenting the rise of the movement and noting its harmony with general, get-tough-on-crime politics of the era); Aya Gruber, *The Feminist War on Crime*, 92 IOWA L. REV. 741, 750 (2007) (describing the feminist criminal law reforms as "a product of conservative tough-on-crime ideology"); Janet Halley, et al., *From the International to the Local in Feminist Legal Responses to Rape, Prostitution/Sex Work, and Sex Trafficking: Four Studies in Contemporary Governance Feminism*, 29 HARV. J. L. & GENDER 335, 337 (2006). *See* Fredrik DeBoer, *Yes, Carceral Feminism Is a Thing*, THE ANOVA BLOG (Oct. 18, 2014), http://fredrikdeboer.com/2014/10/18/yes-carceral -feminism-is-a-thing ("At the end of the most well-intentioned law in the history of laws, there's a cop. That's what we're talking about here. The rest is window dressing."); Victoria Law, *Against Carceral Feminism*, JACOBIN (Oct. 17, 2014), https://www.jacobinmag.com/2014/10/against-carceral-feminism.

[6] Email on file with the author, dated Mar. 13, 2018.

[7] Email on file with the author, dated Mar. 29, 2018.

general case study about the limitations of relying on the criminal law as a vehicle for progressive social reform.

The United States is the world leader in incarceration and it stands as one of the few nations to have ever made it to the "700 club" (700 or more prisoners per 100,000); in Europe there are no nations in the "200 club," and more than half of Europe is not even in the "100 club." As a nation we cage humans at a rate that is 53 percent higher than our closest incarceration rival (Russia).[8] This book challenges the accepted wisdom that efforts to cage ever more humans will lead to greater animal liberation. Social justice and ending oppression for all species requires an interest in reforms that go beyond the cage, and which require departing from the conventional wisdom of mainstream animal protection groups. Such reforms will be difficult for mainstream animal protection groups because, as one scholar has noted, true shifts in policy and behavior are "more evident at the grassroots level than within the high-profile national organizations, where there is greater resistance" to understanding the "interconnectedness of oppression."[9]

To understand the rationale for pursuing criminal punishments as an important part of the animal protection movement's strategy, it is necessary to first appreciate just how divergent, almost to the point of incompatibility, the many strains of animal protection have become. The goals of the groups and persons who wish to reduce or eliminate harm to animals often vary dramatically. For some, protecting companion animals from rogue abusers is the central and defining project of animal protection. The repulsive acts of violence directed toward pets animate this circumscribed interest in companion animal protection. For others, the interest in protecting animals extends beyond these most highly anthropomorphized creatures who share their beds and the label "family,"[10] and includes some of the other most charismatic creatures on earth, such as chimpanzees, cheetahs, rhinos, lions, elephants, and whales. Persons committed to the protection of charismatic wildlife recoil at images of trophy hunting or whaling, and often appreciate the connection between humans and animals in general, but may not oppose in principle zoos or aquariums, dog races and circuses, or the use of billions of animals for food each year. Polling data tends to suggest that a majority of Americans share this highly compartmentalized view of animals – they love many like family, and take for granted the instrumental value of others in satiating dietary cravings, amusement, or research interests. A Gallup poll from 2015 finds that a full one-third of Americans believe animals should have "the same rights as people," and nearly two-thirds of

---

[8] AMERICAN EXCEPTIONALISM IN CRIME AND PUNISHMENT 3 (Kevin R. Reitz ed., 2018).

[9] JONES at 188.

[10] *More Than Ever, Pets Are Part of the Family*: 2015, HARRIS POLL at www.prnewswire.com/news-releases /more-than-ever-pets-are-members-of-the-family-300114501.html (A 2015 Harris poll of 2,225 adults of whom 1,323 had a pet; 95 percent of pet owners consider their pets to be a part of the family); *How People View Their Pets*: 2016, FORTUNE & MORNING CONSULT at http://fortune.com/2016/09/07/pets-are -basically-people/ (A 2016 Fortune-Morning Consult Poll of 2,002 voters of whom 61 percent were pet owners; 76 percent of respondents classified their pets as "beloved members of the family").

Americans support "some rights" for animals, yet more than 90 percent of Americans consume animal products, per capita meat consumption climbs every year to a new record level,[11] the popularity of zoos and animals used in sports and entertainment seems to remain high, and concerns about the use of animals in research seem to be minimal. Animal protection, then, like many features of the human experience, can be shaped by motivated cognition – humans seek protection for animals and pursue policies to protect animals unless and until those policies or norms conflict with existing habits or practices.[12] The western repulsion against dog meat and the consistent (even growing) love for bacon or other pig meat is a microcosm of this motivated cognition. Indeed, research has shown that "while evidence for an animal's mind is generally persuasive [evidence of moral standing], it is not compelling when a person is motivated to defend their use of the animal as food."[13]

Still other persons and groups are concerned about all animals, and not just particularly beloved pets and wild animals. Yet even among those whose concern extends to the less anthropomorphically appealing species, there are notable differences in the chosen means for protecting animals, and perhaps even the goals. Persons concerned with *animal welfare* focus their efforts on ensuring the "humane" treatment of animals, but not the elimination of instrumental uses of animals in the service of human desires. The animal welfare orientation does not seek to eliminate factory farms or zoos, but rather to make them more humane; it is a pursuit not of the elimination but the enlargement of the cages. In 2018, almost no one openly opposes animal welfare protections in the abstract. Even the most persistent defenders of factory farms and research or cosmetic testing facilities acknowledge the abstract notion that, in general, "animals ought to be treated 'humanely' and not subject to 'unnecessary' suffering."[14] Of course, people may disagree about the details of what animal welfare requires in a particular context – industry groups still routinely and vigorously oppose reforms as minimalist as allowing animals such as pigs to live in crates that afford them enough space to turn around. But at the conceptual level, animal welfarists have achieved a victory of almost universal proportions. But it is a pyrrhic victory; the same sort of hollow victory that Edward Bonilla-Silva has identified in the ascendance of colorblindness as America's prevailing racial ideology – "Racism without Racists." Bonilla-Silva has documented that only the most

[11] Catey Hill, *This Chart Proves Americans Love Their Meat*, MARKETWATCH (Dec. 1, 2016), www .marketwatch.com/story/this-chart-proves-americans-love-their-meat-2016-08-15.

[12] For a fascinating study showing this effect, *see* Jared Piazza & Steve Loughan, *When Meat Gets Personal, Animal Minds Matter Less: Motivated Use of Intelligence Information in Judgments of Moral Standing*, 7 SOC. PSYCHOL. & PERSONALITY SCI. 1, 1–8 (2016). The authors find that intelligence plays a critical role in determining the moral status of animals, *unless* the information showing intelligence is "self-relevant." That is, people "disregard relevant information (e.g., intelligence) when it applies to an animal that they consume, and thus avoid a potential moral dilemma." The authors demonstrate through a series of studies that the unique moral status of dogs in society is a product of motivated cognition.

[13] *Id.* at 1–8.

[14] Gary L. Francione, *Animal Rights and Animal Welfare*, 48 RUTGERS L. REV. 397, 398 (1996).

fringe Americans now believe in overt racial discrimination and white supremacy. And yet, racism continues to be a major problem in America. Similarly, very few Americans would seek out the label "animal abuser," or glorify the suffering of animals, and yet the practices and institutions that cause the most suffering to animals on a daily basis persist, and some are even growing. The criminal law entrenches rather than challenges this status quo.

By contrast, a distinct group of people associated with animal rights or liberation share an orientation toward protecting animals by recognizing them as distinct living creatures who are entitled to respect and protection for their own sake. Persons associated with the animal rights as opposed to animal welfare ideology tend to reject the use of animals for the instrumental benefit of humans. The *rights* sought for animals, according to this view, are not the rights to vote or drive, or even to healthcare or participation in contemporary human society, but rather a right to be left alone, and to exist with relative autonomy and self-determination. As a practical matter, animal rights lawyers are only seeking, to date, the "liberation" from inhumane confinement of certain creatures with particularly developed and scientifically established concep-tions of autonomy and self-determination.[15]

The widely varying conceptions of the protections deserved by animals make describing a singular animal protection movement impossible. There is no mono-lithic animal rights or animal protection platform. The orientation and long-term goals evolve over time, vary by group, and even within groups. This book's use of the phrase "animal protection" throughout is meant as an imperfect shorthand for the disparate groups and philosophies that comprise a vast and multifaceted movement. As relevant to this project, persons interested in animal protection are understood to share an interest in reducing the amount of harm suffered by animals, both ones individually identified and animals as a group. Certainly, many animal protection advocates might want more than a reduction in harm – that is, they seek to influence dietary choices and abolish many, or even all institutions that exploit animals. And others who consider themselves interested in animal protection might really only care about select species, or animals they have a personal connection with. But for purposes of this book, the common denominator – from those who merely regard their dogs as family, to the welfarists, to the animal rights people – is a sincere desire to improve the lives of (some or all) animals by reducing the amount of suffering and harm they endure.

Starting from the premise that animal protection scholars and advocates are seeking a net reduction in the total amount of harm suffered by animals, this book interrogates one of the movement's chosen tactics for pursuing this strategy: criminal punishment. Does the increased criminalization of animal cruelty – more crimes,

---

[15] JANE GOODALL, *Forward* to STEVEN M. WISE, RATTLING THE CAGE: TOWARD LEGAL RIGHTS FOR ANIMALS ix, ix-vi (2000).

more enforcement, higher penalties, deportations, and offender registries, among other mechanisms – serve the goal of improving the status of animals in the legal system and reducing their suffering? Alternatively, does incarcerating those who harm animals serve critical human interests in keeping society safe from people who would progress to hurt humans? Are animals or humans better off because of the movement's pursuit of criminal punishment, or instead are neither truly benefitted?

The punitive war on animal cruelty is a dead-end. The seeming victories of the animal protection movement in the realm of individual criminal punishment are a mirage. As Aya Gruber has insightfully observed in the context of women's equality, tethering an interest in rights or equality to the "crime victims' (perceived) interests in retribution" is a fool's errand, more likely to impede than to advance a social movement.[16] Carceral victories do not meaningfully enhance the protection of animals, they do not make humans safer, and the efforts to align the movement, at least at a conceptual level,[17] with the policies and logic of mass criminalization, come at a cost. Propagating the dehumanizing violence of incarceration is not a viable solution to the inhumane treatment of animals. Such a view of the movement – that incarcerating rogue animal abusers will dislodge longstanding social norms about animals – is empirically unfounded and conceptually dangerous. Under this approach the reduction of the suffering of animals is something of a zero-sum game where the increased status of animals is in tension with a less punitive, less carceral approach to criminal justice. Creating the appearance of such a tension is untenable for a group that wants to be perceived as a burgeoning civil rights movement. It is also in tension with creative, radical advocacy within the movement. As one well-established figure explained, anonymously in an interview with me, "we are constantly looking over our shoulders to consider what prosecutors will think of us," and the effect is to stifle some creative or avant-garde advocacy.

The animal protection movement – on an organizational and individual level – regard the fight to secure protections for animals as a civil rights issue. Analogies to women's rights, LGBTQ legal victories, and even the abolition of slavery and the fight against racism are common tropes. But is the movement sincerely interested in civil rights and broad social change? Incarceration is a most unlikely ally for a movement that might earnestly desire far-reaching social reform. Never has a social change or civil rights cause been so thoroughly immersed in the coercive, prosecutorial arm of the State. Indeed, the animal protection movement's commitment to ever harsher criminal punishments and more aggressive enforcement of the criminal law may serve as a case study for understanding how other movements should conceive of their relationship with the carceral state. An alliance with the

---

[16]   Aya Gruber, *A Provocative Defense*, 103 CAL. L. REV. 273, 277 (2015).

[17]   Some may argue that the concern is more conceptual than pragmatic, because it is so rare that a harsh penalty is imposed for animal cruelty. The aspirations and goals of a movement, however, should be taken seriously, and are subject to critique. The movement cannot defend its carceral priorities and then disclaim them as irrelevant insofar as they rarely obtain convictions and longer sentences.

mass criminalization movement and the discredited assumptions that more incarceration leads to less violence are not a good fit for radical social change.

Central to the view of many people connected with animal protection efforts is
the notion that the aggressive prosecution of someone for animal abuse "sends
a signal to other potential abusers in the community" that violence toward animals
will never be tolerated.[18] Aggressive pursuit of incarceration, one leading animal
protection group has explained, is the "blueprint" for using litigation to advance the
status of animals in the law. But such prosecutions may have exactly the opposite
effect. The conduct targeted by the laws is the rare, socially deviant behavior of rogue
animal abusers (mostly companion animals). The ASPCA, for example, has deemed
the production of foie gras to constitute animal cruelty, and yet the organization
leaves unhindered (and unprosecuted) the nation's largest corporate producer of
foie gras whose operations are less than a hundred miles from the ASPCA's head-
quarters in New York. Foie gras prosecutions, the organization seems to conclude,
do not raise money the way that commercials about neglected pets might. More
generally, the enforcement of cruelty laws against individual persons does not trigger
positive changes in social attitudes toward animals and may actually distort the
message that the suffering of all animals matters by reinforcing the dominant view of
most Americans that they are compassionate to animals, and mindful of the need to
reduce their suffering. Cruelty prosecutions allow for a collective transference or
displacement of guilt from mainstream society onto the "other," the socially deviant
animal abuser. As Professor Sherry Colb has observed, it is the lack of personal
sacrifice and the consistency with status quo values, not an evolving social consensus
about animal protection, that explains "why so many people do support anti-animal-
cruelty legislation."[19] Caging cat abusers is much more acceptable than confronting
zoos, much less factory farms.

A failure to imprison one who abuses an animal, under existing thinking, is
a failure to recognize animals as deserving of legal consideration. If we don't punish
(and punish severely) the human who harms animals, regardless of race, age, socioeconomics, or mental health, then we devalue the non-human animal. To imagine
that an animal abuser should get treatment, community service, or strict probation
terms instead of incarceration is regarded as tantamount to disrespecting the entire
animal rights agenda. Even to suggest that one need not be deported from this
country for a prior act of animal mistreatment is regarded as untenably soft-on-
animal-crime. Anything short of maximalist punishments are derided as a "slap on
the wrist," and fundraising and outreach efforts have consistently reiterated the

[18] *No Boundaries for Abusers: The Link Between Cruelty to Animals and Violence Toward Humans*,
ANIMAL LEGAL DEF. FUND, http://aldf.org/resources/when-your-companion-animal-has-been-harmed
/no-boundaries-for-abusers-the-link-between-cruelty-to-animals-and-violence-toward-humans   (last
visited Apr. 23, 2016).

[19] *See e.g.*, Sherry F. Colb, *Whether or Not to Prosecute Animal Cruelty*, DORF ON LAW (Jan. 21, 2015),
www.dorfonlaw.org/2015/01/whether-or-not-to-prosecute-animal.html.

theme to the point that increased criminalization has emerged as a reflexive dogma of the movement. There may be those who are skeptical of this trend, or conflicted about the value of incarceration as a solution to the suffering of animals, but their voices are not part of the academic commentary, much less the blog posts and outreach and press campaigns of animal protection groups.

To date, there has been little publicly vocal opposition, much less reasoned debate about the value of using the criminal law and its punitive power as a central legal tool in service of animal protection.[20] Instead, aggressive criminal enforcement or the lack thereof is one of the most salient themes in animal law. Some of the most important figures in the movement regard aggressive criminal prosecutions as one of the defining elements of animal protection. This book is the first comprehensive effort to subject the vast carceral priorities of animal advocates to scrutiny. By exposing the breadth of the criminal justice efforts sought by animal advocates, and juxtaposing the carceral "successes" of the movement with the well-documented reality that by the turn of this century our "justice system was [already] the harshest in the history of democratic government,"[21] it is possible to better contextualize the criminalization goals of animal protection scholars and advocates. In the social sciences and criminal law literature it is no longer seriously disputed that longer sentences and more punishment often produce criminogenic consequences; indeed, there is a growing body of literature taking stock of the fact that the public's "self-interest" in safety, security, and a thriving community is best served by having lower incarceration rates and a less punitive justice system.[22] These insights have not been infused into the thinking or strategies of many animal protection advocates.

The point is not that animal abuse should be decriminalized; indeed, complete decriminalization would likely be a mistake.[23] However, lobbying and litigating for ever more severe criminal sanctions is not an obvious benefit to the long-term goals of the animal protection movement. Animal protection scholars and organizations devoting resources to the punishment of animal cruelty will likely enjoy a short-term form of masculine[24] (or vengeance-based) satisfaction with each criminal

[20] A notable exception is Wayne Pacelle, the President and CEO of the Humane Society of the United States (HSUS), who wrote a blog post questioning the utility of animal abuse registries. Wayne Pacelle, *Reservations About the Animal Abuse Registry*, HUMANE SOC'Y U.S.: A HUMANE NATION (Dec. 3, 2010), http://blog.humanesociety.org/wayne/2010/12/animal-cruelty-registry-list.html (last visited Jan. 22, 2018).
[21] WILLIAM STUNTZ, THE COLLAPSE OF AMERICAN CRIMINAL JUSTICE 3 (2011).
[22] PAUL BUTLER, LET'S GET FREE: A HIP-HOP THEORY OF JUSTICE 29–30 (2009) (making the case that less punitive polices and policing are in the public interest). *See also id.* at 13 ("No democratic society can incarcerate such a large fraction of its poor population and retain the goodwill of that population."); Jeffrey Fagan & Tracey L. Meares, *Punishment, Deterrence and Social Control: The Paradox of Punishment in Minority Communities*, 6 OHIO ST. J. CRIM. L. 173 (2008).
[23] Existing research shows that criminalization of certain conduct does lead to a decrease in the prevalence of that conduct.
[24] For a well-done discussion of the problem of male dominance and control in the animal protection movement, *see* EMILY GAARDER, WOMEN AND THE ANIMAL RIGHTS MOVEMENT (2011).

punishment victory, but the long-term prognosis is much less clear. It turns out that a punitive, carceral form of animal law is not good for animals, and it may not even be good for human safety.

Chapter 1 provides an overview of the history and conceptual origins of the pro-incarceration tendencies that exist within the modern animal protection movement. Advocates who have adopted a highly punitive approach to protecting animals have not done so in a world of robust, alternative choices. There is considerable path dependence at play here. More than simple errors and oversight, the attraction to criminal punishment might be charitably viewed as an act of desperation by persons and organizations seeking a foothold in a legal world that has proven itself hostile to recognizing animals as deserving of meaningful consideration or protection. It would be facile to suggest that animal advocates have ranked incarceration as their highest priority among a menu of desirable and viable options.

Chapter 2 places the carceral priorities in context, providing a careful overview of the scholarly research on mass criminalization from other fields that have not previously been incorporated into the animal protection debate. To date, animal protection scholars and advocates have not confronted the literature documenting the failures of deterrence and the criminogenic consequences of more aggressive policing and prosecution.

Chapter 3 shifts from the general to the specific, and serves as a detailed typology of the many ways in which animal protection groups pursue more aggressive criminal justice responses to animal cruelty. The efforts are far-reaching, and to those unfamiliar with animal protection's trajectory, quite shocking. The movement has lobbied for more felonies, for aggravated felonies, pursued mandatory minimums, assisted with efforts to deport undocumented persons, and funded prosecutors, to list but a few salient examples. It is fair to describe the animal protection movement as aspiring to be, if it is not already so, a respected arm of governmental efforts to enforce criminal and immigration laws. It is a tough-on-crime movement.

Chapters 4 through 6 and identify a set of overlapping but discrete concerns with the carceral project in animal protection. Chapter 4 applies a critical lens to the overarching efforts at criminalization in this arena and demonstrates the many failures of this project, from a normative and a consequentialist perspective. For example, the success of the movement in obtaining felony cruelty laws masks the fact that many of the same bills that raised animal cruelty to the status of a felony also ushered in exemptions from all cruelty prosecutions for factory farms. Many other discrete objections to the movement's turn to criminal law are also explored in this Chapter.

Chapter 5 takes up the issue of race and the use of criminal law to facilitate the goals of the animal protection movement. This Chapter argues that, even assuming that a more punitive approach to animal law would benefit some pockets of non-human animals by producing less crime, the focus on carceral reforms further isolates the movement from communities of color. An incarceration approach to animal law ignores the growing body of intersectional research in this field and leaves the animal protection movement vulnerable to claims that it would prefer to align itself with a system that has, in the eyes of many scholars, an indelible link to racism, rather than to pursue true anti-oppression reform. The movement risks being viewed as colonialist and racist if its efforts are not more responsive to the realities of tough-on-crime politics. If the animal protection movement truly wants to be an inclusive movement, much less one that has a civil rights orientation and is sensitive to injustice, then pursuing harsher criminal justice responses is a very poor choice of legal tools.

Chapter 6 focuses on the so-called "LINK"[25] as one of the dominant justifications for punishment in modern society. The link, the movement argues, demonstrates the mutuality of advantage in punishing animal abuse more severely – it keeps humans safe. This Chapter suggests that the animal protection movement's use of the link research is critically important to the success of carceral efforts as the link is oftentimes a leading public explanation for the increased criminalization or enforcement of cruelty laws, and yet as this Chapter shows, the movement's deployment of the link research, as with other manipulations of science in the service of criminal prosecutions (such as bogus bite-mark or bullet evidence) is insufficiently nuanced, and misleading. Moreover, even if the strongest versions of the link were accepted as infallible, the notion that human safety is increased by heightened criminal punishment is unsupportable in existing criminology research.

Finally, Chapter 7 briefly anticipates and responds to criticism of the claim that incarceration is not good for humans or animals, and Chapter 8 concludes by offering some tentative possible alternatives for research.

In short, this book breaks from the dominant narrative that a highly carceral approach to animal law is an unmitigated good for the animals it seeks to protect, or good for society, and instead argues that aggressive criminal enforcement should be regarded as a relic of a more desperate, darker period in the history of animal rights. Many in the animal protection movement seek a monumental shift in the social understanding of the human–animal relationship,[26] but such an effort is largely at

[25] The term "LINK" is actually trademarked by the Animal Welfare Institute, and is often written in all-caps. For purposes of this project, the use of the lower-case word "link" means the same thing as the broadly used "LINK" typology. For a discussion of the link's meaning and use in animal protection advocacy, including a summary of the leading research in this field, see Chapter 6.

[26] As Steven Wise has explained in *Rattling the Cage*, there is an impenetrable wall between animal rights and present social understanding: "For four thousand years, a thick and impenetrable legal wall has separated all human from all nonhuman animals. On one side, even the most trivial interests of a single species – ours – are jealously guarded. We have assigned ourselves, alone among the million animal species, the status of 'legal persons.' On the other side of that wall lies the legal refuse of an entire kingdom, not just chimpanzees and bonobos but also gorillas, orangutans, and monkeys, dogs, elephants, and dolphins. They are 'legal things.'" STEVEN M. WISE, RATTLING THE CAGE: TOWARD

odds with efforts to align the movement with the prosecuting power of the State. The money, enthusiasm, and social media attention invested in the carceral project should be redeployed toward efforts that make animal protection more accessible to persons of all classes, cultures, and demographics. The animal protection movement should spend time looking for convergences of interests, affirming the dignity of humans and animals as opposed to inflicting the indignity of incarceration on humans.

Animal rights is often described by its adherents as a philosophy committed to non-violence, an opposition to systemic, institutionalized violence against sentient beings. The support for punitive policies is inconsistent with this philosophy. The critiques that follow are not personal, and they come with a great appreciation for the historically limited set of legal options to protect animals. But the ideology of animal protection via human punishment is dated, inconsistent with a civil rights orientation, and in need of being retired. Perhaps the law's power to effect radical change is limited – maybe the legal system demonstrates the insight of Audre Lourde, that one cannot use the master's tools to destroy the master's house. Or maybe there are ways to infuse legal challenges with a more radical, revolutionary form of advocacy that will shape the media and public narratives, and eventually impact legal norms. Either way, prosecutions are unlikely to be successful tools of radical reform.

LEGAL RIGHTS FOR ANIMALS 4 (2000). *See also*, Steven M. Wise, *Legal Personhood and the Nonhuman Rights Project*, 17 ANIMAL L. 1, 5 (2010) ("I have often written that a high, thick legal wall separates all humans from all nonhumans . . . The goal of the interdisciplinary Nonhuman Rights Project is to change this paradigm.").

Setting the Stage: How Incarcerating Humans Became a Salient Feature of Efforts to Protect Non-Humans

1.1 A PASSION FOR PUNISHMENT – A PRIMER ON CRIMINAL PUNISHMENT IN ANIMAL LAW

Many animal protection groups regard criminal punishment as a valuable way to both advance the status of animals in the law and reduce their overall suffering. One of the founding voices of the movement has put the matter plainly: animal cruelty prosecutions are the "cornerstone of American animal protection."[1] There is an eloquent simplicity to the slogan "Abuse an Animal – Go to Jail." But how was such a simple understanding reached that individual acts of animal abuse are effectively addressed by incarceration? And what makes it obvious to animal protection advocates that seeking lengthy imprisonment terms for human beings engaged in non-institutionalized acts of violence against animals is a net positive for animals? Does this impulse for more rather than fewer cages reflect a heightened sense of empathy for animals, or the absence of empathy for humans? Consider this comment from April 2018 on a social media website hosted by a leading animal protection group, which illustrates the way that a lack of empathy for humans facing incarceration can manifest in classist, othering, even racist policy objectives:

> I think it's about time the human race was more compassionate and started to punish people who think they can abuse animals. We need strick [sic] laws that punish people who inflict abuse on anyone including animals. [W]e are not a third world country where this kind of thing is acceptable. We are supposed to be civilized.[2]

This notion of the animal abuser as the other, the foreigner, and deserving of maximum incarceration is pervasive throughout the comments on websites, and even sometimes in the formal media releases and writings of leading organizations

---

[1] Joyce Tischler, *A Brief History of Animal Law, Part II (1985 – 2011)*, 5 STAN. J. ANIMAL L. & POL'Y 27, 57 (2012).

[2] Debbie Price, Comment on *Bella's Bill*, FACEBOOK (Apr. 1, 2018), www.facebook.com/bellasbill.

in the field. Of course, it is not uncommon for individuals who are emotionally invested in a cause to resort to assuming the utility of criminal punishment, but it is rather remarkable that a movement predicated on notions of empathy holds the prospect of caging humans in such high regard.

Social scientists have come to view animal abusers as people with "an under-developed or compromised capacity to empathize."[3] In summarizing his expert testimony in a criminal case, Randall Lockwood of the ASPCA explained that there is no doubt that "a person's capacity for empathy can be eroded," or that one can have "their empathy beaten or starved out of them." But there is more than a small dose of irony underlying Lockwood's testimony. Lockwood was testifying in support of a prosecutor's motion to force two teens accused of animal cruelty to be tried and sentenced as adults, a practice that many experts and reformers would herald as a social justice abomination. Lockwood's comments are representative of a movement-wide concern about the erosion of empathy among people who harm animals, but the movement appears to be losing sight of whether it is eroding its own empathy by seeking ever more carceral solutions to animal mistreatment. Joi Maria Probus' insights from her essay in *Sistah Vegan* about empathy ring true in the criminal punishment context too: a "lack of empathy is a pathway to the atrocities committed against the oppressed, and in most instances is a justification for the perpetrators."[4]

In rejecting comparisons between human prisoners and animals, the animal advocate will frequently quip that the animals are innocent and beautiful, whereas the incarcerated human is a criminal, even a felon, convicted of cruelty. But this rejoinder is superficial if one contemplates what empathy – and its command to appreciate the circumstances of another – really requires. The movement frequently talks about the power of socialization and enculturation in eroding empathy and therefore providing a framework for understanding how certain people harm animals. Children have to be socialized to disregard the suffering of many animals. But the movement apparently believes enculturation is a one-way street to incarceration. The movement balks, for example, at the idea that animal abuse might be mitigated or treated as less than an act of utter free will; the defendant's upbringing or culture or other mitigating factors that might militate in favor of a reduced sentence are treated as irrelevant.[5] Likewise, leading organizations glamorize prosecutions in publicity surrounding carceral efforts, seemingly heedless of the fact that they may be enculturating the movement's members to view empathy as irrelevant to human punishment.

[3] Lacey Levitt et al., *Criminal Histories of a Subsample of Animal Cruelty Offenders*, 30 AGGRESSION & VIOLENT BEHAV. 48, 55 (2016).
[4] Joi Maria Probus, *Young, Black and Vegan* in SISTAH VEGAN: BLACK FEMALE VEGANS SPEAK ON FOOD, IDENTITY, HEALTH, AND SOCIETY 53, 56 (A. Breeze Harper ed.) (2010).
[5] The movement has called such arguments "absurd" and argued that an interest in one's past, including Michael Vick's, is intolerable in considering the severity of a punishment for animal abuse.

While financial data regarding the expenses pursued in the name of carceral animal law are not publicly available, these carceral efforts probably do not receive the lion's share of resources and funding, despite crime and punishment's cornerstone status. It is likely a small but nontrivial percentage of any organization's total budget. But the resources devoted to prosecution are substantial, they appear to be increasing, and they are in tension not only with funding other projects, but with the very strategic goals of a civil rights movement. In expressing its gratitude to the Humane Society for helping them obtain a conviction that was otherwise impossible, a sheriff's office representative recently explained, "I mean it's unbelievable the hours, the work and the . . . money and resources they've put into" supporting prosecutions.[6] Similarly, the Animal Legal Defense says that it "declared war on cruelty in 1994." It did so by "launching a nationwide campaign for stiffer laws, more vigorous prosecution of animal abusers, and making available the tools to win convictions [and longer sentences]." The groups pay for expert witnesses and consulting experts, they draft pleadings, they provide hands-on services to police, and in many organizations the interest in securing convictions is part of the strategic conversation. Litigation that implicates law enforcement or that might attract the ire of prosecutors is disfavored, and potentially subject to a pro-prosecution veto. The details of these arrangements are discussed in Chapter 4.

Even legal interventions that are unrelated to criminal prosecution by groups that are not generally preoccupied with carceral policies – such as the liberation of an individual animal from squalid conditions – will oftentimes be viewed as *more* successful if criminal prosecution occurs as well. The movement seems to believe that the best interventions have, at least as a secondary consequence, the incarceration of one or more humans. PETA's heroic rescue of Nosey the elephant in December 2017 is illustrative. The release of Nosey to a sanctuary was made possible by the sustained and creative litigation of a team of lawyers. For persons concerned with the well-being of captive wildlife, this was a groundbreaking victory. Notably, however, PETA was not content with saving the elephant, and instead, within hours of obtaining the release of the elephant, was working with authorities to ensure the incarceration of the humans responsible for her captivity. Following celebratory pictures of Nosey experiencing freedom in a sanctuary, PETA's website heralded another reason for celebration: "Another victory was achieved . . . when Liebel and his wife, Franciszka, were arrested and charged with cruelty to animals in relation to their treatment of Nosey."[7] Stories of criminal prosecution extend the news cycle and bring a sense of justice and mainstream success to animal protection efforts.

[6] *Partnership with the Humane Society of the United States*, NAT'L SHERIFF'S ASS'N www.sheriffs.org/content/partnership-humane-society-united-states (last visited Apr. 17, 2018).

[7] Katherine Sullivan, *Victory! Nosey the Elephant Will Remain Out of Reach of Abusive Former Handler, Hugo Liebel*, PETA (Jan. 22, 2018), www.peta.org/blog/victory-nosey-the-elephant-remains-out-of-reach-of-abusive-former-handler (posting the mugshots of the persons charged).

Pointing to the share of animal protection budgets that are devoted to prosecution, many will no doubt argue that carceral animal law policies are but a sideshow, a distraction, and not an important part of the movement. The other litigation in support of animals, they could argue, is the centerpiece of animal protection law. But even the legal work that seems most indicative of the animal protection movement's aptitude to be a force for positive social reform for humans and animals is often tainted by the criminal undertones that the movement has gravitated toward. For example, litigation challenging laws suppressing public debate or whistleblowing, such as challenges to so-called Ag-Gag laws (anti-whistleblower laws that apply within the agriculture industry) and agency secrecy, are earning the movement a deserved reputation as a cohort in the fight for social change through civil rights. But these efforts to ensure transparency on factory farms are routinely deployed by the movement as a strategic means of increasing criminal convictions. Animal protection organizations use criminal convictions as a measure of the success of undercover investigations. In affidavits and briefs filed in court in support of challenges to Ag-Gag laws and other anti-transparency measures, animal protection groups have repeatedly invoked the importance of investigations in bringing about the prosecution of employees of the facility. Ag-Gag laws, the movement argues, are an impediment, not primarily to transparency for the sake of public debate, but to transparency in the service of criminal prosecution. Speaking about the specific dangers of Ag-Gag legislation, the Chief Counsel for the Humane Society explained that, without HSUS investigations, there may not be "law enforcement and [prosecutorial] remedial action" against the low-level workers who abused the animals.

The advocacy of Mercy For Animals, a group dedicated to increasing transparency in food production, is particularly striking in this regard. Following the investigation of a Butterball turkey factory farm, Mercy for Animals posted the mugshots of six men of color on their website as way to memorialize and celebrate the success of the investigation. The mugshots serve as trophies or as the proverbial head on a stake for the movement.

Political scientist Timothy Pachirat, who has done his own undercover work in a slaughterhouse, explained, "To me, there is something deeply saddening about the posting of the mug shots of these six minimum-wage job workers on the website of the animal protection organization that took the undercover footage."[8] As of 2018, the mugshots remain prominently displayed on the organization's website. Indeed, the ability to obtain criminal charges against these men was heralded as evidence par excellence that Mercy For Animals' investigations play a pivotal role in animal protection. These investigations, the organization explained, allow law enforcement to "hold people who abuse animals accountable."[9]

---

[8] Timothy Pachirat, Keynote Address at the Humane Society for the United States Taking Action for Animals Conference (July 2014) (cited with permission of the author).

[9] Nathan Runkle, *More Arrests at Butterball for Cruelty to Animals*, MERCY FOR ANIMALS (Feb. 24, 2012), www.mercyforanimals.org/more-arrests-at-butterball-for-cruelty-to-animals.

The celebratory tone of the animal protection movement with regard to criminal prosecution is unsettling in all cases; incarceration is not a desirable end in and of itself. But the Butterball prosecutions pursued by Mercy For Animals are uniquely problematic and illustrative of the scope of the movement's carceral tendencies. Two of the men were charged, not with felony animal cruelty, but with felony identity theft, presumably for using someone else's social security number so that they could pay taxes and gain employment as undocumented immigrants. Animal protection groups purport to give voice to the voiceless, but jubilation over the prospect of incarceration for immigration offenses and support for deportation proceedings has emerged as an accepted part of the fight to protect animals. Hannah Arendt described citizenship as the "right to have rights." Yet these non-citizen men faced felonies for trying to work in this country, and the animal protection movement applauded their incarceration and almost certain eventual deportation.

The movement's support for deportation is not merely rhetorical; groups actively facilitate the work of immigration officials by, among other things, filing briefs in support of deportation. Other leading animal protection organizations have urged deportation for animal abusers and have even remarked that in cases of animal abuse, deportation is insufficient punishment. When a Chinese man who was told by a New York judge that he would be deported as an "extra dose of punishment," and promised "[y]ou will absolutely, positively be deported from the United States," the animal protection movement's reaction focused on his "light" jail sentence.[10]

When it comes to animal abuse, the movement's stance on incarceration and deportation are on-message with Fox News coverage. Fox News and the animal protection movement's press releases shared a similar celebratory tone over recent news that an illegal immigrant would serve between eight and ten years in prison, and then be deported.[11] Even the pervasive support among progressives for so-called sanctuary cities is challenged in the context of animal abusers. In 2018, The New York Post ran a piece criticizing New York City's sanctuary city policy on the grounds that such a policy might result in some animal abusers not being detained by ICE and deported.[12] Moreover, as a recent change.org petition illustrates, the movement's positive view of deportation is not limited to the United States: "People like this [animal abusers] should NOT be allowed to walk free, let alone be allowed to stay in Australia after committing such a disgusting act."[13]

[10] Gabrielle Fonrouge, *Ex-banker Gets Jail, Deportation for Killing Girlfriend's Dog*, N.Y. Post (Feb. 5, 2018), https://nypost.com/2018/02/05/ex-banker-gets-jail-deportation-for-killing-girlfriends-dog.

[11] Pauline Dedaj, *Illegal Immigrant Who Tortured Dog Gets Prison Time, To Be Deported*, Fox News (Mar. 27, 2018), www.foxnews.com/us/2018/03/27/illegal-immigrant-who-tortured-dog-gets-prison-time-to-be-deported.html.

[12] Seth Barron, *As a Sanctuary City, NYC Protects Dog Killers*, N.Y. Post (Feb. 7, 2018), https://nypost.com/2018/02/07/as-a-sanctuary-city-nyc-protects-dog-killers.

[13] Petition, *Harsher Animal Cruelty Laws! Get Puppy-Abuser Haochen Wang's Dog Removed from His Care!*, CHANGE.ORG, www.change.org/p/the-government-make-harsher-animal-cruelty-laws-get-chinese-student-haochen-wang-who-bashed-his-puppy-for-7-hours-deported-back-to-china (last visited May 5, 2018).

Such comments and active assistance by organizations and lawyers supporting deportation have prompted scholars such as Professor Pachirat to ponder the question of since when "did the animal liberation movement become an appendage of US immigration enforcement?"[4] Professor Pachirat's observation rings true based on his own ethnographic research, which included talking to a man who was tearing up because the US citizen who had been renting him his social security number for "$100 a week out of a paycheck of about $400" had decided to start "demanding $150 each week," and threatening that if the undocumented man did not agree to the increased payment, then he would be "[turned] over to immigration authorities" to be deported.[5] Incarcerating men like this is unlikely to advance the long-term goals of animal protection, and it distorts and undermines the goal of empathy for those invisible to our legal system, something that many people associated with animal protection efforts would identify as a hallmark of the movement. The animal protection movement has no future if it cannot convince people that it is wrong for people to exploit their power over animals; it cannot be convincing in this regard when it completely ignores the power dynamic between an undocumented immigrant and his corporate employer.

Dominant structural, legal, and social norms have impeded the progress of recognizing animals as deserving of legal status. Animal protection groups and scholars are boldly challenging this status quo. But it is time for the animal protection movement to think more carefully and critically about the consequences – intended and unintended – of criminal prosecutions on the lives of humans and animals. The Prosecuting State is not an ally of radical social change, but rather an enforcer of the status quo. As a historical matter, police and prosecutors have been famously engaged in efforts to thwart social change.[16] To take but one striking example, persons were prosecuted in both the North and the South for assisting the Underground Railroad in the nineteenth century.[17] Even after slavery was abolished, at least one commission has documented the malfeasance of prosecutors during the civil rights era in trying to retain the status quo.[18]

---

[14] *Id.*

[15] Timothy Pachirat, Every Twelve Seconds: Industrialized Slaughter and the Politics of Sight 172 (2011).

[16] U.S. Comm'n on C.R., Law Enforcement: A Report on Equal Protection in the South 55–74 (1965) (summarizing frequent mass arrests and prosecutions for demonstrations and protests); *Id.* at 77–8 (describing the trial and sentencing of protesters and noting that protesters were held for weeks without bail or trial and that protesters were routinely convicted and sentenced to the maximum penalty).

[17] Pachirat at 43–55 (documenting law enforcement's tacit approval of violence against African Americans by private citizens and the refusal of prosecutors to prosecute for racially motivated violence).

[18] *Id.* at 94, 97 ("In many areas of Mississippi the failure of law enforcement officials to curb racial violence is largely attributable to the racially hostile attitudes of sheriffs, police chiefs, and prosecuting attorneys.").

In present times, nonviolent civil disobedience in the service of animal protection is regarded as terrorism. People are prosecuted as terrorists for liberating beagles or cats from research labs or farm animals from their cages. One need not believe that these acts spread across species, movements, and time are morally equivalent to appreciate that prosecutors have not been a compelling ally for social change reformers.

Seeking to subvert the very systems of power and dominance that define modern society by resorting to the enforcers of the status quo is unlikely to produce long-term progress. No one seriously doubts the appetite of prosecutors to enforce the growing number of Ag-Gag laws and animal terrorism statutes. And yet, the animal protection movement treats these same prosecutors as natural allies in their fight to break from the socially accepted appropriation and mistreatment of animals. Social movements are most effective when they focus their attention on protecting their members and interests "against a brutalizing state," rather than in support of it.[19] It is the rank and file activist or scholar whose work, whose protests, and whose advocacy has the potential for conceiving of and implementing radical reforms, not the Prosecuting State.

1.2 THE HISTORICAL LACK OF OPTIONS

At the First National Conference on Animal Rights Law in the United States, hosted in New York, NY in 1981, Mark Holzer, the coordinator of the event, said to the audience that the time had come for animal rights in the law. He surmised that the movement's organizations would soon be "considered no differently from [the] . . . already recognized legal action organizations like the ACLU, NAACP, and Sierra Club."[20] Like these other groups, the animal protection movement seeks to displace or shift entrenched social norms and practices. But there has always been something unique about the approach of the animal protection movement. From its very inception, some of the movement's earliest and most celebrated victories have been criminal prosecutions.

For example, it was the criminal prosecution of Edward Taub, a researcher in Maryland, that according to many accounts put the burgeoning legal movement on the map. The Taub prosecution alone "catapulted" PETA and its founders from anonymity into national fame.[21] PETA's founders presented this prosecution as a form of viable animal rights lawyering at the 1981 conference. Other organizations quickly learned that criminal prosecutions of individual actors could generate

---

[19] It is more common for social movements to regard their function as one of policing the police, rather than one of assisting and strengthening the power of police and prosecutors. *See* Jocelyn Simonson, *The Criminal Court Audience in a Post-Trial World*, 127 HARV. L. REV. 2173, 2175 (2014); Jocelyn Simonson, *Copwatching*, 104 CAL. L. REV. 391, 445 (2016).

[20] Joyce Tischler, *The History of Animal Law, Part I (1972–1987)*, 1 STAN. J. ANIMAL L. & POL'Y 1, 12–13 (2008).

[21] *Id.*

massive media and public attention, while making the movement appear mainstream.

According to one careful historical account of animal law by Joyce Tischler, criminal prosecutions "would galvanize the animal rights movement and crystallize" its purpose.[22] From the very beginning, the animal protection movement's use of law included a heavy dose of prosecution. The fame and public attention generated by the Taub prosecution produced considerable free media exposure, and so the movement's interest in criminal prosecutions was not irrational, at least from an instrumentalist perspective.

In modern times, with the rise of the internet, the twenty-four-hour news cycle, and the availability of online petitions, stories describing abuse of beloved animals seem to have emerged as the low-hanging fruit of outreach and fundraising. As a 2010 New York Times story noted about one particular case of abuse in Baltimore, "[i]t was only a matter of hours before the story, made vivid by harrowing video footage of the wounded dog, was disseminated nationwide in newspapers, TV and radio newscasts, and countless Web sites."[23] With that kind of circulation, the movement has rightly identified an area where media attention will push animal protection groups to further sensationalize a story. The movement has complied, generating a motto that is simplistic and publicly digestible: "Abuse an animal – Go to Jail." Hungry for the media attention, the movement has consistently embraced a more-punishment-is-better approach, and left out nuanced discussion of topics like mitigation evidence and the impacts of convictions or incarceration.

It is likely that fundraising campaigns and outreach efforts based on punishing animal abusers resonate with the public in a way that nuanced, multistage civil litigation efforts will not. And with criminal prosecutions, unlike civil cases, win or lose is an occasion for outreach and fundraising. If the prosecutor succeeds in obtaining a record-setting high sentence, mugshots of the person and images of the innocent animal will be emailed around. But likewise, every occasion where a conviction does not obtain, or the prosecutor does not seek a particularly harsh sentence, justifies an equal amount of outreach, this time focused on stoking outrage over the lack of punishment.

There is no comprehensive historical account of the movement's carceral turn. There is not any single narrative that would accurately capture the origin story of the movement's strong impulse to punish abusers. At its earliest stages, animal protection efforts to use the law seem to have been a relatively ad hoc patchwork of strategies. The concerted effort by the movement to oversee the enactment of felony animal cruelty provisions in all fifty states would seem like a promising source of insights into its focus on criminal punishment as a priority. The bulk of that legislative work was done in the early 1990s and beyond. Why was the movement

---

[22] *Id.* at 10.

[23] Charles Siebert, *The Animal-Cruelty Syndrome*, N.Y. TIMES (June 11, 2010) at MM42.

laser-focused on seeking alliances with the Prosecuting State? Ethnographic work focused on these questions should be pursued in future research; the limited answers that emerge based on the cold historical record are relatively unsatisfying. More often than not, available legislative history or contemporaneous statements about the legislation suggest that the felony laws were, above all else, necessary as a means of *protecting people*.[24] It is well documented that, based on the presumed link between animal abuse and subsequent human violence, animal protection groups have, for decades now, urged a more carceral response to animal abuse.

Bracketing for the moment whether the link between human and animal violence is as predictive as the lobbying suggests, and ignoring the false assumption that incarceration will likely break the chain of violence, it is difficult to believe that the primary reason that animal protection groups were pursuing animal cruelty prosecutions as a priority was an interest in helping humans. Rather, the history of the felony cruelty enactments is probably better understood as yet another publicity and outreach campaign. The link was employed as a justification for the felony laws, and the passage of the laws could then be marketed to donors and the public as proof of the movement's progress and effectiveness. The rise of felony laws, then, is probably just another example of the Taub story – an illustration of the public currency that sensational stories of animal abuse carry.

Nonetheless, an account of the movement's gravitation toward criminal prosecution would be incomplete if it focused exclusively on the perceived prospect of public sensationalism and fundraising opportunities. The still relatively nascent movement has not enjoyed many legal tools that could serve the interests of animals. The most straightforward salutary explanation for how pursuing radical social change through felony prosecutions became normalized is the dearth of alternative legal strategies. A well-conceived case filed in the 1980s, *ALDF* v. *Provimi Veal Corp.*, is perhaps the clearest reflection of path determinacy in the movement's early election to embrace criminal prosecutions as a vehicle for social change.

In *Provimi Veal*, an animal protection group demonstrated that the way veal is produced is cruel and inhumane under the plain language of the state animal cruelty statute. Relying on this factual showing, the lawyers for the ALDF brilliantly deployed the Massachusetts consumer protection statute, arguing that veal products should contain a label disclosing that they were produced in violation of state cruelty law.[25] *Provimi Veal* stands as a case of documented cruelty where the criminal infraction was used to produce civil law remedies.

---

[24]   Research may reveal any number of salutary explanations for the carceral turn within the movement. The drawdown of the master's legal prerogative, for example, to exercise physical dominion over the household – the child, the wife, or the pet – through violence. As discussed in later chapters, some have suggested a progressive attribute to the criminalization of violence against the less powerful. To the extent that carceral animal law is ultimately defended on the grounds that it is a progressive reform to protect the powerless, the remainder of this book will challenge that claim as untenable; the war on crime has taught that criminal convictions are never a progressive, anti-oppression form of reform.

[25]   Animal Legal Def. Fund, Inc. v. Provimi Veal Corp., 626 F. Supp. 278 (D. Mass. 1986).

The result was a resounding failure on multiple levels. First, and most significantly, the federal court responded by dismissing the case and explaining that even if the production of veal is criminally cruel, such violations of the criminal law must be "enforced by public officials, not private organizations, no matter how well-intentioned." Of course, ALDF was not seeking to use the criminal law to obtain incarceration for the veal producers, it was simply seeking to influence the labeling or sale of the products, and it was an appropriate plaintiff to do so. Thus, the judge's admonishment was quite wrong. The court labeled ALDF's case an "adroit" effort to use the criminal cruelty laws through the back door of civil consumer protection, and it reminded ALDF that the defining feature of our criminal system is that a "criminal statute [is] enforceable only by public prosecutors."[26]

Despite the creative lawyering that has facilitated ways to work around *Provimi Veal*,[27] decisions like this one have guided animal protection organizations to exercise their political influence to exact more aggressive prosecutions. The recent reliance on prosecutorial pressure and incarceration reflects, at least in part, the lasting effects of judicial efforts to steer animal protection into the criminal justice system. The money spent on carceral animal law, under this view, is targeted to solve concrete problems in precisely the way suggested by courts like *Provimi Veal* – through the criminal justice system. One might say that it is hardly fair to criticize animal protection groups for taking up their cause in the criminal law when courts have explicitly steered them toward carceral solutions.

Both the burnout and fatigue from litigating civil cases and the narrowed set of civil options contributed to a large investment by the animal protection movement in criminal prosecution starting in the 1990s. During the "1970s and 80s, animal law practitioners paid scarce attention to" criminal statutes, considering such laws to be firmly "under the aegis of the criminal justice system." But starting in the 1990s, animal protection groups began to identify opportunities to assist and pressure prosecutors. As Joyce Tischler proudly recounts this development within the movement, the newly "collegial" working relationships with prosecutors "helped in the *move to mainstream animal law* in the legal community."[28] This drive to be considered mainstream and acceptable to the institutional power brokers calls to mind Dr. Martin Luther King Jr.'s critique of the Church as increasingly irrelevant

---

[26] Joyce Tischler has suggested that actually litigating such intensive cases may have exceeded the available bandwidth of the movement at this time, documenting exhaustion, fatigue, and general burnout such that the involved lawyers no longer seemed to want to "stay with the work." Tischler, *The History of Animal Law, Part I (1972–1987)*.

[27] There are many instances where criminal code provisions are relevant to civil liability, including nuisance actions premised on violations of cruelty laws, unfair competition violations where criminal cruelty is the unlawful business practice, civil causes of action based on criminal violations that are available in some states, taxpayer actions where the government waste is animal cruelty, and even negligence per se where the duty owed to the plaintiff arises from the cruelty law.

[28] Tischler, *A Brief History of Animal Law, Part II (1985 – 2011)* at 59.

because of its "fear of being nonconformists."[29] The movement's shift toward the mainstream risks a calcifying effect that breeds complacency.

Yet it is hard to second-guess the wisdom of the movement which hitched its wagon throughout the 1990s to the star of mass criminalization. Legal options were slim to none for a movement that wanted to work within the law. Once the movement had ruled out activist defense, the lessons of *Provimi Veal* seemed to all but preordain a multi-decade entanglement with the popular and mainstream notions of solving problems through increased criminalization and prosecution. The animal protection movement has opted for "governing through crime," which embraces institutionalized, State-centered power at the expense of civil liberties and equality.[30] The introduction to Jonathan Simon's book by this title cautions that Americans have reached a point where even in the face of evidence that crime rates are down, "crime has become so central to the exercise of authority" that it continues to be deployed toward strategic ends.[31] Governing through crime, according to Simon, "fuels a culture of fear" and represses our "capacity for innovation."

1.3 THE CRIMINAL LAW AS CUDGEL IN SHAPING PUBLIC MORALS

Beyond a legal history characterized by limited options, members of the animal protection movement believe that a highly criminalized approach to animal law is a gateway to other successes in the legal system, and perhaps social morality more generally. As Paul Robinson and John Darley have posited, in the absence of any national religion, our "criminal law is, for us, the place we express our shared beliefs of what is truly condemnable." The criminal law, according to this view, plays a "central role in the creation of shared norms."[32] There is no real dispute that decriminalizing conduct entirely will tend to increase the occurrences of such conduct by, among other things, removing the label of social disapproval that attaches to criminal conduct. It stands to reason that animal cruelty should not be entirely decriminalized, because the very "act of criminalization sometimes nurtures the norm," of protecting the well-being of animals.[33]

Certain movements have identified benefits flowing from a more aggressive criminal response. For example, harsher criminal laws and practices helped end the brutal misconception that domestic violence was merely a "private [matter] and

---

[29] MARTIN LUTHER KING JR., LETTER FROM THE BIRMINGHAM JAIL (1963).

[30] JONATHAN SIMON, GOVERNING THROUGH CRIME: HOW THE WAR ON CRIME TRANSFORMED AMERICAN DEMOCRACY AND CREATED A CULTURE OF FEAR 3 (2007).

[31] Noting that the public will tolerate positions taken in the name of "fighting crime" through criminal laws that it will not in other contexts. Criminalizing assaults that cause the death of a fetus, for example, have more to do with the politics of abortion than the underlying crime, and yet "because it is about crime and directed at criminals it can achieve majority support" despite the polarization of the abortion issue more generally. *Id.* at 4.

[32] Paul H. Robinson & John M. Darley, *The Utility of Desert*, 91 Nw. U. L. REV. 453, 468 (1997).

[33] *Id.*

thus inappropriate for legal response."[34] As Tammy Kuennen has explained, the increase in the criminal justice machinery "sent a powerful symbolic message that [the state] takes DV seriously – as a crime that will not be tolerated."[35] A similar message is exactly what the animal protection movement seeks to generate by supporting more and harsher criminal interventions in the realm of animal cruelty. These prosecutions demonstrate that animal suffering matters.

But of course the relationship between social norms and law is complicated. Leading scholars like Aya Gruber and Tammy Kuennen have posited a compelling thesis that the carceral turn in the realm of domestic violence has ultimately been bad for women, particularly women of color. Moreover, as Robinson and Durley acknowledge, the enforcement or creation of a criminal law does not itself create a moral norm, but rather it provides a space for the community to have a discourse about the conduct in question and perhaps eventually settle on a norm that tracks with the criminal code. In this regard examples such as prohibition illustrate the perhaps limited ability of the criminal law to "change norms even when the change is supported by a significant portion of the public."[36] It could be a serious mistake to presume that the criminal law deserves too much credit for the advancing legal status of animals in our society. Indeed, the fact that animal cruelty has been a crime in some states for more than two centuries while the amount of suffering endured by animals during this same period has markedly increased, might suggest that the criminal law has not succeeded in producing the sort of shifts in public norms that one might expect; perhaps it should instead be blamed in part for entrenching such norms.[37]

Closely related to the view of incarceration as a tool for changing social attitudes, the animal protection movement may regard the carceral element of animal law as an important means of public outreach. Perhaps by aligning with people who are primarily concerned with discrete, relatively uncommon acts of horrible pet abuse,

---

[34] Aya Gruber, *The Feminist War on Crime*, 92 Iowa L. Rev. 741, 753–54 (2007) ("[F]eminists moved beyond purely liberal reasoning and asserted that under-enforcement of domestic violence and rape laws represented more than just the failure of the criminal justice system to render formal equality. The lack of enforcement of these laws reified patriarchal views that women are objects and reflected conservative ideology that subordinated women's issues by deeming them private and thus inappropriate for legal response."); *see also* Donna Coker & Ahjané D. Macquoid, *Why Opposing Hyper-Incarceration Should Be Central to the Work of the Anti-Domestic Violence Movement*, 5 U. Miami Race & Soc. Just. L. Rev. 585, 591–92 (2015); Tamara L. Kuennen, *Private Relationships and Public Problems: Applying Principles of Relational Contract Theory to Domestic Violence*, 2010 BYU L. Rev. 515, 526 (2010) (describing the rise in domestic violence prosecutions since mandatory arrest laws have been implemented).

[35] Kuennen at 578 (arguing that feminist legal scholars widely critique the "criminalization strategy" for addressing domestic violence to have been a strategic mistake).

[36] Robinson & Darley at 473.

[37] I have previously documented the ability of formal legal protections for animals to create impediments to social change in support of animal rights. Justin Marceau, *How the AWA Harms Animals*, 69 Hastings L J. 925 (2018) (compiling the social and legal barriers to animal protection generated by the existence and implementation of the AWA).

organizations can tap into an opportunity to expand their base. Perhaps pet cruelty punishment is the gateway drug to animal protection.

But such thinking is wishful in the extreme, and more likely delusional. Aya Gruber has insightfully observed in the domestic violence realm that "[s]ociety and government accept and applaud feminist criminal law reforms, while disparaging feminism generally."[38] Persons will tolerate, even celebrate expansions of the criminal law on issues as divergent as protecting women, protecting fetuses, or barring hate crimes; there is a general social consensus surrounding incarceration for a wide range of issues. But there is much less consensus regarding the underlying issues that serve as the motivation for the expansion of our criminal law. It is one thing for feminism to serve as a justification for more incarceration, but it is quite another matter to expect true changes to social structures and norms.[39] The same is true in the animal protection realm: support for increased deployments of the criminal law is different in kind from support for a general change to social norms regarding the treatment of animals. The notion that punishing animal abuse with aggressive prison sentences will produce spillover victories for the animal protection movement is unsupported conjecture.[40] And the reasoning that because the justice system punishes persons for all variety of petty offenses, it ought to also (or doubly) punish animal abuse is a flawed logic that assumes that criminal prosecution can cure structural social injustices. More is always possible through more crimes and prosecutions according to this thinking.

---

[38] Gruber at 825 (compiling sources noting that true social change for feminists is hard to obtain and not the subject of a simple criminal fix).

[39] *Id.* ("Experience shows society fears movements that seek to change social structure.")

[40] There are correlations between pet ownership and voter support for initiatives that improve animal welfare, like the 2016 Massachusetts initiative that will "prohibit Massachusetts farmers from raising egg-laying hens, breeding pigs and calves raised for veal in spaces that prevent the animals from lying down, standing up, fulling extending its limbs, or turning around freely."

Internal data from the people running the campaign suggest that a majority of dog owners voted in favor of the Massachusetts initiative. But before any firm conclusions could be drawn from this unscientific data, much more research would be needed, ideally research that controlled for variables like occupation, socioeconomics, political affiliations, exposure to farming practices, and most importantly one's views about criminal sanctions for animal abusers. Among pet owners, are those who support factory farming reforms split into subgroups consisting of some who favor and some who oppose more aggressive prosecutions for animal abuse?

2

Putting Carceral Animal Law in Context: An Overview of the Mass Criminalization Problem in the United States

There is no reliable data about how long people are sentenced to incarceration for animal cruelty, or even how often such prosecutions occur. There is no doubt, however, that the leaders of the animal protection movement use prosecutions and more punitive legislation as an important platform in their outreach and education efforts. When the maximum sentences for cases of severe cruelty to animals are less than five or ten years, the leaders in the movement are quick to complain – as one group did in a fundraising letter in 2017, remarking that "the animal cruelty statutes are in desperate need of updating." Newsletters and fundraising material frequently communicate that months or even just a couple of years simply "isn't adequate for the worst cases of animal cruelty." In an outreach email from an animal protection group in March 2018, the Animal Legal Defense Fund explained that an animal abuser "was indicted on a felony-level animal cruelty charge ... the most severe crime he could be charged with – and yet he faces a maximum of just two years in prison."

Criminal punishment is regarded as a necessary and beneficial piece of the movement's legal strategy. It is not the only form of legal advocacy, but leaders in animal law, including Joyce Tischler in a law review article, refer to criminal punishment and legislation as a "cornerstone" of the movement. The rhetoric of the animal protection movement is indistinguishable from the tough-on-crime policies of social conservatives. The movement's own trainings and outreach are doing the bidding of some of the harshest, most classist, regressive, and racist social policy engineers, and they have done so without any internal critique or public rebuke.

The failure to question the vaunted status of carceral policies in animal law is not based on a dearth of relevant research. It is well documented that since World War II the United States has "left an appalling legacy of American exceptionalism in crime and punishment."[1] There is a vast literature of qualitative and quantitative research exploring the realities of the tough-on-crime policies of the United States outside of

---

[1] AMERICAN EXCEPTIONALISM IN CRIME AND PUNISHMENT 1 (Kevin R. Reitz ed., 2018).

the animal protection context. Experts in criminology, law, psychology, and social work, among other fields, have come to regard harsher sentencing practices, registries, and criminal interventions in general as part of the problem, not the solution to violence. This chapter seeks to provide some context for the movement's commitment to incarceration by providing an overview of the key data and scholarly concerns regarding criminalization trends in the United States.

Mass incarceration and criminalization in the United States has reached the point where it is recognized as a human rights issue.[2] The conditions of confinement, disparate application of the justice system based on race and class, and the long-term negative impacts of incarceration all point toward criminal justice as an area that ought to be viewed with great skepticism rather than idealized. As William Stuntz put it, "No democratic society can incarcerate such a large fraction of its poor population and retain the goodwill of that population."[3] At issue is not just goodwill but social mobility and powerlessness, with the impact of incarceration extending generations. As a recent sociology study confirms, "the linkage . . . between parental imprisonment and the production of intergenerational socioeconomic inequality raises human rights issues."[4] Moreover, many of the people caught up in the web of animal abuse are themselves victims. The very data often used to urge the punishment of animal abusers – research showing a correlation between human violence and animal abuse – makes clear that childhood animal cruelty is an "indicator of disturbed family relationships."[5] The correlation between animal abuse and future violence may not be as strong as the correlation between, among other factors, animal abuse and one's own physical abuse or abandonment by a parent.[6] To disregard that connection demonstrates a profound lack of empathy.

Dehumanizing through punishment and publicly shaming a human who has been the subject of abuse in order to raise the status of an abused animal in the eyes of the law is callous. Surely the movement would have sympathy for an abused dog – perhaps a pit bull – who behaves aggressively and inflicts harm on other animals or people in part because the dog was conditioned to violence. Under the carceral logic of many in the animal protection movement, no such compassion is owed to persons who abuse animals after being conditioned to violence by peers, parents, or environment. The remainder of this chapter examines the harm inflicted on individuals and communities when criminal prosecution is celebrated as one of the keystones of animal protection – a movement that advocates for an end to institutionalized, dehumanizing violence.

[2] Human Rights Watch, World Report 2016: United States, www.hrw.org/world-report/2016/country-chapters/united-states (last visited Nov. 16, 2017).
[3] William Stuntz, The Collapse of American Criminal Justice 13 (2011).
[4] Holly Foster & John Hagan, *Maternal and Paternal Imprisonment and Children's Social Exclusion in Young Adulthood*, 105 J. Crim. L. & Criminology 387, 423 (2015).
[5] Stephen R. Kellert & Alan R. Felthous, *Childhood Cruelty Toward Animals Among Criminals and Noncriminals*, 38 Human Relations 1113, 1127–28 (1985).
[6] *Id.*

2.1 THE INCARCERATION EPIDEMIC

The basic facts of mass incarceration[7] in America are not in dispute. The United States incarcerates the largest number of people, and it does so at the highest rate of any nation in the world. The "nation cemented its status as world leader in per capita incarceration – a watershed that occurred around the turn of the century, following a neck-and-neck race with Russia through the 1990s."[8] The United States is estimated to have only five percent of the world's population, but it is home to nearly twenty-five percent of the world's prisoners.[9] The incarceration numbers are "six to ten times those in European nations."[10] In just "a little more than three decades [since the 1980s], Americans first embraced punishment levels lower than Sweden's [one of the least punitive countries in the world], then built a justice system more punitive than Russia's."[11]

Former congressman John Conyers recently published an academic paper putting some of these numbers in context:

> The United States has experienced a precipitous rise in its state and federal prison population over the last forty years. During that period, the number of individuals incarcerated in our nation has risen from approximately 300,000 to more than 2 million. We now have the highest incarceration rate in the world, with more than 700 out of every 100,000 Americans behind bars. Our nation's incarceration rate is roughly 5 times the international average. By comparison, Germany incarcerates 85 per 100,000; France incarcerates 96 per 100,000; and Canada incarcerates 117 per 100,000. Only Rwanda comes anywhere near the U.S. rate, with 595 per 100,000.[12]

As of 2017, roughly 2.3 million people were incarcerated in a United States prison or jail.[13] This includes over 1.3 million state prisoners, 630,000 inmates in local jails, 197,000 federal prisoners, 34,000 youth offenders, 41,000 immigration detainees, 13,000 territorial prisoners, 6,400 people in civil confinement, 2,500 prisoners in Indian country, and 1,400 military prisoners.[14]

---

[7] Mass incarceration or mass imprisonment is a term of unknown origins, but as David Garland has explained, in the tradition of the Soviet Union's infamous Gulag Archipelago, the shift in US criminal justice policy in the 1980s and 1990s "deserves a name of its own . . . America now has 'mass imprisonment' – a new name to identify an altogether new phenomenon." DAVID GARLAND, *Introduction* to *The Meaning of Mass Incarceration*, in MASS IMPRISONMENT: SOCIAL CAUSES AND CONSEQUENCES 1, 1 (David Garland ed., 2001).

[8] KEVIN R. REITZ, *Introduction* to *American Exceptionalism in Crime and Punishment: Broadly Defined*, in AMERICAN EXCEPTIONALISM IN CRIME AND PUNISHMENT at 2.

[9] *Mass Incarceration*, EQUAL JUSTICE INITIATIVE, http://eji.org/mass-incarceration (last visited Nov. 16, 2017).

[10] Foster & Hagan at 394.

[11] STUNTZ at 34.

[12] John Conyersx, Jr., *The Incarceration Explosion*, 31 YALE L. & POL'Y REV. 377, 377–8 (2013).

[13] Peter Wagner & Bernadette Rabuy, *Mass Incarceration: The Whole Pie 2017*, PRISON POLICY INITIATIVE (Mar. 14, 2017), www.prisonpolicy.org/reports/pie2017.html.

[14] *Id.*

Particularly relevant to the crime of animal abuse is the fact that, as rates of incarceration have grown, efforts to treat or rehabilitate inmates have largely been abandoned. States have slashed their already meager budgets for rehabilitation programs.[15] Indeed, the vast majority of inmates are now released back into the community without receiving any rehabilitation "because of reducing funding for rehabilitation programs as well as the closing or scaling back of state mental facilities."[16] The focus on incarceration without comprehensive rehabilitation is particularly troubling because research has shown that rehabilitation and education programs may be especially effective with violent behavior.[17] For example, in San Francisco, two psychiatrists tested the effectiveness of the Resolve to Stop the Violence Project (RSVP), which is "an intensive, 12-hours-a-day, 6-days-a-week program that teaches male-role reconstitution, accountability, empathy, alcohol and drug recovery, creative expression, and awareness of one's contribution to the community."[18] The researchers used RSVP on one dormitory of 52 inmates in a San Francisco jail, 53.8 percent of whom were incarcerated for a violent crime.[19] They used a control group of a different dormitory of 53 inmates in the same jail, 11.4 percent of whom were incarcerated for a violent crime.[20] Prior to RSVP's inception, the RSVP dormitory had 17 "incidents" reported by the sheriffs at the jail; 16 of those were violent.[21] The non-RSVP dormitory had 12 "incidents"; 10 were violent.[22] After implementing RSVP, the RSVP dormitory had one violent incident in the first quarter of the program, and no incidents of any kind after the first quarter.[23] The control dormitory had 35 incidents, 33 of which were violent. Overall, RSVP decreased annual incidents in the dormitory from 24 to 0.8.[24] RSVP costs slightly more than $14 per participant-day, and the researchers estimate that it saves about $732 per inmate per 166-day average stay, as well saving about $4 per inmate per day in medical costs immediately upon its implementation.[25] The researchers also

[15]   *See, e.g.*, Kevin Johnson, *Budget Cuts Silence Programs for Ex-Inmates*, USA TODAY (Feb. 8, 2011), https://usatoday30.usatoday.com/news/nation/2011-02-09-probationviolators09_ST_N.htm (discussing budget cuts for rehabilitation programs in Kansas, Florida, and Texas); Michael Rothfeld, *As Rehab Programs Are Cut, Prisons Do Less to Keep Inmates from Returning*, L.A. TIMES (Oct. 17, 2009), http://articles.latimes.com/2009/oct/17/local/me-rehab17 (discussing how California cut $250 million per year from rehabilitation programs, or over 40 percent of its budget).

[16]   Robert D. Crutchfield & Gregory A. Weeks, *The Effects of Mass Incarceration on Communities of Color*, 32 ISSUES SCI. & TECH 109 (2015).

[17]   *See generally* Bandy Lee & James Gilligan, *The Resolve to Stop the Violence Project: Transforming an In-House Culture of Violence through a Jail-Based Programme*, 27 J. PUB. HEALTH 149 (2005).

[18]   *Id.* at 150.

[19]   *Id.* at 151.

[20]   *Id.* at 151.

[21]   *Id.* at 152.

[22]   *Id.* at 152.

[23]   *Id.* (the study examined the dormitories for two years in total, three quarters before RSVP was implemented, and five quarters after).

[24]   *Id.* at 152.

[25]   *Id.* at 154.

found that participating in RSVP for four months "reduced the frequency of violent reoffending after leaving the jail by 83 percent, compared with a matched control group in a conventional jail."[26] Overall, this amounted to saving "the taxpayers $4 for every $1 spent on [RSVP]."

A recent report from the White House Council of Economic Advisors found that between 1980 and 2014, the incarceration rate in the United States grew by more than 220 percent, while the violent crime and property crime rates both dropped precipitously during the same period of time.[27] Research has even shown that for each additional year a person spends incarcerated, there is a 4 to 7 percent increase in post-release criminal activity.[28] That is, any decrease in crime due to incapacitating an offender is offset (and surpassed according to some studies) by the increased criminal activity that follows longer terms of incarceration. But to say that persons may be more likely to commit a crime after they are incarcerated may actually understate "incarceration's impact on post-release behavior," because research shows that following longer periods of incarceration "criminal activity not only appears to be going up on net, but also becoming more serious."[29] The research cannot fully explain why incarceration causes one to commit more crimes, but leading scholars have posited several hypotheses:

> Incarceration may facilitate the transmission of criminal capital through peer interactions among inmates; penalties to labor market outcomes could increase material hardship, encouraging theft or pursuit of illegal income sources; or, diminished social capital may reduce one's incentives to avoid future incarceration.[30]

A finding entirely at odds with the carceral policies of the animal protection movement is that incarceration does not create less total crime: "*criminal activity actually increases on net after accounting for post-release behavior.*"[31]

By many estimates incarceration costs $30,000 per inmate per year. Much could be accomplished by way of crime prevention if a small piece of the money spent prosecuting and incarcerating could be redirected toward animal protection programs and education. Equally important, in the modern era, children are often prosecuted as adults, leading to sentences that may be grotesquely long relative to sentencing practices dictated by a system that is supposed to recognize the reduced

---

[26] James Gilligan, *Punishment Fails. Rehabilitation Works.*, N.Y. TIMES (Dec. 19, 2012), www.nytimes .com/roomfordebate/2012/12/18/prison-could-be-productive/punishment-fails-rehabilitation-works.

[27] COUNCIL OF ECON. ADVISORS, ECONOMIC PERSPECTIVES ON INCARCERATION AND THE CRIMINAL JUSTICE SYSTEM 3–5 (2016), https://obamawhitehouse.archives.gov/sites/whitehouse.gov/files/documents/CEA %2BCriminal%2BJustice%2BReport.pdf (noting that the leading research finds that the drop in crime is attributable to factors other than incarceration, such as demographic changes and improving economic conditions).

[28] MICHAEL MUELLER-SMITH, THE CRIMINAL AND LABOR MARKET IMPACTS OF INCARCERATION 24–25 (2015).

[29] *Id.* at 26 (addressing recidivism among felony defendants).

[30] *Id.* at 26.

[31] *Id.* at 36.

culpability of juveniles.[32] In addition, prisons are holding far more people than they were designed to house. Federal maximum-security prisons are more than 50 percent over capacity. Overcrowding in prisons has become so acute that the Supreme Court recognized that prisons in this country may be depriving "prisoners of basic sustenance, including medical care," and they may be dramatically increasing the risk of interpersonal violence when they operate at well above their maximum capacities.[33] Alan Esner has found that the psychological impacts of prison overcrowding have reached a point where incarceration in many states may actually increase the rate of recidivism.[34]

Mass incarceration in the United States has fairly been described as a crisis. Leading researchers have concluded that incarceration often has only a small impact on crime reduction, and in some circumstances increased sentences are actually associated with increased the risks of recidivism. Such facts should be of the utmost interest to the budding civil rights activists who claim an interest in protecting animals.

2.2 HARDSHIPS FLOWING FROM CONVICTIONS BEYOND INCARCERATION

2.2.1 *Collateral Consequences*

For many advocates, the sole measure of a crime's significance is the severity of the punishment that it carries. Animal protection advocates respond with outrage when a no incarceration or a minimal term of jail or imprisonment is imposed for animal abuse, and such punishments are routinely referred to as the proverbial "slap on the wrist." In some cases, even felony convictions or years of imprisonment are regarded as insufficient by scholars and advocates. Expanding the scope of felony laws and their sentencing ranges is a priority precisely because it is believed that many offenders are not given a severe enough sentence. Under this view, more felony statutes and higher grades of felonies are essential to ensuring that animal abusers are subjected to a meaningful punishment for their animal abuse. A short term of imprisonment is viewed as tantamount to a direct affront to the animal protection movement.

For criminal law scholars, however, such a view of punishment is divorced from the reality of our justice system. The fact of a conviction may constitute a more lasting punishment than incarceration. One of the leading criminal law scholars of our time, Gabriel Jack Chin, has studied collateral consequences for nearly a decade

---

[32] Jennifer Park, *Balancing Rehabilitation and Punishment: A Legislative Solution for Unconstitutional Juvenile Waiver Policies*, 76 GEO. WASH. L. REV. 786, 792 (2008) (discussing the history of trying juveniles as adults and explaining that "[t]he juvenile court system was created in light of this reduced culpability and a juvenile's greater potential for rehabilitation").

[33] Brown v. Plata, 563 U.S. 493, 509–11 (2011) (approving an order by a lower court ordering California to "reduce its prison population to 137.5 percent of design capacity within two years" as a remedy for overcrowding that was so severe as to inflict serious harm to prisoners).

[34] ALAN ELSNER, GATES OF INJUSTICE: THE CRISIS IN AMERICA'S PRISONS XX (2nd edn.) (2006).

and concluded that the range and scope of these post-release hardships can be analogized to the common law concept of "civil death" or the writ of outlawry,[35] a punishment that is often regarded as worse than incarceration. It is not just the death penalty or mass incarceration that distinguishes the US justice system, but the United States also imposes collateral consequences "with a heavier hand than other developed democracies."[36] The animal protection movement, like most of America, has long overlooked the relevance of collateral consequences as part of the hardship meted out by the justice system. "These sanctions fly below the radar," Kevin Reitz concludes, "and do not attract television drama like a long sentence."[37] But a movement that wants to be taken seriously in the realm of criminal law reform, particularly a movement that purports to oppose institutional violence and oppression, cannot advocate for increased criminalization without addressing collateral consequences.

At common law, one guilty of treason or a felony could be punished with civil death or a writ of outlawry, which involved the "loss of status" as a form of punishment and required the forfeiture of property and chattel. The very "blood of the attainted person was deemed to be corrupt," such that his family was also disgraced and stigmatized.[38] As a common law treatise explained, one who was an outlaw was not merely "a friendless man, he is a wolf."[39] The outlaw had no status in society and likely could be treated as a reviled animal, and perhaps even killed on sight without consequence.[40] The law reduced man to animal. And the modern carceral animal law project has much in common with this phenomenon. Civil death had the effect of lowering the barriers between humans and animals. But this was accomplished by equalizing down, not up. The status of animals was not increased when someone was declared an outlaw, but the status of the human was diminished. The same sort of race-to-the-bottom logic characterizes much of the animal protection movement's carceral logic – the more that animal abusers are caged, dehumanized, and deprived of autonomy, the greater the status of animals in law and society, so the logic goes.

By the middle of the twentieth century, outlawry and civil death were regarded as inhumane and had largely disappeared from the US justice system. But half a

35 Gabriel J. Chin, *The New Civil Death: Rethinking Punishment in the Era of Mass Conviction*, 160 U. PA. L. REV. 1789, 1803–04 (2012).
36 REITZ at 2.
37 *Id.* at 19 (noting that quite often the collateral consequence is more harmful to the defendant than any punishment imposed by the court itself).
38 Chin at 1794 (quoting Avery v. Everett, 18 N.E. 148, 150 [N.Y. 1888]).
39 John Simon, Note, Tennessee v. Garner: *The Fleeing Felon Rule*, 30 ST. LOUIS U. L.J. 1259, 1263 n.28 (1986) (quoting FREDERICK POLLOCK & F.W. MAITLAND, THE HISTORY OF ENGLISH LAW: BEFORE THE TIME OF EDWARD I, at 449 [Cambridge University Press, 2nd edn. 1968] [1898]).
40 James M. Shellow & Susan W. Brenner, *Speaking Motions: Recognition of Summary Judgment in Federal Criminal Procedure*, 107 F.R.D. 139, 141 n.9 (1985) ("The outlaw was considered a 'wild beast,' outlawry being decreed by the pronouncement '*caput gerat lupinum*,' or 'let him bear the wolf's head.'").

century later, just as the animal protection movement was gaining traction through the publication of books like *Animal Liberation* by Peter Singer, a form of civil death began to re-emerge. For reasons entirely unrelated to animal protection, throughout the 1980s and 1990s the formal system of civil death was replicated in substantial ways through the creation of a "pervasive system of collateral consequences applicable to people convicted of crimes."[41] As with civil death, these newly established restrictions and limitations in the form of collateral consequences render people "dead in the eyes of the law" such that, whether guilty of a felony or a misdemeanor, they "suffer the loss of substantial rights."[42] In modern society, even a minor criminal conviction is almost always irreparably life-changing.[43]

The movement regards the length of incarceration imposed as the only suitable yardstick for evaluating whether someone who abuses animals has been sufficiently punished, and yet the cascade of collateral consequences will follow even a mere sentence of probation. The movement's singular focus on incarceration for animal abuse "obscures the reality" that for most convicted persons their "loss of legal status" is more important and more punitive than their term of incarceration.[44] Indeed, the less incarceration imposed, the more important the non-criminal consequences are for an individual:

> If a person is sentenced to twenty-five years imprisonment at hard labor, it likely matters little that she will be ineligible to get a license as a chiropractor when she is released. But to a person sentenced to unsupervised probation and a $250 fine for a minor offense, losing her city job or being unable to teach, care for the elderly, live in public housing, or be a foster parent to a relative can be disastrous.[45]

In "many cases the most important part of the conviction, in terms of both social policy and the legal effect, lies in the collateral consequences."[46] In the most comprehensive study to date, the American Bar Association catalogued more than 46,000 collateral consequences flowing from the fact of a conviction.[47] The consequences of a conviction often include limits on employment and dramatic restrictions on the ability of a low-income person to obtain government assistance.

[41] Chin at 1799.
[42] *Id.*
[43] Of course, there are notable exceptions, usually explained by class and privilege differentials. For example, a congressman from Montana was convicted of physically assaulting a journalist the day before his election; however, he was not rendered ineligible for congressional service or even censured by congress. Margaret Hartmann, *Why Gianforte's Assault Charge Won't Prevent Him from Serving in Congress*, N.Y. Mag (May 26, 2017), http://nymag.com/daily/intelligencer/2017/05/assault-charge-wont-keep-gianforte-from-serving-in-congress.html.
[44] Chin at 1792 (noting that the "degradation of a convict's legal status" has become so extreme as to fairly constitute "the new civil death").
[45] *Id.* at 1806.
[46] *Id.* at 1804–6.
[47] Just. Ctr., Consequence Details, https://niccc.csgjusticecenter.org/consequences/156812/ (last visited Jan. 22, 2018).

Among the most pervasive and devastating forms of collateral consequences are restrictions on employment. Incarceration reinforces and further entrenches class-based divisions with stunning efficacy. The average pre-incarceration income for a male inmate age 27–42 is only $19,650.[48] By contrast, average income for males in the same age range that have not been incarcerated is $41,250.[49] Worse still, a conviction will prevent many people from ever changing their socioeconomic status. Oftentimes any conviction, not even a felony, may prevent people from "working in some of the economy's fastest-growing fields, including education, childcare, private security, and nursing and home health care."[50] One economist found that among those who are incarcerated for "at least two years, at least 40 percent then fail to reintegrate into the labor market after release."[51]

The failure to regain employment is likely due to a number of factors, including the loss of productivity or skillset, and diminished self-worth, but formal, State-imposed collateral consequences are a major factor. For example, a *Wall Street Journal* article provided a detailed account of an Ohio man named Hashim Lowndes whose drug-related conviction from more than a decade earlier rendered him unable to "vote, teach preschool, foster a child, operate a racetrack, cut hair, sit on a jury, provide hospice care, protect game, distribute bingo supplies, deal live-stock, broker real estate – or, perhaps most salient to Mr. Lowndes, obtain a license to become a heating, ventilation, and air-conditioning [HVAC] technician."[52] Apparently there are more than 500 collateral consequences in the Ohio Code, but the inability to get an HVAC license hit Mr. Lowndes hardest as he tried to reestablish himself: "I was scared about taking out a $20,000 loan for a certification that I wouldn't be able to use," said Lowndes.[53]

Mr. Lowndes was only sentenced to three years in prison, a term that many in the animal protection movement regard as inadequate for serious acts of abuse. But a felony conviction carrying a three-year sentence is capable of permanently rendering Lowndes a social outcast based on the collateral consequences and the fact of his conviction.

The "breadth and automaticity"[54] of collateral consequences are paradoxical if the goal of the justice system is to rehabilitate. It is well-documented that "stable employment greatly reduces the chances of a person convicted of a crime breaking

---

48 Bernadette Rabuy & Daniel Kopf, *Prisons of Poverty: Uncovering the Pre-incarceration Incomes of the Imprisoned*, PRISON POLICY INITIATIVE (July 9, 2015), www.prisonpolicy.org/reports/income.html.

49 *Id.*; PEW CHARITABLE TRUSTS, COLLATERAL COSTS: INCARCERATION'S EFFECT ON ECONOMY MOBILITY 11 (2010), www.pewtrusts.org/~/media/legacy/uploadedfiles/pcs_assets/2010/collateralcosts1pdf.pdf (finding that men who were incarcerated make an average of 40 percent less than their peers).

50 Joan Petersilia, *Beyond the Prison Bubble*, NAT'L INST. JUST. J. 268 (Nov. 3, 2011), www.nij.gov/journals /268/pages/prison-bubble.aspx.

51 MUELLER-SMITH at 30.

52 *Id.*

53 *Id.*

54 NORA DEMLEITNER, *Collateral Sanctions and American Exceptionalism*, in AMERICAN EXCEPTIONALISM IN CRIME AND PUNISHMENT at 487.

the law again."[55] A key motivation for animal cruelty prosecutions is the sense that such prosecutions will reduce future criminality and violence by animal abusers. But there is a tension between this goal and the vocal support of restrictions on future employment.[56] Collateral consequences that strip one of any ability to obtain gainful employment may be the strongest guarantee of future arrests and convictions. Criminal prosecutions have criminogenic consequences, a fact that animal protection advocates have not yet confronted.[57]

Employment restrictions are by no means the only significant collateral consequence of a conviction. Housing restrictions are also quite pervasive. Certain crimes place limits on where a person can live in general, but more relevant for purposes of criminal punishment in the animal law context is the impact on low-income housing. Convictions may place one's eligibility for public housing, or even food stamps, in jeopardy.[58] As one scholar has summarized the extensive social disabilities that flow from a conviction:

> Among the widely documented collateral consequences of a felony conviction are ineligibility for public employment; denials of licensure in other occupations; bans on gun ownership; ineligibility for public housing and many other welfare benefits; curtailment of parental rights; exclusion from juries and from public office, and perhaps most infamously, disenfranchisement.[59]

The list of disabilities flowing from a conviction does not end with the formal, government-imposed collateral consequences. Colleges, private employers, and even potential friends or partners will oftentimes "privately" discriminate against individuals with criminal records and reinforce the legal barriers to social reintegration.[60] The social exclusion and humiliation of those convicted of crimes, particularly stigmatized crimes like animal abuse, is facilitated by the fact that information about such convictions is made publicly available, through registries and notifications. In many European countries publicizing information about one's criminal history is viewed as a violation of fundamental privacy, autonomy rights, and the right to rehabilitate. But in the United States, and often at the urging of animal protection groups, the public shaming that renders these individuals as outcasts is celebrated, and efforts to make public registries mandatory are pursued through

---

[55]   *Id.*

[56]   It is not uncommon, for example, for those who feel that the justice system does not take animal abuse seriously to lament the fact that a person convicted of animal cruelty may be able to eventually return to some semblance of a normal, pre-conviction life. Aric Mitchell, *Man Gets 99 Years for Animal Abuse: Here's Why It's Only a Slap on the Wrist*, INQUISITR (Mar. 8, 2015), www.inquisitr.com/1907873 /man-gets-99-years-for-animal-abuse-heres-why-its-a-slap-on-the-wrist (criticizing the fact that Michael Vick was "allowed to resume his career as a highly-paid football star").

[57]   For a full discussion of this point, *see infra* Chapter 5.

[58]   Barbara Mulé & Michael Yavinsky, *Saving One's Home: Collateral Consequences for Innocent Family Members*, 30 N.Y.U. REV. L. & SOC. CHANGE 689, 689 (2006).

[59]   Alice Ristroph, *Farewell to the Felonry*, HARV. C.R.-C.L. L. REV. 1, 1 (2019).

[60]   *Id.* at 44 (discussing the "cumulative effect of various collateral consequences").

legislation. Researchers like Timothy Pachirat are beginning to document that the animal protection movement's public shaming is so dehumanizing that people who are convicted of animal abuse have been driven to greater mental illness or even suicide. Resorting to prosecution as a way to enhance the status of animals in society victimizes humans, many of whom are probably victims of their own past abuse and violence.

In addition to the diminished employment opportunities and the loss of many privileges of citizenship, for non-citizens, a conviction for animal abuse may result in deportation. In some instances, animal protection groups and individuals have not only assisted indirectly with securing deportations by assisting with criminal prosecutions, they have affirmatively worked with immigration officials to directly assist in a deportation. Animal protection organizations view the deportation of an animal abuser as another way to demonstrate the value of animals under US law; securing the removal of a human from the country because of one's abuse of an animal is believed to signal the rising status of animals in the law. Deportation is a way for the movement to signal that human lives do not matter more than animal lives.

To this end, animal protection lawyers are willing to file briefs in support of efforts by federal immigration officials to secure deportation. As a natural progression and correlate of viewing human confinement as serving the goals of animal protection, deportation has emerged as an accepted part of the "animal law" practice. The movement even celebrates convictions for non-animal-related immigration offenses by people who are employed by factory farms. It would be shocking for many outside observers to learn that the animal protection movement is not categorically opposed to permanently exiling someone from their home and family through the use of collateral consequences, but such a position is entirely consistent with the carceral animal law preference to prioritize symbolic legal victories at the expense of entrenching an incarceration system that is regarded as a global human rights issue. It is apt to ask – as political scientist Timothy Pachirat has – when did the animal protection movement become an arm of immigration enforcement?[61] Many persons in the movement agree that the justice system is broken in general, but the cure for animal abuse, apparently, is more of the system. It is what Ben Levin has called criminal law NIMBY-ism.

2.2.2 *Impacts of Conviction on One's Family and Community*

Animal protection is generally conceived of as advocating for an end to injustice against overlooked or forgotten creatures. Criminal prosecution, however, creates a large number of victims who are entirely innocent, and often invisible to the policy makers and people advocating for greater incarceration. Although the collateral consequences of convictions are primarily aimed at the convicted individual, the

---

[61] As one scholar put it, "While less publicized than differentials in incarceration rates . . . the striking difference in scope, breadth and manner of imposition and length of collateral consequences in the United States, as opposed to Europe, exemplify distinct cultural perceptions of criminal offenders and their future in society." DEMLEITNER at 512.

harshness of our justice system also imposes a raft of lifelong hardships on the members of the person's household, including spouses and children.

In some states, all members of a household become "ineligible for food assistance" if anyone in the household is convicted of a large range of offenses. An entire family is rendered permanently ineligible for food assistance based on the crimes of a single parent. It cannot be gainsaid that loss of housing or employment opportunities for a caregiver will create hardships for the entire family. There are countless examples of innocent families being evicted for the criminal misconduct of a co-resident. The impacts of such circumstances on those families, particularly young children, are nothing short of devastating.[62] Animal protection advocates pursuing more criminal convictions and greater severity within these convictions are not contemplating the long-term familial and social consequences of their punitive approach to animal protection.

Criminal punishment also has vast social consequences on one's entire community that should be relevant to the animal protection movement's interest in carceral solutions. As one commentator has explained:

> The damage to social networks starts at the family level and reverberates throughout communities where the families of prisoners are congregated. Locking up someone places an immediate financial and social strain on the rest of the family. . . Dealing with an incarcerated relative causes stress, both from worry about the inmate's well-being and from tension among relatives as they struggle to survive the ordeal. These enormous burdens fall primarily on the shoulders of women caregivers, who customarily shore up families experiencing extreme hardship.[63]

Beyond the diminished opportunities for offenders,[64] the research also increasingly identifies harms flowing from incarceration to *non-convicted persons*, particularly women and children. The impact on many women, though rarely discussed, is so severe that researchers have labeled it "secondary prisonization," and discussed the females in deeply committed relationships as "quasi inmates."[65] These women suffer denigrated status in society that is exacerbated the longer their loved ones remain incarcerated. The "wives, girlfriends, mothers, daughters, and other female

---

[62] "Mrs. Smith, a resident of public housing for 30 years, had eviction proceedings brought against her after her 16-year-old son was found in possession of cocaine several blocks from her apartment. Unable to afford or retain an attorney, Mrs. Smith appeared at her administrative hearing without counsel. Unaware of the law and administrative procedures, Mrs. Smith refused to sign a stipulation agreeing to probation and permanent exclusion of her son from her apartment. . . . The Hearing Officer rendered a determination terminating Mrs. Smith's tenancy. Not knowing what to do, Mrs. Smith prepared to move herself, her children, and her three grandchildren out of the apartment with nowhere to go . . . Routinely, eviction proceedings are commenced against a tenant of record based upon the criminal (usually drug) activity of another household member or guest." Mulé & Yavinsky at 689.

[63] Dorothy E. Roberts, *The Social and Moral Cost of Mass Incarceration in African American Communities*, 56 STAN. L. REV. 1271, 1282 (2004) (quoting ethnographic research).

[64] *See* PEW CHARITABLE TRUSTS.

[65] *Id.* at 18–19.

kin and intimates of prisoners" experience social marginalization and other consequences "even though they are innocent and dwell outside the prison walls."[66] The lives of these women are now understood to be "profoundly transformed," from appearance, to agendas and goals, to all other aspects of their life.[67] Recognizing such spillover or secondary effects is an important piece of understanding the complex ways that incarceration impacts a community beyond merely punishing people for their wrongful acts.[68]

Indeed, even beyond the immediate secondary effects on loved ones, there is a new field of research examining the tertiary or next-generation impacts of incarceration on the loved ones of an incarcerated person. With three decades of mass incarceration behind us, it is now possible to "assess the impact of parental imprisonment on children," all the way through adulthood.[69] Researchers have examined the impacts of incarceration on intergenerational mobility – the American Dream. Research has shown that parental incarceration increases antisocial behavior among adolescents.[70] Moreover, research has shown that the adult children of an incarcerated parent are more likely to experience social exclusion, including "homelessness, political disenfranchisement, and healthcare uninsuredness."[71] If a parent was incarcerated during an individual's childhood, the individual is likely to experience a loss of personal income, household income, and such people are prone to perceptions of powerlessness through their twenties and thirties.[72] Parental incarceration unequivocally "compromises the educational outcomes of children and their prospects for achieving the socioeconomic success that is central to the American Dream." This linkage between parental incarceration and intergenerational socioeconomic harm is one of the reasons modern researchers treat mass incarceration as a human rights issue.[73]

Beyond incarceration, there are collateral consequences even for the proverbial slap on the wrist – a sentence of probation. On the very same day in late 2017 that the Animal Legal Defense Fund was running an online petition calling for a maximum term of incarceration in a cruelty case (so that the punishment would "fit the crime"), Jay-Z, the well-known rap artist and activist, published an op-ed in the *New York Times* that describes probation as a "system that stalks black people."[74] Describing the fact that fellow rapper Meek Mill was sentenced to two to four years in prison for violating probation, he explained:

---

[66] MEGAN COMFORT, DOING TIME TOGETHER: LOVE AND FAMILY IN THE SHADOW OF PRISON 7 (2007).

[67] *Id.* at 15.

[68] Roberts at 15.

[69] Foster & Hagan at 423.

[70] This data is based on findings that either parent spent any amount of time in jail or prison during their offspring's childhood, and the data was part of a longitudinal study.

[71] Foster & Hagan at 390.

[72] *Id.* at 423.

[73] Roberts at 423.

[74] Jay-Z, Opinion, *The Criminal Justice System Stalks Black People Like Meek Mill*, N.Y. TIMES (Nov. 17, 2017), www.nytimes.com/2017/11/17/opinion/jay-z-meek-mill-probation.html.

On the surface, this may look like the story of yet another criminal rapper who didn't smarten up and is back where he started. But consider this: Meek was around 19 when he was convicted on charges relating to drug and gun possession, and he served an eight-month sentence. Now he's 30, so he has been on probation for basically his entire adult life. For about a decade, he's been stalked by a system that considers the slightest infraction a justification for locking him back inside.[75]

It is not only Jay-Z who has noticed that probation is not nearly as non-punitive as it seems. The scale and intrusiveness of probation in the United States is "orders of magnitude greater than in Europe."[76] As Kevin Reitz has explained, "[p]robation used to be considered an instrument of lenity," but it is now recognized that probation is an "important feeder of prison and jail populations."[77] Moreover, the "experience of being on probation is more difficult than commonly understood," and often includes very little rehabilitation, and instead a great deal of "intrusive conditions that any law-abiding citizen would have difficulty satisfying."[78] The original notion of probation was of an opportunity for reform and rehabilitation, but it has moved "away from its rehabilitative origins" in favor of surveillance and strict rule compliance with terms that are far-reaching and difficult to comply with.[79] There seem to be almost no legal limits on the conditions that may be imposed on a probationer. One study found that judges impose on average thirteen conditions, including curfews, drug tests, fees, and geographic monitoring (by ankle bracelet or otherwise), among other things. The conditions are sufficiently onerous that researchers have found that only around 60 percent of people successfully complete their probation. As the animal protection movement doggedly pursues ever-longer sentences, close observers are drawing attention the fact that even the US probation system can be surprisingly harsh, and difficult to escape. People concerned about civil rights have recognized not just a mass incarceration problem, but a "mass probation or mass supervision" problem. Compared to European countries, "US probation exerts an exceptionally punitive reach."[80]

Similarly, criminal law scholar Alice Ristroph has written a timely call for the United States to bid "Farewell to the Felonry" altogether, because the very "classification of persons as felons is central to the mechanics of mass incarceration and to racial inequality."[81] As the animal protection movement is pressing for more felony provisions in order to denote cruelty as a "serious crime," Ristroph painstakingly shows that in fact "there is no essential attribute or internal coherence" to the legal definition of felony, and many of the crimes included in the category are not

[75] *Id.*
[76] EDWARD E. RHINE & FAYE S. TAXMAN, *A Comparative Analysis of Probation in the United States, Scotland, and Sweden,* in AMERICAN EXCEPTIONALISM IN CRIME AND PUNISHMENT at 369.
[77] REITZ at 9.
[78] *Id.* at 9.
[79] RHINE & TAXMAN at 375.
[80] *Id.* at 399–400.
[81] Ristroph at 1.

particularly noteworthy or "wicked." In fact, "it is not usually violence that makes [one] a felon . . . [and] in the federal system, felons are convicted predominantly of drug, immigration, fraud, or gun possession offenses."[82] And yet, because the social meaning of felony is that the crime is uniquely depraved, "discrimination against felons is widely accepted, and even demanded." Felony status is a lifelong disability that leaves little room for rehabilitation.

And this is exactly the point. Any reformer who is interested in "disrupt[ing] broader structural inequalities" must abandon not just the growth of felonies, but the very concept of a felon. The ubiquity of the felony in American law, by this thinking, should be castrated, not coveted. In the nineteenth century the very concept of a felon was used as a means of denoting a social class, much like a caste, perhaps one that would pass on to one's children so that they too would suffer "the same social and political disabilities."[83] It is the stigmatizing effect of the label "felon" that serves to legitimize an "extraordinarily severe criminal justice system."[84] In short, the very vocabulary and priorities of the animal protection movement in casting the expansion of felonies as an affirmative good is incompatible with combatting systemic violence and inhumanity. Supporting criminal prosecution is not apolitical.

For a movement concerned with expanding "Nonhuman Rights," it is striking that some of their cornerstone policies and priorities would entrench a system that is increasingly understood as effecting human rights violations. The movement should think carefully about glorifying the creation of a permanent caste based on felony convictions. Not only do animal rights advocates risk looking like they are out of touch and misanthropic, but the pursuit of tough-on-crime policies may leave the animal movement in the position of chasing its own tail, because incarceration and criminalization threatens to further entrench the class and socioeconomic dynamics that are at least partially to blame for the abuse of innocent animals. Incarceration causes instability in communities, and as Kimberly K. Smith has aptly posited, "there is little reason to believe that animal welfare would be better protected in such destabilized communities."[85] There is every reason to believe that State-sponsored violence and stigmatization will lead to more violence against humans and animals.

2.3 RACE AND MASS CRIMINALIZATION

By 2008, the incarceration rate in the United States had quintupled from that in 1972, and nearly "one in 54 adult males" were incarcerated.[86] But of course, incarceration

---

[82] *Id.* at 38.
[83] *Id.* at 18.
[84] *Id.* at 42.
[85] Kimberly K. Smith, Governing Animals: Animal Welfare and the Liberal State 145 (2012).
[86] Reitz at 3 (noting that the peak of the US incarceration rate appears to have been 2007–2008, but noting that as of 2018 the rate had only "inched" down from about 760 per 100,000 to 711 per 100,000).

rates are not distributed evenly across class or race. Without controlling for rates at which crimes are committed, data shows that African Americans are incarcerated at a rate of about six times that of whites, and Latinos are incarcerated at 2.5 times the rate of whites.[87] The intersection of race and carceral animal law is discussed more fully in Chapter 5, but it warrants a brief introduction at this preliminary point of compiling a general list of critiques relating to tough-on-crime policies.

To put the matter plainly, "race matters in criminal justice."[88] In the twenty-first century, any discussion of the criminal justice system, particularly a conversation about increasing the frequency and severity of punishments, must include a consideration of race and disparate impact. Angela Harris has observed that the modern police officers have grown to understand themselves as "law enforcers in a community of savages, as outposts of the law in a jungle."[89] In this sense, the "criminals as a class" are racialized as non-white, even though, of course, that is not universally true.[90] Encouraging greater reliance on prosecutions without acknowledging ongoing conversations about race and criminal justice reflects a tone-deaf disregard for social dynamics. Animal protection advocates promise that their efforts are colorblind and race neutral, but pursuing increased criminal punishment tends always to be negatively racially inflected.

Although "most Americans seem content to ignore" the problems of race in the criminal justice system and urge the view of America as a post-racist society,[91] distinguished scholars have documented the unfortunate intersections between racial injustice and the administration of our criminal justice system. Any effort to increase the number of crimes, sentences, and range of collateral consequences in our justice system must be considered from the perspective of leading commentators in the field. For example, Michelle Alexander has memorably referred to the system and its epidemic of mass incarceration as "the new Jim Crow."[92] To ignore the saliency of race in modern critiques of mass incarceration is untenable. It is exactly the sort of "colorblind" approach to social change that has led many persons of color, as examined in works such as *Sistah Vegan*, to regard the animal protection movement as racist.[93] For many African American animal advocates, the movement's campaigns "often fail to give a historical context" and come across as insensitive, if not overtly racist. The

---

[87] *Id.* at 4.
[88] Paul Butler, *Racially Based Jury Nullification: Black Power in the Criminal Justice System*, 105 YALE L J. 677, 725 (1995).
[89] Angela P. Harris, *Gender, Violence, Race, and Criminal Justice*, 52 STAN. L. REV. 777, 797–8 (2000).
[90] *Id.* at 797 n.74 (quoting Angela P. Harris, Criminal Justice as Environmental Justice, 1 J. GENDER, RACE & JUST. 1, 17 [1997]).
[91] Michelle Alexander, *The New Jim Crow*, 9 OHIO ST. J. CRIM. L. 7, 7 (2011).
[92] *Id.* at 7, 8.
[93] A. BREEZE HARPER, *Introduction: The Birth of the Sistah Vegan Project*, in SISTAH VEGAN: BLACK FEMALE VEGANS SPEAK ON FOOD, IDENTITY, HEALTH, AND SOCIETY I, XIII-XIV (A. Breeze Harper ed., 2010) (summarizing comments and reactions to animal rights campaigns that the movement regards as race-neutral advocacy).

movement's support for expanding criminal justice responses while positing the irrelevance of race fails to address the critique that the movement is "part of a legacy of white racism" and elitism.[94]

Michelle Alexander has explained that when she began working for the ACLU she had assumed that "the criminal justice system had problems of racial bias, much in the same way that all major institutions in our society are plagued to some degree with problems associated with conscious and unconscious bias."[95] But after working for years as a director of Racial Justice Policy, she came to the conclusion "that mass incarceration in the United States had, in fact, emerged as a stunningly comprehensive and well-disguised system of racialized social control that functions in a manner strikingly similar to Jim Crow."[96] Closely related to the dangers identified by scholars like Jack Chin,[97] Alexander explains:

> Today it is perfectly legal to discriminate against criminals in nearly all the ways it was once legal to discriminate against African Americans. Once you're labeled a felon, the old forms of discrimination – employment discrimination, housing discrimination, denial of the right to vote, and exclusion from jury service – are suddenly legal. As a criminal, you have scarcely more rights, and arguably less respect, than a black man living in Alabama at the height of Jim Crow. We have not ended racial caste in America; we have merely redesigned it.[98]

It is beyond the scope of this chapter to summarize the evidence that scholars have marshaled in support of this conclusion, so I will mention just a couple of data points. More African Americans are incarcerated today (or on probation or parole) than were enslaved in the United States in the years preceding the Civil War.[99] Approximately 60 percent of the persons incarcerated in the United States are persons of color. Felon disenfranchisement laws have stripped the right to vote from more African Americans than the Jim Crow laws did. And the "United States

---

[94] *Id.* at XV.

[95] Alexander at 8.

[96] *Id.*

[97] Indeed, Alexander compliments her analysis with ethnographic research that recounts the toll that collateral consequences impose on people trying to reestablish themselves in a community: "My felony conviction has been like a mental punishment, because of all the obstacles . . . Every time I go to put in a [job] application I have had three companies hire me and tell me to come to work the next day. But then the day before they will call me and tell me don't come in – because you have a felony. And that is what is devastating because you think you are about to go to work and they call you and say because of your felony we can't hire [you]. I have run into this at least a dozen times. Two times I got very depressed and sad because I couldn't take care of myself as a man. It was like I wanted to give up because in society nobody wants to give us a helping hand." *Id.* at 19.

[98] *Id.* at 8.

[99] "In this regard, it is important to keep in mind that most people who are under correctional control are not in prison or jail. As of 2008, there were approximately 2.3 million people in prisons and jails, and a staggering 5.1 million people under 'community correctional supervision.'" Shellow & Brenner at 15.

imprisons a larger percentage of its black population than South Africa did at the height of apartheid."[100]

Beyond quantitative data, people concerned about racial injustice in the United States have levelled powerful qualitative challenges to our systems of incarceration and mass criminalization. For example, in discussing the media coverage of a young black man's criminal trial for kicking a cat in the street accompanied by a photo showing middle-class whites glaring at the defendant, one professor commented that "[w]hen black people look at this picture, they will see the white people and think, 'They probably care less about a young black man being killed by police than they do about this cat.'"[101] Or to quote a leading race and criminal justice scholar, "[i]f it took the white majority more than two hundred years to understand that slavery was wrong, and approximately one hundred years to realize that segregation was wrong (and still many don't understand), how long will it take them to perceive that American criminal justice is evil?"[102] For many scholars, the criminal justice system is an irredeemably negative, racist enterprise.[103]

Moreover, the race problems identified as endemic to the carceral State more generally must be juxtaposed with the perception that animal protection is a mostly "white." A 2005 study of animal welfare organizations found that of the thirteen that responded to the survey, eight had no African American employees, and African Americans made up only 0.8 percent of "highest levels" of employment within these organizations.[104] African Americans are not leading the animal protection movement, and the enthusiasm for tough-on-crime policies by a group that is still overwhelmingly white has an unavoidable racial inflection.

Incarceration and increased criminalization are controversial measures because of their impacts on individuals, families, and communities, as well as their historical connection to oppression. The criminal justice system itself has become a microcosm

---

[100]   ALEXANDER, THE NEW JIM CROW: MASS INCARCERATION IN THE AGE OF COLORBLINDNESS 6 (rev. edn. 2012).

[101]   Tatiana Schlossberg, *Should a Cat-Kicker Go to Jail? Readers Respond*, N.Y. TIMES: CITY ROOM (Sept. 30, 2014), https://cityroom.blogs.nytimes.com/2014/09/30/should-a-cat-kicker-go-to-jail-readers -respond.

[102]   James Forman, Jr., *Why Care About Mass Incarceration?*, 108 MICH. L. REV. 993, 998 (2010) (quoting PAUL BUTLER, *Brotherman: Reflections of a Reformed Prosecutor*, in THE DARDEN DILEMMA: 12 BLACK WRITERS ON JUSTICE, RACE, AND CONFLICTING LOYALTIES 1, 16 [Ellis Cose ed., 1997]).

[103]   Randall Kennedy has posited that "[i]t is entirely plausible that the white-dominated political institutions of America would not tolerate present conditions in jails and prisons if as large a percentage of the white population were incarcerated as is the reality facing the black population. It is surely possible, to many likely, that if the racial shoe were on the other foot, white-dominated political structures would be more responsive than they are now to the terrors of incarceration." RANDALL KENNEDY, RACE, CRIME, AND THE LAW 134 (1997).

[104]   Sue-Ellen Brown, Commentary, *The Under-Represented of African American Employees in Animal Welfare Organizations in the United States*, 13 SOC'Y & ANIMALS 153, 153 (2005) (limiting the study to animal welfare as opposed to "animal rights" groups).

for race-neutral polices that are discriminatory, dehumanizing, and destroying communities. As Kimberly Smith puts it, African Americans often feel anger and distrust toward the "criminal justice system that they feel treats them as animals."[105] The animal protection movement, meanwhile, champions this same system as a means of alleviating the oppression of animals. The mainstream trope of the criminal-human as an animal deserving of extreme punishment undergirds the criminal turn in animal law.

[105] SMITH at 143.

3

A Descriptive Account of the Carceral Animal Law System

3.1 WIDESPREAD SUPPORT FOR CARCERAL ANIMAL LAW

"Abuse an Animal, Go to Jail." This is the slogan of a leading animal protection organization, and it captures the prevailing spirit among the movement more generally.[1] Like many bumper-sticker mantras, what it lacks in nuance or sophistication it makes up for in mass appeal and incisiveness. The slogan works because it cannot be characterized as radical; indeed, the phrase resonates with vastly more Americans than any concerted discussion about changing one's diet, or even wearing fur. A bumper sticker celebrating a plant-based lifestyle is decidedly radical, and yet a call to punish severely those who abuse animals is almost universally accepted. Punishing sadistic animal abusers has become big business for animal protection groups, with organizations seeing many successful fundraising and membership drives based on the visceral reaction people have to abuse. Every time a prominent instance of dog or cat abuse is uncovered, a slew of blog posts from the leaders of the movement follow, along with calls for new offenses, more severe sentencing frameworks, and procedural changes that would make

---

[1] The literature endorsing carceral animal law is long, though its theoretical and doctrinal underpinnings are not typically examined rigorously. *See, e.g.*, Pamela D. Frasch, *The Impact of Improved American Anti-Cruelty Laws in the Investigation, Prosecution, and Sentencing of Abusers*, in THE INTERNATIONAL HANDBOOK OF ANIMAL ABUSE AND CRUELTY: THEORY, RESEARCH, AND APPLICATION 59, 68 (Frank R. Ascione ed., 2008) ("[I]nterviewees generally agreed that the inclusion of a felony level anti-cruelty law was an important step in the ultimate goal of reducing animal abuse in the community."); Megan E. Boyd & Adam Lamparello, *Vulnerable Victims: Increasing Animal Cruelty Sentences to Reflect Society's Understanding of the Value of Animal Lives*, 45 CONNTEMPLATIONS 31, 33 (2013) ("[D]efendants convicted of dogfighting, and other animal cruelty offenses, should receive substantial periods of incarceration."); Kirsten E. Brimer, *Justice for Dusty: Implementing Mandatory Minimum Sentences for Animal Abusers*, 113 PENN ST. L. REV. 649, 669 (2008) ("[O]ne way to ensure violent criminals are prevented from committing further crimes is by implementing mandatory minimum sentences, as both a rehabilitative and deterrent measure . . . If adult [animal] abusers face the possibility of real jail time, they may be deterred from committing acts of animal abuse."); Margit Livingston, *Desecrating the Ark: Animal Abuse and the Law's Role in Prevention*, 87 IOWA L. REV. 1, 3 (2001) ("It is debatable whether modern animal cruelty laws . . . have been effective in

obtaining convictions easier.[2] Likewise, every time cruelty is discovered on a farm, there are calls to prosecute the low-level employees engaged in the misdeeds, heedless of the possibility that such prosecutions may ultimately allow the industry to scapegoat precisely these low-level employees.[3]

Lori Gruen has aptly noted that both "prisons and zoos are paradigm institutions of domination" that ensure lonely, absurd, and unnatural existences.[4] The animal protection movement appears to be concerned with the harms of incarceration on non-humans alone. Yet the "deleterious effects" of incarceration – including feelings of paranoia, anger, and resentment – are common among incarcerated humans and non-humans alike.[5] Traditionally, mainstream society has concluded that the

---

curtailing animal abuse . . . Arguably, the flaw in the legal system lies with inadequate penalties for animal abuse and apathetic enforcement of existing laws."); Jennifer H. Rackstraw, *Reaching for Justice: An Analysis of Self-Help Prosecution for Animal Crimes*, 9 ANIMAL L. 243, 248 (2003) ("[I]t is critical to provide intervention and appropriate treatment and punishment for children and adolescents prone to animal cruelty. Furthermore, adult infliction of animal cruelty must be similarly addressed."); Cass R. Sunstein, *The Rights of Animals*, 70 U. CHI. L. REV. 387, 390 (2003) ("If taken seriously, [state anticruelty laws] would do a great deal to protect animals from suffering, injury, and premature death."); Jacqueline Tresl, *The Broken Window: Laying Down the Law for Animals*, 26 S. ILL. U. L.J. 277, 277–78 (2002) (explaining that the laws needed to help animals are already "on the books" and thus "for lawyers who care about animals, the solution to reducing animal abuse in America is not so much about enacting tougher laws, electing liberal judges, or implementing clandestine 'direct action.'"); *Id.* (concluding that the solution is just more prosecutions and fallaciously asserting that the movement already has the tools it needs to "significantly end animal cruelty this decade").

To date, very few commenters have vigorously contested the rise of carceral animal law. However, some have questioned the outer limits of carceral animal law, such as the introduction of animal abuser registries. *See* Alisha L. Biesinger, *Is Registering as an Animal Abuser in Illinois Abusive to the Offender? An Examination of the Proposed Illinois Animal Abuse Registry*, 39 S. ILL. U. L.J. 299, 318–32 (2015) (discussing the impracticality and ineffectiveness of proposed animal abuser registries and concluding that "[p]rohibiting animal abusers from owning subsequent animals can be accomplished with other less intrusive means"); Wayne Pacelle, *Reservations About the Animal Abuse Registry*, HUMANE SOC'Y U.S.: A HUMANE NATION (Dec. 3, 2010), http://blog.humanesociety.org/wayne/2010/12 /animal-cruelty-registry-list.html (last visited Jan. 22, 2018). *See also* Megan L. Renwick, *Animal Hoarding: A Legislative Solution*, 47 U. LOUISVILLE L. REV. 585, 591–94 (2009) (discussing the ineffectiveness of prosecutions for animal hoarding as "penalties under cruelty laws do not address the underlying causes of hoarding and thus do little, if anything, to prevent recidivism . . . [T]raditional animal-cruelty penalties such as fines, removal of the animals, and even jail time are highly unlikely to deter a hoarder from accumulating more animals in the future, since these punishments fail to address what caused the person to hoard in the first place.")

[2]   *See, e.g.,* Jack Encarnacao, *Puppy Doe Case Highlights Need for Abuse Law Expansion*, BOSTON HERALD (July 24, 2017), www.bostonherald.com/news/local_politics/2017/07/puppy_doe_case_high lights_need_for_abuse_law_expansion (quoting animal protection advocates' surprise in learning that obtaining more felony convictions has not been as smooth or efficient as they had hoped, and reporting on the interest in creating a new offense to fill the gap).

[3]   The majority of the labor of animal agriculture is done by low-income and often immigrant workers who not only bear the physical and psychological brunt of that toil, but also often the only criminal charges filed as a result of undercover investigations at factory farms.

[4]   LORI GRUEN, *Dignity, Captivity, and an Ethics of Sight*, in ETHICS OF CAPTIVITY 231, 237, 243 (Lori Gruen ed., 2014); *Id.* at 240 (recognizing harms to one's dignity from captivity "over and above the impact it has on their well-being").

[5]   *Id.* at 243.

many harms flowing from incarceration are only relevant to human subjects; the animal protection movement has broadened the arc of our social compassion by pointing to the ability of non-humans to suffer. But the animal protection movement condones incarceration when it comes to humans who abuse animals. In an age of mass incarceration, not even the animal rights movement has avoided the temptation to call for more cages and structural State violence against living creatures.

Not every advocate for animals supports incarceration, but the mainstream view seems to be that a more punitive approach to the limited acts of cruelty that are criminalized will help advance the status of animals in law and policy. No less than Gary Francione, doubtlessly one of the most ardent and uncompromising animal rights scholars, has argued that "prosecutions brought under" anti-cruelty statutes will "help to erode the property status of animals."[6] Consistent with this view, the animal protection movement has pressed fervently for more prosecutions, longer sentences, and other criminal justice consequences.

Allegiance to government prosecution is an uncomfortable marriage for a social change movement, given that prosecutors are paid to enforce the status quo. There are empirical and moral reasons to doubt that the uptick in cruelty prosecutions or sentences could ever meaningfully result in an improved status for animals. To take an easy example, the movement has heralded as one of the greatest victories, and a turning point for it, a 2016 criminal case from the Oregon Supreme Court, *Oregon v. Newcomb*. As the Nonhuman Rights Project effused:

> Muhammed Ali stated, "[s]ome mountains are higher than others, some roads steeper than the next. There are hardships and setbacks, but you can't let them stop you. Even on the steepest road, you must not turn back. You must keep going up. In order to reach the top of the mountain, you have to climb every rock." Decisions like *Newcomb* make clear the climb has begun.[7]

The reality is a bit more complicated. *Oregon v. Newcomb* raised the specific legal question of whether law enforcement is permitted to "search" a dog without the owner's consent.[8] Specifically, whether police are required to obtain consent or a warrant before extracting blood or other bodily fluids from a dog in support of a cruelty prosecution.[9] The bodily fluids extracted by a veterinarian were used to support a prosecution for abuse based on malnutrition, and the state's high court held that because the case presented a unique situation in which "the seized *property* was a living animal" the warrantless search that resulted in a conviction was constitutional,

---

[6]   Gary L. Francione, *Reflections on Animals, Property, and the Law and Rain Without Thunder*, 70 LAW & CONTEMP. PROBS. 9, 51 (2007) (explaining that a major limit on the ability of anti-cruelty laws to diminish the property status of animals is the fact that many violations of cruelty laws go unpunished or are charged merely as misdemeanors).

[7]   Sarah Stone, *Making A Legal Difference: Oregon v. Newcomb*, NONHUMAN RIGHTS BLOG (July 2, 2016), www.nonhumanrights.org/blog/newcomb.

[8]   State v. Newcomb, 375 P.3d 434 (Or. 2016).

[9]   *Id.* at 436.

even though a similar search of one's suitcase or other private property would be unconstitutional.[10]

The *Newcomb* case perfectly encapsulates the benefits and drawbacks of the criminal prosecution model of animal law. On one hand, the dog is recognized by the Court as holding a "unique position in people's hearts and in the law . . . that is not well-reflected in the cold characterization of a dog as mere property."[11] On the other hand, the Court's reasoning is best understood as consistent with the American preoccupation with criminal punishment as the *sine qua non* of our society. As a practical matter, the case merely upholds efforts by police and prosecutors to obtain more criminal convictions with fewer constitutional constraints.

It would be a serious mistake to imagine that police and prosecutors think of cases like *Newcomb* as facilitating a radical re-envisioning of the role of animals in the law. These actors were satisfied with and argued for reasoning explaining simply that "not all containers" are the same. According to the Court and prosecutors, a dog is a special, beloved form of property, but it *is of course* nonetheless an item of property; a person who owns "an animal . . . has full rights of dominion and control over it."[12] Such reasoning may well reflect the state of public opinion – animals are loved up to the point that their status conflicts with existing social norms. But there is nothing groundbreaking about cases like *Newcomb*. It is difficult to imagine that many animals' lives will be meaningfully improved by further empowering the Prosecuting State and reducing the scope of the Fourth Amendment.

Moreover, cases like *Newcomb* are jealously limited to their facts by prosecutors and police officers when the shoe is on the other foot. On some occasions recognizing animals as more than mere property could result in acquittals of defendants, or civil liability for law enforcement. For example, in civil rights cases challenging the use of force by police officers against pets, law enforcement and their lawyers consistently argue that pets are mere property, not members of the family or special property deserving of heightened protection. That is, when the property status of an animal limits liability or promotes prosecutorial success, the animal's status as property is celebrated. In a recent case in West Virginia, a law enforcement officer who was captured on video needlessly pointing his gun at a dog's head argued that a family member who tried to protect the dog by grabbing the animal and stepping in front of the officer was, per se, obstructing justice. One might be justified in obstructing an officer who is going to wrongfully seize or injure another person, but it is legally impermissible to obstruct an officer who is attempting to "seize personal property," the state's police force and attorneys have argued. The pattern is not difficult to discern. Law enforcement is always right, and they side with animals only when and to the limited extent necessary to advance the incarcerating power of

---

[10] *Id.* at 439.

[11] *Id.* at 440.

[12] *Id.* at 441 (emphasizing that at the time of the search of the dog in this case the dog had been lawfully seized such that the owner's rights of dominion control had already been substantially reduced).

the State. It is the power of the Prosecuting State, not the animals, that is advanced by supporting criminal prosecutions.

To experienced social change advocates, this pattern should not be surprising. The job of prosecutors and police officers is to enforce the law as it is, not to imagine a better, more just, and socially responsible set of rules. Indeed, prosecutors work to enforce the political victories of the majority. The confrontations between activist reformers and law enforcement and prosecutors throughout history are infamous. There is something suffocating about tying the ambitions of a fledgling, counterculture movement to government action in the form of policing and prosecution,[13] and the state and federal prosecutors and law enforcement have not repaid this fidelity to the criminal system with a sense of mutual respect, loyalty, or shared purpose. During a period when the animal rights movement has championed the justice system as the unsung hero of animal rights, states have passed Ag-Gag laws, often with the support of prosecutors; expanded legislative efforts to criminalize the documentation of hunting practices (for example, by criminalizing photography or videography of hunters); and the federal government has passed a far-reaching anti-terrorism provision directed at property crimes by animal rights activists.[14] The very prosecutors and justice system that is reified by the animal protection movement when it seeks to incarcerate animal abuse will treat a foie gras investigator or a journalist exposing factory farm abuses as criminals or terrorists. The common denominator is a zealous pursuit of convictions, not an underlying drive to improve the status of animals in the legal system. The movement should not be surprised when their support for the "institutional power and authority" of our justice system transforms into support of laws that reinforce the status quo and justify the oppression of animal advocates.[15] In the carceral view of animal law, animals win when prosecutors win. But the only real winner is the entrenched justice system.

Not coincidentally, some of the most innovative litigation seeking animal rights has involved procedural vehicles typically used to check the incarcerating power of the state, such as habeas corpus petitions filed on behalf of non-humans.[16] Habeas corpus is among the most famous bulwarks against prosecutorial overreach and abuse.[17] The legal tools that facilitate civil rights, and potentially animal rights do

---

[13] Failing to note the irony of considering government enforcement of the status quo as radical, commentators have celebrated the work of a particularly "aggressive" prosecutor by noting that he "radically enhanced legal protection for animals." Tresl at 292 (citing other authorities reaching the same conclusion).

[14] 18 U.S.C. § 43 (2006).

[15] Lisa Kemmerer, *Introduction* to Sister Species 16 (2011) (linking the rise of hunter harassment laws to institutionalized "power and authority").

[16] Justin Marceau & Steve Wise, *Exonerating Animals*, in Wrongful Convictions and the DNA Revolution: Twenty-Five Years of Freeing the Innocent 334–54 (Daniel S. Medwed ed., 2017).

[17] A quick comparison is illustrative. There has been recent litigation for true animal rights, such as the litigation for habeas corpus rights for chimpanzees. The primates are amazingly sympathetic and their conditions deplorable, and yet even as they sit solitary, bored, smoking cigarettes and dying, courts are unable or unwilling to grant relief. Nonhuman Rights Project, Inc. v. Presti, 999 N.Y.S.2d 652 (N.Y. App. Div. 2015); People ex rel. Nonhuman Rights Project, Inc. v. Lavery, 998 N.Y.S.2d 248 (N.Y. App.

not involve efforts to prop up the carceral state, but rather involve procedural vehicles for limiting such power.

This chapter provides a taxonomy of the wide-ranging set of criminal justice reforms pursued by animal protection advocates. As detailed below, the animal protection movement's carceral campaign has at least three elements: a media and public relations campaign supporting more prosecutions substantive reforms to the criminal law; and procedural reforms to the criminal law.

3.2 THE RHETORIC OF INCARCERATION: COURTHOUSE ADVOCACY AND PUBLIC RELATIONS CAMPAIGNS

Publicly opining on the importance of severe sentences, talking in the abstract about a need for more "justice," and protesting sentences that appear too lenient have become mainstays of the movement. The case of Sammy, a cocker spaniel in New Jersey, is illustrative.[18] Sammy's case captured the attention of the animal protection movement and was widely covered in the media, garnering international attention based on criminal charges for a married couple's culpable neglect of Sammy. No one alleges that Sammy was harmed through affirmative acts of abuse, but Sammy the dog suffered horribly. The dog was malnourished, uncared for, and unable to walk when law enforcement became involved. For the married couple, the circumstances at the time of the neglect were not much happier. The couple's neglect occurred during a period of extremely difficult personal circumstances, including a divorce, kidney disease, and suicidal tendencies. Through tears, the wife who had moved out of the house explained that "I should have foreseen that Sammy wouldn't have been safe with my husband, but I didn't know he was going to get so sick [with his kidney disease]. . . . If I had foreseen it I would have taken Sammy with me . . . I'm sorry it turned out the way it did." Both the husband and the wife were ultimately fined and sentenced to six months in prison.

The suffering of Sammy is unquestionably horrifying and worthy of concern. But the case is also an example of how aggressive, far-reaching, and seemingly heartless the turn toward carceral animal law can appear. A petition calling for the maximum sentence for the suicidal couple received over 33,000 signatures, and more than 250 people filed into the municipal courtroom wearing shirts demanding justice for Sammy. At one hearing a woman was removed from the courtroom for yelling "go kill yourself" at the man dying of kidney disease and suffering from depression: The prosecuting attorney explained that he was "very satisfied" with obtaining

---

Div. 2014). By contrast, when a dog is badly abused, animal rights advocates can cheer the prosecution and imprisonment of the abuser as a marked success in the societal need to treat animals better.

[18] Douglas A. Berman, *What Message Does Six-Month Prison Sentence in High-Profile NJ Animal Cruelty Case Really Send?*, SENT'G L. & POL'Y (Nov. 19, 2013), http://sentencing.typepad.com/senten cing_law_and_policy/2013/11/what-message-does-six-month-prison-sentence-in-high-profile-nj -animal-cruelty-case-really-send.html.

incarceration for both parties. Such satisfaction is not misguided; there was literally an angry mob of voting constituents calling for a maximum sentence.

Cases like Sammy's are celebrated within the movement as landmark accomplishments. Indeed, the local SPCA called the maximum sentence for the ill, suicidal man "admirable" insofar as it reflected a strong stand against animal cruelty, even though the cruelty took the form of an omission rather than a set of brutalizing, malicious acts. Many other animal protection groups were involved in urging a maximum sentence,[19] and their advocacy likely had a direct impact on the judge, who explained at sentencing that justice would not be served "[u]nless the defendants are sentenced to [maximum] imprisonment for their depraved acts toward Sammy."[20]

In another case of neglect championed by the animal protection movement, an 83-year-old widow who took in stray dogs but could not afford adequate medical care for one of them on her $400-per-month social security check was prosecuted and convicted.[21] Similarly, in March 2016, prosecutors sought three years of imprisonment for a former NFL player who was suffering from severe depression despite a judge's finding that the defendant had definitively not engaged in any intentional acts of abuse.[22] The defense attorney explained that his client's "level of depression is so significant that he's become just isolated," adding that even communication between the lawyer and his client was often ineffectual because of the depression. And yet, despite the mounting evidence of depression among athletes generally, and particularly among former football players, the prosecutor, who has become a hero among animal protection groups, flippantly responded that "I'm sure every defendant awaiting sentencing is depressed."[23] It is nearly impossible to avoid inherent tension, if not outright contradiction, in the movement's call for greater compassion and understanding on one hand and its support for a rigid approach to incarceration that mocks human suffering or frailties that might be relevant to culpability on the other. One might respond that punishment for crimes committed is readily distinguishable from the "punishment" of innocent animals. But even this orientation is a caricature of a justice system that is at war with basic concepts of civil liberty and criminal culpability. Criminal law scholars have documented that a fixation on "actual innocence" even in the human context is shortsighted, callous, and

---

[19] *See, e.g.,* Nicholas Huba, *Brick Couple Avoids Jail Time in Sammy the Dog Case,* JUST. FOR SAMMY (Mar. 18, 2014), https://justiceforsammy.wordpress.com.

[20] Catherine Galioto, *Judge in Dog Abuse Case: We Need to Send a Message to Animal Abusers,* PATCH (Nov. 19, 2013), https://patch.com/new-jersey/brick/amp/20098266/judge-in-dog-abuse-case-we-need -to-send-a-message-to-animal-abusers.

[21] *See* Martinez v. State, 48 S.W.3d 273 (Tex. App. 2001).

[22] *Wouldn't (Severe? Creative?) Alternatives to Incarceration Be the Best Response to Animal Cruelty Convictions?,* SENT'G L. & POL'Y (Mar. 26, 2016), http://sentencing.typepad.com/sentencing_la w_and_policy/2016/03/wouldnt-severe-creative-alternatives-to-incarceration-be-the-best-response-to -animal-cruelty.html.

[23] *Id.*

reductionist.[24] Inflicting suffering – whether on humans or animals, for whatever reason– should be scrutinized.

The prosecutor in the NFL player's case, Adam Lippe, has also gone on the record as stating that it is incontrovertible that one who harms animals will also progress to harm humans: "If you're willing to exert that [control] in a cruel, malicious and vicious way, then you're likely to do that to people, too, who don't have power, like children and vulnerable adults."[25] Chapter 6 details the centrality of the so-called LINK research as a justification for urging more aggressive prosecutions. But the salience of the LINK in publicity campaigns and legislative advocacy also cannot be gainsaid. The common refrain is, as Mr. Lippe puts it, "if you want to keep people safer, punish animal abuse early and severely." Confronted with evidence that cruelty prosecutions *may not* deter future animal violence, or even change social attitudes, a common retort among animal protection advocates is that such prosecutions are nonetheless essential in order to keep people safe. The message is simple: animal abuse prosecutions protect humans. The LINK data has served more than anything else as the rhetorical platform for outreach to policy makers and prosecutors "about the importance of increasing penalties for violent animal cruelty."[26]

The examples of animal abuse discussed above all consisted of horrible suffering by an animal, but the harm was through omission or neglect.[27] When the harm to the animals moves from neglect into the realm of affirmative, malicious acts of abuse, the publicity and calls for incarceration from the movement are intensified. Activists regarded a 90-day jail sentence for an octogenarian who killed a seal in Hawaii insufficient, and pursued and eventually obtained a state law that makes it a felony to harass a monk seal.[28] This is the normal cycle – use a terrible act of abuse as an opportunity to fundraise, and pass harsher, more far-reaching criminal sanctions. Within a year of the new law's enactment in Hawaii, in 2017, a 20-year-old was sentenced to four years in prison for harassing a monk seal while he was extremely intoxicated.[29]

---

[24] Carol S. Steiker & Jordan M. Steiker, *The Seduction of Innocence: The Attraction and Limitations of the Focus on Innocence in Capital Punishment Law and Advocacy*, 95 J. CRIM. L. & CRIMINOLOGY 587 (2005).

[25] Alison Knezevich, *FBI to Start Tracking Animal Cruelty in 2016*, BALT. SUN, Nov. 27, 2015, www .baltimoresun.com/news/maryland/bs-md-fbi-animal-cruelty-20151126-story.html.

[26] Pamela D. Frasch et al., *State Animal Anti-Cruelty Statutes: An Overview*, 5 ANIMAL L. 69, 70 (1999).

[27] Notably, data suggests that neglect of animals is more common than affirmative abuse. Research from the UK RSPCA, for example, shows that there are approximately 750–1,000 prosecutions per year, and the majority "involve neglect rather than violence." HEATHER PIPER & DEBBIE CORDINGLEY, POWER AND EDUCATION, vol. 1 (3) 345 346 (2009).

[28] *See* Haw. Rev. Stat. § 195D-4.5 (2015) (providing for up to five years imprisonment for any acts that harass or harm or attempt to do so to a monk seal).

[29] Megan Cerullo, *Hawaii Man Sentenced to Four Years in Prison for Harassing Endangered, Pregnant Seal*, N.Y. DAILY NEWS (July 27, 2017), www.nydailynews.com/news/national/hawaii-man-sentenced -years-prison-harassing-seal-article-1.3362242 (The prosecutor justified the sentence by noting the link: "Animal abuse is often a precursor to other types of violence and cannot be tolerated.").

Also illustrative is the case of Andre Robinson, a young black man whose criminal prosecution became an international sensation in 2014.[30] Robinson lured a stray cat toward him and then viciously kicked the cat through the air. The video of the kicking is heart-wrenching. Yet without defending his actions, the *New York Times* accurately observed that "[h]ad it been a person he kicked, Mr. Robinson, 22, most likely would have received a quick plea bargain requiring no jail time – if, that is, he had even been arrested."[31] Instead, Robinson found himself mobbed by protesters at every hearing, and the prosecutor did not make a plea offer. Ordinarily misdemeanors do not attract the attention of the *New York Times*, but this 2014 case was newsworthy precisely because it presented a snapshot of the empowered, carceral turn among animal advocates:

> Once dismissed as cat ladies or fringe do-gooders, they have come to wield real power through funding, organization and a focus on legal remedies for animal abuse. They have embraced social-media campaigns; offered rewards to potential witnesses to animal abuse; trained prosecutors; and made inroads in pushing law enforcement across the country to arrest, and seek jail time for, animal abusers.[32]

To be clear, the "real power" animal advocates have come to wield is simply the ability to be heard by prosecutors, a power to press for more and more serious prosecutions. In Robinson's misdemeanor case, crowds of animal protection protesters attended each preliminary hearing, at times "surrounding him."[33] Robinson's case is also exemplary because of the intensity of the social media campaign against him. Animal protection groups provided an international audience with up-to-the-minute details about the case. Rarely do prosecutors have their charging and bargaining decisions carefully scrutinized and subjected to public ridicule, but in Robinson's case animal protection groups contacted and applied pressure to the prosecutors, urging aggressive charging and a pursuit of incarceration. In fact, it was eventually acknowledged by the prosecutor that "behind-the-scenes" advocacy by animal protection groups had influenced the prosecutor's exercise of discretion and prompted him to refuse to offer *any* plea bargains to Robinson. As the reporter put it, the "activists and the pressure they have put on prosecutors have made the defendant's life, and case, much more complicated."[34] After a Facebook page was created to provide updates about the cat, Robinson become a household face. A meme used on a Facebook page shows a young African American man (presumably Robinson) with the caption "when this" and then an illustration of a cat with the caption, "hurts this," followed by jail bars

[30] Stephanie Clifford, *He Kicked a Stray Cat, and Activists Growled*, N.Y. TIMES (Sept. 29, 2014), www.nytimes.com/2014/09/30/nyregion/animal-abuse-gains-traction-as-a-serious-crime-with-jail-more-often-the-result.html.

[31] *Id.*

[32] Haw. Rev. Stat. § 195D-4.5 (2017).

[33] Tatiana Schlossberg, *Should a Cat-Kicker Go to Jail? Readers Respond*, N.Y. TIMES: CITY ROOM (Sept. 30, 2014), https://cityroom.blogs.nytimes.com/2014/09/30/should-a-cat-kicker-go-to-jail-readers-respond.

[34] Clifford at 30.

and the caption "we demand this." The demand for incarceration for a "this" which happens to be an African American male is a jarring and unsettling juxtaposition.

Robinson says he is now recognized in the streets, and when people see him, "they frown their face up." Cases like Robinson's illustrate that criminal punishment and stigma are a normalized aspect of modern animal protection advocacy. Race, class, and social circumstances are of no moment when certain types of animals are harmed. Demanding incarceration for animal abusers has become a dogma of animal protection law. So much so that a black man can be labeled a "this" and promised incarceration as part of a public relations campaign in support of aggressive prosecutions. Evincing this sort of Javert-like sense of justice, one organization sent out a fundraising email in 2017 that laconically summarized the ethos: "Abuse an animal, go to jail. It's as simple as that. . . . With you by our side, we won't rest until anti cruelty laws are robust and strictly enforced."[35]

The prosecution of individuals who harm animals has come to be viewed as one of the centerpieces of a legal system that respects animals. Instances of abuse ignite furious blog posts and media campaigns directed at prosecutors and the public. And the public is receptive to the notion that focusing on criminal punishment is the essence of animal law. This perception is reinforced by public awards and recognitions by the leading organizations. In giving out awards, it is not uncommon for organizations to honor prosecutors who have taken aggressive positions or secured difficult convictions as the top "Animal Defenders" in the country.[36] In an almost Orwellian twist, prosecutors are treated as the paradigmatic defenders of animals. To deny the centrality of criminal prosecution to the animal protection movement at this point in history is to engage in willful blindness. No doubt slogans will change, and priorities will shift, but it will be years, maybe decades before the movement seriously confronts its legacy of tough-on-crime politics.

3.3 THE SUBSTANTIVE LAW OF INCARCERATION: MORE CRIMES AND INCREASED SENTENCES

The earliest limits on animal cruelty were borne of a desire to protect human interests.[37] The laws protected either a property interest in one's animals against

---

[35] Email from Animal Legal Defense Fund (July 13, 2017) (on file with author).

[36] *America's Top 10 Animal Defenders*, ANIMAL LEGAL DEF. FUND, http://aldf.org/national-justice-for -animals-week/national-justice-for-animals-week-2014/americas-top-10-animal-defenders/ (last visited Nov. 16, 2017).

[37] The extent to which animal cruelty provisions did, in fact, protect people can scarcely be overstated. Animal cruelty provisions and the ASPCA, the organization that was initially instrumental in the protection of animals, provided the inspiration for the first child abuse statutes and organizations dedicated to preventing child abuse. *See, e.g.*, Howard Markel & M. D., *Case Shined First Light on Abuse of Children*, N.Y. TIMES (Dec. 14, 2009), www.nytimes.com/2009/12/15/health/15abus.html (discussing a case brought by the ASPCA in 1874 on behalf of an abused child when no laws protected children from physical abuse from their parents); John E. B. Myers, *A Short History of Child Protection*, 42 FAM. L.Q. 449, 451–52 (2009) (discussing how an animal protection advocate helped

deprivation,[38] or a more general sense of morality based on the notion that permitting animal abuse to go on unabated would debase our communities. As Professor Gary Francione explains this second rationale, anti-cruelty laws reflect classic Victorian Era moral legislation, and the underlying "purpose of the statutes is to improve human character and not to protect animals."[39] In 1896, the Colorado Supreme Court treated the cruelty laws as serving a dual purpose:

> [L]aws, such as the one under consideration, have been enacted by the various states having the common object of protecting these dumb creatures from ill treatment by man. Their aim is not only to protect these animals, but to conserve public morals, both of which are undoubtedly proper subjects of legislation.[40]

Many laws codifying Victorian morality, such as sodomy bans and pornography restrictions, have been struck down entirely or limited substantially, but animal cruelty laws are thriving and expanding.

The first wave of anti-cruelty statutes preceded any organized animal protection movement in the United States by more than a century; New York passed an anti-cruelty law in 1828. By 1913, every state had enacted its own anti-cruelty law; however, animal protection interests did not begin to infuse the legislative drafting until 1868, when the politically connected founder of the ASPCA, Henry Bergh, secured the enactment in New York of a new, more robust anti-cruelty law.[41] Bergh pursued a reform of the New York system because although the cruelty law had been on the books for almost half of a century, "no one could remember that it had ever been used."[42] Bergh's successful reforms in New York proved contagious and started anew an interest in criminal anti-cruelty laws, with other states soon following New York's lead.[43]

---

create the New York Society for the Prevention of Cruelty to Children, the first organization devoted to the protection of children).

[38] Luis E. Chiesa, *Why Is It a Crime to Stomp on a Goldfish? – Harm, Victimhood and the Structure of Anti-Cruelty Offenses*, 78 MISS. L.J. 1, 8–9 (2008) (discussing "an 1846 Vermont statute made it a crime to 'willfully and maliciously kill, wound, maim or disfigure any horse, or horses, or horse kind, cattle, sheep or swine, of another person'").

[39] GARY L. FRANCIONE, ANIMALS, PROPERTY, AND THE LAW 123 (1995). *See also* Amie J. Dryden, *Overcoming the Inadequacies of Animal Cruelty Statutes and the Property-Based View of Animals*, 38 IDAHO L. REV. 177, 212 (2001) (relying on and discussing Francione's work). However, this is not to suggest that animal cruelty was permitted in every state prior to the codification of these laws. For example, the Puritans of Massachusetts provided a "Body of Liberties" in 1641, and Liberty 92 provides "No man shall exercise any Tirrany or Crueltie towards any bruite Creature which are usuallie kept for man's use." GERALD GARTH JOHNSON, PURITAN CHILDREN IN EXILE: THE EFFECTS OF THE PURITAN CONCEPTS OF THE ORIGINAL SIN, DEATH, SALVATION, AND GRACE UPON THE CHILDREN AND GRANDCHILDREN OF THE PURITAN EMIGRANTS LEADING TO THE COLLAPSE OF THE PURITAN PERIOD 243 (2002).

[40] Waters v. People, 46 P. 112, 113 (Colo. 1896).

[41] EMILY STEWART LEAVITT ET AL., ANIMALS AND THEIR LEGAL RIGHTS: A SURVEY OF AMERICAN LAWS FROM 1641-1990 X (4th edn. 1990).

[42] *Id.*

[43] BRUCE A. WAGMAN ET AL., ANIMAL LAW: CASES AND MATERIALS 70 (4th edn. 2010) (describing Bergh as the "catalyst" for this new wave of laws).

At the risk of oversimplifying the diverse legislative outcomes across the states, the reforms central to this new wave of animal cruelty laws were twofold: (1) criminal penalties applied to the abuse of animals, regardless of ownership, thus changing the tradition of only protecting animals from abuse by someone other than their owner; and (2) the laws expanded the scope of the criminal prohibitions so as to include non-intentional acts of abuse, such as mere neglect or the failure to provide adequate care. It appears that the sentences for crimes during this period remained relatively constant.

Although a precise estimate is difficult because of gaps in legislative history and the fact that some states reformed their cruelty codes numerous times during the twentieth century, it appears that between Bergh's reforms in 1868 and 1980 there were a total of about twenty-six states that had reformed their cruelty codes. Thirteen more states did so during the 1980s, and nine more in the 1990s. By 2000, roughly forty-eight states had revised their original animal cruelty codes at least one time in dramatic ways. The remaining two, Kansas and North Dakota, did so in 2010 and 2013 respectively. Important distinctions remain between the laws, but today, because of the efforts of animal protection advocates beginning with Henry Bergh, some version of modernized[44] animal cruelty is recognized as a crime in all fifty states, the District of Columbia, Guam, the Virgin Islands, Puerto Rico, American Samoa, and the Northern Mariana Islands.[45]

By one measure, modern animal cruelty laws reflect a legislative victory for the animal protection movement, and the championing of criminal cruelty laws is understandable. No other legislative success comes close to measuring up to the widespread acceptance of cruelty laws. But the success in achieving criminalization represents the very beginning, not the end, of the carceral animal law story. Animal protection groups are eager for additional reforms, noting that among their top legislative priorities in modern times is further "[s]trengthening anti-cruelty laws and related penalties."[46] In addition, smelling victory on the criminalization front, in recent years, more and more conduct involving animals is finding its way into the criminal code.

Without the efforts of animal protection groups drafting model criminal codes[47] and lobbying for an expanding range of crimes, there would be fewer states with

[44] Not every state adopted all of the Bergh reforms, even as they modernized their cruelty codes. Iowa, for example, continues to define animal abuse in the antiquated fashion as applying only to harm to an animal "owned by another person" and without the "consent of the person owning the animal."

[45] For a thorough history of animal cruelty laws, *see* David Favre & Vivien Tsang, *The Development of Anti-Cruelty Laws During the 1800s*, 1993 Det. C.L. Rev. 1 (1993). According to some accounts, the first criminal law prohibiting harm to animals was in Maine in 1821. Allie Phillips & Randall Lockwood, Nat'l Dist. Att'ys Assoc., Investigating and Prosecuting Animal Abuse 13 (2013); Favre & Tsang at 8 (describing the Maine statute as "the earliest yet uncovered").

[46] *Public Policy*, Am. Soc'y for Prevention of Cruelty to Animals, www.aspca.org/animal-protection /public-policy (last visited Jan. 24, 2018).

[47] Such as the Animal Legal Defense Fund's model codes. *See* Stephen K. Otto, *Model Animal Protection Codes*, Animal Legal Def. Fund (2010), http://aldf.org/downloads /ALDF_Model_Laws_v15_0.pdf.

animal crimes, and the provisions themselves would not be as broad in scope. Most such provisions can be characterized as broadening, if only trivially, the definition of animal cruelty by prohibiting things like bestiality[48] or pet tattoos,[49] or tethering a dog for extended periods.[50] Other provisions seek to criminalize the sale or trade of items that contain animal products from exotic animals, or they criminalize the harassment of a particular wild animal. This is not intended to trivialize these acts, which can be harmful and even deadly to animals. The point is a more straightforward one: the range of criminal prohibitions relating to the treatment of animals is expanding and is lauded as a key legislative victory by many animal protection groups.[51]

Having achieved the power to incarcerate animal abusers in every state, the natural next step for animal law was to focus on increasing the penalties that result from animal cruelty convictions, or to make it easier to convict people of these crimes.

The latter example, seemingly at odds with the due process underpinnings of a democratic society, has been explicitly advocated for by commentators in animal law. One commentator published an article arguing that the requirement of a mens rea in animal cruelty statutes is imposing an unnecessary and "extra burden on prosecutors."[52] The candor of advocating this position is commendable, but such a view of the criminal law is out of touch with the underpinnings of our justice system's requirement of moral fault. And yet, in the view of some animal law commentators and many public supporters of animal protection, animal cruelty should be a strict liability offense – that is, a conviction could be sustained even without any showing of a culpable mental state. Mainstream animal protection groups have not made advocating for strict liability a legislative priority, but neither have they distanced themselves from such proposals.

In defense of strict liability, Jeffrey Holland, an Ohio attorney, explained that defense attorneys in cruelty cases are currently allowed to "twist the words of the

---

[48] *Id.* at 8.
[49] Sherry F. Colb, *New York State Bans Tattoos of Companion Animals*, VERDICT (Jan. 21, 2015), https://verdict.justia.com/2015/01/21/new-york-state-bans-tattoos-companion-animals.
[50] *See* Rebecca F. Wisch, *Table of State Dog Tether Laws*, ANIMAL LEGAL & HIST. CTR., www.animallaw.info/topic/table-state-dog-tether-laws (last visited Jan. 24, 2018) (compiling state dog tethering laws).
[51] They are not the only legislative victory, just the most pervasive and non-controversial. Recent ballot initiatives in a handful of blue states reveal successful efforts in other areas, such as Massachusetts' 2016 initiative that bans farms in the state from raising "any egg-laying hen, breeding pig or calf raised for veal in a way that prevents the animal from lying down, standing up, fully extending its limbs, or turning around freely," and banning the sale in-state of such products produced through the prohibited means by out-state farms. But such laws are few and far between, and often passed only in states where the agricultural industry's presence is minimal. Karin Brulliard, *Massachusetts Voters Say No to Tight Quarters for Hens, Pigs and Calves*, WASH. POST (Nov. 9, 2016), www.washingtonpost.com/news/animalia/wp/2016/11/09/massachusetts-voters-say-no-to-tight-quarters-for-hens-pigs-and-calves/?utm_term=.116be33b2e38 (noting that the law only directly implicated a few thousand egg-laying hens that reside in Massachusetts).
[52] Tresl at 288.

reckless standard" to facilitate acquittals.[53] For this reason a bill was introduced in Ohio in 1998 that would have made animal cruelty a strict liability offense for which "proof of a culpable state of mind is not required."[54] This bill did not pass, but the very fact of such legislation on behalf of the movement's stated interest in protecting animals is illustrative of just how far the animal protection movement has treaded outside of mainstream thinking on fairness in criminal law. Advocating for more strict liability offenses reveals the movement's willingness to treat criminal punishment in this realm as unrelated to the general critiques of the justice system.

One of the most famous articulations of the importance of mens rea in the criminal law involved a potential act of animal abuse. Noting that under well-settled principles of criminal law dating back centuries, the criminal law must require an "evil" or culpable frame of mind in addition to a voluntary act, Oliver Wendall Holmes, Jr. famously observed that even a dog would recognize the difference between "being stumbled over and being kicked."[55] And yet a strict liability animal cruelty statute would not credit the dog's own recognition on this count. The Supreme Court has explained that there is an overriding presumption against strict liability even when the most grammatical reading of a statute would allow for it because of the strong presumption against punishing persons who lack sufficient mental culpability.[56] Contrary to the emotion-laden, ahistorical claims of some animal protection lawyers, preserving the hallowed protection of mens rea in animal cruelty crimes is not an affront to animal protection, it is the *sine qua non* of criminal responsibility.[57] Demolishing the pillars of criminal responsibility is an intolerable vehicle for pursuing the protection of animals.

In addition to efforts to erode the fundamental structure of criminal liability, obtaining longer sentences has emerged as a major priority of the movement and on this score, the animal protection movement has achieved considerable success. As Scott Heiser, the former director of the criminal justice program for the Animal Legal Defense Fund, put it, most states' "sentencing requirements for animal abusers aren't tough enough." As one potential work-around, he advocates the controversial prosecutorial practice by which multiple charges are stacked in a single case "in hopes of getting a longer sentence."[58] Among criminal justice scholars, particularly those focused on wrongful convictions, charge stacking is treated as one of the symptoms of the justice system's unfairness. It has been documented that in cases where prosecutors stack charges in order to create

---

[53]   *Id.* at 300 (interviewing attorneys on this question).

[54]   House Bill 108 (H.B. 108).

[55]   OLIVER WENDELL HOLMES, JR., THE COMMON LAW 2 (1881).

[56]   *See, e.g.,* United States v. X-Citement Video, Inc., 513 U.S. 64, 72 (1994).

[57]   Some prosecutors and commentators have advocated for "at least" reducing the mens rea standard to negligence. Tresl at 311 (quoting a prosecutor, "To overcome this hurdle, the mens rea of animal cruelty statutes needs to be changed, minimally, from a reckless standard to one of negligence.").

[58]   *See, e.g.,* Boyd & Lamparello at 34; Patrick Ronan, *Puppy Doe Case Puts Animal-Abuse Laws in Spotlight*, ENTERPRISE (Oct. 31, 2013), www.enterprisenews.com/article/20131031/NEWS/310319781.

a frighteningly long potential sentence, innocent people can be intimidated into pleading guilty in order to benefit from a supposedly "generous" plea bargain. Charge stacking is often viewed as an overly aggressive, bullying tactic that disproportionately impacts low-income individuals and increases the risk of innocent people pleading guilty, but it has been explicitly endorsed by leaders in the animal protection movement. One of the most respected criminal law scholars in modern history, William Stuntz, has described the modern obsession with criminal law as pathological, and noted that the expanding range of the criminal law can "utterly undo the accuracy-enhancing features of the law of criminal procedure," and the "ability to stack charges puts" the accuracy of convictions in serious doubt.[59]

In the animal law field, however, leading academics, including Joan Schaffner, have ignored this literature and instead argued that the status of animals in the law will never be improved unless harsher sanctions are available, and people are prosecuted "to the fullest extent of the law."[60] The sentiment is nearly ubiquitous among public commentators and organizations in support of animal protection, which frequently decry what they call the "alarmingly lenient" sentences for animal cruelty offenses.[61] Some commentators have gone so far as to view effective animal advocacy as *best* served through expansion of the range of animal crimes and the possible penalties for these crimes. As one commentator put it, "*The* role of the animal law attorney, therefore, must be to strengthen, endorse, and enforce state anti-cruelty statutes."[62]

Emblematic of the very pathology that Stuntz found so troubling, one of the major goals of the animal protection movement in the early 2000s was to have animal abuse categorized as a felony in all fifty states. Like the criminalization of cruelty, the animal protection movement cannot take credit for the first wave of felony provisions, which predated the movement itself and corresponded to an interest in protecting the moral purity of mankind and protection of property rights.[63] In 1804, Massachusetts enacted the first law that made animal cruelty a felony.[64] Following Massachusetts, Oklahoma enacted a felony animal cruelty law in 1887, then Rhode Island followed suit in 1896, and Michigan in 1931. No other state enacted a felony provision until the 1980s. Three states enacted felony laws in the 1980s, nineteen in the 1990s, and the final twenty-four states (and the District of

---

[59]   Willliam J. Stuntz, Reply: Criminal Law's Pathology, 101 Mich. L. Rev. 828, 829 (2002).

[60]   Joan E. Schaffner, *Laws and Policy to Address the Link of Family Violence*, in The Link Between Animal Abuse and Human Violence 231 (Andrew Linzey ed., 2009).

[61]   Boyd & Lamparello at 34.

[62]   Tresl at 295 ("If an attorney wants to make people listen, she should concentrate her efforts on revising and strictly enforcing her state's animal cruelty statutes.").

[63]   *See Animal Cruelty Facts and Statistics*, Humane Soc'y U.S., www.humanesociety.org/issues/abuse_neglect/facts/animal_cruelty_facts_statistics.html (last visited Jan. 24, 2018) (stating that the first four states to enact animal cruelty laws did so before 1931).

[64]   Animal cruelty was deemed a crime against nature. "Whoever commits the abominable and detestable crime against nature, either with mankind or with a beast, shall be punished by imprisonment in the state prison for not more than twenty years." Mass. Gen. Laws ch. 272, § 34 (2017).

Columbia) enacted felony laws after 2000. South Dakota was the last state to enact a felony cruelty law, and it did so on March 14, 2014.[65] The enactment of new felony laws in all fifty states is regarded as a decisive and critical victory for which the animal protection movement proudly takes credit. The Humane Society described the expanding felony codes as a "significant milestone for animal protection,"[66] and the Executive Director for the Animal Legal Defense Fund explained, "When I joined the Animal Legal Defense Fund 15 years ago [in 1999], getting all states on the felony anti-cruelty map was a major goal. At that time, only about thirty states had these provisions."[67] In fact, the organization's widely publicized 50-state rankings on animal welfare was specifically designed to draw embarrassing media attention to those states that had failed to pass felony laws, or had failed to keep up, by passing new, more severe felony provisions.

Creating more felonies was never the end goal. Although all fifty states now have felony anti-cruelty laws, there is still an overriding consensus within the movement that the laws are insufficiently punitive. The problem is not just underenforcement, say the leaders in the movement, but the insufficiently high statutory maximum sentences. Some of the felony cruelty laws, deemed inadequate, are only triggered if the individual has a prior conviction (or in one state two prior convictions)[68] for animal abuse.[69] Others require some particularly egregious or sadistic abuse before felony liability attaches. Such limits on felony liability are treated by the Humane Society and the ASPCA, among other groups, as urgently in need of being "upgraded."[70] In the world of animal protection, then, the restrictions on felonious liability are treated as a concrete statement of disinterest in the well-being of

[65] Chris Berry, *All 50 States Now Have Felony Animal Cruelty Provisions!*, ANIMAL LEGAL DEF. FUND (Mar. 14, 2014), http://aldf.org/blog/50-states-now-have-felony-animal-cruelty-provisions/.

[66] *See South Dakota Lawmakers Enact Stronger Animal Cruelty Penalties*, HUMANE SOC'Y U.S. (Mar. 14, 2014), www.humanesociety.org/news/news_briefs/2014/03/south-dakota-lawmakers-enact-stronger-animal-cruelty-penalties-031414.html ("The enactment of [the South Dakota felony animal cruelty law] is a significant milestone for the animal protection movement . . . Today, due to the hard work of animal advocates and lawmakers . . . every state and the District of Columbia has some form of a felony animal cruelty law.").

[67] Stephen Wells, *Legally Brief: Felony Laws Are a Victory for Animals*, ANIMAL LEGAL DEF. FUND (Mar. 27, 2014), http://aldf.org/blog/legally-brief-felony-laws-are-a-victory-for-animals/; *see also id.* (video link explaining that the lack of a felony charge was an "injustice" because it trivialized animal abuse).

[68] Idaho is the only state that requires two prior offenses before abuse is a felony.

[69] Six have second-offense felonies (Iowa, Mississippi, Ohio, and Pennsylvania have felony laws that apply only on the second offense; Texas and Virginia have second-offense felonies, depending on the situation). *Animal Cruelty Facts and Statistics* ("The HSUS believes all states should allow felony charges for egregious cruelty regardless of whether the perpetrator has a prior conviction.").

[70] *Idaho Felony Animal Cruelty Bill Praised as Step in the Right Direction*, HUMANE SOC'Y U.S. (Mar. 30, 2012), www.humanesociety.org/news/press_releases/2012/03/idaho_felony_animal_cruelty_033012.html. *See also South Dakota Lawmakers Enact Stronger Animal Cruelty Penalties* ("The Humane Society of the United States strongly supported both upgrades to the [South Dakota animal cruelty] laws.").

animals. More felonies, more first-offense felonies, and greater use of felony charges are central pieces of the animal protection movement's modern advocacy.

Even in states with felony provisions for first-offense animal abuse, animal protection groups have continued to devote considerable lobbying resources and campaigns in service of the goal of increasing the penalty of felony abuse. For example, Massachusetts, at the urging of animal protection groups, passed a statute in 2014 (dubbed the Puppy Doe bill) that increased the maximum penalty for animal abuse from five years to seven years for first offenses, and to ten years imprisonment for second offenses.[71] In 2018, there is a bill pending that would establish a new round of Puppy Doe "updates" that will increase the punitiveness for animal cruelty. Other states have considered or adopted similar expansions in the maximum penalties. It is not uncommon for the animal protection movement to be involved in the drafting of revisions to enhanced criminal provisions. In other contexts, advocates have urged sentencing enhancements for animal violence when the abuse is carried out in the context of domestic violence.

Beyond increasing the reach of the criminal law and expanding the number of felonies, animal protection scholars and groups are also resolutely in favor of other draconian substantive reforms. Advocates have endorsed imposing mandatory minimum sentences for animal abuse crimes. A mandatory minimum sentence is a means of cabining a prosecutor or sentencing judge's discretion by imposing an inflexible floor, below which a sentence for a particular crime may not fall. Mandatory minimum sentences became popular during the war on drugs throughout the 1990s. Mandating an automatic minimum prison term regardless of the circumstances has a harsh dehumanizing effect. For most of this nation's history, sentencing judges enjoyed virtually unlimited sentencing discretion – they could tailor the punishment to the crime and the individual. Mandatory minimums make such tailoring, and individualized sentencing, impossible. As noted conservative criminal law scholar Paul Cassell has explained, the "'no escape' feature of the mandatory minimums can lead to possible injustices in particular cases."[72] In light of the inability of mandatory minimum sentencing regimes to allow for a sentence to be tailored to the circumstances, they are widely considered to be inhumane, sparking frequent litigation about whether mandatory minimums violate the Eighth Amendment bar on cruel and unusual punishment. More recently, the recognition of their harshness has led to high-profile, bipartisan support for eliminating or reducing the number of mandatory minimums.

---

[71] *See, e.g., ASPCA Commends Mass. Lawmakers for Passing "Puppy Doe" Bill*, AM. SOC'Y FOR PREVENTION CRUELTY TO ANIMALS (Aug. 14, 2014), www.aspca.org/about-us/press-releases/aspca -commends-mass-lawmakers-passing-puppy-doe-bill (applauding "Massachusetts lawmakers for passing a measure to increase maximum jail time and monetary penalties for animal cruelty.").

[72] Paul G. Cassell, *Too Severe?: A Defense of the Federal Sentencing Guidelines (and a Critique of Federal Mandatory Minimums)*, 56 STAN. L. REV. 1017, 1018 (2004).

Nonetheless, scholars in the field of animal law have advocated for an animal protection regime that would include mandatory minimums. For example, Joan Schaffner, the founder of the section for animal law within the Association of American Law Schools conference, has explained that in order to "reflect the seriousness of [animal cruelty] properly, the law should impose a minimum sentence."[73] Another legal commentator noted that "mandatory minimums are not guaranteed to solve all of the many problems with prosecuting animal abusers," but such reforms are desirable insofar as they will have the apparently salutary effect of giving the prosecution a "significant bargaining chip" that will ensure quick plea bargains and harsher sentences.[74] Many in the animal protection movement would likely appreciate that mandatory minimum sentences are illustrative of the unfairness of the justice system's operation, but they support this very system when it targets those who harm animals. It is animal law exceptionalism.

Similarly disorienting, animal protection groups have also been supportive of charging children as adults for crimes relating to animal mistreatment. The criminal law has historically separated juveniles from adults in considering the appropriateness of a particular conviction or punishment. Children are understood to have reduced culpability because, in part, they are less capable of impulse control and reasoning than fully matured adults. Children have greatly reduced culpability until their brain is fully developed, which appears to be around age 25. For this reason, children are typically prosecuted in juvenile courts, where the focus is supposed to be on treating the delinquency rather than punishing for criminal deviance. Yet in stark contradiction to the science about brain development and the norms of criminal law, states are increasingly willing to permit prosecutors to charge juveniles as adults and subject them to the same range of criminal punishments. This impulse to "get tough" on crime by treating kids as adults has been roundly criticized by humanitarian groups. The Equal Justice Initiative, for example, has explained that:

> Many young children in America are imperiled by abuse, neglect, domestic and community violence, and poverty.... Sadly, many states have ignored the crisis and dysfunction that creates child delinquency and instead have subjected kids to further victimization and abuse in the adult criminal justice system. Across the United States, thousands of children have been sentenced as adults and sent to adult prisons.... Some 10,000 children are housed in adult jails and prisons on any given day in America. Children are five times more likely to be sexually assaulted in adult prisons than in juvenile facilities and face increased risk of suicide.[75]

Just as one would not impute malice to animals who misbehave or mistreat each other, it seems odd to impute adult liability to young persons who are not fully culpable. Nonetheless, when animal abuse occurs at the hands of juveniles, advocates have

---

[73] Schaffner at 137.

[74] Brimer at 665.

[75] *Children in Prison*, EQUAL JUST. INITIATIVE, https://eji.org/children-prison (last visited Jan. 24, 2018).

urged that the children be charged and sentenced as adults. The advocacy group Last Chance for Animals, for example, has publicly lamented the state law barriers for prosecutors in California to charge juveniles as adults for animal cruelty, describing it as unfortunate that state law "shields minor defendants by statutorily limiting what types of crimes a minor can be deemed fit to be charged as an adult." Being sentenced as a juvenile is treated as allowing the children to get off with a mere "slap on the wrist."[76] Other groups and campaigns share this perspective.

Online petitions seeking to have teenagers charged as adults are not uncommon. In 2018, a change.org petition, "Justice for Thor," was nearing 75,000 signatures in support of charging a teenager who had horrifically slashed the throat of a puppy as an adult. Repeating the folk psychology myth that if one can commit acts that would be criminal as an adult, one must be treated as an adult, the petition's author explained, "If he can make the decision to deeply cut an innocent baby animal's throat . . . he can be charged as an adult!!!" In 2009, even a pregnant 14-year-old was deemed an appropriate target for abandoning the historic practice of treating juveniles as deserving special compassion, and at the urging of animal protection advocates, she was charged as an adult with felony animal abuse in New York.[77]

For persons and groups concerned with civil liberties, subjecting children to adult punishment is antiquated and unacceptable, but this is not a radical position within the animal protection movement. Leading figures from the movement have testified as experts for the prosecution in hearings urging that a judge allow a juvenile to be treated as an adult.[78] Leading animal protection groups even devote resources and file legal briefs in support of the imprisonment of children. In one illustrative 2017 brief, in a case from Massachusetts, an animal protection organization explained that it "is clear that felony animal cruelty [should permit an] indictment as an adult," because, among other reasons, there exists a "longstanding, strong public policy of animal protection in the Commonwealth."[79] The brief argued that "Child animal abusers . . . are ticking time bombs whom society needs to *address* at the earliest possible moment" by punishing them as adults.[80] It is both callous and unproven to assume that by imprisoning children as young as 14 as adults, society will effectively

---

[76] *The Correlation Between Animal Cruelty and Violent Offenders*, LAST CHANCE FOR ANIMALS, www.lcanimal.org/index.php/campaigns/other-issues/animal-cruelty-a-violent-behavior/teen-animal-abuser-convicted (last visited Jan. 24, 2018).

[77] Lisa Colangelo, *Teen Accomplice in Kitten Roasting Case Charged with Felony Animal Cruelty*, N.Y. DAILY NEWS (June 17, 2009), www.nydailynews.com/news/crime/teen-accomplice-kitten-roasting-case-charged-felony-animal-cruelty-article-1.379420; *Petition to Have Cheyenne Cherry Tried as Adult*, CARE 2 PETITIONS, www.thepetitionsite.com/332/petition-to-have-cheyenne-cherry-tried-as-adult/ (last visited Jan. 24, 2018).

[78] Charles Siebert, *The Animal-Cruelty Syndrome*, N.Y. TIMES (June 11, 2010) at MM42 (noting that Randall Lockwood from the ASPCA "was asked to testify at the pretrial hearing in which a judge ruled that Tremayne and Travers Johnson would be tried as adults for the burning of Phoenix in Baltimore.").

[79] Massachusetts case, Comm. v. a Juvenile, SJC 12277, Amicus Brief of ALDF, at 12.

[80] *Id.* at 19 (emphasis added).

address any mental illness or defect. But the same brief goes on to argue that only by punishing juveniles as adults will it be recognized in law that "animal life is valuable in and of itself." By imprisoning young people in a way that is not in accord with their culpability, the movement presumes that greater appreciation for all sentient life will be achieved. The paradoxical notion is that the caging of children will liberate animals.

3.4 STRUCTURAL OR PROCEDURAL REFORMS IN THE SERVICE OF INCREASED INCARCERATION

If substantive criminal law reforms are the "cornerstone" of American animal law, as Joyce Tischler has called them, the procedural reforms sought in support of more and longer convictions are the foundation. Recognizing that new criminal laws represent formal but not necessarily functional success, the animal protection movement has committed significant resources to ensuring that the criminal laws relating to animals are actually used, and that when they are used, they are effective in securing convictions and sentences. The parameters of this procedural advocacy include arguing for narrow constructions of constitutional rights, assisting police and prosecutorial efforts to obtain maximum sentences, creating victim advocates, and pursuing offender registry legislation.

3.4.1 *Limiting Constructions of the Federal Constitution*

The animal protection movement has advocated for a number of very narrow constructions of constitutional rights that, divorced from an agenda of maximizing prosecutorial success would be inconceivable. Behind-the-scenes advocacy and trainings put on by animal protection groups have likely shaped the views of prosecutors about the reach of the constitution in animal cruelty cases, but such impacts are difficult to measure. However, animal protection groups also take public positions against expansive interpretations of the constitution in litigation, especially through amicus briefs.[81] The narrow view of the constitution adopted by animal protection advocates through amicus briefs in cruelty cases has received essentially no scrutiny. Without attempting to fully catalogue the range of efforts the movement has pursued in the service of limiting constitutional rights, examples include expanding the power of police to enter and search without warrants, urging an expansion of the category of speech that is "unprotected" under the First Amendment, and advocating that the targeting of political minorities is constitutionally permissible. These briefs provide some insight into the dissonance between the animal protection movement and civil rights more generally.

---

[81] Richard H. Fallon, Jr., *Scholars' Briefs and the Vocation of a Law Professor*, 4 J. LEGAL ANALYSIS 223, 223 (2012) (arguing that many professors compromise their integrity by joining such briefs too promiscuously).

3.4.1.1 Freedoms Against Political Targeting

Church of the Lukumi Babalu Aye v. *City of Hialeah* has emerged as a landmark decision protecting political minorities from overt, animus-inspired legislation.[82] The case involved the City of Hialeah's efforts to criminally proscribe religious animal slaughter by people of the Santeria religion. Of enduring import, the Court definitively rejected the contention that a statute's *facial neutrality* is determinative as to its constitutionality, and thus confirmed that legislative motive is relevant to an assessment of a statute's constitutionality. As the Court explained, the Constitution protects against "government hostility which is masked, as well as overt."[83] The decision's significance in this regard is evidenced by a federal court of appeals decision striking down President Trump's ban on refugees from certain Muslim-majority countries. It also comes up in every challenge to an Ag-Gag law or any other provision singling out animal rights activists for disadvantage. The first federal appellate court to rule on Trump's refugee ban explicitly invoked the *Lukumi* decision as authority for considering illicit motives on the part of government officials, noting that "It is well established that evidence of purpose beyond the face of the challenged law may be considered in evaluating Establishment and Equal Protection Clause claims."[84]

The record in the *Lukumi* case left no doubt that the city council's emergency session and subsequent criminal ordinances were borne out of animus to the Santeria religion.[85] Indeed, this is precisely why this case has been described as "simple" and why it was decided unanimously. Determining whether a law is neutral (or generally applicable) can be outcome-determinative in legal challenges, and it will sometimes involve fine-grained judgment calls, but where a law is found to directly target a particular religion or group, and when it exempts other groups, the argument for neutrality is futile. Examining the targeting that occurred by the city in this case, James Oleske has compiled the findings by the Supreme Court:

> The Court . . . observed that the ordinances were "enacted . . . in direct response to the opening of the church," and described the context in which the gerrymandered ordinances were drafted. "The prospect of a Santeria church in their midst was distressing to many members of the Hialeah community, and the announcement of the plans to open a Santeria church in Hialeah prompted the city council to hold an emergency public session." Against that background, and in light of the text and operation of the resulting ordinances, the Court had little difficulty concluding that "Santeria alone was the exclusive legislative concern" of the City Council. And the

---

[82]   Church of Lukumi Babalu Aye v. City of Hialeah, 508 U.S. 520 (1993) [hereinafter *Lukumi*].

[83]   *Id.* at 534.

[84]   Washington v. Trump, 847 F.3d 1151, 1167 (9th Cir.), reconsideration en banc denied, 853 F.3d 933 (9th Cir. 2017).

[85]   *Lukumi*, 508 U.S. at 534 ("The record in this case compels the conclusion that suppression of the central element of the Santeria worship service was the object of [Hialeah's] ordinances.").

concern was obviously not benign: "The pattern we have recited discloses animosity to Santeria adherents and their religious practices."[86]

The hostility to the Santeria was so patent that during the legislative debate the religion was condemned as "barbaric devil worship."[87]

In spite of this uniquely explicit legislative history, nearly every major animal rights group filed amicus briefs urging the Supreme Court to view the law as facially neutral, and therefore constitutional. Indeed, many of the briefs take the position that a facially neutral law – that is, one that does not single out the Santerias by name in the text of the law – is absolutely immune from constitutional scrutiny. Many of the briefs in support of the animal protection movement argued by analogy from cases from prior eras that were grounded in overt racism and discrimination. For example, the animal protection movement's many briefs frequently cited an 1879 decision, *U.S. v. Reynolds*, as the controlling authority for their argument. *Reynolds* was a case upholding bigamy laws against free exercise challenges by, in large part, noting the historical connection between polygamy and less "civilized" non-whites: "Polygamy has always been odious among the northern and western nations of Europe, and, until the establishment of the Mormon Church, was almost exclusively a feature of the life of Asiatic and of African people."[88] As subsequent courts and scholars have recognized, the defining feature of *Reynolds* was its finding that "polygamy [was] harmful merely because it was a non-Western practice."[89] But perhaps more than any other single case, *Reynolds* was central to nearly every brief filed by the animal protection movement. As the brief on behalf of the Humane Society and the ASPCA put it, *Reynolds* guarantees that a state law does not run afoul of the "Free Exercise Clause even if it was promulgated in specific response to moral objections to a religious practice."

The animal protection groups and scholars sought to defend the legislation targeting Santeria practices, which included animal sacrifice, by undermining some of the foundational constitutional protections for oppressed political minorities. For example, leading animal law scholar Gary Francione wrote a brief for PETA and other groups urging the Court to hold that despite the animus against a discrete religious minority in the legislative record, the laws must be regarded as generally applicable and constituitonal. The Humane Society filed a brief that was even more direct, claiming that as a legal matter the Court should hold that the city council members' subjective intent in enacting the laws was entirely irrelevant. The Humane Society urged an understanding of the Constitution that would treat legislative "motive" as something that courts are prohibited from considering;

---

[86] James Oleske, Jr., *Lukumi at Twenty: A Legacy of Uncertainty for Religious Liberty and Animal Welfare Laws*, 19 ANIMAL L. 295, 303 (2013).

[87] KIMBERLY K. SMITH, GOVERNING ANIMALS: ANIMAL WELFARE AND THE LIBERAL STATE 130 (2012).

[88] Reynolds v. United States, 98 U.S. 145, 164, 25 L. Ed. 244 (1878).

[89] Maura I. Strassberg, *Scrutinizing Polygamy: Utah's Brown v. Buhman and British Columbia's Reference Re: Section 293*, 64 EMORY L.J. 1815, 1822 (2015).

according to the HSUS brief, the "improper or discriminatory motive" of proponents of these laws is not something courts should or can consider in reviewing a government action. Of course, the argument that improper legislative motive is irrelevant to the validity of the statute is self-serving, because the legislative record was tainted by animus from the movement itself. An HSUS expert testified in the trial court, for example, that Santeria was a "bloody cult . . . whose continued presence further blights the image of South Florida."[90] But more generally, the legal positions staked out by the movement's leading lawyers and academics in this case, had they been successful, would have proven devastating for constitutional litigation by all social justice litigation in support of protecting minority, or oppressed political groups.

As Kimberly K. Smith has explained, "We can expect, in a majoritarian political system, that the dominant cultural perspective will usually be reflected in our laws."[91] For this reason, constitutional liberties against, for example, a targeted attack on a group whose practices and worldview are "very much at odds with those of the majority" are critical to protecting the rights of emerging or non-majority political constituencies. The animal protection movement is still very much a small, politically nascent movement. By seeking to insulate politically motivated legislation from constitutional scrutiny, the movement was willing to forfeit a major source of protection for their own advocacy and outreach. Animal protection lawyers and scholars were willing to forego a long-term broadly conceived set of constitutional protections against animus and political targeting in order to ensure jail time for a handful of religious minorities, persons generally identified by Kimberly K. Smith as "dark-skinned, working class" immigrants, who engage in ritual animal abuse.

For legal scholars, the folly of this approach should have been patent. Not only is the importance of opposing legal oppression deeply entrenched in social change lawyering, but the legal doctrine at issue is critical to combatting such oppression. The importance of demonstrating that an otherwise facially valid law could be rendered unconstitutional because of improper legislative motive is of nearly canonical importance to social justice lawyers. Facially neutral efforts to restrict minority voting, no less than legislation aimed at disadvantaging lesbians and gays, were held unconstitutional only because of the underlying, improper legislative motives. Oftentimes the statute did not specify a race or minority by name, but rather targeted them with legislative precision and the veneer of neutrality. The same issue is also directly relevant to some of the key animal law concerns in recent years. For example, Ag-Gag laws, tainted as they are by the farm industry's explicit effort to cripple the animal protection movement, do not single out animal protection groups

---

[90] David M. O'Brien, Animal Sacrifice and Religious Freedom: Church of the Lukumi Babalu Aye v. City of Hialeah 41, 83 (2004). More generally, the legislative record was replete with condemnation for the "devil-worship," and a recognition that not all ritual slaughter, for example kosher slaughter, was prohibited.

[91] Smith at 133.

as reviled or disfavored on the plain text of the law, just as Hialeah did not explicitly draft legislation targeting the Santeria. And juxtaposing the legal arguments in each instance reveals a striking similarity among animal protection arguments in the Santeria case and the arguments of the prosecuting attorneys in attorneys general offices defending Ag-Gag laws. The Humane Society argued in its brief in support of the Hialeah that:

> By citing to selective portions of the minutes of the City Council's meetings, petitioners misdirect the Court's inquiry from the *purpose* of the ordinances to the subjective *motivations* of concerned citizens and a few Council members. This Court, however, has recognized the important distinction between legislative purpose and motive.[92]

Likewise, in defending their state's far reaching Ag-Gag law, the State of Idaho explained that the interest of the legislature in targeting animal activists was irrelevant:

> As a matter of law, the *motives* of individual legislators in supporting or opposing a bill should not be considered in identifying its purpose . . . and more generally the law precludes this Court from psychoanalyzing the Idaho legislature as a whole or individual legislators to extract a subjective *"motive"* for enacting the Ag-Gag law.[93]

Had the more than a dozen animal protection groups that supported the City of Hialeah persuaded the Supreme Court that the underlying illicit motivation for government action was constitutionally irrelevant, their victory would stand as a major obstacle to free speech, equal protection, and other constitutional claims of the sort brought by politically disfavored groups, including the animal protection movement, who are unfairly singled out for disadvantage in our political system.

Sometimes lawyers represent clients whose interest in a particular case is at odds with the long-term development of the social movement.[94] But the many scholars and animal law lawyers who came to the defense of Hialeah did so not as lawyers for the City, but as amici offering their unsolicited and unnecessary legal input. Not bound by the restrictions that flow from representing a client in a particular case, the leaders in the animal law field nonetheless seized the opportunity to argue that the constitutional protections prohibiting illicit political targeting should be abandoned, or at least greatly reduced. Had the movement's defense of a set of criminal laws succeeded, the state of constitutional law might look much different today. Few legal arguments are more at war with an effort to facilitate anti-oppression efforts

---

[92]   Brief for The Humane Society of the United States et al. as Amici Curiae Supporting Respondents at 12–13, Church of the Lukumi Babalu Aye v. City of Hialeah, 508 U.S. 520 (1993) (No. 91-948) (arguing that it was settled law that an otherwise constitutional law should not be struck down based on illicit motive).

[93]   ALDF v. Wasden, State of Idaho, Opening Br. 9th Cir at p.54.

[94]   There is a robust academic literature about the tensions between lawyering for a "cause" and lawyering for a particular "client."

through the legal system. Fortunately for animal advocates and every other social justice movement, their arguments in favor of ignoring improper government motive were not adopted by the Supreme Court.

3.4.1.2 Narrowing the Scope of Constitutional Defenses Available to Defendants

There is open hostility among animal protection advocates and scholars to constitutional protections that limit the ability of prosecutors to secure convictions for animal cruelty. In summarizing a recent decision limiting the scope of Fourth Amendment protections, advocates said things like, "Animals seem to be winning important cases in . . . the criminal justice system." There is an unmistakable sense that limiting constructions of the Fourth Amendment are "good news for animal welfare, [and] [b]ad news for lowlife scum animal abusers."[95]

There is a widely accepted notion that a more narrowly construed set of search and seizure rights will help protect animals by ensuring that people guilty of animal abuse do not escape conviction. Many advocates do not think about the impact on their own activism, or that of more radical elements of the movement, on reducing the footprint of the Fourth Amendment. Indeed, many seem to imagine that their advocacy occurs in a vacuum. They act as though the limits on the Fourth Amendment apply only to cases of animal cruelty. But in reality, the limits on unreasonable searches and seizures do not vary by the type of crime. Similarly, there is a common retort among animal advocates that the abuser is guilty, but, of course, the Fourth Amendment means very little if it is only a protection for persons who turn out to be innocent. As the Supreme Court has repeatedly recognized, a "Fourth Amendment protection, reserved for the innocent only, would have little force in regulating police behavior toward either the innocent or the guilty."[96]

The Fourth Amendment generally prohibits warrantless searches or seizures. Entry onto private property, or the seizure of private property without a warrant or consent is presumptively unconstitutional. As the Supreme Court recently explained, the basic rule is that "searches conducted outside the judicial process, without prior approval by judge or magistrate, are *per se* unreasonable under the Fourth Amendment – subject only to a few specifically established and well-delineated exceptions."[97] The Fourth Amendment stands as the bulwark against general warrants, sweeps of a community for crime, and intrusions on privacy by the investigative arm of the government. The animal protection movement, however, focuses considerable resources and attention toward the goal of expanding the

---

[95] *Pets Are Not Mere Objects Oregon Supreme Court Rules*, THE POODLE AND DOG BLOG (June 20, 2016), http://thepoodleanddogblog.typepad.com/the_poodle_and_dog_blog/2016/06/pets-are-not-mere -objects-oregon-supreme-court-rules.html
[96] Minnesota v. Carter, 525 U.S. 83, 110 (1998).
[97] Arizona v. Gant, 556 U.S. 332, 338 (2009) (quoting Katz v. United States, 389 U.S. 347, 357 [1967]).

number and scope of the supposedly "specifically established and well-delineated exceptions." In this endeavor, the movement has found considerable legal "success."

First, and perhaps least controversially, the animal protection movement has successfully urged courts to expand the so-called "emergency exception" to the warrant requirement. In Massachusetts, animal protection groups authored and submitted amicus briefs to the state supreme court that were cited in support of the holding of the court recognizing an expansion of the emergency exception to the warrant requirement.[98] With the support of animal protection groups, other state supreme courts have reached the same conclusion.[99] To a certain extent it is hard to find folly in a rule that simply reduces barriers to saving the life of a helpless animal. But the critical feature of these decisions and the advocacy supporting them is an overriding enthusiasm for prosecutions. An expansion of the exceptions to the Fourth Amendment will result in very few animal lives actually being saved, if for no other reason than police officers are busy and not generally in a position where their decision to enter without calling first to get a warrant will mean the difference between life and death for an animal.

Instead, what expanded emergency exceptions do is provide law enforcement with a larger range of after-the-fact explanations for entering one's home without a warrant. The wider the range of exceptions to the warrant requirement, the more frequently a police officer's entry into a home will be treated as reasonable. Law enforcement officers can get warrants by phone or email in a matter of minutes, so the emergency aid exception does not serve a glaring, unaccounted for need. Even if one assumes that an agent of law enforcement will necessarily need to enter homes on short notice in order to rescue an animal (perhaps a dog left on a balcony without shade or sustenance), the emergency aid exception to the Fourth Amendment is primarily necessary as a means of ensuring that the entry does not limit or preclude a subsequent prosecution. The rule is one that simply ensures that inculpatory evidence is not suppressed at trial and makes a conviction more likely. Of course, what the expanded emergency exception does not do, which might result in a substantial alleviation of animal suffering, is allow any private person who is in a position to rescue an animal (and not necessarily to bring a prosecution) to enter private property (at least a field, yard, or car) and save an animal. Indeed, many states don't even explicitly recognize a right of private citizens to break the window of a hot car to rescue an animal, much less provide an affirmative defense against prosecution for one who enters private property to save an animal from imminent death. If the priority is not prosecution but the rescue of imperiled animals, activists and the movement might prioritize laws like those in California, which allow for one to lawfully enter private property to provide care to an animal in need. The much more

---

[98] *See* Commonwealth v. Duncan, 7 N.E.3d 469, 469 n.1, 474-75 (Mass. 2014) (noting that several animal rights organizations had submitted amicus briefs and concluding that "the emergency aid exception [to the Fourth Amendment] encompass[es] warrantless searches to protect nonhuman animal life").

[99] State v. Fessenden, 333 P.3d 278, 279 (Or. 2014).

limited popularity and prevalence of these entry for care laws, which provide *limits on prosecuting* private persons as opposed to assistance to police and prosecutors, is a telling reminder of the priorities of the movement.

Beyond expanding the range of instances where police may enter private property, animal protection advocates have also supported and celebrated a narrow definition of the term "search" as used in the Fourth Amendment. In *State* v. *Newcomb*, the Oregon Supreme Court embraced the position urged in amicus briefs by the animal protection movement and held that the "defendant had no protected privacy interest in [his dog's] blood that was invaded by the medical procedures performed."[100] The "search" of a dog through a blood draw, in other words, is treated as a non-search. This case was heralded in blogs and press releases as a significant milestone because it was, as the Animal Legal Defense Fund's blog reported, judicial recognition that "Animal sentience matters!" But notice the relevance of sentience. Because the dog was sentient, somehow the court felt justified in reaching a decision that those familiar with the Fourth Amendment would find quite concerning. To be sure, the conclusion that a pet's owner does not enjoy some sort of constitutionally enshrined right to prevent his animal from receiving emergency veterinary care (and losing the animal) is positive and deserving of cheer from the animal protection movement. However, *Newcomb*'s holding that the removal of blood or bodily fluids from an animal is not a search goes much further.

Under *Newcomb*, could police seize the cats of a woman who they suspect deals cocaine or methamphetamine and, without a warrant, test the animals' skin, saliva, and blood for traces of the drug to use as evidence of drugs passing through the house? The celebrated reasoning of *Newcomb* concludes that the removal of bodily fluids from an animal is not a search, and yet the clearly established law is that blood draws from humans (one's self or one's children) are definitely a search.[101] In one sense, the notion that subjecting animals to invasive medical testing is not a search is a diminishment of an animal's status. A decision that truly emphasized the importance of animal sentience might reflect on the deprivation of the animal's bodily integrity, as the cases do in the context of evaluating medical procedures or searches of a human's body. Instead, *Newcomb* is the worst of both worlds. It treats the dog as the property of the human owner, thus considering the dog's interests irrelevant, and also holds that there is no search of the human owner's property because the property is special. It is also very difficult to rationalize the court's decision that though the dog is the property of the owner, there was no trespassory search in this context.[102]

Notice, then, what a recognition of sentience by courts achieves in the criminal law context – the successful conviction and incarceration of a person. Sentience in the eyes of the movement has become a means of securing convictions with fewer constitutional limits. But it is worth pondering what this status of animals as special

---

[100]   *Newcomb*, 375 P.3d at 442.
[101]   Schmerber v. Cal., 384 U.S. 757 (1966).
[102]   U.S. v. Jones, 565 U.S. 400 (2012).

evidence means. What does the special status of animals portent if animals are assumed to consent to searches of their body when such searches might lead to the prosecution of persons associated with the animal? Could an FBI agent who is lawfully present at an animal sanctuary and sees a pig he suspects was rescued (i.e., stolen) from a factory farm cut off the tip of the animal's ear, swab his genitals, or remove blood with a syringe to obtain a DNA sample? In 2017, federal agents did just this in Colorado.[103]

Does the celebrated status of animals in *Newcomb*, which special status makes them available as evidence to the prosecution over their caretaker's objection, really advance the goals of the animal protection movement? It would seem that cases like *Newcomb* play an important role in protecting the ability of prosecutors to incarcerate abusers, but they do very little to advance the status or protect the autonomy of animals. Only a lawyer could love the notion that the sentience of a pig is more respected by allowing that its ear may be removed or its blood tested as evidence of the animal's theft from a factory farm (or its abuse by its owner).

In other areas of constitutional criminal procedure, the voice of the animal protection movement can also be found advocating for limits to constitutional protections. The movement has argued that defendants in abuse cases receive too much constitutional protection under the confrontation clause of the Sixth Amendment.[104] Likewise, the movement has urged constructions of statutes that would limit the applicability of the double jeopardy protections against multiple punishments for the same crime.[105] Ensuring that every harm to an animal can be prosecuted as a separate offense to a separate "victim" has emerged as a defining feature of the animal law agenda, but this too promises little meaningful change for animals. Ultimately this sort of animals-as-victims victory is nothing more than the old law professor hypothetical about whether stealing a six pack of soda constitutes one crime, or six crimes. If the answer is six, the soda (and the shopkeeper) are not any better off, but the offender will go to jail for a longer period of time.

The point is not that the positions taken by the animal protection movement as to the scope of criminal procedure rights are nefarious or even necessarily incorrect. However, the movement's advocacy on issues of constitutional law has been oriented toward increased incarceration, and that does not necessarily lead to

---

[103] The Colorado example is distinguishable because the agents had a warrant. But the notion of the animals as evidence, from *Newcomb*, was still salient. As a form of special evidence it was deemed appropriate to remove portions of a pig's ear to bring it for DNA testing.

[104] *See* Scott Heiser, *Playing with Fire*, Animal Legal Def. Fund (May 10, 2010), http://aldf.org/blog /playing-with-fire (discussing potential Confrontation Clause issues with admitting veterinary reports, especially if those reports were created specifically for trial for animal abuse).

[105] *See* Amicus Curiae Brief of Animal Legal Def. Fund, State v. Nix, 283 P.3d 442 (Or. Ct. App. 2012), *vacated on procedural grounds by* State v. Nix, 345 P.3d 416 (Or. 2015) (arguing that harming multiple animals is, as a matter of state statutory law, multiple offenses because each animal is a separate victim); *see also* Scott Heiser, *Great News in Oregon: Each Animal Counts!*, Animal Legal Def. Fund (Aug. 3, 2012), http://aldf.org/blog/great-news-in-oregon-each-animal-counts (discussing how ALDF "was delighted" to submit an amicus brief arguing that each abused animal was a separate victim).

a safer world for animals or a meaningfully improved legal status for animals. It also warrants mention that at the same time the movement has been pursuing criminal justice reforms that diminish the reach of the constitutional protections available to criminal defendants, its leading organizations have assiduously avoided doing criminal defense representation for activists. Joyce Tischler, the founder of the Animal Legal Defense Fund, explained that in the 1980s her organization came to regard the civil rights defense of activists as having "drawbacks."[106] First, the defense of activists requires resources to be diverted away from impact litigation in the civil realm. Second, ALDF grew "increasingly uncomfortable" with "being perceived as aligning with acts of civil disobedience." Thus by end of the 1980s groups began to disassociate from criminal defense work; indeed, the national organizations were often more likely to condemn than legally defend activists engaged in civil disobedience.

Nearly thirty years later, the fear of aligning with "civil disobedience" remains, and most of the movement is steadfastly opposed to providing legal representation to such activists, thus leaving those who commit acts of civil disobedience to fend for themselves in the court system. But the first justification identified by Tischler for abandoning criminal defense work – avoiding the costs and resources associated with non-impact cases defending individuals – has been jettisoned in favor of participating in criminal cases, *but on the other side.* There is no general aversion to non-impact, criminal cases against an individual. Instead, there is simply a desire to avoid sullying the movement's reputation by aligning with persons or entities despised by the police and prosecution. The movement would rather spend resources assisting in the prosecution of a low-level employee at a factory farm, and ensuring his deportation, than it would spend those same resources defending an activist who rescues a baby piglet from its imminent death at a factory farm. Criminal law in support of prosecutors is no more impact litigation than criminal law in support of defendants, but because the goal is to avoid civil disobedience and to appear mainstream, then only supporting prosecutors is tolerated.

In short, the animal protection movement is no longer on the sidelines of criminal law; it has chosen a side, and not the side of civil liberties or social change. The mainstream animal protection groups have sought alliances with law enforcement while distancing themselves from activists who trespass or rescue animals from factory farms. Animal protection groups are notorious for bringing a wide range of cases, some of which have almost no chance of success. But notably absent from the docket of *every* major animal protection group is any litigation to keep people who are charged with crimes out of jail. Perhaps the movement's connections to law and lawyers have made it overly conservative. The movement – a movement that should hold a coveted, radical position in social change advocacy – now seems to be afraid

[106] Joyce Tischler, *The History of Animal Law, Part I* (1972–1987), 1 STAN. J. ANIMAL L. & POL'Y 1, 25 (2008).

of appearing too radical; it has taken a decidedly strong stance against supporting the sort of nonviolent crime that is famously credited with many civil rights successes, instead supporting prosecutions for animal abusers by, among other things, urging courts to adopt narrow constructions of the constitutional amendments that limit police or prosecutor behavior.

3.4.1.3 Restrictions on Free Speech

At one level, the animal protection movement understands that robust free speech protections are necessary "for the bringing about of political and social changes."[107] Weaponizing free speech is an essential component of social change efforts; it is through speech that less politically powerful movements communicate ideas and norms that do not resonate with mainstream culture. The far-reaching and some-times offensive campaigns of the animal rights movement are underwritten by First Amendment protections. When speech protections are less robust, animal protec-tion efforts suffer. For example, animal protection organizations have had cam-paigns and advertisements banned in countries across Europe where speech protections are somewhat more limited. Moreover, the reduced protection of poten-tially defamatory speech in many industrialized countries has led to the destruction of animal advocacy organizations by, for example, bankrupting them for their speech criticizing factory farms or the fur industry.[108] The absence of greater protections for free speech in other nations have literally been the source of demise for movements and organizations.

Nevertheless, free speech is not sacrosanct among animal protection advocates and scholars, particularly when the pursuit of convictions is contingent on restricting the First Amendment. It seems likely that many in the movement would not object to a wide range of limitations on pro-animal exploitation speech and speech-related activities. On the contrary, it is unlikely that animal protection lawyers would concede the possibility that trophy hunting or wearing fur, for example, might conceivably fall within the contours of expressive activity covered by the First Amendment. If San Francisco's recent ban on selling fur had also included wearing fur, one would be hard pressed to find an animal protection advocate standing up for the potential free speech intrusion. Likewise, the movement is highly supportive of government laws compelling industry speech – for example, the movement has advocated and litigated in support of a variety of mandatory labeling rules. By the same token, it would not be far-fetched to imagine the movement supporting a viable legislative path in favor of limiting pro-industry propaganda. It is not uncommon at animal law conferences, even academic conferences, to hear repeated calls for restrictions on the speech of pro-industry or pro-farm groups.

[107]   New York Times Co. v. Sullivan, 376 U.S. 254, 269 (1964).
[108]   David Connett, *Lynx Anti-Fur Group Faces Extinction After Libel Loss*, INDEPENDENT (Dec. 24, 1992), www.independent.co.uk/news/uk/lynx-anti-fur-group-faces-extinction-over-libel-loss-1565298.html.

Too often the movement conceives of free speech as a positive good, but only after the content of the speech is approved.

The recent case of *U.S. v. Stevens* reflects a concrete example of the movement's circumscribed appreciation for the importance of protecting free speech. In *Stevens*, the Supreme Court was confronted with a federal statute that criminalized the acts of knowingly creating, selling, or possessing any "depiction of animal cruelty," and a depiction of "animal cruelty" was defined as one "in which a living animal is intentionally maimed, mutilated, tortured, wounded, or killed," if that conduct violates federal or state law where "the creation, sale, or possession takes place."[109] The catalyst for the law was the disgusting practice of creating "crush videos," or videos depicting small animals being tortured and crushed under one's body or shoe. The Supreme Court held that outlawing crush videos could be criminalized through a more narrowly drafted statute,[110] and it struck down the federal statute in question as unconstitutionally overbroad, because the Court identified a number of instances where the law made criminals out of persons who possessed other media depicting the killing or maiming of animals. For example, the statute had the effect of criminalizing "any magazine or video depicting lawful hunting that is sold in the Nation's Capital."[111]

Stevens is almost universally lamented as wrongly decided, if not catastrophically so, by the leading lawyers and scholars in the field. Commentators have written blogs, briefs, and entire books decrying the decision as further evidence of our speciesist culture. But these reflexive reactions are badly mistaken.

The effort to protect animals from crush videos is laudable, but the legislative vehicle for doing so was bungled, and the Court was right to strike it down. Even assuming criminalization, in general, might serve to protect the lives or status of animals in our society, the animal protection movement should have more humility when it comes to matters outside their expertise. The crush video ban that was supported so fervently by the movement was also opposed by some of the leading civil rights experts in the country. Several of the most preeminent free speech scholars in the country, including Erwin Chemerinsky, Jack Balkin, and Geoffrey Stone all opposed the law and supported the Supreme Court's decision in *Stevens*. Likewise, leading media groups authored amicus briefs in support of reversing Stevens' conviction. These groups were not expressing solidarity with animal abusers, though the movement suggested as much in media campaigns, but rather, as the amicus brief from the Reporters Committee for Freedom of Press put it:

> The goal of preventing crush videos and other animal cruelty is certainly a worthy one. It is this very interest in protecting animals from abuse that makes speech about their treatment so valuable. Press coverage serves the community by exposing

---

[109]   United States v. Stevens, 559 U.S. 460, 464–65 (2010).

[110]   Indeed, Congress drafted a narrower statute focused on crush videos and the law has survived constitutional challenge in the lower federal courts.

[111]   *Stevens*, 559 U.S. at 461.

animal cruelty such as crush videos, animal fighting and the mistreatment of animals at some puppy mills and slaughterhouses. At the same time, the press regularly covers fishing, hunting, and other broadly accepted activities which, in some cases, fall within the scope of the statute.[112]

Two aspects of the *Stevens* decision warrant particular attention. First, the decision striking down the law turned on the Court's unwillingness to accept calls by advocates to expand the category of so-called "unprotected speech." Both the prosecutors and the animal protection organizations pleaded with the Court to simply dispose of the case by holding that "these depictions are outside the reach of that Amendment altogether – that they fall into a 'First Amendment Free Zone.'"[113] Specifically, animal protection groups filed a panoply of amicus briefs in support of the prosecution, which argued that coverage of the First Amendment should be contingent on a case-by-case balancing of the harms and benefits flowing from a particular type of speech. Illustratively, the Animal Legal Defense Fund submitted an amicus brief arguing for a new free speech framework under which any act of expressive value or benefit would be weighed against its harms or cost to society. Only speech that was sufficiently valuable – whose value outweighed its costs – would deserve free speech protection. Striking the same chord, the ASPCA authored a brief that stated blithely that "[w]hether a category of speech warrants First Amendment protection requires balancing the governmental interest in restricting the speech against the value of the speech." The animal protection movement apparently endorsed a government censor sitting in the wings, waiting to engage in a balancing test to determine whether one's speech is sufficiently valuable so as to deserve constitutional protection.

Summarizing the movement's collective disbelief when the Court ultimately refused to treat the criminalized conduct as wholly outside the coverage of the First Amendment, prominent animal law scholar David Cassuto remarked that the Court's rejection of an "ad hoc balancing test" in this context was strangely "off topic." In Cassuto's mind and the minds of animal protection lawyers who advocated in favor of upholding the statute in the Court, the Court was simply too dismissive of the horrific nature of crush videos and animal cruelty more generally. After all, Cassuto explained, "No one and least of all the government in its briefs pretended that the issue of curtailing speech was a matter to be taken lightly." A brief by free speech scholars, however, pointedly disagrees and describes the animal protection movement's advocacy as an "approach [that] would jettison seventy years of First Amendment jurisprudence and would inject unprecedented judicial discretion into the definition of low value speech." Simply put, the animal protection lawyers were on the wrong side of history, arguing for a limitation on speech

---

[112] Brief of The Reporters Committee for Freedom of the Press et al. as Amici Curiae Supporting Respondent, United States v. Stevens, 559 U.S. 460 (2010) (No. 08-769).
[113] *Stevens*, 559 U.S. at 469.

rights even in the face of some of the movement's potentially greatest allies – media advocacy groups, civil rights lawyers, and free speech experts. A win for the animal protection groups in *Stevens* would have marked one of the largest rollbacks in speech protections in over a century.

Stevens stands as one of the most important modern free speech cases. Bucking the suggestion of the animal protection movement, the Court erected a strong safety net against government efforts to simply cast disfavored or low-value speech as "non-speech." Under *Stevens*, the inquiry is grounded in history such that very few categories of expression will be categorically declared non-speech. As the Court explained, "From 1791 to the present . . . the First Amendment has permitted restrictions upon the content of speech in a few limited areas, and has never include[d] a freedom to disregard these traditional limitations." Today social change lawyers, including those defending such practices as investigative journalism, rely on *Stevens* to protect their tactics, which can involve using misrepresentations to produce powerful exposés. In no small part, the Supreme Court's subsequent decision recognizing the protection of lies in *U.S. v. Alvarez*[114] is derivative of the important holding in *Stevens* that, other than a small set of historically proscribed forms of speech, content-based restrictions are subject to heightened scrutiny.

The second notable feature of the *Stevens* decision is its application of the ever-enigmatic overbreadth doctrine to strike down a federal statute. Animal law scholar David Cassuto also lamented this part of the decision, saying "there is little good here," and complained that the Court spends "too little time analyzing the law as it relates to Mr. Stevens," and "instead focuses on the law's potential applications to other cases not currently before it."[115] The effect of such an analysis of cases or hypotheticals not before the Court is, in his view, is an "opinion [that] runs far into the weeds." More trenchantly, Cassuto laments that

> [T]he Court struck down the law as over-broad by manufacturing fanciful hypotheticals in which the law might be applied unconstitutionally. . . . [A]ny law can be applied unconstitutionally. Law professors make a living dreaming up hypotheticals in which a given statute might be applied in a manner that violates the Constitution. The fact that we can do this is not reason enough to void a law. The issue is (or should be and traditionally has been) whether the law applies unconstitutionally to the party challenging that law.

Though his analysis is often right on the mark, on this score Cassuto is descriptively and doctrinally incorrect. As a doctrinal matter, protecting the rights of third parties not before the court is precisely the purpose of the overbreadth doctrine. Because of the risk that restrictions on expressive activity will "chill" otherwise lawful activity both by persons before the court and those who are not, the Court has created the

---

[114]   567 U.S. 709 (2012).
[115]   David Cassuto, *U.S. v. Stevens: The Post Mortem*, ANIMAL BLAWG (Apr. 22, 2010), https://animalblawg .wordpress.com/2010/04/22/u-s-v-stevens-the-post-mortem/.

overbreadth doctrine as a safeguard; its very purpose is to consider the speech impacts of persons not before the Court.[116] Overbreadth provides a vehicle for striking down a speech-restrictive law even if the law does not unconstitutionally infringe the speech rights of a person before the court. Moreover, practicing lawyers know that the core of a viable overbreadth claim is a long list of speech that, though not necessarily engaged in by the party before the Court, falls within the restrictions of the statute. Far from a frivolous diversion, the enterprise of generating "fanciful hypotheticals" is the very legal legwork required by the constitution to make out an overbreadth claim. As Erwin Chemirnsky has put it, overbreadth is demonstrated by "showing a significant number of situations where a law could be applied to prohibit constitutionally protected speech."[117] Overbreadth, then, is all about getting into the seemingly irrelevant "weeds," and the Court's willingness to do so in this case, over the objections of leading animal protection advocates, ensured that overbreadth retained vitality as an independent protection of free speech.

The continued salience of the overbreadth doctrine is not of merely passing concern to the animal protection movement. The overbreadth doctrine allows activists challenging hunter harassment or Ag-Gag laws to target the laws' application not just to their own efforts, but those of credentialed undercover journalists, labor unions, or environmental groups. As the Court usefully explained in *Stevens*, a law is over-broad whenever "a substantial number of its applications are unconstitutional, judged in relation to the statute's plainly legitimate sweep."[118]

Indeed, a shocking number of free speech cases turn, at least in part, on the reasoning of *Stevens*. In the absence of *Stevens*, the current landscape of free speech protections would look very different in the United States. And yet, even today, many animal protection scholars and lawyers treat the *Stevens* decision as deviant and misguided. In book-length arguments, scholars have argued that, at the very least, the Court should have deferred to prosecutorial discretion. But the movement is badly mistaken in its assurance that such deferral would have limited the statute's reach to the most egregious situations. As the Court cogently explained, "the First Amendment protects against the Government; it does not leave us at the mercy of *noblesse oblige*. We would not uphold an unconstitutional statute merely because the Government promised to use it responsibly."[119]

Had the animal protection advocates and prosecutors succeeded in getting their way in *Stevens*, the free speech protections of the Constitution would look very different today. The realm of unprotected speech would be vastly larger, and the doctrine of overbreadth would be abandoned as an unnecessary diversion. A First Amendment that applied only to those forms of speech that achieved a favorable

---

[116] Virginia v. Hicks, 539 U.S. 113, 124 (2003) (noting "overbreadth doctrine's concern with 'chilling' protected speech").

[117] ERWIN CHEMERINSKY, CONSTITUTIONAL LAW: PRINCIPLES AND POLICIES 991 (5th edn. 2015).

[118] *Stevens*, 559 U.S. at 460, 473.

[119] *Id.* at 460, 473.

outcome on an ad hoc weighing of costs and benefits would be radically different and less protective than current doctrine. The animal protection movement was correct to argue that preventing animal abuse is a compelling government interest; where it went astray was voicing its general preference for a poorly and broadly drafted statute at the expense of seminal speech protections. The animal protection movement should be more introspective about what it might mean when the nation's premiere media and free speech scholars all oppose the movement's understanding of the First Amendment, even when such an interpretation might result in fewer persons being incarcerated for animal abuse.

***

When an animal interest is at stake, particularly in instances of sadistic abuse, the movement has been too willing to abandon would-be alliances with civil rights leaders and seek narrow constructions of the Constitution. The point is not that each narrowing construction of the Constitution urged by the animal protection attorneys is wrong or reflects poor judgment. Reasonable people could agree with some of the positions taken by animal rights advocates in each of the cases discussed above. The point, rather, is that animal protection groups are now in the unique role of a civil rights movement that has consistently urged narrowing interpretations of the fundamental rights enshrined in the Bill of Rights.[120]

3.4.2 *Victim Advocates: Court-Appointed Advocates Who Urge Incarceration*

Another procedural reform, heralded as a sea change in the way animal abuse cases are handled, is the appointment of a victim advocate to speak on behalf of an abused or neglected animal. Such reforms reflect the tireless ingenuity of those who care about animals and seek to increase the probability and duration of incarceration in cases of animal cruelty. Although victim advocates are not universally available for children victims of crime, a recently enacted law in Connecticut entrenches the view of animals as high-status victims by permitting courts to appoint advocates for the animals in cases of animal abuse or neglect.

The Connecticut system, signed into law in 2016, is the first of its kind in the country. Law professor Jessica Rubin, whose advocacy prompted the reform, describes the advocate model as a way of addressing the prosecutorial and judicial tendency to prioritize cases with human victims.[121] The law treats animal advocates

---

[120]   To be sure, there are scholars who argue that a variety of constitutional rights should yield to the urgent need of protecting vulnerable victims. *See, e.g.,* Danielle K. Citron & Mary Ann Franks, *Criminalizing Revenge Porn,* 49 WAKE FOREST L. REV. 345, 374–86 (2014) (arguing that revenge porn can be criminalized without violating the First Amendment); Nancy Leong & Joanne Morando, *Communication in Cyberspace,* 94 N.C. L. REV. 105, 131–35 (2015) (discussing how cyberharrasment can be criminalized without violating the First Amendment).

[121]   Pat Eaton-Robb, *In One State, Abused Animals Get a Legal Voice in Court,* DENVER POST (June 3, 2017), www.denverpost.com/2017/06/03/connecticut-animals-legal-voice.

as official parties to a criminal case. The advocates have the authority to do investigations in support of the prosecution, such as interviewing witnesses or compiling evidence, and they write briefs and even make recommendations to the judge. For obvious reasons, the prosecutors pursuing harsher sentences for animal abuse have been quick to describe the law as a significant development, with one prosecutor saying, "It has really assisted me in doing my job."[122]

The animal protection movement has been scrupulously watching the initial results in Connecticut and gauging the efficacy of replicating the provision across the country. Early support for the law is overwhelming. David Rosengard, a staff lawyer at the Animal Legal Defense Fund, for example, explains that "this is really a groundbreaking law." It is too early to tell whether convictions and sentences will materially tick upward, but there is widespread optimism that putting two parties advocating for incarceration (the prosecutor and the advocate) before the judge will cause these cases to be taken more seriously. Indeed, the sponsor of the Connecticut law, Diana Urban, has explained that the very reason she sponsored the animal advocates law was to see higher sentences; the law itself is colloquially known as Desmond's Law, named after a dog abuse case that prompted national outrage when the abuser was sentenced to treatment rather than incarceration.

Among legislators like Senator Urban, there is a love for companion animals and an overriding sense that abuse crimes are underenforced. For example, advocates point to data suggesting that 47 percent of animal abuse in New York goes unprosecuted, and the rate of non-prosecution may be even higher in other states. The figures are striking, but less so when put in context: some studies estimate that only about 20 to 40 percent of sexual assaults and rapes are prosecuted, and only about 60 percent of murders. The Department of Justice's most recent data shows a national arrest and prosecution rate of 64 percent of murder offenses, 40 percent of rape offenses, and 29 percent of robbery offenses.[123] An animal cruelty prosecution rate that is higher than the rate of prosecution for sexual abuse, and only slightly lower than the murder prosecution rate does not sound like the greatest injustice facing animals. Of course, even if the rates of animal cruelty prosecutions are higher than animal protection advocates might like to acknowledge, this does not suggest that the animal advocate model will be ineffectual. Quite the contrary, it seems very likely that the presence of skilled, high-profile attorneys, such as Professor Rubin, will impact the disposition of many cruelty cases, if for no other reason than the judge is forced to understand that members of the community, and even parties in addition to the prosecutor's office, desire incarceration.

---

[122]   *Id.*
[123]   *Crime in the United States 2013*, Fed. Bureau Investigation: Uniform Crime Reporting, https://ucr .fbi.gov/crime-in-the-u .s/2013/crime-in-the-u.s.-2013/offenses-known-to-law-enforcement/clearances/clearancetopic_final (last visted Jan. 24, 2018).

More generally, the movement's support for a legal system that includes animal advocates seems intuitively correct. As David Rosengard puts it, "To get justice, a third voice is needed in that [court]room."[124] The third voice then speaks for the animal and makes sure that animal cruelty is taken seriously, resulting in severe, carceral penalties. Another way of framing the task of the animal advocate is that of a human lawyer who is able to give voice to the voiceless animals. On the surface, this seems entirely unobjectionable and long overdue.

But upon reflection, it is not clear whether the system entrenches greater respect for animal autonomy, or merely a greater likelihood of incarceration. Through the advocacy of a court-appointed advocate, it seems that animals will be given a monolithic voice that assumes that all animals have one message: "The more prison the better." Such a system assumes that all animals would support the harshest penalty and would unflinchingly reject calls for mercy regardless of the circumstances surrounding the abuse. It assumes, for example, that a dog who suffers horribly from neglect at the hands of a dying elderly person would always want maximum retribution against this person.

But such an approach raises a host of under-theorized questions about the agency of a non-human animal who is vested with the right to a court appointed advocate. As Catherine MacKinnon has posited, many forms of animal protection adopt a model that "makes animals objects of rights in standard liberal moral terms [but] misses animals on their own terms."[125] When it comes to asserting a right for animals to have a person advocate for greater punishment for the animal's abuser, MacKinnon might reply, "Who asked the animals?"[126]

That humans dominate animals is not in dispute, and that the notion of a court-appointed advocate is an earnest effort to reduce that domination is also beyond question. But as a practical matter, such a system is just a different form of domination. The notion that a human-appointed advocate speaks for the animal when requesting increased punishment is a story of reinforcing domination. The love for animals motivating such domination is believed to mitigate or eliminate the domination, but such legal advocacy is itself a form of domination: the "speaking for the other problem."

[124] Rick Rojas, *Abused Dogs and Cats Now Have a (Human) Voice in Connecticut Courts*, N.Y. Times (Aug. 27, 2017), www.nytimes.com/2017/08/27/nyregion/animal-abuse-connecticut-court-advocates .html.

[125] Catherine MacKinnon, *Of Mice and Men: A Feminist Fragment on Animal Rights*, in Animal Rights 263, 264 (Cass Sunstein & Martha Nussbaum eds., 2004).

[126] Other scholars have thoughtfully confronted the problem of attributing thoughts and emotions to animals while advocating for human law reform. *See, e.g.*, Jessica Eisan, *Beyond Rights and Welfare: Democracy, Dialogue and the Animal Welfare Act*, 51 Mich. J. L. Ref. 101, 134–37 (2018); Jessica Eisan, *Animals in the Constitutional State*, 15 Int'l J. Const. L. 909, 938–40 (noting the enforcer-beneficiary gap in animal protection efforts); *Id.* ("even if there were a constitutional system that allowed enforcement by animals themselves, any legal assertions would necessarily be made through a guardian ad litem or similar legal representative," thus stepping right into the gap between the interests of the enforcer of rights and the beneficiary).

Moreover, it is not clear that court-appointed human advocates are particularly well-suited to speak for the animal victims. Ethologist Marc Bekoff has described animals as ambassadors for forgiveness, and Frans De Waal has documented submissive behaviors and kissing among chimpanzees as a token of forgiveness in the immediate aftermath of some gruesomely violent encounters. In fact, some consider the almost mythical ability of dogs to forgive and move on after even the most horrific acts of abuse or neglect an inspiration for the betterment of humanity. At the very least, it is far from obvious that every animal would reflexively prefer incarceration to treatment and rehabilitation. If advocates could truly decipher the wishes of their animal clients, they might be surprised to learn that the animals might frequently prefer forgiveness to a degree beyond that of which many humans are capable. Put differently, whether one judges an animal's propensity for forgiveness as a sign of a higher or lower biological status, the fact remains that they might be more forgiving than their human-appointed advocate. Or as MacKinnon has put it in a separate context, "[r]eferences to what animals might have to say are few and far between."[127]

This is precisely the problem with an animal advocate model in a criminal case. The "voice" provided to the animal "client" is actually just a judicially sanctioned opportunity to advocate for the thoroughly human interest in maximal punishment. As an illustration, animal advocates in Connecticut have already been documented invoking the presumed LINK between animal abuse and subsequent human violence as a justification for incarceration. On such logic, the victim animal desires maximalist punishment in order to prevent the animal abuser from graduating or moving on to human victims. The façade becomes almost laughable if it is examined carefully: in the guise of speaking for an *animal*, court-appointed *human* advocates are urging maximal incarceration in order to protect *humans* from potential violence at the hand of the accused. The voice of the animals ends up looking very similar to the voice of the carceral form of animal law embraced by humans in the animal protection realm. As Catherine MacKinnon has observed, people frequently appoint themselves as the "animals' representatives without asking and have often" understood their role in the social hierarchy as the protectors.

The guardian ad litem context of protecting young children and advocating for their "best interests," even if it is against the child's expressed preference, seems at first blush a useful analogy. If courts can appoint persons to speak about the best interests of a child even when it means disagreeing with the child, then perhaps there is nothing unseemly about asking a human to speak for an animal without knowing exactly what the animal wants. But the analogy is of limited utility for several reasons. First, guardians are deployed in order to help children find safe homes and to protect the child from future neglect or abuse; they do not speak for the child in criminal proceedings. The guardian ad litem does not opine over the

---

[127]   MacKinnon at 270.

objection of a child that one's abusive mother must be sent to prison for a maximum term. There is a material difference between using a court-appointed advocate to ensure the safety of a vulnerable being and using a court-appointed advocate to insist on retribution in the name of the victim. One form of advocacy has protection of the vulnerable as its central purpose, and the other is a step or two removed from protecting, focused instead on backward-looking punishment for past misdeeds.

Second, where there is a lack of resources or training such that guardians ad litem are incapable of accurately gauging the best interests of the child, everyone agrees that the court proceedings can be devastating in their departure from what is actually in that child's best interests.[128] Where an advocate is unable to fully investigate the situation or meet with the child, researchers have found that the promise of having a representative of the child present is the worst of all worlds because it "gives the illusion that abused and neglected children have their own advocate when in fact they do not."[129] The absence of a good relationship with the child or the absence of a deep understanding of the child's personal interests and needs is essential to effective guardianship work, and it is impossible to obtain this sort of information from an animal. Put differently, if the hallmark of competent legal representation is, in part, truly understanding what the client wants, the process of lawyers acting as advocates for the interests of animal-clients by pursuing maximum incarceration seems to promise too much.

The analogy to human victim advocates in criminal cases fares even worse. Victim advocates "do not have the right to make decisions for victims," and it is generally understood that "[m]aking decisions for the victim fails to understand that effective advocacy values a victim's right to make his/her own decisions."[130] It would be a terrible irony if by inserting a human "voice" to speak for the animals, court-room advocates would once again be using animals to serve characteristically human interests in revenge or in the name of preventing future violence against humans.

It could be that nearly every abused animal would seek a maximum sentence for its abuser, but the difficulty with empowering animal advocates to assist the prosecution as representatives of the victim is that the advocate cannot actually communicate with the abused animal. Animal advocates may turn out to provide a meaningful promise of greater rates of incarceration, but it is a bit fanciful to pretend that such advocates present an explicit reflection of anything other than the human advocates' wishes. In the end, human lawyers speaking for animals and insisting that the animal wants punishment based on human interests is a classic

---

[128] Hollis R. Peterson, *In Search of the Best Interests of the Child: The Efficacy of the Court Appointed Special Advocate Model of Guardian Ad Litem Representation*, 13 Geo. Mason L. Rev. 1083 (2006).

[129] Robert Kelly & Sarah Ramsey, *Do Attorneys for Child Protection Proceedings Make a Difference?- A Study of the Impact of Representation Under Conditions of High Judicial Intervention*, 21 J. Fam. L. 405, 452 (1983).

[130] Ronald B. Adrine & Alexandria M. Ruden, *The Role of the Victim Advocate*, Oh. Domestic Violence L. § 17:2 (2016).

illustration of noblesse oblige – we demonstrate how "good we are to be good to them."[131]

Would a cruelly caged primate like a chimpanzee, above all else, prefer to see its captor replace it in a cage? Or is this a projection of human interests and goals onto animals? Might the chimp prefer the money and effort to be devoted elsewhere? It seems beyond doubt that every abused animal would prefer not to be abused again, and domestic animals likely prefer to be loved by humans as opposed to being alone. But imbuing the innocence and victimhood of an animal with the human proclivity to incarcerate does not reflect an unequivocal advancement of the law's respect for the interests and well-being of animals. Instead, it risks being a self-referential exploitation of animals in the service of the distinctly human preference to cage other humans.[132] The movement must "avoid reducing animal rights to the rights of some people to speak for animals against the rights of other people," and the victim advocate model fails this test.[133]

3.4.3 *Immigration Enforcement*

In addition to assisting prosecutors, some in the animal protection movement have become receptive to the idea of limiting immigration, or even assisting with the deportation of immigrants who were involved in animal mistreatment. There is a sense that if the movement cares about animal suffering and regards animal cruelty as a crime of violence, then deportation is an appropriate penalty for animal cruelty.

Immigration can come up in the context of animal cruelty in a number of ways. First, simply pursuing criminal punishment for animal abusers will mean that, in many cases, people convicted of animal cruelty will be deported. Several high-profile cases within the last six months feature stories of men whose animal abuse conviction will result in their removal from the country at the completion of their term of imprisonment. A direct result of advocacy making clear that animal cruelty is treated as a more serious offense is the deportation of more persons. The case of Marco Chavez, a former Marine who was honorably discharged, is illustrative. Chavez, who was brought to the United States as an infant and did not speak Spanish, was convicted of animal cruelty in 1998. As a result of the conviction, Chavez served 15 months in prison, and was then deported to Mexico.[134] In December 2017, Chavez was allowed to

---

[131] MacKinnon at 266.

[132] Much has been written about the difficulty in understanding whether a domestically owned and controlled animal could ever meaningfully consent to sexual relations with a human, even when the animal appears to be consenting. If consent in these circumstances is fraught, certainly the lawyer-advocate's ability to discern consent to seek maximalist punishment of a human (perhaps against a human who engaged in bestiality) is even more fraught. MacKinnon at 268 (noting that animals can be "and are trained to make it appear that they enjoy doing what people want them to do").

[133] MacKinnon at 270 (observing that "lawyers have devoted little attention to the emerging rules and forms of governance in animal societies").

[134] *Marine Who Was Deported to Mexico Gets to Return to U.S.*, L.A. Times (Dec. 21, 2017), www.latimes .com/local/lanow/la-me-marine-deport-20171221-story.html

return to the United States where his family continues to reside, but only because of help from the ACLU and a pro bono attorney who helped Chavez secure a pardon from California Governor Jerry Brown. The only reason Chavez was allowed back in the country was that lawyers and a major national non-profit joined forces in order to remove the animal cruelty conviction from Chavez's record.

Well beyond the mere fact of deportation as a consequence of one's criminal conviction, some supporters of animal protection efforts propound narratives grounded in a sense of ethnic or cultural superiority. Within the movement, there exist ethnocentric criticisms of other cultures as inherently less concerned with animals. As a recent letter to the editor of a local Texas paper by an animal advocate put it, it is impossible to support "immigration without siding to some degree with animal cruelty."[135]

Other examples of similarly insensitive comments about immigration can be found within the animal protection movement. It is argued by some, for example, that reduced immigration is a positive development for efforts to protect animals. Some point to data suggesting that persons who immigrate from lower-income countries into countries with a higher socioeconomic standing tend to increase their intake of meat and dairy.[136] Studying this process of dietary assimilation among people who immigrated to the United States, one researcher documented that common changes in diet included increased consumption of junk food and meat.[137] Even industry trade journals have tied the "increase in consumption" of meat in the United States primarily to immigrant communities.[138] Because of this connection, some people stake out an animal protection stance that opposes immigration, particularly from lower-income countries.

No animal protection group of national acclaim appears to have endorsed any restrictions on immigration policy publicly, and many animal protection groups, particularly the Animal Legal Defense Fund, have attempted to coordinate with workers' rights and immigration groups in order to provide education about the hardships faced by immigrants who work in the agricultural sector. Bringing attention to the workplace safety and health hazards associated with agricultural work is

---

[135] Charles P. Stephens, Letter to the Editor, *Immigration, Animal Cruelty Go Together*, AMARILLO GLOBE-NEWS (Jan. 8, 2017), http://amarillo.com/opinion/2017-01-08/letter-immigration-animal -cruelty-go-together.

[136] *See, e.g.*, Gerd Holmboe-Ottesen & Margareta Wandel, *Changes in Dietary Habits After Migration and Consequences for Health: A Focus on South Asians in Europe*, 56 FOOD & NUTRITION RES. 18891, 11891 (2012). World Bank research shows that among immigrant children there is an "increased consumption of fats, meats, and milk." John Gibson, David McKenzie & Steven Stillman, *What Happens to Diet and Child Health When Migration Splits Households? Evidence from a Migration Lottery Program*, 36 FOOD POL'Y 7, 9 (2011).

[137] Ilana Redstone Akresh, *Dietary Assimilation and Health Among Hispanic Immigrants to the United States*, 48 J. HEALTH & SOC. BEHAV. 404 (2007).

[138] Other News, *What's the Next Big Meat? Immigrant Population Driving Up Goat Demand*, FARM & DAIRY (Feb. 11, 2014), www.farmanddairy.com/news/immigrant-population-driving-goat-demand /175438.html.

unquestionably advocacy that benefits animals, and benefits the immigrant communities; indeed, 76 percent of agricultural workers are Hispanic/Latino.[139]

On the other hand, animal protection groups have not been averse to working with immigration officials in a variety of capacities in order to facilitate the deportation of persons who have a conviction relating to animal abuse. Major animal protection organizations have filed amicus briefs in support of government efforts to deport people convicted of animal cruelty. It is also not uncommon for the movement to highlight the immigration status of a person accused of animal abuse, or who works at a factory farm, in order to increase media attention surrounding a particular case. So, at least part of the animal protection movement's identity in enhancing the status of animals through the criminal law includes efforts to remove people from the country through deportation.

3.4.4 *Influencing Police and Prosecutors*

The criminal law is not self-executing; it is instead predicated on something approximating absolute discretion.[140] It has been said that "[t]he decision to prosecute is one of the most solitary and unfettered exercises of power in the American political system."[141] Overseeing and assisting with a fundamental reworking of the substantive and procedural law of animal protection will not ensure higher rates of incarceration if animal protection advocates cannot convince police and prosecutors to devote resources, bring cases, and seek maximal sentences in the realm of animal abuse.[142] The movement's ability to influence and infiltrate the prosecutorial ranks is another astonishing example of their unique commitment to a vision of social justice through incarceration.

3.4.4.1 Externally Influencing Prosecutorial Discretion

As one scholar has observed, "the ability to decide whether and what to charge gives the prosecutor perhaps the most power of any single actor in the criminal justice process."[143] Confronted with evidence of a crime, a prosecutor may simply decline

---

[139] Farmworker Just., Selected Statistics on Farmworkers (2014).

[140] Inmates of Attica Corr. Facility v. Rockefeller, 477 F.2d 375, 380 (2d Cir. 1973) ("In the absence of statutorily defined standards governing reviewability, or regulatory or statutory policies of prosecution, the problems inherent in the task of supervising prosecutorial decisions do not lend themselves to resolution by the judiciary.").

[141] James Stewart, The Prosecutors: Inside the Offices of the Government's Most Powerful Lawyers 9–10 (1987); Michael A. Caves, *The Prosecutor's Dilemma: Obligatory Charging Under the Ashcroft Memo*, 9 J. L. & Soc. Challenges 1, 23 (2008) (citing Stewart for the same proposition).

[142] Tresl at 302–03 ("[N]o matter how many statutes are written, no matter how strict the language, unless there is a prosecutor willing to prosecute, the statutes will be meaningless because they will not be enforced.").

[143] Roger A. Fairfax, Jr., *Delegation of the Criminal Prosecution Function to Private Actors*, 43 U.C. Davis L. Rev. 411, 428, 430 (2009) ("[P]rosecutors can effectively nullify a law in a jurisdiction").

to prosecute for any number of reasons, including that she is too busy, or simply does not deem the crime in question a high enforcement priority. Commentators have observed that prosecutorial discretion is "an area of the law that social movements have almost never infiltrated."[144] The animal protection movement, however, due in no small part to the presumed link between human and animal violence and the outreach and training that has been done on these issues, enjoys a uniquely influential relationship with local prosecutors. For well over a decade the animal protection community has been fostering connections with the prosecutor community, and those relationships are designed to facilitate an interest in a more punitive approach to animal protection.[145]

The movement has engaged in a wide variety of advocacy and expenditures designed to attract prosecutorial attention and affection. The outreach takes three general forms: (1) assistance with a specific case by providing resources or lawyers; (2) trainings on animal cruelty prosecution; and (3) awards, accolades, and the hiring of former prosecutors.

First, lawyers in the animal protection movement provide trainings to prosecutors, and work on joint statements regarding the importance of prosecuting animal abuse to the full extent of the law. For example, the American Association of Prosecutors in conjunction with animal protection groups issued a 2014 joint statement of "principles regarding the prosecution of animal abuse." The then president of the APA, David LaBahn, aptly summarized the key ingredient of the document: "There is a link between animal abusers and other types of interpersonal violence including child abuse, domestic violence and elder abuse," and prosecutors must seek maximum incarceration in order to address this link.[146] The alliance of animal protection groups and leading prosecutors emphasized the empirically unfounded conclusion that lenient penalties for animal abuse are "correlated to a host of corrosive societal ills" as a way of jolting lower-level prosecutors into caring more about animal abuse crimes.[147] More concrete than a statement of principles, in 2013, the ASPCA donated $10,000 to the National District Attorneys Association to fund a center dedicated to training and supporting prosecutorial efforts.[148] The Humane

---

[144] Rebecca T. Engel, *"An Existential Moment of Moral Perception": Declarations of Life and the Capital Jury Re-Imagined*, 31 QUINNIPIAC L. REV. 303, 312 (2013).

[145] Tischler at 42–43 (describing how in 2005, the Humane Society of the United States started contracting with local governments to help prosecute animal cruelty cases).

[146] *Prosecutors and Animal Welfare Advocates Develop Principles to Combat Animal Cruelty*, AM. SOC'Y FOR PREVENTION OF CRUELTY TO ANIMALS (Mar. 3, 2014), www.aspca.org/about-us/press-releases/pro secutors-and-animal-welfare-advocates-develop-principles-combat-animal.

[147] As discussed in Chapter 5, there is no empirical data about the impact of incarceration on decreasing or exacerbating any of the presumed correlations between animal abuse and human violence.

[148] The funding was earmarked to "cover the cost of technical assistance, research, strategy discussions with prosecutors, and training requests – including a wide array of webinars." *ASPCA Grants $10,000 to National District Attorneys Association*, AM. SOC'Y FOR PREVENTION OF CRUELTY TO ANIMALS (July 22, 2013), www.aspca.org/about-us/press-releases/aspca-grants-10000-national-district-attorneys -association.

Society, the Animal Legal Defense Fund, and other national organizations have also hosted and funded dozens of training seminars and webinars for prosecutors and police officers in just the past several years.

Beyond arm's-length case involvement through training programs and public statements, animal protection groups are investing valuable attorney hours doing the legal work of prosecutors on a *pro bono* basis.[149] The Animal Legal Defense Fund is famous for its amicus briefs in support of the prosecution in nearly any high-profile case of animal cruelty that does not end in plea bargain. Similarly, the Humane Society promises to prosecutors that whenever needed, their attorneys will provide *pro bono* work in the form of "detailed and reliable memoranda of law . . . includ[ing] advice and assistance with research on case law or legal issues as you prepare for trial."[150] The organizations also maintain lists of potential expert witnesses, and in many instances the non-profits will even pay for the expert witness's involvement in the case.

It is difficult to imagine another realm in which prosecutors can rely upon such a wealth of external resources in the form of both financial and in-kind services. Certainly, many cash-strapped offices do not enjoy this level of external support for any other type of case, including crimes of rape or murder. In many cases, the movement is so eager to have a case prosecuted that it will do anything short of actually prosecuting the case itself. And where local rules and culture permit it, the organizations may be involved in the actual criminal prosecution.[151] Animal protection attorneys have appeared as special prosecutors and have prosecuted defendants for animal abuse.[152] The commitment to incarceration is truly full-service.[153]

As one legal commentator has explained in advocating for further support of prosecutors in this realm, "creative manipulating of existing laws can mean the difference between" a conviction and an acquittal;[154] "[w]hen lawyers use creative legal strategies to tap the potential" for convictions and incarceration, they will increasingly see results in the form of more and longer sentences. There is a perception that more regular, punitive, and innovative theories of prosecution will help avoid the desperation reflected by "support [for] clandestine, illegal

---

[149] Perhaps no assistance to the prosecution is more meaningful than efforts to reduce the cost of prosecution. By adding a free forensic team, or providing pro bono assistance with a briefing, as discussed in subsequent chapters, prosecutors get a huge advantage over public defenders.

[150] *Resources for Prosecutors*, HUMANE SOC'Y U.S., www.humanesociety.org/issues/abuse_neglect/prosecutors_resources.html?credit=web_id113230553#Prosecutor_Training (last visited Jan. 24, 2018).

[151] Tresl at 302 (stating that under Ohio law a county humane society may appoint an attorney to aid in the prosecution of "any person guilty of an act of cruelty to . . . animals").

[152] *Id.* (stating that Jeffrey Holland was a special prosecutor in the state of Ohio).

[153] See *Animal Cruelty Prosecutor Jake Kamins Takes on Oregon Animal Abuse*, ANIMAL LEGAL DEF. FUND, http://aldf.org/resources/the-animals-advocate/the-animals-advocate-fall-2014/animal-cruelty-prosecutor-jake-kamins-takes-on-oregon-animal-abuse/ (last visited Jan. 24, 2018) (discussing how ALDF awarded a three-year grant in order to fund a prosecution unit devoted to animal cruelty crimes in Oregon); Tischler at 58–59 (stating that animal rights groups provide training on the link between animal abuse and domestic violence).

[154] Tresl at 303.

activities aimed at liberating animals."[155] Indeed, much of the support for prosecutorial activities amounts to a not-so-subtle rebuke of activists engaged in open rescues
and more radical forms of civil disobedience. Some activists and commentators now
treat a robust support of prosecutors and incarceration as "direct action" in support
of animal protection in a stunning departure from the historical moorings of the
phrase as it came be understood in the civil rights context,.[156] It would no doubt
strike Martin Luther King, Jr. as surprising to see the term "direct action" used as
a proxy for greater deference or support for the police state and the power of
incarceration.[157] But as the "Guide for Activists" explains direct action, "What can
you do? Call or write your local prosecutor's office and demand that all animal
abusers . . . be given the maximum sentence possible under the laws of your state."[158]

Embracing prosecution as the salient form of activism, some commentators identify
the Animal Legal Defense Fund as the "most legally effective organization for animals
in America," because of their "Zero Tolerance for Cruelty" campaign, which is
"intended to strengthen and aggressively enforce the already existent anti-cruelty statutes
across America."[159] This vision of animal protection success is explained thusly:

> By aggressively prosecuting animal cruelty cases, the legal consciousness of
> Americans will be raised. The result will be that citizens' perceptions about animals
> will change, this alteration in perception will ripple over into state capitols, and
> legislators will be motivated to write tough anti-cruelty laws. With tougher laws in
> place, lawyers, judges, and prosecutors can unify their voices in order to, unequi-
> vocally and jurisprudentially, condemn cruelty, neglect, and torture to animals.[160]

Consistent with the fanciful and ahistorical view of the prosecution as the wellspring
or catalyst for effective social change, it has become commonplace for animal
protection groups to celebrate the work of prosecutors with awards, accolades,
banquets, and free media attention.[161] The lists of animal law's greatest heroes
published by animal protection groups, for example, feature the prosecutors who

---

[155] *Id.* at 277.
[156] *Id.* at 277.
[157] MARTIN LUTHER KING, JR., LETTER FROM BIRMINGHAM JAIL (Aug. 1963) ("In any nonviolent campaign there are four basic steps: collection of the facts to determine whether injustices are alive, negotiation, self-purification, and direct action."); *Id.* ("we had no alternative except that of preparing for direct action, whereby we would present our very bodies as a means of laying our case before the conscience of the local and national community.")
[158] ANIMAL LEGAL DEF. FUND, FIGHTING ANIMAL ABUSE, HONORING ANIMAL VICTIMS: A RESOURCE GUIDE FOR ACTIVISTS AND COMMUNITIES 11 (2013), http://aldf.orgdownloads/AnimalAdvocates ResourceGuide2013.pdf.
[159] Tresl at 280.
[160] *Id.* at 281.
[161] *See, e.g., America's Top 10 Animal Defenders* (listing ALDF's top 10 animal defenders, many of whom are prosecutors); *Jail Time for Dog Abuser, Send Thanks to Prosecutor*, ANIMAL LEGAL DEF. FUND (Sept. 24, 2008), http://aldf.org/cases-campaigns/action-alerts/action-alert-archive/2008-2/jail-time-for-dog-abuser-send-thanks-to-prosecutor/ (encouraging people to send thank-you letters to a prosecutor who obtained a conviction for an animal abuse crime); Sherry Ramsey, *Justice for Abused Donkey*, HUMANE SOC'Y U.S. (Aug. 21, 2014), www.humanesociety.org/news/news/2014/08/donkey-abuse

press the legal limits of the animal cruelty law with creative theories and stacked charges, and obtain unusually high sentences. One group has created a top ten list of animal defenders.[162] The names of the honorees are foreign to animal law or animal rights conferences and are anything but household names to the lawyers on the ground doing social justice litigation – the honorees are not running sanctuaries or bringing civil rights cases for animal rights, and they are certainly not people engaged in civil disobedience in support of the movement. Frequently the public acclaim is awarded to prosecutors and police officers. Such awards and accolades are mutually beneficial – the prosecutor gets a stroke to the ego, free press celebrating their work, and support with a potential reelection campaign. Likewise, the animal protection movement gets an opportunity to dialogue and curry favor with the persons vested with the most discretion in our justice system.[163]

In addition to targeted recognition of individual prosecutors, it is also increasingly common for animal protection groups to sponsor national conferences for prosecutors, including the American Prosecutors Association and the National District Attorneys Association. Although it is best to avoid over-generalizing based on the movement's support for these organizations, at least one casual observation is in order. The animal protection movement – in the service of instilling greater empathy toward non-human animals – is providing funding for and aligning itself with NGOs that, among other regressive policies, still actively support the death penalty for humans in the United States and oppose eliminating mandatory minimums.[164] The animal protection movement has allied itself with groups that continue to spend considerable resources urging incarceration for drug crimes including the use or possession of marijuana, and who provide trainings for prosecutors on how to be more effective in

-justice-082114.html (congratulating a prosecutor on obtaining a conviction in an animal cruelty case).

[162] *America's Top 10 Animal Defenders.*

[163] *The History of Human-Animal Interaction The Twentieth Century*, LIBR. INDEX, www.libraryindex .com/pages/2155/History-Human-Animal-Interaction-TWENTIETH-CENTURY.html (last visited Jan. 24, 2018) ("Many [animal rights] groups publicize cases on their Web sites and ask members to lobby prosecutors for stiff sentences.") Activists are instructed to make it clear that they will vote for the most aggressive animal abuse prosecutor in upcoming election cycles. *Id.*

[164] *See, e.g., Animal Cruelty Prosecutor and Judicial Training*, HUMANE SOC'Y U.S. (June 24, 2015), www .humanesociety.org/about/leadership/subject_experts/prosecutor_training.html (listing several prosecution oriented events that HSUS and other animal rights groups have sponsored or participated in); Maurice Chammah, *The Unfolding Campaign to Save the Death Penalty*, MARSHALL PROJECT (Nov. 19, 2015), www.themarshallproject.org/2015/11/19/the-unfolding-campaign-to-save-the-death -penalty#.6uz3k8QkT (discussing prosecutors' efforts to fix the death penalty); Lora Dunn, *Reporting from the 4th National Animal Cruelty Prosecution Conference of the Association of Prosecuting Attorneys*, ANIMAL LEGAL DEF. FUND (May 5, 2014), http://aldf.org/blog/reporting-from -the-4th-national-animal-cruelty-prosecution-conference-of-the-association-of-prosecuting-attorneys (discussing ALDF's presence at the Association of Prosecuting Attorneys conference); Scott Heiser, *National Animal Cruelty Prosecution Conference*, ANIMAL LEGAL DEF. FUND (Apr. 7, 2014), http://aldf .org/blog/national-animal-cruelty-prosecution-conference/ ("[T]he Animal Legal Defense Fund is proud to sponsor the 4th National Animal Cruelty Prosecution Conference in Atlanta, in partnership with the Association of Prosecuting Attorneys.").

convincing a jury to impose a death sentence. Summarizing the role of these associations of prosecutors, Udi Ofer, director of the Campaign for Smart Justice at the American Civil Liberties Union, said that these groups "all too often act as a roadblock to significant reforms," and according to Ofer, "[i]n state after state, we've seen DA associations hold back [criminal justice] reforms that are supported by Democrats and Republicans alike."[165] The National District Attorneys Association even reacted angrily and dismissively to a national report on "Forensic Science in Criminal Courts," which documented shortcomings with several types of forensic evidence commonly used, such as bite marks and shoe prints, that scientists had discredited. Some of the movement's most coveted allies, it turns out, are among those most responsible for blocking meaningful criminal justice reforms across the board. Money is fungible, and by funding trainings for these organizations and crediting their moral authority, the animal protection movement is culpable for further empowering some of the most ardent enemies of equitable criminal justice reform.

More generally, the schmoozing and wooing of prosecutors has emerged as a mainstay for many animal protection groups. To date, no one has suggested anything ethically improper has occurred in any of these relationships, and certainly the animal protection community exerts far less pressure over most prosecutors than other politically motivated and highly resourced groups. Nonetheless, these ventures raise ethical flags for good governance advocates. In other contexts, organizations with political agendas have come under increasing scrutiny from legal scholars and journalists for their efforts to attract the allegiance of elected prosecutors.[166] In 2014, the *New York Times* ran an explosive exposé detailing the previously un-scrutinized efforts of companies like Pfizer and AT&T to lobby prosecutors to enforce laws in a way that was beneficial to their financial well-being and worldview.[167] Such practices of lobbying prosecutors are notable because, though prosecutors are the representatives of the State in court, they are not held to the same standards as individual legislators when it comes to ethics rules regarding gifts and favoritism. What could be an impeachable act for a legislator has become business as usual for many prosecutors.[168] As the *New York*

[165] Jessica Pishko, *Prosecutors Are Banding Together to Prevent Criminal-Justice Reform*, THE NATION (Oct. 18, 2017), www.thenation.com/article/prosecutors-are-banding-together-to-prevent-criminal -justice-reform/

[166] Mike Koehler, *The Uncomfortable Truths and Double Standards of Bribery Enforcement*, 84 FORDHAM L. REV. 525, 549 (2015) (explaining the trend of pressure on prosecutors by big business).

[167] Eric Lipton, *Lobbyists, Bearing Gifts, Pursue Attorneys General*, N.Y. TIMES, Oct. 28, 2014 (noting that "routine lobbying and deal-making [with prosecutors] occur largely out of view").

[168] Neal Devins & Saikrishna Bangalore Prakash, *Fifty States, Fifty Attorneys General, and Fifty Approaches to the Duty to Defend*, 124 YALE L.J. 2100, 2143 (2015) ("Elected attorneys general pay more attention to the needs of their political base than to the institutional or political interests of other parts of the executive branch, including the governor."); *see also* Koehler at 549 (explaining that big corporations use campaign contributions, personal appeals at lavish corporate-sponsored conferences, and other means to push prosecutors to drop investigations, change policies, negotiate favorable settlements, or pressure federal regulators).

Times reported, some prosecutors have formally declined prosecutions after receiving awards, trips, and other recognition from the potential targets of such prosecutions.[169]

Typically, the lobbying of prosecutors is used as vehicle for avoiding civil or criminal enforcement efforts, but the animal protection movement has turned this agenda on its head. There is no record of a concerted campaign to pressure prosecutors to forego charges against, for example, activists in the movement who participate in civil disobedience. Rather, the courting of prosecutorial favor is in service of an ethos of more and longer sentences for animal cruelty. Such advocacy remains ethically dubious. Undoubtedly, for example, if Pfizer used its influence with prosecutors to urge greater restrictions on the prosecution of animal cruelty against pharmaceutical researchers, or if it lobbied for more creative ways to prosecute activists who oppose all biomedical research on animals, the movement would rightfully protest the company's undue influence on prosecutors and challenge the neutrality of the exercise of prosecutorial discretion. Indeed, following in the footsteps of the animal protection movement it appears that a concerted push to externally fund agricultural crimes prosecutions may be well under way.[170]

The paid-for dinners, events, and awards mentioned above are all forms of not-too-subtle lobbying, or at least means of gaining access. But the *New York Times* exposé also documented another effective means of gaining access to prosecutorial power and discretion – having in-house representatives from the prosecution, ideally former colleagues. It turns out that "unlike the lobbying rules covering other elected officials, there are few revolving-door restrictions or disclosure requirements governing"[171] state prosecutors. The revolving door is not nearly as well-entrenched in the animal protection movement, but one could speculate that if financial resources were less of a constraint, or perhaps more saliently if the movement could attract more senior prosecutors into animal protection movement, there would be a much greater representation of former prosecutors holding senior positions within the animal protection movement. At this point, unlike in other areas of crime, there are relatively few senior prosecutors with consistent experience in the realm of cruelty prosecutions. Certainly, animal protection organizations have recognized that hiring people of influence in the prosecutorial community can be money well-spent toward the goal of greater incarceration for animal-related crimes, and indeed whenever possible they have hired key, well-connected prosecutors. In terms of access to the criminal justice community, hiring an elected DA or senior prosecutor who is well-known across the

---

[169] *See, e.g.*, Corey Hutchins, *New York Times Investigation Sparks Local Scrutiny of State Attorneys General*, COLUM. JOURNALISM REV. (Nov. 7, 2014), www.cjr.org/united_states_project/nytimes_attorney_general_inves.php (discussing reactions to Lipton's piece in the *New York Times*); Lipton at 167 (exposing lobbyists' efforts to woo attorneys general).

[170] Daniel P. Mears et. al, *A Process and Impact Evaluation of the Agricultural Crime, Technology, Information, and Operations Network (ACTION) Program*, at 119 (2007) (calling for "vertical integration" of industry and prosecutors, including the private funding of prosecutors so that more attention can be devoted to crimes against farmers), available at www.ncjrs.gov/pdffiles1/nij/grants/217906.pdf.

[171] Lipton.

country and has connections in the national prosecutor organizations such as the National District Attorneys Association is money well spent.

In what is perhaps the best example of such a hire, the Animal Legal Defense Fund hired a former elected district attorney, Scott Heiser, who was the state president of the district attorneys' association and had an executive-level position on the board of a national prosecution organization.[172] Heiser was one of the most powerful lawyers in one of the most important animal protection groups in the country; he enjoyed a leadership position that allowed him to opine on the strategy and tactics of the entire organization. In describing his work for the organization, this former prosecutor notes:

> [W]ith over 60 years of prosecution experience among them [the criminal justice program attorneys] regularly provide training to law enforcement officers and prosecutors across the country. . . . Under [his] leadership, ALDF has forged partnerships with both the Association of Prosecuting Attorneys (APA) and the National District Attorneys Association (NDAA) to provide the training necessary to ensure that prosecutors get the results these cases deserve.[173]

Other groups have also invested heavily in the capital of former prosecutors: the ASPCA put out a press release in 2013 celebrating the hiring of both a long-time police officer and a seasoned prosecutor to assist with efforts to liaise with local police and prosecutors in the region.[174] And what is notable about the hiring of a prosecutor into an animal protection organization is that the lawyer is virtually never assigned to engage in or oversee litigation, as they might be in a general counsel or law firm position.[175] Their litigation background is not important to their work. The hiring of such prosecutors into non-litigation roles is a transparent effort to make connections with prosecutors and gain credibility. These former prosecutors and police officers are explicitly and intentionally deployed to integrate the animal rights community within the prosecutorial network. "We are one of you. We are part of your team," pleads the movement to the nation's leading prosecutors.

---

[172] Scott Heiser, ANIMAL L. CONF., http://animallawconference.org/scott-heiser/ (last visited Jan. 24, 2018). Heiser has since returned to the ranks of the prosecutorial world, leaving open the possibility that the revolving door is functioning.

[173] *Id.*

[174] *ASPCA Bolsters Partnership with NYPD with Two Key Hires*, AM. SOC'Y FOR PREVENTION OF CRUELTY TO ANIMALS (Oct. 1, 2013), www.aspca.org/about-us/press-releases/aspca-bolsters-partnership-nypd -two-key-hires.

[175] In the world of white-collar crime, it is very common to hire prosecutors to serve as well-connected defense lawyers. *See* KENNETH H. MANN, DEFENDING WHITE-COLLAR CRIME: A PORTRAIT OF ATTORNEYS AT WORK 22 (1985); Matthew Goldstein, *Point72 Hires Ex-Prosecutor as General Counsel*, N.Y. TIMES (May 6, 2015), www.nytimes.com/2015/05/07/business/dealbook/point72-hires-ex -prosecutor-as-general-counsel.html (discussing hiring "a former federal prosecutor to send a message to the federal authorities that his firm would not tolerate the kind of aggressive behavior that resulted in his former hedge fund, SAC Capital Advisors, pleading guilty to insider trading charges.").

3.4.4.2 Paying for Prosecutions

Even hiring a leading prosecutor is no guarantee that the person will remain effective years later in influencing the discretion of new prosecutors. Connections grow stale and perhaps the prosecutor will move on to a more lucrative lobbying position. The only way to ensure that prosecutors remain steadfast in their commitment to prosecute animal cruelty is to pay a prosecutor to bring such cases. To most students of the American legal system, this would seem an impossibility. After all, a hallmark of the American justice system is that *only* the government can bring criminal charges against an individual.[176] As a testament to their creativity and tenacity, animal protection groups have nonetheless achieved notable success in this effort as well.[177]

In Ohio, county humane societies are authorized to appoint persons to aid in the prosecution of individuals charged with animal cruelty.[178] At least one attorney has served as a private attorney general prosecuting animal cruelty under this statute.[179] The attorney became well known in the state for his ambitious and aggressive animal cruelty prosecutions, and he was paid his usual rate from private practice by the Ohio Humane Societies. He made just as much money prosecuting cruelty cases as he did billing private clients and had no qualms about noting that he preferred prosecution to his normal civil docket. By all accounts, this arrangement has been advantageous to the funders because the attorney "has been remarkably successful in getting convictions."[180]

Moving beyond special prosecutors, however, the Animal Legal Defense Fund has set the gold standard for "bankrolling" prosecutions.[181] The organization has created, funded, and apparently selected a full-time prosecutor in Oregon whose

[176] There are no truly private prosecutions. The closest the US system comes are *qui tam* actions. *See* Evan Caminker, *The Constitutionality of Qui Tam Actions*, 99 Yale L.J. 341, 341 (1989) ("In [qui tam] action[s], a private person maintains a civil proceeding on behalf of both herself and the United States to recover damages and/or to enforce penalties available under a statute prohibiting specified conduct."); Michael Edmund O'Neill, *Private Vengeance and the Public Good*, 12 U. Pa. J. Const. L. 659, 683 (2010) ("[M]ost jurisdictions have either disallowed privately managed prosecutions completely, or severely limited the role a private prosecutor may play.").

[177] Tischler at 59 ("[A]nimal law practitioners have experimented with efforts to civilly enforce cruelty laws and assist with private prosecutions in states where such approaches are allowed").

[178] Ohio Rev. Code Ann. § 1717.06; Ohio Rev. Code Ann § 2931.18.

[179] Tresl at 302. ("It is through [Ohio law] that [Jeffrey] Holland has acted as private attorney-general and special prosecutor.") Jeffrey Holland has tried several animal cruelty cases under Ohio law. *Id.* ("Whenever there is a case of animal cruelty in the area, a humane society or a local prosecutor often thinks to call Holland before calling anyone else . . . Holland has been remarkably successful in getting convictions.")

[180] *Id.* at 302–03 (applauding Holland's "creative manipulating" of the law in order to obtain unlikely convictions).

[181] *See, e.g., Animal Cruelty Prosecutor Jake Kamins Takes on Oregon Animal Abuse*; Nigel Jaquiss, The Animal Lawyer, Willamette Wk. (Dec. 2, 2014), www.wweek.com/portland/article-23626-the _animal_lawyer.html ("[Jake Kamins, the Oregon Animal Cruelty Deputy District Attorney] is being paid for by a three-year, $300,000 grant from the Animal Legal Defense Fund, a California advocacy group.").

only job is to prosecute animal related crimes.[182] The prosecutor, Jake Kamins, is a fully-sworn member of the district attorney's office, but his salary is funded entirely by ALDF, and he prosecutes only animal cruelty or neglect cases. The terms of his funding, as revealed in the contract between him and ALDF, make clear that the continued funding of the position is tied, at least informally, to the success he has in obtaining more and longer terms of incarceration. ALDF expects some returns on their investment, and presumably a prosecutor who was dismissing charges, suggesting treatment instead of incarceration, or otherwise offering lenient plea bargains would not expect their funding to continue. There are very few, if any, true analogues to such an arrangement in the United States, and one could reasonably speculate that the movement will soon look to fund other prosecutor positions across the country.

3.4.4.3 Assisting and Conducting Police Investigations

Animal cruelty prosecutions can present challenging evidentiary issues and raise complicated forensic questions, all of which cost money and time. If police do not investigate the cases, and investigate them properly, no prosecutor – not even one paid for by the non-profits – will be able to bring a successful prosecution. Animal protection groups support law enforcement cruelty investigations in a variety of ways that mirror the role they play in prosecutors' offices.

First, the animal protection organizations conduct trainings seemingly for every police department that will host them, and they provide free training materials to assist law enforcement.[183] Beyond training, some groups actually assist law enforcement at crime scenes by providing them with direct investigative support. For example, the ASPCA has a "Field Investigations Team" comprised of cruelty experts who "assist in all aspects of criminal investigation[s] and provide expert testimony as needed."[184] Even more impressive, the Humane Society has its own "mobile animal crimes lab," which is described as a vehicle "manufactured to contain the latest forensic equipment to help law enforcement at animal fighting or abuse crime

[182] Bennett Hall, *DA Honored for Animal Rights Work*, CORVALLIS-GAZETTE-TIMES (Mar. 4, 2014), www
.gazettetimes.com/news/local/da-honored-for-animal-rights-work/article_fae5e8aa-a32b-11e3-8a51
-0019bb2963f4.html ("Funded by a three-year grant from the Animal Legal Defense Fund, the position was filled in September by Jake Kamins.").

[183] *See, e.g., Animal Cruelty Prosecutor and Judicial Training* (listing training events for prosecutors); Heiser ("Joining the all-star faculty for this three-day training [on prosecuting animal cruelty cases] are ALDF's veteran prosecutors."); *Law Enforcement Training on Animal Cruelty Crimes*, HUMANE SOC'Y U.S., www.humanesociety.org/issues/animal_rescue/law-enforcement-training.html (last visited Jan. 24, 2018) (discussing free training for law enforcement offered by HSUS).

[184] *ASPCA Field Investigations and Response Team*, AM. SOC'Y FOR PREVENTION OF CRUELTY TO ANIMALS, www.aspca.org/fight-cruelty/field-investigations-and-response-team/field-investigations-team (last visited Jan. 24, 2018). The Humane Society even maintains an "Animal Rescue Team" comprised of animal cruelty experts who "assist with the investigation and prosecution of every type of animal abuse."

scenes."[185] This "new weapon in the fight against animal cruelty" is apparently being made available to law enforcement officers free of charge. As the HSUS describes it, "This cutting-edge vehicle is an innovative tool in the arsenal of resources that we offer to law enforcement to crack down on animal fighting criminals and other abusers . . ."

It is no longer uncommon for notable animal abuse prosecutions to originate from the investigative work of a privately funded animal welfare organization. Increasingly, the lines between government action and non-profit advocacy are inextricably inter-twined. Indeed, courts and criminal lawyers in some states have become accustomed to having privately employed persons conduct arrests and investigations in animal cruelty cases.[186] As the Oregon Supreme Court recently explained, "The state has not disputed that Special Agent Wallace qualified as a government actor under the circumstances of this case [despite the fact that] Special Agent Wallace was employed by the Oregon Humane Society, a private nonprofit entity, rather than a state or local law enforcement agency."[187] Across the country animal protection organizations are paying private police officers (SPCA or "humane" officers) who are deputized to investigate animal abuse.[188] To an even greater extent than they have accomplished within the prosecutorial ranks, animal protection groups pay for and provide the very officers "charged with investigating and enforcing the animal cruelty laws of [a state]."[189] These privately funded[190] and privately selected officers take pains to emphasize that they are "real" cops. The Humane Society of Rochester promotes its privately funded officers by explaining that "[o]ur law enforcement officers are

---

[185]   *The HSUS Unveils Iowa-Built Mobile Animal Crimes Investigation Lab*, HUMANE SOC'Y U.S. (Apr. 28, 2010), www.humanesociety.org/news/press_releases/2010/04/crime_investigation_vehicle_042810 .html (noting that the Humane Society teamed up with Animal Rescue Club to create the van that includes "two fully-functional rooms for examining dogs and documenting their injuries, equipment for evidence packaging, ultra-violet lights for spotting body fluids, entomology kits, a latent print lift kit and devices for identifying suspected blood.").

[186]   *Newcomb*, 375 P.3d at 436 (noting that the privately employed persons certified as police officers are termed "humane special agents" under Oregon law).

[187]   *Id.*

[188]   *See Humane Investigations*, ANIMAL HUMANE SOC'Y, www.animalhumanesociety.org/rescue/humane -investigations (last visited Jan. 24, 2018).

[189]   *Law Enforcement at Lollypop Farm*, LOLLYPOP FARM, HUMANE SOC'Y GREATER ROCHESTER, www .lollypop.org/site/c.clKUI9OQIoJcH/b.7795697/k.D8B2/Investigating_Animal_Cruelty.htm (last visited Jan. 24, 2018); *see also Cruelty Investigations*, R.I. SPCA, https://rispca.com/services/animal -cruelty-investigations/ (last visited Jan. 24, 2018) (stating that the Rhode Island SPCA supports law enforcement with its on investigator); Penny Ellison, *Three Common Misconceptions About SPCA's*, HAND2PAW (Mar. 18, 2015), www.hand2paw.org/animal-shelters/three-common-misconceptions -about-animal-shelters/ ("In Pennsylvania, neither the Pennsylvania SPCA nor any local SPCA bearing the name of the County where it is located receives any funding from the government."); *Frequently Asked Questions*, MASSACHUSETTS SPCA, www.mspca.org/cruelty-prevention/law -enforcement-faqs/ (last visited Jan. 24, 2018) (providing requirements for MSPCA law enforcement officers).

[190]   There are not any absolute rules in most states regarding where the funding comes from for animal abuse investigators, and accordingly the funding structure takes on a variety of forms, ranging from purely government-funded to purely privately funded, as well as hybrid funding systems.

certified state peace officers with the authority to make arrests – not 'dogcatchers' or animal control officers."[191]

Animal protection groups also engage in the more mundane details of assisting police by, for example, staffing hotlines where people can report potential animal abuse,[192] paying for and hosting software that allows animal abuse to be reported anonymously online, and offering cash rewards of tens of thousands of dollars for information leading to arrests in abuse cases.

****

There is longstanding sense among many senior figures in the animal protection world that cruelty prosecutions are among the most important part of animal law. By prosecuting more people more severely, there is a hope that the legislatures will gain interest and create even more crimes with even higher penalties. Over time these prosecutions and longer sentences, it is argued, will result in a widespread acceptance of animals as enjoying a more significant legal status. There is a sense that as long as states diligently pursue a more punitive approach to animal cruelty, the moral and legal standing of animals will be indelibly improved. It remains to be seen whether this strategy will yield any material benefits to animals, much less society in general, which is the subject of the chapters that follow. But what cannot be doubted is that animal protection groups have secured a remarkable foothold within the criminal justice system. Through awards, trainings, free legal assistance, expert witnesses, amicus briefs, and even the private funding of police officer and prosecutor positions, animal protection groups have done their best to increase the likelihood that non-institutionalized animal abuse will be punished more frequently and more severely. The uncompromising phrase "abuse an animal, go to jail" really does reflect the mainstream ethos of the modern movement, at least when it comes to rogue acts of pet abuse as opposed to institutionalized animal suffering.

---

[191] *Law Enforcement at Lollypop Farm* (commenting favorably on the number of arrests made by the officers in a single year).

[192] See *LiveSafe: Mobile App to Report Animal Cruelty*, ANIMAL LEGAL DEF. FUND, http://aldf.org /resources/when-you-witness-animal-cruelty/aldf-livesafe-mobile-app-to-report-animal-cruelty (last visited Apr. 21, 2016) (announcing ALDF integration in a crime reporting app that allows users to report animal cruelty directly to ALDF); *Report Animal Cruelty*, HUMANE SOC'Y U.S. (May 27, 2015), www.humanesociety.org/issues/abuse_neglect/tips/cruelty_action.html (stating that the Humane Society offers phone lines to call if someone's community does not have adequate resources to handle an animal abuse complaint).

4

General Critiques of the Carceral Turn in Animal Protection

A leading animal law textbook observes that humane association officers tasked with enforcing cruelty laws are frequently "reluctant to seize animals without a warrant (even if there is immediate danger) because they are concerned the seizure will be invalidated later."[1] The "hesitation" prompted by a concern with the admissibility of the evidence "can result in abused animals dying." This anecdote is a microcosm of the problems with the prosecution-based focus of the movement. There is a willingness to prioritize practices that strengthen the criminal case against a perpetrator even at the expense of actually saving animals. It is inevitably posited that only through the rigid enforcement of animal cruelty laws will animals ever be truly safe, and yet the reality is that keeping animals safe is oftentimes a secondary concern to securing a conviction.[2]

---

[1] The textbook's authors invoke this scenario as evidence of the technicalities that may encumber a criminal prosecution. However, the fact that animals are dying in order to benefit a prosecutor's chances of obtaining a conviction is in tension with any claim that animal cruelty laws are primarily protections for animals. WAISMAN ET AL., ANIMAL LAW 79 (5th edn. 2013). Perhaps animal protection groups would serve the interest of the non-humans best by training the officers to immediately seize animals that are in imminent danger even if the prosecution would be jeopardized, and to promote civil proceedings that would ensure the animal does not return to an abusive situation.

[2] Certainly, there are means of keeping an abused dog from returning to a dangerous owner through civil proceedings or protection orders. An illegal seizure by the police of stolen property or drugs does not entitle the person who was subjected to the police misconduct to have the contraband returned to them. Similarly, to the extent the victim-animal is still alive, there are a variety of means of protecting that particular animal, including confiscation, restraining orders and the like, which do not turn on incarceration or even prosecution. *See, e.g.,* Ariz. Rev. Stat. Ann. § 13–4281 (allowing the state to terminate the ownership rights of an animal and transfer them to the state); 510 Ill. Comp. Stat. Ann. § 70/3.04 (allowing for the forfeiture of an animal before a criminal conviction); Asheville North Carolina Ordinance Section 3–30 (allowing for seizure of an animal if a person violates Section 3–12); *see also* Margreta Vellucci, *Restraining the (Real) Beast: Protective Orders and Other Statutory Enactments to Protect the Animal Victims of Domestic Violence in Rhode Island*, 16 ROGER WILLIAMS U. L. REV. 224, 241–42 (2011) (arguing for the expansion of Rhode Island law that would include animals in protection orders); Joshua L. Friedman & Gary C. Norman, *Protecting the Family Pet: The New Face of Maryland Domestic Violence Protective Orders*, 40 U. BALT. L.F. 81, 82 (2009) (arguing for protective orders for companion pets who were victims of animal abuse).

This chapter shows that the carceral approach to animal law is conceptually and logically flawed. By aligning itself with the imprisoning state and the tough-on-crime approach to solving social problems, the animal protection movement is risking serious self-inflicted wounds.[3] Similar carceral approaches have been deployed in other contexts including drugs, domestic violence, and sex offenses, and the animal protection movement would be well-served to take seriously the lessons learned in these contexts.

4.1 THE LEGISLATIVE COST OF FELONY CRUELTY LAWS: THE CORRELATION BETWEEN PASSING FELONY LAWS AND EXEMPTING AGRICULTURAL CRUELTY

Even the most sanguine assessment of increased policing and prosecution in the realm of animal protection cannot overcome a basic empirical reality – enacting felony provisions correlated with the creation of the single biggest loophole in state cruelty codes. The creation of felony provisions appears to have been a tradeoff for state exemptions for institutional abuse such as common agricultural practices. The movement's "success" in achieving legislative victories in the form of more severe cruelty laws, then, has come at a massive and unacknowledged cost to the protection of animals – that is, triggering the largest exemption from animal cruelty laws in the United States.

This section provides an overview of the operation of customary agricultural exemptions from animal cruelty and their impact on animal protection. Next, it details the findings of an exhaustive original study of the legislative history surrounding the creation of felony cruelty laws, which demonstrates that the movement's coveted felony provisions were often part of a legislative package that included the decriminalization of institutionalized, agricultural abuse.

4.1.1 *Customary Agricultural Practices Exemption*

As of 2017, forty states exempt abuse to any animal raised for food from the definition of animal cruelty so long as the acts in question are "deemed 'accepted,' 'common,' 'customary,' or 'normal' farming practices."[4] These exemptions for agricultural uses of animals render the suffering of billions of animals per year invisible to the criminal law. Factory farms in most states are largely insulated from liability for acts that unquestionably cause tremendous suffering to animals. As David Wolfson has aptly observed, "These statutes have

---

[3] *See, e.g.*, JONATHAN SIMON, GOVERNING THROUGH CRIME: HOW THE WAR ON CRIME TRANSFORMED AMERICAN DEMOCRACY AND CREATED A CULTURE OF FEAR 4, 15 (2007) (detailing the get-tough-on-crime approach to policing).

[4] David J. Wolfson, *Beyond the Law: Agribusiness and the Systemic Abuse of Animals Raised for Food or Food Production*, 2 ANIMAL L. 123, 123 (1996).

given the farming community the power to define cruelty to animals in their care."[5] Stated more bluntly, through these exemptions, "[l]egislatures in the United States have endowed agribusiness with complete authority to decide what is, and is not, cruelty to animals under their care ... In effect, state legislatures have granted agribusiness a legal license to treat farm animals as they wish."[6] If a practice becomes generally accepted or customary, no matter how cruel, it cannot, as a matter of law, serve as the basis for an animal cruelty prosecution in forty states.

To appreciate the force of such an exemption, it is important to realize that animals used for food make up more than 90 percent of all domestic animals and thus comprise the vast majority of animals that suffer at human hands. Moreover, the animal cruelty tolerated as customary agricultural practices is among the most brutal animal mistreatment that animals endure. One need not take the word of animal activists that animal cruelty permeates the factory farm. One of the most famous defamation cases in history pitted McDonalds against some protesters in the U.K. who held signs and passed out leaflets that, among other things, described McDonalds as responsible for animal "torture." Despite the historically relaxed standard for defamation liability in the United Kingdom as compared to the United States, McDonald's failed to establish liability for the claim that it had contributed to animal cruelty because, as factual matter, the company was actually culpable for the torture and abuse of animals. In one section of the opinion the court concluded that "McDonald's [was] responsible for torture and murder." Judge Bell concluded that in many instances it was factually accurate to treat McDonald's as responsible for cruelty to animals.[7] Explaining that a large number of accepted animal husbandry practices are in fact cruel, the court noted that "[o]f course, the commercial urge to rear and slaughter as many animals as economically and therefore quickly as possible may lead to cruel practices ... which could be avoided if less attention was paid to profit and high production and more to the animals."[8] McDonald's spent more than $16 million in legal fees bringing the

---

5   *Id.; see also* Luis E. Chiesa, *Why Is It a Crime to Stomp on a Goldfish? – Harm, Victimhood and the Structure of Anti-Cruelty Offenses*, 78 Miss. L.J. 1, 10 (2008) (noting also that even when the anti-cruelty law might be applied to animals raised for food, the penalties for cruelty to dogs and cats are often higher). According to one commentator, "[o]nly Minnesota, Oklahoma, and Mississippi do not permit any exemptions to their cruelty statutes." Jacqueline Tresl, *The Broken Window: Laying Down the Law for Animals*, 26 S. Ill. U. L.J. 277, 290 (2002).

6   Wolfson, *Beyond the Law*, at 123.

7   The decision goes through numerous examples of alleged cruelty and torture and finds that many such allegations are factually true, but does conclude that some of the allegations of suffering and cruelty were not accurate. "Claims that McDonald's bore responsibility for starvation in the third world, the destruction of vast areas of rainforest, and that it served food with a very real risk of cancer, heart disease and food poisoning, were not proven to be true." David J. Wolfson, *Mclibel*, 5 ANIMAL L. 21, 33 (1999).

8   Chief Justice Bell, *The Verdict Section 8: The Rearing and Slaughtering of Animals*, www.mcspotlight .org/case/trial/verdict/verdict_jud2c.html (last visited Oct. 31, 2017).

defamation case, and a couple of unrepresented[9] protesters were able to convince a court that allegations of animal cruelty were not factually false.[10]

If two nearly pro se litigants can convince a court over the objections of a global law firm that the ordinary practices of meat and dairy production are oftentimes cruel, then the fact of such cruelty is probably not fairly in dispute. Nonetheless, for persons unfamiliar with standard animal husbandry practices it is useful to highlight several examples of practices that fall outside of the animal cruelty statutes because of the exemptions for customary agricultural practices:

- Animals raised for food may be exempted from general requirements for shelter, including minimal protection from the weather.
- Animals may be confined in cages or crates so small that the animal cannot even turn around.
- Animals may have their testicles and tails removed, or they may be branded, all without anesthetic.
- Chickens have their beaks removed without anesthetic.
- Chickens may be starved in order to induce a new egg laying cycle.
- Cows as young as a day old may be removed from their mothers and housed in veal crates that preclude exercise or play.
- Chickens are killed at rates that make minimally careful handling impossible, with many facilities striving for line speeds in excess of 140 birds per minute (meaning that each worker has to hang the birds by their feet upside down on a moving conveyor belt at a rate of about 30–45 birds per minute).

It does not take an act of radical anthropomorphism to imagine that sentient creatures would suffer a great deal from any of these customary farming practices. More importantly, however, the sort of daily suffering that is imposed on animals at any large, industrial facility cannot fully be captured by a list. An accepted means of killing off unwanted fowl is drowning them in foam ; the USDA explicitly approved asphyxiation through foam, though it was noted that death may not occur for fifteen minutes.

Nathan Runkle's biography gives another vivid anecdote about a so-called "standard agricultural practice" that shaped his life's trajectory.[11] Runkle describes an experience with his high school science teacher who doubled as a hog farmer. The science teacher brought a bucket of dead baby piglets to class for dissection. Apparently one of

[9] The defendants were "offered limited pro bono assistance." Wolfson, *Mclibel*, at 23–24.
[10] *Id.* ("Perhaps the most important aspect of the McLibel decision is the contradiction Mr. Justice Bell exposed: many common farming practices in the United States and the United Kingdom are held to be cruel and yet, at the same time, these practices continue because they do not fall within the statutory definition of cruelty.")
[11] Nathan Runkle, Mercy for Animals 21–23 (2017).

the pigs was not dead and was trying to climb out of the bucket. With the approval of the teacher, "a senior student in the class . . . proceeded to grab the baby animal by her hind legs and, in full view of the other students, slam her head-first into the concrete floor. Twice."[12] The science teacher was charged with animal cruelty for approving such abuse, but the judge immediately dismissed the charges because "slamming piglets headfirst in to the ground is, in fact, standard agricultural practice."[13] The judge was not wrong. Indeed, the practice of "thumping" or grabbing baby pigs who are small or otherwise unlikely to thrive by their back legs and killing them by blunt force trauma caused by striking their skulls against the floor is an accepted practice in the pork industry, according to the American Veterinary Medical Association.[14] The exemption for agricultural practices in Runkle's home state of Ohio (and the thirty-nine other states that have such an exemption) insulates the institutional practice of killing pigs by bashing their skulls repeatedly against the ground.

Similarly, leading animal protection advocate Jon Lovvorn has astutely observed that there is no recourse for the tens of thousands of hens crammed into a processing shed without light, clean air, or room to move, but "if someone kills or injures a single blue jay in the rafters of a factory farm, he could be fined $15,000 and sentenced to six months in jail."[15] Likewise, undercover investigations that reveal the daily conditions endured by animals in transport or in production leave little room to doubt that oftentimes the most common, daily events on a factory farm cause horrific suffering. Most of Timothy Pachirat's profound book *Every Twelve Seconds* focuses not on exposing and detailing animal suffering, but rather he emphasizes the banality and geography of a massive slaughterhouse. Yet Pachirat's lucid writing and his focus on other issues make the couple of short vignettes regarding animal suffering particularly chilling.[16] In one passage, for example, Pachirat describes his work on the chute that leads cows from their transport to slaughter:

> Forty minutes after we return from morning break a third cow collapses in the chute . . . The cow struggles to right itself, but with the narrow passageway and downward slope slick with feces and vomit, it cannot get up. It soon lies still, breathing heavily and jerking its head back and forth . . . Gilberto grabs a pair of metal rings off the wall behind him and tosses them to Fernando . . . Fernando

---

[12]   *Id.* at 21.
[13]   *Id.* at 23.
[14]   In 2012, the American Veterinary Medical Association (AVMA) rationalized that "[b]ased upon current data, the AVMA Panel on Euthanasia has determined that manually applied blunt force trauma to the head is an acceptable method of euthanasia for suckling pigs." Gail Golab, *Hot on Facebook: Euthanasia of Suckling Pigs Using Blunt Force Trauma*, AMVA (July 21, 2012), http://atwork .avma.org/2012/07/21/hot-on-facebook-euthanasia-of-suckling-pigs-using-blunt-force-trauma/.
[15]   Feinberg, note 3.
[16]   TIMOTHY PACHIRAT, EVERY TWELVE SECONDS 154 (2011).

inserts the rings through the cow's nostrils, clamps them shut and attaches them to a yellow rope, which he jerks heavily, trying to make the cow, now lying flat on its back, sit up and flip over onto its legs. Steve and several line workers from inside who have been alerted to the problem by the knocker join in the pulling. The pressure on the rope stretches the cow's nostrils until they are almost translucent. Finally, the men pull so hard they rip the cow's nostrils and the nose rings fly out, hitting Juan in the hand . . . Steve motions to Gilberto to begin driving the cattle over the downed cow . . . With electric prods Gilberto and Fernando push the remaining cattle over the downed cow, and they stomp on its neck and underbelly trying to escape the electric shock.[17]

The suffering inflicted on billions of animals per year on factory farms is categorically not cognizable as animal cruelty in forty states for one reason: the customary agricultural practices exemption that has been added to state cruelty codes.

4.1.2 *The Connection Between the Agricultural Exemptions and Felony Cruelty Laws*

Among the animal protection movement's most celebrated legislative victory has been the adoption of felony cruelty provisions in all fifty states. The last state's adoption of a felony provision in 2014 – South Dakota – is heralded as a "significant milestone in an undeniable trend favoring humane treatment of animals."[18] Missing from this narrative of landmark success and milestones, however, is the fact that a full one-third of the states with exemptions for factory farming practices enacted these exemptions in conjunction with passing their felony laws. Whether wittingly or unwittingly, the movement struck a deal with the devil – the felony provisions for rogue acts of abuse came at the cost of exempting widespread acts of animal abuse against billions of animals per year.

Despite the recognized connection between customary farm practices and immense animal suffering discussed immediately above, the vast majority of states explicitly exempt from the statutory definition of animal cruelty acts that are consistent with customary farming practices. The chart below lists the forty states with broad exemptions as of 2018 (other states, including New Hampshire have less sweeping exemptions), and provides the date of the original enactment of the exemption, as well as the date of any revisions to those exemptions.

---

[17] *Id.* at 154–55.
[18] Chris Berry, *All 50 States Now Have Felony Animal Cruelty Provisions*, ANIMAL LEGAL DEF. FUND (Mar. 14, 2014), http://aldf.org/blog/50-states-now-have-felony-animal-cruelty-provisions/.

Animal Cruelty Exemption Laws – Date of Enactment

STATE	EXEMPTION	YEAR
Illinois	510 ILCS §70/13,/3.03	1973/1999
Wisconsin	§§951.015,.09,.14	1973
Kentucky	§525.130(2)(b),(d)	1974/2003
Maryland	§10–603(1)	1975
Kansas	§21–6412(c)(6)	1977/2006
Ohio	§§959.13(A)(2),(A)(5),(B)	1977
Arizona	§§13–2910.05,.06	1979/1998
Rhode Island	§4–1-5(b)	1981
Louisiana	§14:102.1.C	1982/2008
Washington	§16.52.185	1982/2006
Missouri	§578.007(8)	1983
Pennsylvania	§18–5560	1984/2017
Virginia	§§3.2–6570.C,.D	1984/1999
Oregon	§§167.315,.320,.335	1985
Florida	§828.125(5)	1986
Maine	§§17–1031.2.D,1037-A	1987
South Carolina	§47–1-40(C)	1988
Nevada	§574.200(f)	1989
Vermont	Tit. 13 §351(b), 352	1989/1998
Colorado	§18–9-201.5 (1)	1990
Montana	§45–8-211(4)(b)	1991
South Dakota	§40–1-17	1991/2014
Tennessee	§39–14-202(f)(1)	1991
Utah	§76–9-301(1)(b)(ii)(C)	1991
West Virginia	§61–8-19(f)	1991
Indiana	§35–46-3–5(a)(5)	1993
Idaho	§25–3514(2), (5)	1994
Iowa	§§717.2	1994/2000
Michigan	§§750.50(11)	1994
Wyoming	§6–3-203(m)(ii)	1994
Connecticut	§53–247(b)	1996
New Jersey	§§4:22–16(e),-16.1	1996
Alaska	§11.61.140(c)(3)	1998
North Carolina	§14–360(c)(2)	1998
New Mexico	§30–1-18(I)(4)	1999
Georgia	§16–12-4(g)	2000
Texas	Penal Code §42.09(f)(2)	2001
North Dakota	§36–21.2–03(3)(a)(1),(2)	2007/2013
Arkansas	§§5–62-105(a)(5), (b)	2009
Nebraska	§§54–902(4), 54–907(4),(5)	2010

The chart below lists the ten states that passed felony cruelty laws, but have not enacted an agricultural practices exemption.

States that Have Felony Laws but No Agricultural Exemption

STATE	FELONY
Alabama **	§13A-11-14.1(c)(1)
California	Penal Code § 559c
Deleware	Tit. 11, §1325
Hawaii*	§711–1108.5
Massachusetts	§272–77
Minnesota*	§343.21 Subd. 9
Mississippi	§97–41-1; §97–41-15
New Hampshire	§644–8.III(a)
New York*	Agr & Mkts §353-a
Oklahoma	§21–1685

* Denotes that the state's felony law only applies to pets, horses and/or service animals.
** Denotes a felony law that exempts from felony coverage customary agricultural practices.

The sense of accomplishment surrounding the success of the movement in lobbying for felony cruelty laws is in tension with the realization that all but ten states have exempted from the definition of cruelty (not just felony cruelty) acts of abuse that are accepted as customary agricultural practices. For years, animal protection groups have published 50-state rankings for animal cruelty. Those rankings heavily penalized states which did not have a felony provision, and yet little or no attention is paid to the creation of sweeping criminal exemptions for institutionalized abuse.

One might fairly criticize the movement for prioritizing legislative efforts to create felony violations instead of efforts to end legislative exemptions for farming practices. However, the actual story is even more damning. The untold story of successfully obtaining felony laws in every state is *actually* the story of creating exemptions for farm animal abuse in many states.

Of the forty states that have exemptions for customary farming practices, twelve of these states added those exemptions at the exact same time (often through the same legislation) that added a felony provision. Approximately one out of every three states with an exemption for farm abuse added the exemption in the same bill or at the same time that it passed (or expanded) its felony cruelty law. The felony bills opened the door to farm bureaus and agricultural lobbyists to reform the cruelty code so as to exempt their practices from criminal oversight.

Off-the-record conversations with leaders of the movement who have asked to remain anonymous but who have direct knowledge of this history have confirmed that the addition of farm exemptions was not entirely unexpected. Some have suggested that decision-makers in the movement recognized the implicit trade-off, but pursued felony laws anyway. There were probably very few explicit bargains whereby the movement agreed to support the exemptions in exchange for the felony law, but in many states "the felony cruelty laws were held hostage" by supporters of big agriculture who would not allow such provisions to pass without codified concessions, including agricultural cruelty exemptions. The exact terms of these arrangements varied by state, but it is safe to say that the contemporaneous enactment of felony laws and agricultural exemptions was not simply an unhappy coincidence.[19] The movement is culpable for some of the most sweeping statutory prohibitions on holding factory farms accountable.

The chart below provides a list of the states that enacted exemptions for customary farm practices (or materially expanded existing agricultural exemptions) at the same time that they passed a provision recognizing certain forms of animal cruelty as a felony.

Contemporaneous Enactment of Farm Cruelty Exemptions & Felony Cruelty

	State	Felony Provision	Exemption	Year	
1.	Florida*	§828.125(1)	§828.125(5)	1986	Exemption for "recognized livestock husbandry practices or techniques."
2.	Michigan	§750.50b(3)	§750.50(11) §750.50b(8)	1994	Exemption for "lawful killing of livestock or a customary animal husbandry or farming practice involving livestock."
3.	North Carolina	§14–360(b)	§14–360(c)(2)	1998	Exemption for "activities conducted . . . for purposes of production of livestock or poultry." The exemption was **expanded** the following year (1999) to include aquatic species.
4.	Vermont	§13-352a,-353	§§13-351b(3), 13–352(3)	1998	Exemption for "livestock and poultry husbandry practices" was initially limited to cruelty relating to a section pertaining to tying/tethering or restraining an animal, but the exemption was **expanded** to all animal cruelty offenses.
5.	New Mexico	§30–18-1 (D),(F)	§30–18-1(H)(4)	1999	Exemption for "commonly accepted agricultural animal husbandry practices."
6.	Virginia	§3.2–6570.B	§3.2–6570.D, .F	1999	Exemption for dehorning cattle **expanded** to include an exemption for all "farming activities."
7.	Georgia	§16–12-4(e)	§16–12-4(g)	2000	**Expanding** the exemption from "killing animals raised for the

(continued)

---

[19] Painting the movement's strategic decisions in this realm in the most favorable light, one could imagine that they perceived very little harm flowing from the enactment of an agricultural exemption given that factory farm prosecutions were unheard of.

(continued)

	State	Felony Provision	Exemption	Year	
					purpose of providing food" to a more general exemption for all "agricultural, animal husbandry, butchering, food processing."
8.	Maine	§17–1031.1-B	§17–1031.5	2001	Exemption added in 2001 for "disposal of farm animals using an acceptable animal husbandry practice."
9.	Kansas	§21–6412(b)(1)	§21–6412(c)(6)	2006	Exemption for "normal or accepted practices of animal husbandry" **expanded** to include "the normal and accepted practices for the slaughter of such animals for food or by-products and the careful or thrifty management of one's herd or animals, including animal care practices common in the industry or region."
10.	Arkansas	§5–62-103(f)	§5–62-105(a) (5), (b)	2009	Exemption for "generally accepted animal husbandry practices."
11.	North Dakota	§36–21.2–03(1)	§36–21.2–03(3)	2013	Exemption for "customary practice in production agriculture" **expanded** to include all "production of food, feed, fiber, or ornament, including all aspects of the livestock industry," as well as breeding, feeding, raising of animals.
12.	South Dakota	§40–1-2.4	§40–1-17	2014	Exemption for "agricultural pursuits or animal husbandry practices"; **expanded** to specify that "all aspects of the livestock industry" are exempt.

---

* Florida law has subsequently eliminated its general exemption for customary husbandry practices, but retained the exemption for the separate offense of cow or horse abuse. So the table is accurate as to contemporaneous enactments, but it appears possible under existing Florida law for one to be prosecuted for general, misdemeanor cruelty even for customary practices. In addition it should be noted that Alabama does not appear in the chart because its enactment of a contemporaneous exemption was limited to the felony abuse provision.

Before elaborating on the significance of these findings, it is worth noting a few caveats about the data displayed in the chart. First, as made clear in the column elaborating on the exemptions, some of the exemptions are expansions of the previous farmed animal exemption. Specifically, of the twelve states that passed exemptions as part of the package of legislation that included a felony cruelty provision, seven were expansions of preexisting agricultural exemptions, and five represented the first farm practice exemptions in the state. The list does not include states which merely reworded or re-codified their exemption. Only material expansions of the agricultural exemption are reflected in the list of thirteen states. South Dakota is illustrative of the sort of expansion that was treated as relevant. The state went from a longstanding exemption of certain husbandry practices to, with the enactment of the felony law, a general exemption for "all aspects of the livestock industry." Similarly, in Virginia the dehorning of cattle was exempted from the cruelty code in 1984, but in 1990, when the felony provision was added, the legislature exempted all "farming activities" from cruelty prosecutions. Most of these determinations regarding whether a change to an exemption could be characterized fairly as an expansion of the exemption were straightforward. The closest call in categorizing a change as an expansion to an exemption was Kansas, which changed its preexisting exemption for "normal or accepted practices of animal husbandry" such that the law now exempts all "normal or accepted practices of animal husbandry and the normal and accepted practices for the slaughter of such animals for food or by-products and the careful or thrifty management of one's herd or animals, including animal care practices common in the industry or region." It seems clear that Kansas meant for its already broad exemption to more clearly encompass a wider range of common practices.

It is also worth noting that at least one of the states listed in the chart, Maine, already had one or more felony provisions in the cruelty code prior to the date listed in the chart. For such states, the date listed in the chart corresponds not with the enactment of the state's first felony law, but with an increase in the number of felony provisions. Moreover, it is worth noting that one state, New Jersey, actually went against the grain and added an exemption for customary livestock practices in 1996 when the offense was reduced in grade from a misdemeanor to a disorderly person offense.[20] This appears to be the only state that added an exemption at the same time that it reduced the grade of its cruelty offense.

Beyond the simple fact that many of the current exemptions were enacted contemporaneously with felony provisions, an examination of the date range for the exemption enactments is even more revealing. Of the twelve exemptions (or expansions of exemptions) passed at the same time as a felony provision, ten were enacted in 1998 or later. Only two states passed a felony provision and an agricultural exemption

---

[20]   N.J. Stat. Ann. §§4:22–16(e),-16.1 (1996).

simultaneously prior to 1994. Tying felony cruelty to an agricultural exemption was a distinctly modern phenomenon.

Moreover, after 2005, there were a total of nine states that passed felony anti-cruelty laws for the first time: Alabama, Arkansas, Alaska, Connecticut, Idaho, Kansas, North Dakota, South Dakota, and Pennsylvania. Of these nine states, nearly fifty-percent (4 out of 9) simultaneously added or expanded exemptions for agricultural practices. In addition, of the four states that most recently added or expanded an agricultural exemption (Alabama, Arkansas, North Dakota, and South Dakota), other than Alabama, each state enacted the exemption at the same time that the state was, for the first time, creating a felony animal cruelty provision (and Alabama exempted customary agricultural practices from felony cruelty). When the last wave of states passed felony laws, they tended to do so in conjunction with the passage of an agricultural exemption.

Equally illuminating, as the chart below illustrates, of the most recent fourteen states (of the forty total) to enact agricultural exemptions, nine such exemptions were passed at the same time that a felony provision was added. That is to say, roughly two-thirds of the fourteen most recent agricultural exemptions were passed *at the same time* that the state was adopting or expanding its felony cruelty laws.

Animal Cruelty Exemption Laws Enacted Since 1999

	STATE	EXEMPTION	YEAR
1.	Arkansas	§5–62-105(a)(5), (b)	2009
2.	Georgia	§16–12-4(g)	2000
3.	Kansas	§21–6412(c)(6)	2006
4.	Kentucky **	§525.130(2)(b),(d)	2003
5.	Louisiana **	§14:102.1.C	2008
6.	Maine	§17–1031.5	2001
7.	Maryland **	§10–603(1)	pre-2001
8.	New Mexico	§30–1-18(H)(4)	1999
9.	North Dakota	§36–21.2–03(3)	2013
10.	South Dakota	§40–1-17	2014
11.	Texas**	Penal Code §42.09(f)(2)	2001
12.	Vermont	§§13-351b(3), 13–352(3)	1998
13	Virginia	§3.2–6570.C, .D	1999
14.	Washington**	§16.52.185	2006

** Indicates that the exemption was not enacted contemporaneously with a felony cruelty law.

This data leads to an unmistakable conclusion. In the modern era of animal law, when the push for animal cruelty felony provisions was strongest, nearly every state that was adding a felony provision was simultaneously adding a customary farming practices exemption. Passing a felony law was perhaps the best predictor of whether a state would exempt customary agricultural practices from animal cruelty. And as noted above, this was not merely a coincidence. Leaders in the animal protection movement understood that the legislative cost of the coveted felony cruelty laws was often the adoption or expansion of a law exempting customary farm practices. The suggestion is not that the movement celebrated or pursued the exemptions, but that it was some-times willing to "hold its nose" and accept the exemptions in exchange for the passage of felony cruelty laws. The movement's dirty secret is that its obsession with enacting felony cruelty laws paved the way for agricultural exemptions.

Although the movement has never publicly acknowledged its role in the enactment of modern agricultural exemptions, the media coverage surrounding certain enact-ments tend to confirm what has been shared with the author off the record. For example, the enactment of the Arkansas felony law was preceded by media coverage quoting animal protection groups and supporters of the legislation who made clear that, because of the broad exemption for all "accepted livestock management prac-tices," the Citizens for a Humane Arkansas reported that they were "100% confident" that the new felony law presented no "threat to Arkansas livestock industries or producers."[21] Adding additional clarification, one animal protection spokesman explained that agriculture had nothing to fear: the felony law is "not about agriculture at all, but about people who burn puppies [or] cut the heads off of cats."[22]

Similarly, the North Dakota felony provision was heralded in the press because it enjoyed the support of both animal protection organizations and the state farm bureau and cattlemen's association. But the reason that such an alliance was possible is that the animal protection organizations did not oppose expansions to the agricultural exemption. In a news story summarizing the opposition of agricultural interests to an earlier version of the felony provision, a person sympathetic to the industry was quoted as saying that the felony provision was problematic because, in general, ranchers "really feel like the industry is best served by self-monitoring."[23] In the end, the animal protection movement capitulated and supported "self-monitoring" as the rule for institutionalized animal abuse. The industry referred to the expansion as a "clarified" version of the agricultural exemption, which allowed them in turn to support the felony provision. A similar story is likely true in many of the states that added felony provisions after about 2000. As one agricultural industry advocate describes the process of obtaining exemptions in exchange for felony laws, "It turns out that finding common ground was easier than we might have guessed."[24]

The data presented in this part undermine the narrative that the enactment of felony provisions in all fifty states was an unmitigated good, much less a vaunted milestone for the movement. The enactment of felony laws has been a bait-and-

---

[21] *Advocates of Animal Cruelty Act Speak Out*, PARAGOULD DAILY PRESS (Sep. 5, 2002).

[22] *Id.*

[23] *Animal Groups Offer Alternative to Proposed Ballot Initiative*, N.D. DEP'T OF AGRIC., www.nd.gov /ndda/news/animal-groups-offer-alternative-proposed-ballot-initiative (last accessed Sept. 25, 2018) (the initiative would make some animal cruelty a felony).

[24] *S.D. Panel Approves Making Animal Cruelty a Felony*, DEVILS LAKE JOURNAL (Devils Lake, ND) (Feb. 2, 2014), 2014 WLNR 3969093.

switch – we celebrate the victory of a felony provision that made it possible for the industry to render the most common and sustained abuse of animals invisible to the animal cruelty code.

4.2 INCARCERATION AS INEFFECTUAL IN SECURING CIVIL RIGHTS: LESSONS FROM TOUGH-ON-CRIME POLICIES

The unasked question underlying the impulse to seek punishment for animal cruelty is whether the harsh treatment of human defendants through the criminal justice system will result in benefits to animal protection efforts. By analyzing the efficacy of the criminalization campaigns surrounding the war on drugs and domestic violence, this section raises serious doubts about the efficacy of criminal justice efforts as tools for securing long-term advances for the animal protection movement. Outside of animal law, leading thinkers on all sides of the political spectrum have come to treat carceral solutions as ineffectual and antiquated.[25] The number of crimes and the severity of the punishment has been described by Hadar Aviram "as a veritable human rights crime of massive proportions."[26] At the very moment in history when the animal protection movement is seeking out ever more draconian criminal justice reforms, mainstream culture appears poised to reform or abandon tough-on-crime policies.[27]

Resorting to incarceration or tough-on-crime policies as a means to achieve social change is not a particularly novel strategy. Advocates against domestic violence, drug abuse, and child sexual abuse have previously urged and obtained significant criminal law reforms, many of which mirror aspects of the current policies of animal advocates.[28]

---

[25] See, e.g., Alec Karakatsanis, *Policing, Mass Imprisonment, and the Failure of American Lawyers*, 128 HARV. L. REV. F. 253, 254 (2015) (explaining lawyers' responsibilities in contributing to mass incarceration); Stephano Bibas, *The Truth About Mass Incarceration*, NAT'L REVIEW (Sept. 16, 2015), www .nationalreview.com/article/424059/mass-incarceration-prison-reform (arguing that mass incarceration is not an effective deterrent because most criminals do not consider long-term consequences when they are committing crimes).

[26] See, e.g., Hadar Aviram, *Mass Incarceration on Trial: A Remarkable Court Decision and the Future of Prisons in America*, 49 LAW & SOC'Y REV. 295, 296 (2015).

[27] See, e.g., Dorothy E. Roberts, *The Social and Moral Cost of Mass Incarceration in African American Communities*, 56 STAN. L. REV. 1271, 1300 (2004) ("The empirical evidence of community-level damage caused by the spatial concentration of mass imprisonment supports a radical rethinking of dominant justifications for prison policy and related crime control and sentencing reforms."); Bruce Western & Christopher Wildeman, *Punishment, Inequality, and the Future of Mass Incarceration*, 57 U. KAN. L. REV. 851, 876 (2009) (explaining the harms of mass incarceration and offering ways to solve the problem of mass incarceration).

[28] See, e.g., Alafair S. Burke, *Domestic Violence As a Crime of Pattern and Intent: An Alternative Reconceptualization*, 75 GEO. WASH. L. REV. 552, 553 (2007) (illustrating the criminal law reforms in Domestic Violence Cases); Andrea Lofgren, *A Sign of Things to Come? Drug Policy Reforms in Arizona, California, and New York*, 14 N.Y.U. J. LEGIS. & PUB. POL'Y 773, 775 (2011) (exemplifying the change in mindset on criminal prosecution of low-level drug criminals with examples of Arizona, California, and New York laws); Jessica E. Mindlin, *Child Sexual Abuse and Criminal Statutes of Limitation: A Model for Reform*, 65 WASH. L. REV. 189, 195 (1990) (outlining the expansion in child sexual abuse laws in order to protect children from their abusers).

The lessons learned from these prior reform efforts should, at a minimum, give the movement pause about its current assumptions regarding the viability of curing social problems with incarceration.

4.2.1 *The Domestic Violence Analogy – Mandatory Arrest*

The animal protection movement believes that crimes against animals are under-enforced. This is an assumption without empirical data to support it, but it drives policy decisions within the movement. Because of this fear of underenforcement, many in the animal protection movement support mandatory reporting and man-datory arrest laws. Mandatory reporting requires certain professions, usually medical professionals, to report all suspected acts of animal abuse, and the failure to do so can result in the non-reporter being prosecuted and jailed. Mandatory arrest, by contrast, strips discretion from a police officer and requires "that a police officer arrest suspected [abusers] when there is probable cause to believe that abuse has occurred," regardless of whether the abuse was observed by the officer first-hand.[29]

Animal protection is not the first movement to consider mandatory arrest a possible solution to the disfavored status of a class of victims. After enduring decades of complacency toward domestic violence, in the 1980s battered women's advocates pursued a number of criminal law reforms.[30] Plagued by a culture where domestic violence was considered a "family matter" such that arrests and convictions for assault and battery were virtually nonexistent, reformers focused on ways to force arrests and impose harsher sentences.[31] The battered women's advocates achieved many successes in the form of legislation that required mandatory reporting of abuse and, most notably, mandatory arrest laws.[32]

---

[29] Amy M. Zelcer, *Battling Domestic Violence: Replacing Mandatory Arrest Laws with a Trifecta of Preferential Arrest, Officer Education, and Batterer Treatment Programs*, 51 AM. CRIM. L. REV. 541, 546 (2014).

[30] See, e.g., Elaine Chiu, *Confronting the Agency in Battered Mothers*, 74 S. CAL. L. REV. 1223, 1229 (2001) (explaining that criminal reforms can be placed into three categories: "1) Policies that deny the choices of battered women 2) Policies that empower women by giving or even requiring them to make choices 3) Policies that evaluate the decisions made by battered women, mostly in hindsight, and punish allegedly bad ones.")

[31] Emily J. Sack, Battered Women and the State: The Struggle for the Future of Domestic Violence Policy, 2004 Wis. L. Rev. 1666, 1667, 1669 (2004) (describing the movement for stronger police policies when confronting domestic violence complaints, including a Minneapolis study where mandatory arrests lowered the recidivism rate of domestic violence); Tara Urs, *Coercive Feminism*, 46 COLUM. HUM. RTS. L. REV. 85, 90 (2014) (comparing the American model of domestic violence policy, where we use police to resolve domestic violence, with the Cambodian domestic violence policy, where they use restorative justice techniques to resolve domestic violence).

[32] See, e.g., Dennis P. Saccuzzo, *How Should the Police Respond to Domestic Violence: A Therapeutic Jurisprudence Analysis of Mandatory Arrest*, 39 SANTA CLARA L. REV. 765, 776–77 (1999); (providing five reasons for mandatory arrest laws: 1) they control police behavior; 2) they provide protection from immediate violence; 3) they have a general deterring effect; 4) they send a strong message to society; 5) they provide a redistributive function of police assets); Marion Wanless, *Mandatory Arrest: A Step Toward Eradicating Domestic Violence, But Is It Enough?*, 1996 U. ILL. L. REV. 533, 535 (1996)

Citing similar concerns, animal protection advocates have urged mandatory arrest laws for animal cruelty, and have succeeded in obtaining such reforms in some states. For example, the much-celebrated Oregon cruelty code provides that, "[i]t shall be the duty of any peace officer to arrest and prosecute any violator of [animal cruelty statutes] for any violation which comes to the knowledge or notice of the officer."[33] The enthusiasm for the provision is borne out of the same thinking that led to mandatory arrest provisions in the domestic violence context – the notion that without such provisions the crime would not be taken seriously.

In the domestic violence context, mandatory arrest and reporting reforms did spur change. The number of domestic violence arrests increased rapidly under the mandatory reporting and mandatory arrest policies.[34] But the increase in arrests has not been recognized as an unequivocal good.[35] Leigh Goodmark, for example, has provided a detailed examination of research finding that the mandatory arrest laws have had a disparate racial impact, resulting in higher arrest rates in African American communities.[36] More stridently, Miriam Ruttenberg has explained that despite their superficial appeal, mandatory arrest laws "also perpetuate racist law enforcement."[37] As one commentator explains, "Social justice advocates have observed that domestic violence law reform has resulted in an expanded oppressive police presence that 'decimate[s] poor communities and communities of color,' [and] increased the rate of incarceration."[38] The conservative prosecutors enforcing these provisions have actually had the effect of "reifying" cultural and gender stereotypes.[39]

("Supporters believe mandatory arrest laws will curtail domestic violence and signify that society finally recognizes that domestic violence is a crime.").

[33] Or. Rev. Stat. § 133.379(1) (2015).

[34] Sack at 1671 ("Mandatory arrest policies have significantly increased the number of arrests of batterers for domestic violence crimes."); Urs at 96 (describing how the number of arrests increased as mandatory arrest policies became more common).

[35] *See* Nancy Durborow et al., Compendium of State Statutes and Policies on Domestic Violence and Healthcare 2–4 (2010), www.acf.hhs.gov/sites/default/files/fysb/state_compendium.pdf (discussing the negatives of mandatory reporting laws and stating "[u]nfortunately, applying mandatory criminal injury reporting laws to domestic violence cases is most often not helpful to domestic violence victims").

[36] Leigh Goodmark, *Law Is the Answer? Do We Know That for Sure?: Questioning the Efficacy of Legal Interventions for Battered Women*, 23 St. Louis U. Pub. L. Rev. 7, 37–38 (2004).

[37] Miriam H. Ruttenberg, *A Feminist Critique of Mandatory Arrest: An Analysis of Race and Gender in Domestic Violence Policy*, 2 Am. U. J. Gender & L. 171–72 (1994).

[38] Deborah M. Weissman, *Rethinking a New Domestic Violence Pedagogy*, 5 U. Miami Race & Soc. J. L. Rev. 635, 637 (2015), quoting *Safety and Justice for All: Examining the Relationship Between the Women's Anti-Violence Movement and the Criminal Legal System*, Ms. Foundation for Women 1, 15 (2003), available at http://files.praxisinternational.org/safety_justice.pdf.

[39] G. Kristian Miccio, *A House Divided: Mandatory Arrest, Domestic Violence, and the Conservatization of the Battered Women's Movement*, 42 Hous. L. Rev. 237, 241 (2005) (arguing that the conservative, prosecutorial element within the battered women's movement has had the effect of "reifying the cultural stereotypes").

In addition, there is research suggesting that mandatory arrest has the unintended consequence of forcing persons other than the true bad actors into the justice system. For example, in the domestic violence context there is data showing that the mandatory arrest laws have led to a dramatic increase in the number of women arrested for domestic violence.[40] One scholar has observed that "[m]andatory arrest laws increasingly result in the arrest of heterosexual women, members of the LGBT community, and people who exhibit mental illness, substance abuse, poverty, and other contextual problems."[41] In the realm of animal abuse, this may correspond to an unproductive diversion of resources toward minor cases of neglect or abuse and away from the more costly and time-consuming investigations of systemic abuse. A 2001 Department of Justice (DOJ) study of family violence found, for example, that "a majority of suspects discontinued their aggressive behaviors even without an arrest, [thus suggesting] that policies requiring arrest for all suspects may unnecessarily take a community's resources away from identifying and responding to the worst offenders and victims most at risk."[42]

More generally, the mandatory arrest approach to violence prevention has been criticized as the type of solution that creates more problems than it solves.[43] As Pamela Blass has explained, by emphasizing criminal enforcement, "society has ignored the fact that the overwhelming reality is that it is a social problem [and thus] [r]ather than looking progressively to a comprehensive plan to modify how women are viewed and treated by men, society has shifted the responsibility to the criminal justice system."[44] By the same token, the abuse of animals is caused by complex social phenomena that may be masked more than they are cured by criminalization policies like mandatory arrest. There is no reason to assume that these broad sociological issues concerning the use of mandatory arrest and mandatory reporting laws will be less trenchant in the animal protection context. One

---

[40]   Michelle Carney et al., *Women Who Perpetrate Partner Violence: A Review of the Literature with Recommendations for Treatment*, 12 AGGRESSION & VIOLENT BEHAVIOR 108, 112 (2007).

[41]   Carolyn B. Ramsey, *The Stereotyped Offender: Domestic Violence and the Failure of Intervention*, 120 PENN ST. L. REV. 337, 341 (2015); *Id.* at 373 (describing a "feminist batterer intervention curricula that discourage[s] inquiry into other contributors to intimate-partner abuse.").

[42]   U.S. DEP'T OF JUST., ATTORNEY GENERAL'S TASKFORCE ON FAMILY VIOLENCE, FINAL REPORT 22 (1984), www.eric.ed.gov/PDFS/ED251762.pdf.

[43]   *See, e.g.*, Pamela Blass Bracher, *Mandatory Arrest for Domestic Violence: The City of Cincinnati's Simple Solution to a Complex Problem*, 65 U. CIN. L. REV. 155, 181 (1996) (explaining domestic violence as a societal problem rather than just a criminal justice problem); EVE S. BUZAWA & CARL G. BUZAWA, *The Scientific Evidence Is Not Conclusive: Arrest Is No Panacea*, in CURRENT CONTROVERSIES ON FAMILY VIOLENCE 337, 347 (Richard J. Gelles & Donileen R. Loseke eds., 1993) (stating that mandatory arrests are focused on deterrence rather than on rehabilitation to solve the domestic violence problem).

[44]   *See, e.g.*, LINDA G. MILLS, INSULT TO INJURY: RETHINKING OUR RESPONSES TO INTIMATE ABUSE 32 (2003); Bracher at 181 ("All fifty states have made domestic violence illegal conduct, but the criminal justice system alone has not reduced, much less ended, domestic abuse."); Thomas L. Hafemeister, *If All You Have Is a Hammer: Society's Ineffective Response to Intimate Partner Violence*, 60 CATH. U. L. REV. 919, 1001 (2011) (providing a new system to help solve domestic violence problems that identifies personal characteristics of the couple and when the violence is occurring).

could anticipate that the increased police presence and enforcement of animal crimes will have similarly disparate class and race outcomes in communities.

Moreover, research has shown that when a victim is certain that abuse will result in arrest, rates of reporting the crime may actually drop. Robert Peralta and Meghan Novisky published a study in 2015 which cautions that people may perceive the cost of reporting abuse in such regimes to be too high.[45] There is a risk that the wrong person will be arrested for the abuse, that immigration consequences will flow from the call,[46] and that, more generally, some people are deterred from reporting by virtue of the simple fact that they want to have an abuser treated or stopped, but not jailed. And based on an increasing amount of research on this topic, this preference is not irrational. In 2015, the Journal of Experimental Criminology published a study that found that domestic violence victims were "64% more likely to have died of all causes if their partners were arrested and jailed" rather than warned or treated for acts of violence and allowed to remain at home.[47] Based on the finding that the arrest of one's partner for abuse-related charges was linked to premature death, the authors of this study called for a reconsideration of mandatory arrest laws across the states.

Even bracketing the human costs flowing from mandatory arrest that are mentioned above, there is a growing consensus that such policies do not work – that is, they are ineffective in producing lower rates of domestic violence. Despite an initial study, known as the Minneapolis Study, suggesting that the mandatory arrest policies were actually reducing domestic violence and favorably impacting deterrence,[48] subsequent research has almost universally reached less favorable conclusions. As one researcher has explained, "studies have failed to show a nexus between arrest and deterrence."[49] The general consensus now is that mandatory arrest policies for violence do not have a significant impact on rates of repeated domestic violence.[50] In fact,

---

[45] M. A. Novisky & R. L. Peralta, *When Women Tell: Intimate Partner Violence and the Factors Related to Police Notification*, 21 VIOLENCE AGAINST WOMEN 65–86 (2015).

[46] Interestingly, the animal protection movement facilitates such fears by, among other things, seeking to have violence against animals treated as a crime of violence that triggers removal from the country for undocumented persons.

[47] Lawrence W. Sherman & Heather M. Harris, *Increased Death Rates of Domestic Violence Victims From Arresting vs. Warning Suspects in the Milwaukee Domestic Violence Experiment*, 11 J. OF EXPERIMENTAL CRIMINOLOGY 1–20 (2015).

[48] Lawrence W. Sherman & Richard A. Berk, *The Specific Deterrent Effects of Arrest for Domestic Assault*, 49 AMER. SOC. REV. 261 (1984) (explaining the initial findings of the Minneapolis Study).

[49] Bracher at 178.

[50] *See, e.g.*, Franklyn W. Dunford, David Huizinga & Delbert S. Elliot, *The Role of Arrest in Domestic Assault: The Omaha Police Experiment*, 28 CRIMINOLOGY 183 (1990) (discussing the Omaha study that revealed that arrest, on its own, failed to deter battering); J. David Hirschel et al., *The Failure of Arrest to Deter Spouse Abuse*, 29 J. RES. CRIME & DELINQ. 7, 29 (1992) (concluding that arrest is no more effective than temporary separation of the couple or issuing a citation); Joan McCord, *Deterrence of Domestic Violence: A Critical View of Research*, 29 J. RES. CRIME & DELINQ. 229 (1992) (critiquing legitimacy of prior research methods on domestic violence yielding results indicating efficacy of mandatory arrest); Richard J. Gelles, *Perspectives on Family Law and Social Science Research: The Politics of Research: The Use, Abuse, and Misuse of Social Science Data – The Cases of Intimate Partner Violence*, 45 FAM. CT. REV. 42, 47 (2007).

research suggests that in some instances mandatory arrest may actually lead to an increase in offender recidivism.[51] Indeed, the efficacy of aggressive arrest policies has been so thoroughly called into question that even the lead author of the original Minneapolis Study has concluded that the "compelling implication" of additional research is that mandatory arrest laws should be repealed.[52] As one researcher explained in the context of family violence, "In some cases, recidivism not only occurred, but actually occurred with increased severity" following the enactment of mandatory arrest policies.[53] There is no reason to suggest that the "alarmingly high" rate of repeat (or aggravated) abuse following mandatory arrests would be less in the context of animal abuse; indeed, the greater ease of access to animal victims might make recidivism even more likely.[54] Scott Heiser once quipped that, "You don't have to be a vegan" to recognize that mandatory arrest laws for animal abuse are "very good."[55] But this sanguine assessment of mandatory arrest laws is at odds with the research regarding mandatory arrest in the domestic violence context.

4.2.2 *Harsher Sentences As a Cause Not a Cure for Crime*

The United States is a world leader in incarceration, boasting less than five percent of the world's population but the largest prison population in the world[56] – more than twenty-five percent of the world's prisoners are in the United States.[57] In less than a century the United States has gone from questioning whether federal criminal jurisdiction existed,[58] to living under a federal criminal code containing more than 4,500 federal crimes alone.

---

[51] Dunford at 187 (explaining that the Omaha study shows mandatory arrest may lead to higher recidivism, in direct conflict with the Minneapolis Study).

[52] Janell D. Schmidt & Lawrence W. Sherman, *Does Arrest Deter Domestic Violence?*, in Do Arrests and Restraining Orders Work? 41 (1996).

[53] Zelcer at 548.

[54] Hirschel et al. at 29–30; *see also* Sherman & Berk at 777–78 ("There is little doubt that mandatory arrest will sometimes have negative or unintended consequences."). There does appear to be some evidence suggesting that symbolic shifts in attitudes from the changes in the law cause a general, though not a specific deterrent advantage. *See* Deborah Epstein et al., *Transforming Aggressive Prosecution Policies: Prioritizing Victims' Long-Term Safety in the Prosecution of Domestic Violence Cases*, 11 Am. U. J. Gender Soc. Pol'y & L. 465, 466 (2003) (observing general deterrence benefits).

[55] Scott Heiser, Memorandum for Prosecuting Attorneys (June 29, 2008), available at www .prosecutingattorneys.org/wp-content/uploads/A-Quick-Overview-for-Oregon-Prosecutors-Animal -Abuse-Neglect-Hoarding-and-Fighting.pdf.

[56] *See, e.g.,* Brittany Bondurant, *The Privatization of Prisons and Prisoner Healthcare: Addressing the Extent of Prisoners' Right to Healthcare*, 39 New Eng. J. on Crim. & Civ. Confinement 407, 421 (2013).

[57] *See, e.g.,* Robert F. Muse, *In Pursuit of Simple, Ordinary Justice*, 51 Am. Crim. L. Rev. 317, 319 (2014) (explaining the stark prison numbers in America); *Incarceration*, The Sentencing Project, www .sentencingproject.org/template/page.cfm?id=107 (last visited Apr. 21, 2016) (explaining that, following a 500-percent increase in the prison population in the last thirty years, the United States is currently the world's leader of incarceration).

[58] *See, e.g.,* Sara Sun Beale, *Federalizing Crime: Assessing the Impact on the Federal Courts*, 543 Annals Am. Acad. Pol. & Soc. Sci. 39, 40 (1996) (providing the evolution of federal criminal jurisdiction, including the rise of federal criminal law in the 1950s-60s); Andrew Weis, *Commerce Clause in the*

As described in previous chapters, the animal protection movement has announced a war on animal cruelty. The war on cruelty is not justified by any data, but rather an intuition that more punishment in this realm will produce the desired social change. But animal advocates are not the first to use incarceration as a means of fighting a "war" against undesirable conduct. In an effort to curb the perceived harms associated with drug use, lawmakers dramatically increased the role of incarceration in combatting drug addiction in what has famously been dubbed by multiple presidents as the "war on drugs."[59] One judge has defined the war on drugs as an effort to combat illegal drug use through a "program of massive prisons [and] demonization."[60] Not coincidentally, social scientists have documented that during the war on drugs, incarceration in the United States "accelerated dramatically, increasing more than five-fold between 1971 and 2000."[61]

Animal protection advocates have implicitly embraced the war on drugs as a model for advancing the status of animals. It is an attempt to engage in social change lawyering through prosecution. The war on animal mistreatment is much more recent and less entrenched in our statutory laws than the war on drugs, but it turns on a similar philosophy – that is, the notion that a heightened response by every element of the criminal justice system is necessary and beneficial. In the war on drugs, legislation has shifted many drug crimes from misdemeanors to felonies,[62] has increased the maximum sentences for felony crimes,[63] and has added mandatory

Cross-Hairs: The Use of Lopez-Based Motions to Challenge the Constitutionality of Federal Criminal Statutes, 48 STAN. L. REV. 1431, 1436 (1996) ("Since the New Deal, the pace of federalization has accelerated and continued almost unabated and has gradually reversed the long-standing pattern of state and local authority over criminal conduct.").

59   *See generally* JONATHAN SIMON, GOVERNING THROUGH CRIME: HOW THE WAR ON CRIME TRANSFORMED AMERICAN DEMOCRACY AND CREATED A CULTURE OF FEAR (2007) (discussing the legislative changes that led to the war on crime); David Schultz, *Rethinking Drug Criminalization Policies*, 25 TEX. TECH L. REV. 151, 153 (1993) ("Seeking to discourage illegal drug use, as well as confining criminal activity surrounding the marketing of illegal drugs, is what is referred to as the 'drug problem' in the United States.").

60   JAMES P. GRAY, WHY OUR DRUG LAWS HAVE FAILED 6 (2001).

61   Marie Gottschalk, *Dismantling the Carceral State: The Future of Penal Policy Reform*, 84 TEX. L. REV. 1693 (2006); J. M. Kirby, *Graham, Miller, & The Right to Hope*, 15 CUNY L. REV. 149, 155 (2011) ("As a result of lengthy mandated sentences under both the drug war and a general 'tough-on-crime' approach, the national average prison population increased six times over from 1972 to 2003.").

62   *See, e.g.*, Ark. Code Ann. § 5–64-419 (2012) (classifying possession of controlled substances from a Class A misdemeanor to a Class D felony level based on weight and substance); Ark. Code Ann. § 5–4-401 (2014) (identifying minimum sentences for each class of felony); Ga. Code Ann. § 16–13-30 (2010) (establishing sentencing ranges for felony offenses based on weight, as well as considering whether the substance has been mixed or otherwise combined with other substances); Utah Code Ann. § 58–37-8(2)(b) (2017) (classifying the criminality of marijuana possession based on weight). Shima Baradaran, *Drugs and Violence*, 88 S. CAL. L. REV. 227, 244–53 (2015) (outlining the legislative efforts in passing mandatory minimums for drug crimes).

63   *See, e.g.*, Margaret P. Spencer, *Sentencing Drug Offenders: The Incarceration Addiction*, 40 VILL. L. REV. 335, 344 (1995) (stating that the 1988 amendment to the 1986 Anti-Drug Abuse Act "increased the other maximum sentences and increased the monetary penalties previously prescribed in the 1986 Act"); The Honorable William W. Wilkins, Jr. et al., *Competing Sentencing Policies in A "War on Drugs" Era*, 28 WAKE FOREST L. REV. 305, 318 (1993) (describing that the Senate pushed for longer maximum sentences for drug crimes when enacting the 1986 and 1988 Anti-Drug Abuse Acts).

minimum sentences to some crimes.[64] These same reforms have already been obtained or are being actively pursued by animal protection groups because, in the words of one animal law scholar, such changes are necessary in order for the legal system to properly "reflect the seriousness of the offense[s]."[65]

Notably, the carceral turn in animal law coincides with a recently emerging consensus that the tough-on-crime approach has been ineffective, if not counter-productive. Summarizing the data, the White House Council of Economic Advisors explained that "[e]merging research finds that longer spells of incarceration increase recidivism," noting that the findings show "that each additional sanction year causes an average increase in future offending of 4 to 7 percentage points."[66] More color-fully, Dan Baum wrote that the war on drugs and its concomitant emphasis on incarceration is an illustration of government at its most "expensive, ineffective, delusional, and destructive."[67] Baum mocks the supposedly well-intentioned efforts, explaining that for decades the government has been "on a rampage, kicking in doors and locking people up in the name of protecting its citizens from illegal drugs."[68] But the protection, he argues, has been illusory while the harm to our communities has been concrete. Increasingly, there is "growing public dismay over the crushing economic costs of incarcerating more than two million people on any given day and monitoring millions more on parole and probation."

Groups like the National Association for the Advancement of Colored People (NAACP), the American Civil Liberties Union (ACLU), and the Sentencing Project, among countless others, have spent the last two decades making the case to courts, legislatures, and the public that a basic respect for civil rights is incon-sistent with an overly carceral state. The animal protection movement has not, to date, engaged with any of the literature or trends regarding incarceration (or other civil penalties including deportation). By ignoring these histories, and proceeding enthusiastically in support of ever more carceral solutions, the movement risks repeating or exacerbating the mistakes of other eras and movements. In recent years states have experimented with repealing mandatory minimums, have "expanded the number of people in prison eligible for early release," and have

---

[64] Christopher Mascharka, *Mandatory Minimum Sentences: Exemplifying the Law of Unintended Consequences*, 28 FLA. ST. U. L. REV. 935, 936 (2001) ("The brunt of federal mandatory minimum sentences is aimed at drug crimes. This trend is mirrored in the states, as many states now have mandatory provisions for drug possession."); Whitley Zachary, *Prison, Money, and Drugs: The Federal Sentencing System Must Be More Critical in Balancing Priorities Before It Is Too Late*, 2 TEX. A&M L. REV. 323 (2014) ("In the 1980s, the federal government began a 'war on drugs' and Congress passed a number of drug statutes that carried mandatory minimum penalties for offenders.").

[65] JOAN E. SCHAFFNER, *Laws and Policy to Address the Link of Family Violence*, in THE LINK BETWEEN ANIMAL ABUSE AND HUMAN VIOLENCE 230 (2009).

[66] The White House, *Economic Perspectives on Incarceration and the Criminal Justice System* (Apr. 2016). https://obamawhitehouse.archives.gov/sites/default/files/page/files/20160423_cea_incar ceration_criminal_justice.pdf.

[67] DAN BAUM, SMOKE AND MIRRORS: THE WAR ON DRUGS AND THE POLITICS OF FAILURE (1996).

[68] *Id.* at vii.

been looking for "enhanced treatment options," as well as ways to grant judges *greater* discretion to issue sentences other than incarceration for felonies.[69] Thus, even as society more generally is taking seriously alternatives to aggressive prosecution, the animal protection movement is locked in the dated logic of incarceration.

Even the political rhetoric in support of the war on animal cruelty is reminiscent of the concerns raised by drug war advocates. The marijuana-as-a-gateway-drug theory, for example, resembles in significant ways the LINK-based, graduation theory – the notion that dangerous people start by harming animals. The gateway drug theorists, according to Dan Baum, are misleading the public in ways relevant to the misuse of LINK data, because their research looks

> in only one direction, asking heroin users and cocaine users if they first used marijuana and predictably finding that many had. They didn't ask, though, whether the addicts had first used alcohol, tobacco or caffeine – any of which might also be described … as the gateway. More important, the researchers failed to track marijuana smokers on how many graduate to harder drugs.

As discussed in Chapter 6, many violent criminals have engaged in animal cruelty, but even if every killer had previously harmed animals, this would still not justify sweeping generalizations about the predictive power of animal abuse. To a certain extent, flawed empirical conclusions that are championed as scientific support for incarceration undergird both the war on drugs and the carceral animal law framework.

Both movements have also emphasized personal accountability, directing blame squarely at the individual and ignoring potential societal causes. William Bennett, one of the most famous drug czars of the 1990s, explained that the "corrupt values" of individual people were primarily responsible for every social evil, from teen pregnancy to homelessness, and drug use. The story is always one of individual people making bad choices. The same type of narrative dominates discussions about the importance of the criminal war on animal cruelty – animal mistreatment is the result of corrupt, depraved individuals, not a predictable result of child abuse, family strife, or other issues, and the solution to such personal failures is always a more robust penological response.

Understanding antisocial behavior in this way leads one to reject any mitigating factors that might humanize the defendant and justify calls for mercy. In this vein, references to one's poverty or one's childhood abuse are often dismissed out of hand as irrelevant or worse. Indeed, Scott Heiser, while serving as the director of the Criminal Justice Program for the Animal Legal Defense Fund disparaged efforts to "induce empathy" for a defendant by titling a blog post on the topic, "What the hell are they thinking?"[70] It is beyond imagination, according to people like Heiser, that

---

[69]   Marie Gottschalk, *Dismantling the Carceral State: The Future of Penal Policy Reform*, 84 TEX. L. REV. 1693, 1698 (2006).

[70]   Scott Heiser, *What the Hell Are They Thinking?*, ANIMAL LEGAL DEF. FUND (Sept. 10, 2007), http://aldf .org/blog/what-the-hell-are-they-thinking/.

culpability for animal abuse might vary depending on one's upbringing and personal circumstances. The animal protection movement has no shortage of its own William Bennett-like apostles of incarceration – more prosecution is always better, and mercy or empathy (when it comes to human abusers) is a childish distraction. For a movement that decries the absence of empathy as an important source of animal suffering, it is striking to see empathy so quickly dismissed as irrelevant when it comes to the criminal sentencing of humans.

Presently, many animal protection advocates would insist that the problem with incarceration for animal abuse is that there is simply not enough of it. Because of this perception, many animal advocates would argue that there is simply no comparison between the war on drugs and the war on animal cruelty (other than the moniker the movement itself selected of "war"). But even the war on drugs escalated gradually, through a process of accretion over time. There were, of course, critical moments that took on enhanced significance, but the massive expansion of incarceration was a long-term "product of the hopes, fears, and ambitions of people with varying motives and disparate points of view."[71] Strange bedfellows formed alliances to make the war on drugs possible – it was Democrats and Republicans reaching across the aisle in support of mass incarceration; it was groups seeking to protect children and victims; and it was people motivated by other more nefarious or ethnocentric reasons. Likewise, the carceral animal law project is bipartisan and has found support among psychologists, social workers, animal lovers, police, and prosecutors. It is the combination of law-and-order prosecutors who love dogs, cynical people who support more incarceration across the board, and people with a true animal protection orientation that gives the carceral animal law project momentum. There also exists a body of support for these carceral policies that are overtly racist, advocating for higher penalties for animal cruelty because of the assumption that non-whites commit the majority of such "barbaric" acts. Over time, and with far-reaching alliances among social interest groups, the range of crimes and the severity of penalties is increasing, all in the service of a war on animal cruelty that is presumed to be in the interest of the animals and the public.

Researchers have documented that drug arrests have increased during the war on drugs, and not just "on their own terms but relative to overall arrest numbers," with drug crimes accounting for "5.9% of all arrests in the United States in 1980 and 11.1% of all arrests by 1990."[72] It is also notable "that arrests for simple possession – particularly marijuana possession – were chiefly responsible for the rise in drug arrests after 1990."[73] This focus on crimes that were perhaps more common but reflect less culpability could be gainfully analogized to the fact that the majority of animal cruelty reports are for neglect rather than affirmative acts of abuse.

---

[71] Baum at viii.
[72] Alex Kreit, *Drug Truce*, 77 Ohio St. L.J. 1323, 1339 (2016).
[73] *Id.* at 1340.

Apparently, when it comes to drugs or animal abuse, the less culpable range of crimes plays an oversized role in tough-on-crime campaigns.

Nonetheless, it must be acknowledged that it is too simplistic to suggest that American exceptionalism in the realm of incarceration is purely (or even primarily) a product of the war on drugs.[74] The war on drugs is but a symptom of a larger cultural preoccupation with incarceration. As John Pfaff has documented, even at the "peak of drug incarcerations, in 1990, approximately 22% of all inmates were drug offenders – or, phrased more starkly, over three-quarters of all state prisoners were serving time primarily for non-drug offenses."[75] Contrary to the public assumption, it is not the fact of incarceration for drug crimes that has been the primary driver of mass incarceration, but rather the habits and practices of prosecutors and police that were formed during this war on crime era. Likewise, it was the revisions to sentencing measures during the tough-on-crime era, including mandatory minimums, that empowered prosecutors to exercise their charging and sentencing discretion in ever harsher, more aggressive ways. The drug war has meant that more "people convicted of drug offenses receive prison sentences," and the "average sentence for drug offenders ... increased by 17% between 1988 and 2004."[76] More generally, from the early 1980s through the early 2000s, the number of drug arrests tripled, and there was a 1100-percent increase in the number of drug offenders incarcerated.[77] Simply put, starting in the 1980s more people arrested for drug offenses went to jail or prison, and they went for longer times because of the war on drugs.

Sitting on the outside, many in the animal protection movement look enviously at these increases in arrest and sentencing rates. To have a culture of aggressive policing, more incarceration, and longer terms of incarceration is the core goal of the criminal justice projects operating within the animal protection movement. But even if the human costs of such schemes could be dismissed as irrelevant to efforts to secure social change, the simple reality is that the more aggressive criminal justice system has not yielded the success that was anticipated. The war on drugs' successes in the punishment column have not translated into meaningful results in the public safety or changed behavior columns. Gil Kerlikowske, the director of the Office of National Drug Control Policy under President Obama, observed that, "In the grand scheme, [the drug war] has not been successful. Forty years later, the concern about drugs and drug problems is, if anything, magnified, intensified."

---

[74] JOHN PFAFF, LOCKED IN (2017) (rejecting this narrative, which he calls the "standard story").

[75] John F. Pfaff, *The War on Drugs and Prison Growth: Limited Importance, Limited Legislative Options*, 52 HARV. J. ON LEGIS. 173, 180 (2015); *see also* John F. Pfaff, *The Micro and Marco Causes of Prison Growth*, 28 GA. ST. U. L. REV. 1239, 1272 (2011) (noting that "increases in drug incarcerations explain only a fraction of prison growth, so any reduction in drug commitments will have only a moderate effect on prison population size.").

[76] Kreit at 1341.

[77] Id.

This conclusion is generally shared by empirical researchers who have documented that the intensive and sustained criminal war on drugs has actually made the
problem worse, not better. Although drug prices have gone up, which could be
counted among the victories of the war on drugs, researchers have consistently found
that the rate of drug addiction has remained relatively constant, while the expense of
combatting drug crimes in dollars, incarceration, and the general erosion of civil
liberties have skyrocketed. In his book, "Drugs, America's Holy War," economist
Arthur Benavies summarizes and compiles data regarding the war on drugs and
makes an impassioned case for viewing the war on drugs as affirmatively *harming*
society.[78] Benavies surveys research finding that the increased criminal response
may not have had an impact on drug use, but that it did disrupt communities and
correlate with an upsurge in other crimes. Just as animal cruelty seems to be
associated with other antisocial behaviors, it seems that tough-on-crime policies
also have criminogenic consequences.

Of course, not every negative externality of the drug war can fairly be expected to
have application in the context of a war against animal cruelty. For example, the
black markets, turf wars, and cartel activities that have defined drug (and alcohol)
prohibitions do not lend themselves to easy analogues in the animal protection
context. But the existing data from other realms should be a sobering reminder for
animal advocates that increased criminalization – efforts to "crack down" on certain
behaviors – have impacts on society beyond the individual who is punished.
Moreover, it is far from clear that the crackdowns are successful even in decreasing
the prevalence and social acceptability of the targeted activity. During the period of
increasingly harsh criminal penalties and aggressive prosecution for illegal drug use,
the rate of illegal drug addiction has remained roughly constant at about 1.5 percent,
but during this same time the amount of money spent on drug control ballooned
from less than $2 billion annually to $20 billion. Researchers have also documented
that in important ways, the harms of drug use have increased rather than decreased
under the war on drugs. For example, the rate of drug overdoses has increased
dramatically during the war on drugs:

> In 1971, two years before the creation of the DEA, the Centers for Disease Control
> and Prevention (CDC) reported that slightly more than 1 death per 100,000 people
> in the United States was related to drug overdose. This figure rose to 3.4 deaths per
> 100,000 people by 1990 (see Figure 1). By 2008, there were 12 overdose deaths per
> 100,000 people.[79]

Commentators have also observed that the harsh criminal response to drug use has
"not reduced illicit drug use in dramatic or even significant terms in the United

[78] ARTHUR BENAVIES, DRUGS: AMERICA'S HOLY WAR (2009).
[79] Christopher J. Coyne & Abigail R. Hall, *Four Decades and Counting: The Continued Failure of the
War on Drugs*, CATO INSTITUTE (Apr. 12, 2017), www.cato.org/publications/policy-analysis/four
-decades-counting-continued-failure-war-drugs.

States," despite its significant personal and financial costs.[80] As Andrew Leipold has put it, "Exact numbers are hard to come by, but it appears that the increase in costs associated with drug use over the last decade or two has not led to a corresponding decrease in drug use itself."[81] Arthur Benavies makes the same claim more stridently: "There is no evidence that the war has reduced the consumption or abuse of the banned drugs."[82] The data that most strongly suggests that the drug war has had success in reducing drug use, data produced by the very office tasked with administering the federal drug war, the Office of National Drug Control Policy (ONDCP), suggests only very modest success, and has been subjected to a book-length, stinging critique by Matthew Robinson and Renee Scherlen.[83] Robinson and Scherlen show that the government reports of success through ONDCP are greatly overstated, because, among other findings, any declines in the use of illicit drugs documented by the agency do not reflect the benefits of the war on drugs (under ONDCP) because among other reasons, figures consistently show rates of drug use higher than those in 1988, the year that ONDCP was created. In other words, if rates of drug use declined as compared to rates in the early and mid-1980s (when drug use rates were at their all time highs), they did so for reasons other than the creation of the ONDCP and its drug war.[84] More precisely, studying the drug war from 1989 through 1998, Robinson and Scherlen, found that over this period there: (1) "clearly were no declines in lifetime drug use," (2) the current use of illicit drugs did not decline, and (3) the current drug use among school age children increased.[85]

In addition, a review of recent publications from ONDCP itself reveals that the percentage of people admitting to the use of illegal drugs has remained relatively constant during recent decades.[86] According to the Center for Disease Control, in 2015 10.1 percent of Americans over twelve admitted to using illegal drugs within the last month, a figure that is entirely consistent with the drug use rates throughout the

---

[80] MaryBeth Lipp, *A New Perspective on the "War on Drugs": Comparing the Consequences of Sentencing Policies in the United States and England*, 37 Loy. L.A. L. Rev. 979, 1031 (2004) (noting that there was a decline in drug use between 1979 and 2000, but positing that even these declines might be better explained by reference to socioeconomic and other factors); *Id.* (describing relatively "constant rates of drug abuse" over time).

[81] Andrew D. Leipold, *The War on Drugs and the Puzzle of Deterrence*, 6 J. Gender Race & Just. 111 (2002).

[82] Arthur Benavies, Drugs: America's Holy War 111 (2009).

[83] Matthew B. Robinson & Renee G. Scherlen, Lies, Damned Lies, and Drug War Statistics: A Critical Analysis of Claims Made by the Office of National Drug Control Policy 60–92 (2007).

[84] Robinson and Scherlen document the largest drops in drug use in the years immediately prior to 1988, at which time drug use leveled off and has remained somewhat consistent.

[85] *Id.* at 156–59.

[86] Perhaps the most accurate way to summarize the data regarding drug use is to note that drug use increased throughout the 1960s and 1970s and peaked in 1979, at which point it declined until 1988, and "then remained relatively constant since." *Id.* at 6, 9 (condemning the research of the Office of National Drug Control Policy [ONDCP] as ideological and misleading insofar as it uses statistics to justify the "nation's drug war").

1990s.[87] Likewise, the perceived availability of cocaine, heroin, and other drugs by American twelfth-graders has gone up, sometimes dramatically since the 1980s.[88] The perceived availability of some drugs has steadily increased.[89] Trends regarding the prevalence of drug use also suggest that rates have remained relatively constant over time.

On a more positive note, the lengthy duration of the war on drugs has had at least one salutary consequence: it has created a robust dataset from which researchers can study the effectiveness of more punitive, law-and-order policies on crime control. The findings from this data do not support the animal protection movement's decision to pursue a war on crime approach to animal cruelty. At a level of generality, it is accepted that the existence of a criminal justice system and the criminalization of undesirable behavior decreases the amount of that behavior. In the absence of any criminal penalties, everyone seems to agree that crime would likely increase substantially. But this simply supports the view that one need not set out to decriminalize animal cruelty entirely. The presence of a criminal sanction likely does produce a "norm nurturing" effect that may be beneficial. But the critical important question is whether increasing the severity of criminal punishments will produce any marginal benefit for animal well-being. The assumption is that by increasing the severity of punishments, crimes against animals will decrease, but this assumption is at war with the available data.

There seems to be an emerging consensus that evidence does not support the conclusion that harsher penalties reduce crime.[90] In fact, some of the leading researchers in the field blame incarceration for slowing the decline in crime by as much as three percent.[91] In terms of specific deterrence, incarceration has been shown to have either no effect, or to actually increase the odds that a person will reoffend.[92] Based on this data, criminologist Daniel Nagin has concluded that

[87] *Id.* There is some data suggesting materially higher rates of drug use among certain populations in the late 1970s and early 1980s, but since a low point around 1992, the prevalence of drug use seems to have spiked again. The same researchers have had conflicting findings regarding the perceived dangerousness of various drugs by school age children over time. *Monitoring the Future, Figures and Statistics*, NAT'L INST. ON DRUG ABUSE (last visited Nov. 8, 2017), http://monitoringthefuture.org/data/16data/16drfig1.pdf.

[88] *Id.* (perception of cocaine as readily available went from 37 to 54.5 percent and for heroin it went from 24.2 to 34.9 percent).

[89] *Id.*

[90] Anthony Doob, *Sentencing Severity and Crime: Accepting the Null Hypothesis*, 30 CRIME & JUSTICE 143–95 (2003); Daniel S. Nagin, *Deterrence in the Twenty-First Century*, 42 CRIME & JUST. 199 (2013); *see also Five Things About Deterrence*, OFFICE OF JUSTICE PROGRAMS, https://nij.gov/five-things/pages/deterrence.aspx#addenda (last visited Nov. 10, 2017); Martin H. Pritikin, *Fine-Labor: The Symbiosis Between Monetary and Work Sanctions*, 81 U. COLO. L. REV. 343, 345 (2010) ("Indeed, excessive reliance on incarceration may be actually increasing crime rates through increased recidivism and disruption of family and community bonds, among other things."); Sonja B. Starr, *Evidence-Based Sentencing and the Scientific Rationalization of Discrimination*, 66 STAN. L. REV. 803, 858 (2014).

[91] Oliver Roeder et al., *What Caused the Crime Decline?*, COLUMBIA BUSINESS SCHOOL RESEARCH PAPER NO. 15–28, 1, 22 (Feb. 12, 2015), http://dx.doi.org/10.2139/ssrn.2566965.

[92] Nagin at 201.

policies supporting lengthy terms of incarceration cannot be justified on a deterrence-based model of crime prevention.[93] Similarly, Linda Fetiman has concluded that there is no evidence the imposition of severe penalties through "highly visible prosecutions" leads to even a marginal increase in either general or specific deterrence.[94]

The failure of the war on drugs in the United States should serve as a cautionary tale for the animal protection movement.[95] Tough-on-crime is not synonymous with changing social mores, much less reducing undesirable conduct. As the White House Council of Economic Advisers recently concluded, "research shows that further increasing the incarcerated population is not likely to materially reduce crime."[96]

It also bears noting that research has revealed a connection between the severity of a crime and the likelihood of a wrongful conviction. Sociologists have found that the more serious the crime, the more likely the fact-finding process will be tainted with errors such as false confessions, perjury, eyewitness mistakes, or defective forensic methods.[97] "[A]s the seriousness of a crime increases, so too does" the risk of a wrongful conviction.[98] Scott Phillips and Jamie Richardson, for example, pro-duced an empirical study that shows that the worst crimes often result in convictions based on the "worst evidence," and they speculated about the possibility of a linear relationship between the heinousness of the crime and the erroneousness of the evidence used to produce a conviction. Although this is likely only a peripheral concern at this point because the penalties do not make animal cruelty among the most serious offenses, as animal crimes become more serious (with no clear limiting principle in sight), the animal protection movement should be mindful of the data

---

[93] Incapacitation is posited as the only viable explanation for lengthy incarceration. *Id.*

[94] Linda C. Fentiman, *Rethinking Addiction: Drugs, Deterrence, and the Neuroscience Revolution*, 14 U. PA. J.L. & SOC. CHANGE 233, 239 (2011).

[95] Decades ago the United States and Portugal took diametrically different approaches to the drug problem. Rather than embarking on a criminal punishment campaign, Portugal legalized all drugs, even cocaine and heroin, and invested in treatment, education, programs, and outreach. After more than fifteen years, the results are as starkly contrasting as the approaches: "The United States drug policy failed spectacularly, with about as many Americans dying last year of overdoses – around 64,000 – as were killed in the Vietnam, Afghanistan and Iraq Wars combined . . . In contrast, Portugal may be winning the war on drugs – by ending it. Today, the Health Ministry estimates that only about 25,000 Portuguese use heroin, down from 100,000 when the policy began ... The number of Portuguese dying from overdoses plunged more than 85 percent ... It's not a miracle or perfect solution. But if the U.S. could achieve Portugal's death rate from drugs, we would save one life every 10 minutes. We would save almost as many lives as are now lost to guns and car accidents combined." Nicholas Kristof, *How to Win a War on Drugs*, N.Y. TIMES (Sept. 22, 2017), www.nytimes.com/2017/09/22/opinion/sunday/portugal-drug-decriminalization.html?mcubz=3.

[96] The White House, *Economic Perspectives on Incarceration and the Criminal Justice System.*

[97] Samuel R. Gross, *The Risks of Death: Why Erroneous Convictions Are Common in Capital Cases*, 44 BUFF. L. REV. 469, 476–81 (1996).

[98] Scott Phillips & Jamie Richardson, *The Worst of the Worst: Heinous Crimes and Erroneous Evidence*, 45 HOFSTRA L. REV. 417, 421 (2016).

suggesting that the increased seriousness of an offense will be unlikely to produce changes in social behavior, but will yield a greater risk of wrongful convictions.[99]

Finally, moving beyond the quantitative data, qualitative research has also found fault in the tough-on-crime approach. Researchers have observed that, like any war effort, the foundation is a thorough demonization of the enemy. The problem, according to scholars like Benavies, is that all too often such campaigns are predicated on misinformation, or misleading constructions of the existing data. Not unlike the carceral animal law movement's use of anecdotes about animal abusers growing into serial killers, the advocates for the war on drugs have long predicated the need for more and harsher punitive responses on the need to keep society safe. Indeed, the war on drugs preys on moral panic, creating a narrative about drugs as instantly addictive and no less dangerous than the "plagues of medieval times." By generating moral panic – a sense that society at large is in imminent danger – it is possible to construct an exaggerated criminal response. The war on drugs and the war on cruelty both employ social constructions of the problem that are potentially "blown out of proportion," and the resulting moral panic affords policy-makers considerable latitude in ratcheting up penalties.[100] Take just one example of a publication on the war on drugs by the Bureau of Narcotics in the 1930s, explaining the danger of marijuana:

> Prolonged use of Marihuana frequently develops a delirious rage, which sometimes leads to high crimes, such as assault and murder. Hence Marihuana has been called the "killer drug." The habitual use of this narcotic poison always caused a marked deterioration and sometimes produces insanity ... [Moreover], its effects upon character morality are even more devastating. The victim frequently undergoes such moral degeneracy that he will lie and steal without scruples.[101]

In 2018, with marijuana legalization spreading, this summary may seem laughably naïve or hyperbolic. But the fearmongering was an important part of engineering a social and legislative response. The animal protection movement's obsession with the presumed connection between animal mistreatment and human harm, discussed in detail in Chapter 6, works similarly in creating fertile ground for a war on crime. The problem is exaggerated and the carceral solution unfounded. Incarceration does not promise a solution to the predicted dangers of animal cruelty or drug use. Tough-on-crime polices are "good politics, [but] ... terrible government."[102] Or as Judge

---

[99]   Some scholars speculate that there may be an abundance of wrongful convictions among the least serious crimes as well, albeit for different reasons. Alexandra Natapoff, *Misdemeanors*, 85 S. CAL. L. REV. 1313, 1338, 1346 (2012).

[100]   Robinson & Scherlen at 11 (outlining some of the common myths about the dangers of drug use).

[101]   *Id.* at 11 (quoting a publication by the Bureau of Narcotics); *Id.* at 19 (explaining that the United States has been engaged in a series of drug wars of varying intensity since at least the early twentieth century, and potentially dating back to the prohibition on the opium trade with China in the 1880s); *Id.* at 27–29 (describing the modern drug war as starting with Nixon and intensifying under Reagan).

[102]   JAMES P. GRAY, WHY OUR DRUG LAWS HAVE FAILED AND WHAT WE CAN DO ABOUT IT 4 (2001).

James P. Gray said in relation to the war on drugs: "We pursue it not because it is effective, but because it is 'fundable.'"[103] A war on animal cruelty has also proven to be fundable and publicly popular, but history and existing data does not suggest that this war will reduce animal cruelty, much less meaningfully improve the lives of most animals. Instead, like the war on drugs, a sustained war on animal cruelty will amount to "a war against the people of this nation and against our fundamental freedoms."[104]

4.3 ANIMAL ABUSE REGISTRIES ARE HARMFUL TO ANIMAL PROTECTION EFFORTS

In recent years, publicly available animal abuse registries have become a legislative priority for the animal protection movement.[105] In response to lobbying by animal protection advocates, New York City enacted a registry in 2014,[106] several counties have recently enacted registries,[107] and the first statewide registry went online in the state of Tennessee in January 2016.[108] Advocates have made it clear that the success in Tennessee in obtaining a publicly accessible, online registry will serve as the template for other statewide abuse registries. As one of the pioneers of pressing for incarceration as a lever to advance animal rights, Scott Heiser, put it, the movement hopes Tennessee's law will "pave the way for other states to adopt similar registries."[109]

---

[103] *Id.* at 4.

[104] Ross C. Anderson, *We Are All Casualties of Friendly Fire in the War on Drugs*, 13-Nov. UTAH B.J. 10, 10–11 (2000).

[105] One group proudly notes that it has "offered start-up grants to establish state-level registries in Michigan, Texas, and Arizona this year – and offered to donate $10,000 to offset the costs of establishing a registry in New York City – which has just become the largest jurisdiction in the nation to protect its citizens with an animal abuser registry." Stephen Wells, *Legally Brief: Christmas Comes Early for Animals – as Abuser Registry Takes Hold in NYC*, ANIMAL LEGAL DEF. FUND (Dec. 20, 2013), http://aldf.org/blog/christmas-comes-early-for-animals-as-abuser-registry-takes-hold-in-nyc/.

[106] *See* Chris Green, *NYC Creates City-Wide Animal Abuser Registry!*, ANIMAL LEGAL DEF. FUND (Feb. 5, 2014), http://aldf.org/blog/nyc-creates-city-wide-animal-abuser-registry/.

[107] *See, e.g.*, SUFFOLK CTY. CHARTER § 299-42, www.ecode360.com/15405586 (creating an animal abuser registry in Suffolk county); Ian Carr, *Albany County, NY Passes Nation's Third Animal Abuser Registry Law*, ANIMAL LEGAL DEF. FUND (Oct. 12, 2011), http://aldf.org/blog/albany-county-ny-passes -nations-third-animal-abuser-registry-law/ (celebrating Albany County's new animal abuser registry); Chris McKenna, *Animal Abuse Registry Law Passes in Orange County Legislature*, TIMES HERALD-RECORD (May 8, 2015), www.recordonline.com/article/20150508/NEWS/150509435 (announcing animal abuser registry in Orange County); Stephan Otto, *Rockland County, New York Unanimously Approves Animal Abuser Registry!*, ANIMAL LEGAL DEF. FUND (May 18, 2011), http://aldf .org/blog/rockland-county-new-york-unanimously-approves-animal-abuser-registry/ (celebrating Rockland County's new animal abuser registry); *Nassau County Animal Abuse Registry*, NASSAU COUNTY SPCA, www.nassaucountyspca.org/nassaucountyanimalabuseregistry.cfm (last visited Apr. 23, 2016) (describing Nassau County's animal abuser registry).

[108] Laura Moss, *Tennessee Launches Nation's First Statewide Animal Abuse Registry*, MOTHER NATURE NETWORK (Jan. 5, 2016), www.mnn.com/family/pets/stories/tennessee-launches-nation-first-statewide -animal-abuse-registry.

[109] Arin Greenwood, *Tennessee Will Soon Have First Statewide Animal Abuse Registry*, HUFF. POST (Nov. 4, 2015), www.huffingtonpost.com/entry/tennessee-animal-abuse-registry_us_56392877e4b0411 d306eaf90 (quoting Scott Heiser saying he is "very pleased with the new Tennessee law").

Registries are heralded by animal advocates as important victories in the struggle to advance the status of animal in the law.[110] The sponsor of the Tennessee registry, Senator Richard Briggs, explained that "these animals become members of our family and they need to have some of the same protections as the people who become attached to them."[111] It is perverse that the first rights or "protections" that lawmakers would extend across species lines to non-humans is the right to have a publicly available offender registry; it is difficult to imagine that such a right would be on any person's top ten list of coveted protections.

Legal commentators have also posited that the creation of abuse registries will help reduce violence to animals and, based on the presumed link between human injury and animal violence, reduce the amount of human violence.[112] Accepting this line of reasoning, the Animal Legal Defense Fund announced an effort to protect humans and the public alike through its ongoing campaign titled "Expose Animal Abusers," which urges the adoption of public abuse registries in every state.

In 2017 alone, there were more than a dozen bills introduced for statewide animal abuse registries. The bills often emphasize the need for detailed information about the abusers to be made public in order to protect animals. As one commentator explained, an animal abuser registry should include the:

> [a]buser's legal name and aliases, date of birth, Social Security number, driver's license number, gender, race, current address, place of employment, parole officer, information about whether minors live with the abuser, a photograph, fingerprints, and descriptions of any tattoos, scars, or distinguishing marks.[113]

The availability of demographic and background information might be useful for law enforcement, and certainly for researchers.[114] But the posting of pictures and addresses online is not a necessary element of data collection, or law enforcement tracking; indeed, without the benefit of a public registry, the FBI began collecting and compiling data regarding state animal abuse statistics in 2016. The central thrust of registry efforts has been to render the "criminal element more knowable" to law enforcement,[115] but

[110] *See, e.g.,* Carr; Otto; Wayne Pacelle, *Big News: FBI to Start Tracking Animal Cruelty Cases,* A Humane Nation (Sep. 17, 2014), http://blog.humanesociety.org/wayne/2014/09/animal-cruelty -uniform-crime-report.html ("The decision is also significant in affirming, at the highest levels of our government, that animal cruelty is a vice just like so many other violent crimes. It is the latest tangible gain in our effort to make opposition to animal cruelty a universal value in our society.").

[111] Leslie Ackerson, *Tennessee's Animal Abuse Registry One Year Later,* 10NEWS (Feb. 8, 2017), www.wbir .com/news/local/animal-abuse-registry-one-year-later/404322256.

[112] Charlotte A. Lacroix, *Another Weapon for Combating Family Violence: Prevention of Animal Abuse,* 4 Animal L. 1, 32 (1998).

[113] Stacy Nowicki, *On the Lamb, Toward a National Animal Abuse Registry,* 17 Animal L. 197, 237 (2010).

[114] A quick review of some registries reveals that the racial demographics for animal abuse crimes may reflect, as in other areas of the law, a dramatically disparate impact on persons of color. As of the time of writing, the Hillsborough Registry, for example, was comprised entirely of men of color and one female. Every person on the Tallahassee registry was a person of color.

[115] Wayne Logan, Knowledge as Power: Criminal Registration and Community Notification Laws (2009).

upsides for law enforcement from publicizing the registry seem to be de minimis. The public access to this information, however, does come with severe downsides, including humiliation and, according to a Human Rights Watch report, documented vigilante attacks that include killings.[116]

The enthusiastic support for animal abuse registries as a valuable means of protecting animals is belied by existing research. As with a tough-on-crime approach to sentencing, animal protection advocates did not invent the idea of an abuse registry. Indeed, a national animal protection group urged support for the 2017 bills that would produce statewide registries by explaining that the laws "are modeled on registries kept for convicted sex offenders."[117] The registries are designed to "function similar to the sex offender registries that [already] exist,"[118] and thus sex offender criminal registries serve as "models for a national animal abuse registry."[119]

Sex offender registries, however, are far from a template for effective criminal justice reform. After years of study, the existing criminal registries are largely deemed ineffective, if not affirmatively harmful by social scientists. Sex offender registries[120] grew out of the intuition that sex offenders were a uniquely dangerous class of offenders insofar as they were more likely to recidivate than other criminals.[121] The fear of repeat offenders was the primary motivation for implementing registry requirements. It turns out that the hypothesis that sex offenders recidivate at a higher rate than other criminals has been debunked,[122] but sex offender registries have remained, and even increased in popularity.[123] Data has been largely treated as irrelevant and sex offender registries continue to serve as a model for other registries.

---

[116] CHARLES EWING, JUSTICE PERVERTED 104–05 (2011) (quoting and discussing the Human Rights Watch Report).

[117] *State Animal Abuser Registries Proposed in 2017*, ADVANCING SCIENCE WITHOUT HARMING ANIMALS, www.navs.org/new-state-animal-abuser-registries-proposed-2017/#.Wc6TWdFrxzo (last visited Nov. 10, 2017); Danielle K. Campbell, *Animal Abusers Beware: Registry Laws in the Works to Curb Your Abuse*, 48 VAL. U. L. REV. 271, 328 (2013) (arguing that by "identifying animal abusers to the public other crimes can be deterred as well").

[118] *Id.* at 294 (quoting the *Model Animal Protection Laws*, ANIMAL LEGAL DEF. FUND 21–22 (2010), http://aldf.org/downloads/ALDF_Model_Laws_v15_0.pdf).

[119] Stacy Nowicki, *On the Lamb, Toward a National Animal Abuse Registry*, 17 ANIMAL L. 197, 202 (2010).

[120] It has been observed that a number of registries predated sex offender registries, but these registries were deemed ineffectual and largely abandoned over the course of the twentieth century. Elizabeth Reiner Platt, *Gangsters to Greyhounds: The Past, Present, and Future of Offender Registration*, 37 N.Y.U. REV. L. & SOC. CHANGE 727, 728 (2013).

[121] Wayne A. Logan, *A Study in "Actuarial Justice": Sex Offender Classification Practice and Procedure*, 3 BUFF. CRIM. L. REV. 593, 593 n.4 (2000) (compiling the legislative findings in support of sex offender registries and showing that legislatures across the country were deeming such legislation necessary because "sex offenders pose a high risk of reoffending after release from custody").

[122] In fact, the recidivism rate for sex offenders is no higher, and may actually be lower than the rate for other crimes. RICHARD TEWKSBURY ET AL., SEX OFFENDERS: RECIDIVISM AND COLLATERAL CONSEQUENCES 10 (2012), www.ncjrs.gov/pdffiles1/nij/grants/238060.pdf ("The results are consistent with previous research which has argued that sex offenders have relatively low rates of recidivism, typically *significantly lower* than non-sex offenders.").

[123] New York City passed a city ordinance creating an animal abuse registry in 2014, Daniel Mescon, *Animal Abuse Registry Survives Bloomberg Veto*, N.Y. WORLD (Feb. 5, 2014), www.thenewyorkworld

Over time, the recidivism rationale has given way to simple politics and symbolism: registries have become a popular way of signaling that one is "tough on crime" and cares about an issue. During the debate over a federal sex offender registry bill in 1991, a Senator remarked that empirics did not matter, and explained that if the law would "assist law enforcement authorities in one criminal apprehension . . . I believe it is worth implementing."[124] Presently, legislatures are considering a wide variety of offender registries, from methamphetamine abuse to drunk driving registries.[125] If a legislator cares about drunk driving, drug abuse, or sex crimes, so the logic goes, she will certainly support an offender registry related to the offense.[126] Animal abuse registries arise from this same intuition – if a politician cares about animals, they must support an abuse registry, even if the marginal benefits of the registry are outweighed by the marginal costs.[127]

There is a common-sense appeal to the idea of a registry – by forcing one to register, we make it less likely that the public will be harmed. It is speculated that the offender will both be deterred from committing the same crime again (the crime for which he is registered), and because of increased public and police scrutiny, it is less likely that he will commit other crimes as well. As the Arizona Department of Public Services put it, "An informed public is a safer public!"[128] There is a sense that monitoring offenders is a simple, "common sense" means of protecting the public against repeat violence.[129]

The animal protection movement has applied the same logic to arrive at the conclusion that animal abuse registries are beneficial. As one legal commentator explained, "[A]nimal abuser registry laws have the potential to do more than protect animals; they have the potential to provide greater safety to society as a whole – maybe even saving some lives along the way."[130] A representative of People for the

---

.com/2014/02/05/animal-abuse-registry-survives-bloomberg-veto/, and the first statewide registry took effect in January 2016. Talia Kaplan, *Tennessee Becomes First State to Release Animal Abuse Registry*, WKRN2 (Jan. 1, 2016), http://wkrn.com/2016/01/01/tennessee-becomes-first-state-to-release-animal -abuse-registry/ ("On Friday, Tennessee became the first state to release an animal abuse registry.").

[124] Logan, *A Study in "Actuarial Justice": Sex Offender Classification Practice and Procedure* at 129 (quoting Senator Durenberger during debate on the Wettlering Act).

[125] Platt at 738–39 (compiling types of existing and proposed registries).

[126] There is rarely an organized opposition. As is often the case, increased criminalization is politically costless because the people who bear the costs are socially marginalized groups. *See* Nicola Lacey, *The Machinery of Criminal Justice* 126 HARV. L. REV. 1299, 1321 (2013) (book review) ("Tough law-and-order policies are electorally attractive – and politically costless. This is a powerful recipe for, loosely speaking, a 'prisoners' dilemma' in which competing political actors – including voters – become locked into policy choices that would be in their individual, and the overall social, interest to avoid.").

[127] *See, e.g.,* Carr (noting that Albany County unanimously passed an animal abuser registry and that "[b]y enacting an animal abuser registry, Albany County sends a clear and unambiguous message that animal abuse will not be tolerated!"); Green (identifying specific legislators who strongly supported or spoke for an animal abuser registry).

[128] *Sex Offender Information*, ARIZONA DEPT. OF PUBLIC SAFETY, www.azdps.gov/services/sex_offender / (last visited Apr. 24, 2016).

[129] EWING at 92 (compiling courts and legislators invoking common-sense appeal of registries).

[130] Campbell at 328; Platt at 745.

Ethical Treatment of Animals (PETA) urged support for animal abuse registries by explaining: "Such people [who abuse animals] are commonly repeat offenders who pose a threat to all living beings, from dogs and cats to humans."[131] In a sense, the public registries play the role of a modern-day scarlet letter, alerting neighbors and any passersby of the deviant past of the individual.

Under empirical scrutiny, however, the common-sense public safety rationale for registries crumbles. Both in regards to specific deterrence – the effectiveness of registries in preventing an offender from returning to crime – and general deterrence – the ability of the registry to provide enough additional marginal punishment so as to deter others from engaging in the crime – there is no support for the claim that registries are an effective means of reducing crime. The view among scholars is that when it comes to offender registries as a tool for crime prevention, "the emperor has no (or very few) clothes," because the "consensus of empirical research is that these sex offender registration and notification laws have no statistically significant effect."[132]

As to specific deterrence, decades' worth of research has shown that there is no statistically significant drop in recidivism between registered and unregistered offenders.[133] The data led one commentator to explain that the existing "[e]mpirical studies repeatedly arrive at the same conclusion: Sex-offender registry and notification laws are ineffective deterrence tools."[134] But even more strikingly, some of the research now shows that persons are actually *more likely* to "recidivate when [they are] subject to community notification [registries]."[135] Amanda Agan has explained that her research shows a registered offender "appears to behave no differently, or possibly worse, than one who did not have to register. If anything, registered offenders have higher rates of recidivism."[136] As another commentator summarized the recent research: "[O]ffender registries, and the crushing collateral consequences that often accompany them, may actually increase rather than deter the incidence of recidivism."[137]

---

[131] Story Hinckley, *Massachusetts Proposes Animal Abuser Registry. How Would that Work?*, Christian Science Monitor (Oct. 21, 2015), www.csmonitor.com/USA/USA-Update/2015/1021/Massachusetts-proposes-animal-abuser-registry.-How-would-that-work (quoting PETA cruelty casework director Stephanie Bell).

[132] *Id.* at 115.

[133] Nowicki at 209–10 (compiling sources); Iowa Dept. of Hum. Rights, The Iowa Sex Offender Registry and Recidivism 10 (2000), https://humanrights.iowa.gov/sites/default/files/media/SexOffenderReport%5B1%5D.pdf; Roxanne Lieb, *Community Notification Laws: "A Step Towards More Effective Solutions,"* 11 J. Interpersonal Violence 298, 298 (2006).

[134] Molly J. Walker Wilson, *The Expansion of Criminal Registries and the Illusion of Control*, 73 La. L. Rev. 509, 523 (2013).

[135] Amanda Y. Agan, *Sex Offender Registries: Fear Without Function?*, 54 J.L. & Econ. 207, 213 (2011); J.J. Prescott, *Do Sex Offender Registries Make Us Less Safe?*, 35 Regulation 48, 55 (2012) ("Notification regimes, with their attendant impositions, appear much more likely to increase the probability that released sex offenders return to crime, all else equal, than to reduce it.").

[136] Agan at 231.

[137] Platt at 748.

Similarly, Charles Ewing's insightful book on the treatment of sex offenders notes that while registries and similar reforms have "enjoyed great popular and political support," they have not had an impact in "reducing crime," and the existence of registries has "actually increased the likelihood that sex offenders will recidivate."[138] Another commentator reached a similar conclusion, explaining that "[w]hile nearly all the data suggests the offender registries are ineffective at reducing, and may even increase crime, registry laws continue to be passed by legislators and upheld by courts."[139] Such findings are consistent with a 2012 study funded by the National Institute of Justice and submitted to the DOJ that found that public registries are "not likely to be an effective deterrent for sex offender recidivism and may produce" collateral consequences that inhibit rehabilitation.[140] It has been observed that "community notification may increase recidivism through increased stress caused to offenders by threats of bodily harm, termination of employment, on-the-job harassment, and forced instability of residence."[141] It turns out that the stress, exclusion, disruptions to social stability, and the ridicule that accompany public registries may make the public feel good about being tough on crime, but shaming humans is unlikely to save animals (or people) from crime.[142]

The research regarding general deterrence is more nascent and less clear-cut. There are so few studies on this point that to date there has not been enough data for meta-analysis. One unpublished study did report a two-percent decrease in the number of reported rapes when a public registry was created.[143] Such a finding, if true, however, may be explained by research showing that registries may actually discourage family members or close friends from reporting crimes that require public registration.[144] Researchers have

---

[138]   EWING at 205 (noting also the harm to our civil liberties by stretching the constitution to permit regimes like registries and civil detention); *Id.* at 95–96 (identifying one study from 2005 that found a possible connection between reduced recidivism rates and public registries [Barnoski], but noting that when subjected to a meta-data analysis the overall findings from the body of research in this field show that there is no decrease in recidivism rates).

[139]   Platt at 782.

[140]   TEWKSBURY ET AL. at 12.

[141]   Agan at 213.

[142]   Prescott at 50 (noting that "[r]egistration laws, by enhancing the efficacy of police supervision, seem likely to reduce recidivism of registered offenders by increasing the probability of detection," but explaining that the data betrays this assumption); Jill S. Levenson et al., *Megan's Law and Its Impact on Community Re-Entry for Sex Offenders*, 25 BEHAV. SCI. & L. 587, 598 (2007).

[143]   Ewing at 94 n.87 (citing L. Shao and J. Li, The Effect of Sex Offender Registration Laws on Rape Victimization [2006]).

[144]   Melissa Hamilton, *Public Safety, Individual Liberty, and Suspect Science: Future Dangerousness Assessments and Sex Offender Laws*, 83 TEMP. L. REV. 697, 712 (2011) ("Stigmatization of offenders and families may lead to reduced rates of reporting of sexual victimization, particularly when the perpetrators are non-strangers."); Heather R. Hlavka & Christopher Uggen, *Does Stigmatizing Sex Offenders Drive Down Reporting Rates? Perverse Effects and Unintended Consequences*, 35 N. KY. L. REV. 347, 363 (2008); Michael Vitiello, *Punishing Sex Offenders: When Good Intentions Go Bad*, 40 ARIZ. ST. L.J. 651, 685 (2008) (noting the risk of decreased reporting that flows from sex offender laws). *See also* Aya Gruber, *The Feminist War on Crime*, 92 IOWA L. REV. 741, 761 (compiling research on the issue).

posited that "reporting rates for non-stranger sexual assault may be decreasing in response to the public stigmatization associated with sex offender registration and notification."[145] If family members and loved ones follow a similar pattern in the context of an animal abuse registry, then one might expect to see lower total rates of reported animal abuse without any corresponding drops in the actual rates of animal abuse. Registries might be expected to have the effect of driving animal abuse further underground.

On the other hand, one recent study of the relationship between registries and general deterrence was conducted by J. J. Prescott and John Rockoff, who found that registries might have a statistically significant general deterrent effect. They summarize their findings by noting that there is some "evidence that registration reduces the frequency of sex offenses."[146] On this basis alone, many might argue that registries are sound policy. After all, even if the benefits are small, how can it hurt to simply have a registry that allows the police and public to keep closer tabs on a past offender. But this assumption is dangerous because it ignores the risk of increased recidivism discussed above. There exists a basic tradeoff: "[W]hereas some nonregistered or potential offenders may be deterred by the threat of notification and its associated costs, the ex post imposition of those sanctions on convicted offenders may make them more likely to recidivate."[147] Thus, even assuming the general deterrence benefits of a registry, such benefits are more than offset by the crimogenic, recidivist-producing harms of public notification.[148]

On a more general level, advocates of registries often point to registries as a way of protecting their family from potentially dangerous neighbors. If one knows that his neighbor has a history of offending, so the logic goes, his children or pets will be safer. As with the other assumptions about registries, however, the notion that the availability of such information will reduce crime is betrayed by the existing data. Some have pointed out that the proliferation of registries has actually made it more difficult for law enforcement to carefully monitor and track those persons who may be the most dangerous. Moreover, Amanda Agan has found that "knowing where a sex offender lives does not reveal much about where sex crimes, or other crimes, will take place."[149] The fact that a past offender lives in a particular area does not predict whether there will be more or less crime in that neighborhood. In fact the residence of an offender may be a red herring because research suggests that if they are tempted to reoffend these persons have "always been careful not to reoffend in close proximity to their homes."[150] Similar findings have led Agan, among others, to conclude that existing

---

[145]   Hlavka & Uggen at 363.

[146]   J. J. Prescott & Jonah E. Rockoff, *Do Sex Offender Registration and Notification Laws Affect Criminal Behavior?*, 54 J.L. & ECON. 161 (2011).

[147]   Prescott at 181.

[148]   EWING at 93 (describing the general deterrence benefits as "more than overcome by the negative effects of notification laws").

[149]   Agan at 234.

[150]   Jill Levenson & Leo P. Cotter, *The Impact of Sex Offender Residence Restrictions*, 40 INT'L J. OFFENDER THERAPY & COMP. CRIMINOLOGY 168, 173 (2005); EWING at 101 (surveying literature on residency restrictions including Grant Duwe, et. al, *Does Residential Proximity Matter?*, 35 CRIM. J. AND BEHAV. 484, 501 (2008)).

data "does not support the conclusion that sex offender registries are successful in meeting their objectives of increasing the safety of neighborhoods by providing public notification of precisely where past offenders reside."[151] It is simply untrue that information about where an offender resides is a reliable predictor of where the crime (even the registered offense) will occur. Perversely, then, people may take comfort in the safety of their neighborhood by reviewing the local offender registries, but numerous studies have shown that this is a false comfort.[152] Registries may simultaneously increase the risk that one will recidivate, while also failing to predict where the crime will occur.

Confronted with a choice between these empirical realties and popular policy, some animal protection advocates might argue that animal abuse registries are still justified insofar as they are likely to deter other crimes. That is to say, even if the registry does not specifically reduce recidivism of the crime in question, the added police scrutiny will surely cause a registered person to commit fewer crimes (other than the registered crime). This represents a strange rationale for legislation supposedly pursued in order to protect animals. But it is a rationale that is already being given voice. As one legal commentator rationalized the issue, the "animal abuser registry laws have the potential to" save human lives.[153] Another commentator posited that "[o]ne of the reasons for creating an animal abuser registry ... is the relationship between animal abuse and other forms of violence."[154] There is an assumption that an offender registry, at the very least, will prevent other types of crimes in the future as the offender is under greater scrutiny.[155] With the benefit of an abuse registry, they argue, perhaps a mass shooting, for example, could be prevented. These assumptions also turn out to be unfounded. As one recent study reports:

> [G]eneral recidivism trends are largely unaffected by [registry status] as well ... Sex offenders are under greater surveillance and have an increased number of restrictions once released to the community, so there is *the potential* that this policy would also provide a specific and/or general deterrent benefit for both sex and non-sex recidivism ... [T]his study is the first of its kind to demonstrate that [registries] as a policy [have] little effect on two related and socially important recidivism outcomes using the trajectory methodology: 1) reducing/deterring sexual recidivism; and 2) reducing/deterring recidivism in general.[156]

---

[151]   Agan at 235.
[152]   Charles Ewing explains that even if the most notable defects were fixed, public registries do not assist in crime prevention or community safety. EWING at 113 (noting that the people who take the time to learn about each offender in their neighborhood would not be those "to whom he poses the most, if any, risk").
[153]   Campbell at 328.
[154]   Nowicki at 214.
[155]   *Id.* at 214.
[156]   TEWKSBURY ET AL. at 57 (emphasis added).

In short, there is no basis for concluding that a mandatory, public registry will reduce the total amount of registered crimes *or* other crimes. Recidivism rates across the board have simply not improved, leaving one to fairly wonder what value such registries have as part of the animal protection movement. Beyond vengeance and harm to the human perpetrator, there may not be much more that can be expected. And if there is any opposition by animal protection leaders to animal abuse registries, it is because too few people are registered. There is a growing sense among some organizations, including the ASPCA, that resources are better spent enhancing the penalties for animal cruelty or paying for prosecutions, but only because the existing registries contain so few people. As Randall Lockwood, a Senior Vice President for the ASPCA has explained, registries are not a good investment relative to "strengthening" felony cruelty laws "given the limited scope, reach and utilization of animal abuse registries."

As Justice Souter explained in his concurrence to a judgment upholding Alaska's sex offender registry, the widespread dissemination of the offender's identifying information serves to "humiliate and ostracize the convict," and it results in their "exclusion from jobs or housing."[157] The registries trigger a long-term and profound sense of humiliation and isolation among offenders.[158] In the words of a commentator, "notification laws also demonize sex offenders and punish them beyond their prison sentence."[159] There is also a well-documented and intentional strand of vigilantism at the foundation of support for public registries. As author and political commentator Doug Giles has explained, the value of criminal registries is that they are capable of making offenders "shake in their boots." The goal of running their faces on the TV and in the newspaper on a daily basis in the places where they reside, Giles explains, is to make them "very uncomfortable."[160] Not surprisingly, among registered offenders in one Florida study, "57 percent reported having trouble finding housing; 48 percent said they suffered financially; and 60 percent said they suffered emotionally."[161]

Undergirding the persisting interest in registries is a sincere desire to stigmatize, torment, demonize, and otherwise psychologically shame and humiliate the offender. Stripped of its crime control pretense, an animal abuse registry is best thought of as an explicit effort to *dehumanize* offending humans in order to demonstrate the law's willingness to extend *humanity* to animals.[162]

---

[157]   Smith v. Doe, 538 U.S. 84 (2003) (Souter, J., concurring).

[158]   E.B. v. Verniero, 119 F.3d 1077, 1102 (3d Cir. 1997).

[159]   Michael P. Griffin & Desirée A. West, *The Lowest of the Low? Addressing the Disparity Between Community View, Public Policy, and Treatment Effectiveness for Sex Offenders*, 30 LAW & PSYCHOL. REV. 143, 165 (2006).

[160]   EWING at 69 (quoting Doug Giles blog).

[161]   *Id.* at 101 (citing Jill Levenson & Leo P. Cotter, *The Impact of Sex Offender Residence Restrictions*).

[162]   It is plausible that registries that are not public, but rather function as a no-adopt list for pet sellers, would represent a meaningful improvement in protecting animals. There is no public stigma and, though empirically untested, it seems likely that it would make it more difficult for animal abusers to obtain animals. Of course, such registries may simply shift the abuse to non-adopted animals like strays or animals belonging to neighbors.

Animal abuse registries arise out of an "understandably visceral response"[163] to sadistic acts of animal abuse, but the data does not support extending the model of sex offender registries to the realm of animal abuse. Sex offender registries as a template for reform represent a sad irony: the registries were enacted because of the flawed assumption that sex offenders are more likely to recidivate, but the fact of public registries is now documented to be the cause of increased rates of recidivism. The registries "have not reduced the number of sex offenses in the United States or even the rate of sex offenses among previously convicted sex offenders who have been the direct target of the laws."[164] Registries make the public "less rather than more safe."[165] One researcher has designated offender registries as "one of the worst policies enacted with regard to the larger concern of sex offender treatment and decreasing sexual assault in this country."[166] The animal protection movement's enthusiasm for a criminal justice reform that is explicitly modeled on the failed system of sex offender registries is symptomatic of the broader disease of carceral animal law. Empirical data and compassion are cast aside in favor of an ever more punitive, even if not more effective system of animal protection. As researchers studying other criminal registries have observed, a key effect of registries is the creation of a false sense of safety among the public. Registries may actually make communities more dangerous.[167] The investment in publicly available abuse registries will go down as a shameful part of the movement's history, and an illustration of the irrelevance of data to criminal-animal-law reforms.

4.4 THE PRINCIPLE OF DISINTERESTED OR NEUTRAL PROSECUTORS AND ANIMAL CRUELTY PROSECUTIONS

Recent events have highlighted the unsavory intersection of money or influence and prosecutorial discretion. The Manhattan District Attorney, for example, declined to prosecute members of the Trump family for their allegedly criminal real estate dealings, and it was subsequently revealed that the lawyer for the Trumps donated $25,000 to the prosecutor's reelection campaign. Movie mogul Harvey Weinstein was not prosecuted for various allegations of sexual misconduct, and months later his lawyer donated $10,000 to the district attorney. It is entirely possible that nothing approaching a quid pro quo occurred in either instance, and that nothing unseemly was afoot. As a matter of appearances, however, the prospect of individuals and

---

[163] Levenson & Cotter at 114; *Id.* (supporting a limited scheme of mandatory registration that is not publicly available because such registries may be useful in a "small number of cases").

[164] *Id.* at 109.

[165] *Id.*

[166] Michael P. Griffin & Desiree A. West, *The Lowest of the Low? Addressing the Disparity Between Community View, Public Policy, and Treatment Effectiveness for Sex Offenders*, 30 LAW & PSYCHOL. REV. 143, 165 (2006); *Id.* (compiling literature in support of registries); *see also*, Eric Tennen, *Risky Policies: How Effective Are Restrictions on Sex Offenders in Reducing Reoffending?*, 58 FALL B. B. J. 25, 27 (2014).

[167] EWING at 109.

entities swaying prosecutorial discretion is deeply problematic. As Bruce Green and Fred Zacharias explained, at a minimum, prosecutorial neutrality must include "independence from actors who wish to influence prosecutorial decisions, objectivity in weighing evidence, and freedom from political agendas."[168]

Of course, purchasing prosecutorial mercy is only one side of the coin. John Pfaff has issued a series of stinging rebukes to the longstanding body of literature that mistakenly equates longer drug sentences with the rise in incarceration.[169] As Pfaff explains, "[T]he primary engine of prison growth, at least since crime began its decline in the early 1990s, has been an increased willingness on the part of district attorneys to file felony charges against arrestees."[170] Prosecutorial discretion, more than the creation of new crimes or penalties, is the predictor par excellence of incarceration rates. The staggering rate of incarceration in the United States, Pfaff finds, is primarily driven by increased "prosecutorial toughness."

Not surprisingly, advocacy and financial outreach to prosecutors in the hopes of buying such "toughness" has emerged as a priority for animal protection leaders. The animal protection movement has labeled political influence and the financial support of prosecutors who promise aggressive enforcement of animal cruelty laws the "grassroots community level" activism that "can make the biggest impact."[171] The non-profits are barred, at the risk of forfeiting their tax exempt status, from making direct financial contributions to a political campaign, but the organizations encourage their members to financially support politicians and prosecutors who evince a tough-on-crime mentality, and the organizations themselves contribute considerable sums of money and in-kind services to prosecutors on an annual basis. For example, animal protection groups provide *pro bono* legal services to prosecutors in the form of legal and expert advice, they contribute money and resources to investigations and prosecutions, and they sponsor awards, trainings, and even conferences for prosecutors. Equally significant, the movement takes great pride in avoiding any association with criminal acts, even de minimus crimes of civil disobedience. At some large national organizations, legal strategies are vetted with prosecutors and made to conform to the goals and ideals of prosecutors. Out of a fear of angering prosecutors, the movement is even opposed to helping activists obtain defense lawyers when they are facing criminal charges.[172] Any litigation – civil or

---

[168]   Bruce A. Green & Fred C. Zacharias, *Prosecutorial Neutrality*, 2004 WIS. L. REV. 837, 851 (2004).

[169]   John F. Pfaff, *The War on Drugs and Prison Growth: Limited Importance, Limited Legislative Options*, 52 HARV. J. ON LEGIS. 173, 198 (2015) ("Prosecutors are paid for [and elected by] the county, but prisoners are paid for by the state. A prosecutor thus reaps the full political benefit of each incarceration but does not have to pay much of the financial cost – in fact, this moral hazard problem incentivizes prosecutors to send people to prison rather than jail, since jail is a county expense as well.").

[170]   *Id.* at 198.

[171]   Tresl at 281.

[172]   Glenn Greenwald, *The FBI's Hunt for Two Missing Piglets Reveals the Federal Cover-Up of Barbaric Factory Farms*, THE INTERCEPT (Oct. 5, 2017), https://theintercept.com/2017/10/05/factory-farms-fbi -missing-piglets-animal-rights-glenn-greenwald.

criminal – that might raise the ire of the prosecution bar is reflexively deemed impermissible.

In general, a prosecutor's decisions regarding whether and what to charge are accorded a "virtually conclusive presumption of propriety."[173] Injecting private money into the supposedly neutral office of the prosecutor is an unseemly and dangerous game, and one that does not promise lasting benefits for animals.

4.4.1 *The Historical Context of Privatized Prosecutions*

Efforts to privatize or outsource the prosecutorial function are not altogether new. As a historical matter, privately funded prosecutors were the norm in England at least through most of the nineteenth century.[174] As one commentator explained, "Although the usual norms characterizing a criminal prosecutor most often encompass . . . a full-time government attorney elected directly by the people of a particular political subdivision, such a norm is unique to the United States and is of recent invention."[175] Even in early colonial America, as it was in Britain, prosecution was often a private matter such that the victim was responsible for hiring a lawyer to prosecute alleged crimes.[176] As one leading scholar on the topic, Roger Fairfax, has explained, in the colonial system, "aggrieved victims who could afford to engage counsel would retain a lawyer to initiate criminal proceedings against an accused. Those complainants without access to counsel would have to manage the criminal case without a lawyer."[177] But the colonial justice system rather quickly diverged from its English roots and "public prosecutors came to dominate American criminal justice systems far ahead of any English counterparts."[178] As one leading historian poetically put it, the "concept of public responsibility for prosecuting criminals rang a bell in the colonial [American] mind that for unknown reason, failed to toll on the other side of the Atlantic."[179]

---

[173] *Private Prosecution: A Remedy for District Attorneys' Unwarranted Inaction*, 65 YALE L.J. 209, 218 (1955).

[174] Bruce P. Smith, *The Emergence of Public Prosecution in London, 1790–1850*, 18 YALE J.L. & HUMAN. 29 (2006) (noting that leading historians have concluded that the "typical prosecution" in the eighteenth and early nineteenth century was at the initiative of the crime victim, and noting that England did not even establish a public prosecutor's office until 1879); *Id.* at 32 (noting that there was skepticism about centralizing prosecuting authority in the hands of the state, but finding that between 1790 and 1850, public prosecutors played a "considerable" role in prosecuting misdemeanor crimes).

[175] Maybell Romero, *Profit-Driven Prosecution and the Competitive Bidding Process*, 107 J. CRIM. L. & CRIMINOLOGY 161, 169–70 (2017).

[176] *See, e.g.*, ANGELA J. DAVIS, ARBITRARY JUSTICE: THE POWER OF THE AMERICAN PROSECUTOR 9–10 (2007).

[177] Roger A. Fairfax, Jr., *Delegation of the Criminal Prosecution Function to Private Actors*, 43 U.C. DAVIS L. REV. 411, 423–24 (2009) (compiling scholarly literature on pre-revolution prosecution).

[178] Maybell Romero, *Profit-Driven Prosecution and the Competitive Bidding Process*, 107 J. CRIM. L. & CRIMINOLOGY 161, 169–70 (2017).

[179] Bruce Smith at 32 (quoting LAWRENCE FRIEDMAN, CRIME AND PUNISHMENT IN AMERICAN HISTORY 30 [1993]).

4.4.2 *The Privatization of the Animal Cruelty Prosecutor*

There are examples of prosecutorial functions being delegated to private parties in recent decades.[180] Some jurisdictions contract out the prosecutorial function to a private lawyer through the traditional "request for proposal" or bidding process that one would see with other types of government outsourcing. Generally these lawyers have no employment relationship with the retaining government entity, but rather function as classic independent contractors.[181]

These delegations of prosecutorial authority, though in tension with the ideal of a truly public prosecutor, are often driven by a desire to save money. As with other acts of privatizing government functions, the state believes it can perform the function at lower cost through outsourcing. But even when the motive for privatization is purely financial as opposed to partisan,[182] scholars and courts have lamented that "prosecutors hired pursuant to this method of outsourcing ... have little in common with the popular cultural conception" of prosecutors as neutral and disinterested.[183]

In the animal law context, the privatization of the prosecution function has moved beyond simply outsourcing to private attorneys as a means of saving money.[184] Animal protection groups devote considerable resources to support prosecutors, both on individual cases for which they have a vested interest, and more generally to prosecutors who are willing to take seriously animal cruelty prosecutions. Although the notion of a prosecutor representing the victim of a crime is a concept foreign to the modern US justice system, the animal protection groups unquestionably view themselves as the "voice" of the animal victims. The passion of the animal protection community in pursuing a prosecution is likely just as intense as the average victim of crime who seeks prosecution, and probably much more intense than the lust for prosecution experienced by many victims of crime.

As noted immediately above, at common law victims often had to hire prosecutors, and in England, even today, there are famous examples of victims who fund a private prosecution in order to overcome perceived or real discriminatory or arbitrary prosecution policies. Advertising themselves as an important safeguard for victims when the "authorities do not help," a British website, private-prosecution.co.uk, explains that "[e]very individual has the right, entrenched in law, to prosecute another who has committed a criminal offence."[185] Scorn for prosecutors who would consider a sentence other than incarceration for an animal

---

[180]   Fairfax at 415.

[181]   *Id.* at 416–17.

[182]   In the context of prosecutorial neutrality, scholars have defined nonpartisanship to include both "objectivity in weighing evidence, and freedom from political agendas." Green & Zacharias at 851.

[183]   Maybell Romero, *Profit-Driven Prosecution and the Competitive Bidding Process*, 107 J. CRIM. L. & CRIMINOLOGY 161, 166 (2017).

[184]   *Id.*

[185]   It has been observed that such a system creates a two-tier justice system with the wealthy affording more justice than the poor.

abuser has become a defining feature of animal protection advocacy, and the movement is, in effect, pursuing a system that is more like the UK model in which private groups or individuals can purchase a prosecution.

While victim-funded prosecutions are not permitted in most US jurisdictions,[186] perceiving themselves as assisting aggrieved victims, animal protection groups have invested in individual prosecutions by, among other things, providing the funding for expert witnesses, investigations, or specialized forensic analysis.[187] Animal protection groups will pay for the most expensive aspects of a criminal prosecution. In addition, several animal protection organizations have standing offers to provide free legal research and media coverage to interested prosecutors.[188] Any measure that will reduce the cost of prosecution and encourage public prosecutors to bring more – and more aggressive – animal cruelty cases will find substantial financial and in-kind support from the animal protection movement. There are even animal protection organizations that employ multiple full-time lawyers who do not carry an active caseload, but rather exist primarily to provide free legal research, sample pleadings, jury instructions, motions, or briefs in support of prosecutors who are committed to the "vigorous prosecution of animal abusers."[189]

When a case of animal cruelty appears in the news, the lawyers in these organizations actively solicit the relevant prosecutors and volunteer to provide free legal assistance or funding to support the case. These lawyers, working behind the scenes, will sometimes secretly serve as trusted, integral parts of the prosecution team. In support of prosecutors, the lawyers in some animal protection organizations are paid to provide volunteer assistance as special district attorneys in prosecutor offices across the country. As one Memorandum of Understanding puts it, the non-profit is willing to provide "every form of support necessary for [the prosecution] to achieve the best possible outcomes in Animal Cruelty cases free of charge."[190]

It is difficult to imagine that a prosecutor who avails him or herself of free legal assistance and funding from an animal protection organization would not realize that refusing to seek incarceration in that particular animal cruelty case would be disqualifying for any efforts to obtain funding and support in a future case. The funding and support come with an implicit promise that the accused will be aggressively prosecuted. Thus, the decision between obtaining external resources in

---

[186] See John D. Bessler, *The Public Interest and the Unconstitutionality of Private Prosecutors*, 47 Ark. L. Rev. 511, 515 (1994) (noting that some jurisdictions still allow a private attorney to be retained or appointed to assist in a criminal prosecution).

[187] *Criminal Justice Program*, Animal Legal Def. Fund, http://aldf.org/about-us/programs/criminal-justice-program/ (last visited Apr. 24, 2016).

[188] *Resources for Prosecutors*, Humane Soc'y of the U.S. (Dec. 11, 2015), www.humanesociety.org/issues/abuse_neglect/prosecutors_resources.html?credit=web_id92274750#Help_with_Cruelty_Cases (last visited Nov. 10, 2017).

[189] *Criminal Justice Program*, Animal Legal Def. Fund, http://aldf.org/about-us/programs/criminal-justice-program/ (last visited Apr. 24, 2016).

[190] Memorandum of Understanding between Oregon District Attorneys Association and ALDF, Jan. 21, 2013 (on file with author).

support of a case and considering less than a maximalist sentence in that case has to be made up front, without the benefit of knowledge about the details of the case or the defendant. To put the matter plainly, it may be the case that some prosecutors do not have the resources to prosecute animal cruelty cases without the support of animal protection organizations, but it cannot be gainsaid that such support will necessarily color the prosecutor's discretion at a point in the process before he or she has had a chance to assess the context and possible mitigating factors surrounding the crime. Prosecutors who are interested in prosecuting cruelty cases in order to ensure that a person receives treatment rather than incarceration would not expect to be eligible for funding and assistance from an animal protection non-profit. The very rationale for funding lawyer positions whose job it is to assist prosecutors on a *pro bono* basis is to ensure that cruelty cases result in maximalist enforcement and sentencing. As the Animal Legal Defense Fund has explained, the organization "provides assistance to prosecutors nationwide," because it is "dedicated to ensuring more animal cruelty cases are prosecuted to the fullest extent of the law."[191] Support is not given for an individualized assessment of whether incarceration is warranted for a particular defendant; it is given to make an example of the person.

Beyond robust external support for public prosecutors, some animal protection groups have also taken the rather unprecedented step of funding the salaries of prosecutors who will aggressively enforce animal abuse crimes. For example, a law enforcement non-profit named "Safer Dallas Better Dallas" provides funding for an "animal cruelty prosecution unit." The money was sufficient to completely cover the first year of salary for a prosecutor and support staff that are dedicated to the enforcement of animal cruelty laws. Safer Dallas Better Dallas is not an animal protection non-profit, but there is no question that the animal protection movement had a strong financial and strategic influence on the organization's decision to fund this unit. Animal protection groups and law enforcement were described as "banding together to launch what is likely the first animal cruelty unit in a North Texas district attorney's office."[192] The county commissioner who first spearheaded the effort explained the funding in terms that resemble the animal protection movement's talking points: "People who abuse animals abuse other people, too . . . A lot of children who abuse animals are your future murderers."[193] Describing her support and enthusiasm for the Dallas plan, Allie Phillips, the then director of the National Center for Prosecution of Animal Abuse noted that "[w]hen you address the animal abuse, you never know what you will have prevented in the future."

[191] *Top 5 Prosecuted Animal-related Crimes*, Animal Legal Def. Fund, http://aldf.org/press-room/press-releases/top-5-prosecuted-animal-related-crimes/ (last visited Nov. 14, 2017).

[192] Brandon Formby, *Dallas Officials, Nonprofit Raising Money to Prosecute Crimes Against Animals*, Dallas News (Dec. 2012), www.dallasnews.com/news/news/2012/12/02/dallas-officials-nonprofit-raising-money-to-prosecute-crimes-against-animals.

[193] *Id.*

A prosecutor who is funded by donations from a groups with a particular interest in one type of crime would seem to have difficulty retaining the image of a disinterested, neutral public prosecutor with "professional independence."[194] If the funder is not a partisan group, but rather a politically neutral group interested in crime control, there would be some buffer against accusations of improperly political prosecutions. By contrast, the ability of a prosecutor to retain neutrality and independence would be substantially degraded if the prosecutor was funded, not by a general law enforcement non-profit, but rather a partisan advocacy group, such as an animal protection group. Such a funding practice is now under way in at least one jurisdiction.

The Animal Legal Defense Fund prides itself on "working behind the scenes" with its team of lawyers who support prosecutors, but it has also provided the funding for at least one fully-sworn prosecutor in Oregon, Jake Kamins. ALDF crafted the position in way that allows Kamins to be housed in a single district attorney office, while having the authority to prosecute animal abuse cases in any of Oregon's 36 districts. In the words of ALDF, the funding of this position is "a cutting-edge program intended to make sure that no criminal gets off the hook for animal cruelty."

The Memorandum of Understanding between ALDF and the Oregon District Attorney's Association, which was obtained through an open records request, reveals several of the notable features of this public-private partnership. The private animal protection group agreed to pay a "base salary" of up to $8,333.00 per month, or $100,0000 per year for a "highly experienced prosecutor who is dedicated to prose-cuting Animal Cruelty cases for those District Attorneys who want the free help."[195] So by its plain terms, the agreement anticipates that the individual will be a fully-sworn state prosecutor, but he will also remain something of an outsider to the district attorneys, because he will make himself available to provide "free help" with their cases. The county district attorney's office is vested with the ultimate hiring and firing authority for this "special deputy district attorney."

The Memorandum of Understanding makes clear the goal of the funding arrange-ment: "[E]nsuring the vigorous prosecution of Animal Cruelty cases." In other words, the animal protection group providing the funding could interpret the exercise of leniency in a case as a material breach of the contract. The district attorney's office is on notice that the failure of the special district attorney to focus exclusively on animal cruelty cases, or the failure to do so with sufficient aggressive-ness, provides a basis for their funding to be withdrawn. The contract also provides ALDF with access to "all records necessary to assure conformance with the terms and conditions of this Agreement." The prosecutors have guaranteed access to their

---

[194] Green & Zacharias at 861.
[195] A subsequent "Renewal of Memorandum of Understanding" dated September 26, 2016 increases the monthly payment to $8,750 per month, or $105,000 per year.

case files, as requested, in order to evaluate whether they are pursuing prosecutions with sufficient zeal.

In addition, the appointed special district attorney is required to provide quarterly reports detailing the number of cases filed, the number of cases closed, and the outcome of each case. Both ALDF and the Oregon District Attorneys Association are given the authority to "terminate this agreement, without cause" with one-year advance notice, and either party may do so with 30 days' notice if there is a failure by either party to cure a material breach of the agreement. The agreement also specifies that the contract will only be renewed if both parties agree to an extension in writing.

It is also interesting that the employment contract between Jake Kamins, the special prosecutor funded by ALDF, and the county specifies that Kamins will "act as an independent contractor." It is a true mix of private and public prosecution. An outside organization has been permitted to fund an independent contractor who is given full prosecutorial authority, but by contract is limited to the enforcement of animal cruelty laws. The details of this arrangement are unheard of in modern history, and betray the image of the disinterested prosecutor conveyed in the legal scholarship regarding the prosecutorial function.[196]

Even aside from the particular details of the arrangement, the example of Jake Kamins as a privately funded prosecutor underscores the fact that focusing on animal cruelty prosecutions is a sort of head-in-the-sand approach to animal protection. As noted above in Section 4.1.1, the majority of modern felony animal cruelty laws were enacted in conjunction with a criminal exemption for all customary agricultural practices. One is hard-pressed to find prosecutors who publicly object to these exemptions.[197] Kamins was recently invited to do an online discussion regarding his role in the animal rights community.[198] When asked specifically whether "existing animal cruelty laws are sufficient" or whether he would like to see any changes to laws in order to better protect animals, his answer was that he would like to see an animal abuse registry and some other procedural changes.[199] Kamins supports mandatory minimum sentences and registries, but he is not troubled by the exemption for accepted husbandry practices in his home state of Oregon (or the forty-plus other states that have such an exemption) as problematic.

[196] Kamins's employment contract does include a boilerplate covenant in which he agrees that he "has no interest and shall not acquire any interest, direct or indirect, which would conflict in any manner or degree with the performance of services."

[197] *But see* Pamela Frasch & Holli Lund, *The Unequal Treatment of Animals by Species and Practice in the United States: A Moral and Legal Dilemma* (2008), www.derechoanimal.info/images/pdf/Frasch-Lund-Unequal-Treatment-Animals-USA.pdf (questioning why companion animals receive greater protections than farm animals in the legal system).

[198] Kamins was asked to do an IAmA on reddit.com, where users posted questions and he responded to those questions. To read the IAmA in its entirety, *see* www.reddit.com/r/IAmA/comments/3ripsc/iama_statewide_animal_cruelty_prosecutor_ama/.

[199] Jake Kamins (AnimalDDA), REDDIT.COM (Nov. 2015), www.reddit.com/r/IAmA/comments/3ripsc/iama_statewide_animal_cruelty_prosecutor_ama/cwogan6.

In fact, Kamins explicitly and unapologetically invoked the agricultural exemption later in the same forum in order to explain why the forced impregnation of dairy animals by metal racks is not legal cruelty warranting prosecution.[200]

As the figurehead for animal-protection-funded prosecutions, Kamins illustrates the inherent conservatism of this model of law reform. Kamins embodies the notion of the prosecutor as a representation of the status quo; he pursues incarceration divorced from any serious effort to change the status of animals in the law. When asked publicly whether he thinks dietary choices have an impact on animal welfare, Kamins replied, "[m]y practice focuses on criminal animal cruelty in Oregon, which doesn't impact the eating of animals in a general sense," and when pressed on the issue he responded more curtly by explaining that he is not vegan:

> I'm sure there's no answer [explaining why I'm not vegan] I could give that wouldn't spark a larger debate, which I'm not really interested in. Suffice it to say that it would involve a significant lifestyle change that I'm not able to undertake.[201]

The idea that modern animal protection efforts will be lastingly advanced through an ideology that treats dietary choices as too onerous, and incarceration as essential gives lie to the notion that carceral animal law is a far-reaching modality of reform. As a prosecutor paid for by ALDF, Kamins's advocacy paints a painfully limiting picture of the prospects of animal protection through prosecution.[202] Imprisoning people is socially acceptable and mainstream, but if Kamins is the face of carceral animal law, the movement has to question its implicit premise that animal cruelty prosecutions serve as a gateway or critical nexus to an expanding arc of compassion for non-human animals.

Prosecution is a publicly acceptable solution precisely because it does not require any "significant lifestyle change[s]." And if the leading prosecutors who support

---

[200] *Id.* at www.reddit.com/r/IAmA/comments/3ripsc/iama_statewide_animal_cruelty_prosecutor_ama/cwokynq; *see id.* at www.reddit.com/r/IAmA/comments/3ripsc/iama_statewide_animal_cruelty_prosecutor_ama/cwogv4i.

[201] *Id.* at www.reddit.com/r/IAmA/comments/3ripsc/iama_statewide_animal_cruelty_prosecutor_ama/cworowv.

[202] A look at the prosecutions that Kamins has pursued provides little to no reassurance that his position affords much protection to animals other than pets. He has prosecuted numerous cases of horse neglect, and abuse to dogs and cats, but only on a couple of occasions have animals used for food been the victims. *See Animal Cruelty Prosecutor Jake Kamins Takes on Oregon Animal Abuse* (discussing several of Kamins's prosecutions in 2014, all of which involved animal neglect). During his Reddit IAmA, Kamins was asked whether he had prosecuted any factory farms, and if not, what it would take for him to do so. He responded that he had not, and that "the borders of [animal cruelty] get narrower" when dealing with "lawful farming/livestock operations." Kamins at www.reddit.com/r/IAmA/comments/3ripsc/iama_statewide_animal_cruelty_prosecutor_ama/cwogrmq. He expanded on his answer by saying that, based on current Oregon law and exceptions for husbandry, "livestock raising and processing in a general sense is not in my purview." *Id.* Even the prosecutions that do involve cows or pigs tend to be the exceptions that prove the rule of general indifference to these animals. *See e.g., Cattle Operations Get 120 Neglect Convictions,* KOIN6 (Oct. 7, 2014), http://koin.com/2014/10/07/cattle-owners-get-120-animal-neglect-convictions/ (discussing Kamins's prosecution of two commercial cattle operators).

carceral animal law strategies (including those funded by animal protection organizations) are not convinced that advancing the status of animals in the law requires
more than aggressive prosecutions, it is a bridge too far to imagine that the public
who is roused to celebrate and support these prosecutions will perceive the strategy
differently. It is simply not the case that a prosecutorial orientation is a gateway to
greater compassion for animals, or a path toward recognizing animals as enjoying
a heightened legal status. Carceral animal law promises incarceration of humans,
but not much more than that.

4.4.3 *The Ethical and Constitutional Problems with Special Interest Prosecutors and Prosecutions*

The animal protection movement is not alone in providing funding for an interest-
group-oriented prosecutor, but examples of such a practice in modern America are
extremely rare, have been the subject of biting critiques, and are distinguishable.

One such arrangement was identified as unique in a story by the American Bar
Association, which reported that a non-profit comprised of local business leaders in
Altoona, Pennsylvania had raised money to fund "a drug prosecutor."[203] The non-
profit apparently funnels upwards of $100,000 to the local prosecutor's office
each year in order to fund a sort of privatized, local war on drugs. The money
funds a full-time prosecutor who is referred to as the "drug prosecutor" and a support
staff for that prosecutor. A local newspaper has suggested that the private funding has
had an impact on the manner and number of local prosecutions, and concerns have
been raised that the private drug prosecutor might be spurred "to bring marginal
cases to satisfy financial backers."[204] But setting aside ethical concerns, if the goal is
more prosecution the privately secured funding appears to be working. The district
attorney noted that with the benefit of a privately funded prosecutor, the city has
earned "[a] kind of a reputation up here. We've put people in jail for 35 or 40 years"
for drug crimes.

There are also periodic examples of private parties covering part of the expense of
a particular case, such as an expert witness's fees. Such cases have resulted in
challenges to the financial arrangements, the resolution of which is often fact-driven,
turning largely on whether it was reasonable to conclude that the defendant was
actually prejudiced by the financial support from the victim. Where a financial
arrangement can fairly be understood to create pressure, or a sense of obligation on
the part of prosecutor, a conflict of interest exists. The leading case is *People*

---

[203] Debra Cassens Weiss, *Nonprofit Funds Drug Prosecutor and Cops, Who Turn Addicts into
        Informants*, ABA J. (Dec. 1, 2014), www.abajournal.com/news/article/nonprofit_funds_drug_prosecu
        tor_and_cops_who_turn_addicts_into_informants/.

[204] Rich Lord, *Privately Funded Prosecutor Pursues Drug Case in Altoona*, Pittsburgh Post-Gazette
        (Nov. 30, 2014), www.post-gazette.com/news/state/2014/12/01/Privately-funded-prosecutor-pursues
        -drug-cases-in-Altoona/stories/201411300089.

v. *Eubanks,* a California Supreme Court decision that held that a prejudicial conflict to the defendant resulted from the decision by a prosecutor to solicit $13,000 from the victim of a crime in order to pay for expert witness fees already incurred by the prosecutor.[205] Of particular note, the *Eubanks* court rejected the notion that only financial arrangements that would inhere to the personal interest of a prosecutor by benefitting that person's own "pocketbook" could give rise to an impermissible conflict. Instead, the Court held that a prosecutor's impartiality could "be impaired by institutional interests" just as much as by personal ones, and noted in particular that "a prosecutor may have a conflict if institutional arrangements link the prosecutor too closely to a private party, for example a victim."[206]

Providing financial support for a prosecutor, the Court in *Eubanks* recognized, creates the dangerous possibility that a public prosecutor would be in "a position of attempting at once to serve two masters." As the Court put it, "[p]rivate influence . . . is a conflict of interest . . . if it creates a reasonable possibility the prosecutor may not act in an evenhanded manner." Arguably, in *Eubanks* the financial arrangement was particularly problematic because it appeared that continued prosecution of the case may have been contingent on the victim coming up with the necessary financial support. But the support provided is likely less than animal protection groups have provided on numerous occasions to prosecutors (both financial and in-kind support), and the *Eubanks* decision is fairly read as standing for the more general proposition that "justice simply should not be for sale."[207]

Similarly, in *State* v. *Culbreath*, the Tennessee Supreme Court upheld the dismissal of criminal charges in a pornography case where a private anti-pornography organization had funded the investigation of adult entertainment facilities and provided funds to the prosecutor's office to pay for the prosecution. The fact that the compensation for the special prosecutor came from a "special interest group," was critical to the Court's conclusion that the prosecution was so lacking in neutrality as to be "fundamentally unfair." In *Culbreath* the Court emphasized that financial entanglements can leave an attorney unable to exercise "his or her independent professional judgment free of compromising interests and loyalties."[208]

In an argument that one could imagine prosecutors using to defend the private funding of animal cruelty prosecutions, the state in *Culbreath* defended the use of the privately funded prosecutor on the grounds that "there was no conflict of interest because [the private attorney] and the prosecution had the same interest –

[205] *See, e.g.,* People v. Eubanks, 927 P.2d 310 (Cal. 1996).
[206] *Id.*
[207] Hambarian v. Superior Court, 88 Cal. App. 4th 163, 105 Cal. Rptr. 2d 566, 582 (Sills, P. J., dissenting), review granted and opinion superseded sub nom. Hambarian v. Orange Cty. Superior Court, 25 P.3d 1078 (Cal. 2001), and aff'd, 27 Cal. 4th 826, 44 P.3d 102 (2002), as modified (June 12, 2002)
[208] State v. Culbreath, 30 S.W.3d 309, 312 (Tenn. 2000). In *Culbreath* the private prosecutor was paid on an hourly basis, which the court regarded as an aggravating factor, because it gave him a financial incentive to enhance the duration and complexity of the case.

eradicating sexually-oriented businesses."[209] Under this line of argument, if the private funding is put toward the goal of eradicating a crime, then there is never a conflict of interest.[210] But the Tennessee Supreme Court summarily rejected such an argument, noting that a "prosecutor's discretion about whom to prosecute and to what extent they should be prosecuted . . . is vast" and, thus, efforts to influence this discretion present untenable conflicts of interest. In a passage that is relevant to assessing whether the animal protection movement's involvement in prosecutions is forbidden by the rules of professional ethics, the *Culbreath* Court explained exactly how funding or assistance that alter prosecutorial priorities can create an impermissible conflict of interest:

> A prosecutor exercises considerable discretion in matters such as the determination of which persons should be targets of investigation, what methods of investigation should be used, what information will be sought as evidence, which persons should be charged with what offenses, which persons should be utilized as witnesses, whether to enter into plea bargains and the terms on which they will be established.[211]

Ultimately the Court concluded in *Culbreath* that the appearance of impropriety was so strong when criminal charges were facilitated by the involvement of a privately funded prosecutor as to warrant an outright dismissal of the case. The Court analogized the private funding of a prosecutor to a more obvious conflict of interest where the "prosecutor presented charges to a grand jury while at the same time representing the victim's family in a corresponding civil action."[212] When criminal charges are pursued by a privately funded prosecutor, or when a privately funded prosecutor is an integral part of the prosecution team, courts have recognized a conflict of interest that injects intolerable unfairness into the case.

Courts have also identified ethical problems with special interest groups funding a more general scheme in support of prosecutions of a certain type, as opposed to funding or supporting a particular prosecution.[213] One such case arose in Florida where a non-profit was funding drunk-driving prosecutions. The system of private funding was eventually abandoned when a lawyer challenged the funding process in a federal case. Describing the rationale for challenging the case, attorney Jiulo Margalli asked, "Do you want the motivation to be justice . . . or do you want the motivation of the prosecutor to be a guilty verdict so that that [office] could continue

---

[209] *Id.* at 316.

[210] Scholars have observed that "[e]thically, there is nothing wrong with a prosecutor wanting to convict someone he sincerely believes is guilty. However . . . the question becomes whether a prosecutor has become so obsessed," that impartiality is impossible. Laurie L. Levenson, *High-Profile Prosecutors & High-Profile Conflicts*, 39 LOY. L.A. L. REV. 1237, 1242–43 (2006).

[211] *Culbreath*, 30 S.W.3d 309, 312 (quoting Young v. U.S. ex rel. Vuitton, 481 U.S. 787, 807 (1987)).

[212] *Id.* at 318.

[213] On the other hand, there are insurance fraud departments in state prosecutor offices that are funded largely, if not entirely, by the insurance industry.

to receive funding from the organization who paid them?"[214] Expressing the same sentiment, leading legal ethics scholar Bruce Green has opined that the reason privately or special interest funded prosecutions are uncommon in modern times is "we want disinterested prosecutors who answer to the public, and not to individuals."[215]

For similar reasons, it is hard to square the animal protection movement's funding of prosecutors with the ideal of a neutral prosecutor. Prosecutors funded by the animal protection movement know that their decisions will be scrutinized by the movement and adjudged according to a standard whereby more incarceration is better – that is the very reason for the financial support. Such a prosecutor cannot operate with true objectivity, because to consider a novel, non-carceral solution such as treatment or a diversion program, or even just to take into account the life circumstances of an animal abuser would undermine the very purpose of the financial grant funding the prosecutor.

Even more so than in *Eubanks*, where the victim simply paid for an expert witness, where a prosecutor's entire position is funded by the special interest, there could well be a personal as well as an institutional interest in impressing and placating the funding organization. Even assuming the integrity and independence of the prosecutors who receive such money, the appearance and reality of influence is unavoidable.[216] As Judge Friendly once explained, a prosecutor "is not disinterested if he has, or is under the influence of others who have, an axe to grind against the defendant."[217] Funding from a special interest group creates the possibility for a "sense of obligation" on the part of the prosecuting attorney.[218] Even the most ethical prosecutor could not help but feel pressure to perform in a way that appeases the funder.

Probably the closest modern day analogy to the private funding for prosecutors by the animal protection movement is the relationship between prosecutors and the insurance industry. Aviva Abramovsky described the relationship between the insurance industry and prosecutors as an "unholy alliance," and the parallels to the animal protection movement's attempts to coordinate and fund prosecutors are notable.[219] Like animal cruelty, insurance fraud cases are said to be "complex and frequently expensive," and yet the prosecution of these crimes is believed to be

---

[214]   Lord.
[215]   Walter Olson, *When Prosecutors Collect Private Grants*, OVERLAWYERED (Mar. 5, 2015), www.overlawyered.com/2015/03/private-grants-to-assist-prosecution/.
[216]   On the other hand, courts have explained that "no one factor will compel disqualification in all cases; 'the entire complex of facts' must be reviewed to determine 'whether the conflict makes fair and impartial treatment of the defendant unlikely.'" Hambarian v. Superior Court, 44 P.3d 102, 108 (Cal. 2002); *Id.* Rejecting a rigid requirement of prosecutorial recusal whenever "the victim is paying for a prosecutorial expense that otherwise would have been incurred by the District Attorney's Office."
[217]   Wright v. United States, 732 F.2d 1048, 1056 (2d Cir. 1984).
[218]   *Hambarian* 44 P.3d at 104 (2002) (quoting People v. Eubanks, 927 P.2d 310 (Cal. 1966)).
[219]   Aviva Abramovsky, *An Unholy Alliance: Perceptions of Influence in Insurance Fraud Prosecutions and the Need for Real Safeguards*, 98 J. CRIM. L. & CRIMINOLOGY 363, 371 (2008).

capable of yielding far-reaching public benefits. Likewise, because of the risk that the crime will go "under-prosecuted," an interest in locating funding to support such prosecutions outside of "the state's general revenues" has become a popular idea. Specifically, although the details vary by jurisdiction, nearly every state has mandated by statute that insurance providers fund prosecutors and investigators that are able to bring insurance fraud prosecutions. The most common model is funding prosecutors in the state Attorney General's office through a legislatively mandated special assessment on insurance revenues.

Legal scholars and civil liberties groups, including the ACLU, have decried the private funding of insurance prosecutors as an inappropriate conflict of interest. To date, the regimes have withstood legal challenges, but the factors that have been relied upon to uphold such provisions seem to cut against the legality of the arrangements between animal protection groups and prosecutors. For example, the Massachusetts Supreme Court upheld the insurance-assessment model of funding prosecutors, but it did so in large part because of the lack of any evident personal loyalty between prosecutors and the insurance industry. Moreover, the funding scheme at issue was legislatively mandated. The court explained that if it was examining a legal challenge to a funding scheme for prosecutors "that was not endorsed by statute, the appearance of the possibility of improper influence would be far clearer."[220] The court went on to say that when assessing the propriety of a private entity funding a prosecution, the inquiry is very different when the "legislature has endorsed the plan, [and] has supervisory authority over it."

The creation of a tax or assessment on a particular industry, in short, should be viewed as fundamentally different than a private organization's voluntary (and revocable) donation.

It has also been treated as legally relevant that the funding by the insurance companies for prosecutions comes from the industry in general, rather than from certain self-selected organizations or companies. Legal scholars and judges have explained that such collective funding schemes have the benefit of diluting the influence of individual organizations on particular cases. An insurance fraud prosecutor working in a state with dozens of insurance companies paying into a general assessment will, one imagines, have less of a "client-like" relationship with any one of the companies.[221] There is little likelihood that a single insurance company could exert particular influence in support of its particular prosecution goals.

Notably, however, even in the context of a generalized insurance fund, prosecutors who bring insurance fraud cases against consumers have identified a conflict of interest that precludes them from prosecuting the insurance industry itself for fraud. That is to say, the state attorneys who are funded by insurance proceeds have deemed themselves conflicted off of any case alleging fraud on the part of their funding

---

[220]   Commonwealth v. Ellis, 708 N.E.2d 644, 652 (Mass. 1999).

[221]   Aviva Abramovsky, *An Unholy Alliance: Perceptions of Influence in Insurance Fraud Prosecutions and the Need for Real Safeguards*, 98 J. Crim. L. & Criminology 363, 383 (2008).

sources. Of course, in the context of a single organization funding a particular prosecution or a particular prosecutor, the loyalty and financial interests in zealously pursuing the interests of that organization make the potential for an intolerable, client-like relationship considerably more likely. No judge would disagree that serious concerns would arise if a prosecutor has pledged loyalty "to a party interested only in a conviction."[222] So the only question is how close to the line of clear impermissibility has the animal protection movement treaded. The private funding arrangement in Oregon, which the movement seems poised to replicate elsewhere, has arguably gone farther toward creating a clear conflict of interest than any ongoing modern privatized prosecution scheme in this country.

Beyond concerns regarding conflicts of interest, financial and in-kind support for a prosecution like that provided by the animal protection movement can also give rise to violations of constitutional safeguards afforded by due process. Roger Fairfax has studied the issue carefully and concluded that private funding arrangements, even without any partisan or substantive motivations, present a "a serious barrage of modern constitutional challenges." While the case law on this question is virtually nonexistent, fundamental fairness would seem to dictate that if a prosecutor is paid in whole or in part for "his prosecutorial services by the victim or an organization allied with the victim," the conflict of interest is sufficient to violate due process.[223] In the most analogous case to be decided to date, *Young v. United States ex rel. Vuitton*, the Supreme Court held that it was a structural error for a trial judge to appoint a prosecutor who was counsel for an interested party in a contempt prosecution.[224]

The animal protection movement's "infusion of a payer independent from the state's general revenues" injects a serious danger of unconstitutionality and "improper conflicting interests influencing the prosecutor's discretion."[225] The public has an interest in prosecutors who are "free from the potential conflict of loyalties" that arise when special interests or victims fund a prosecution.[226] It has been observed that the very source of "legitimacy for the criminal justice system" in our country is the "notion that criminal prosecution authority properly rests exclusively with the state" and not with private actors or special interests.[227] It is perverse that in the pursuit of "justice" for animals, the animal protection movement is undermining

---

[222]   *Ellis*, 708 N.E.2d at 652.
[223]   Gerald F. Uelmen, *Fighting Fire with Fire: A Reflection on the Ethics of Clarence Darrow*, 71 FORDHAM L. REV. 1543, 1556–57 (2003); *Id.* (quoting Judge Friendly for the point that a prosecutor is never appropriately disinterested if "he has, or is under the influence of others who have, an axe to grind against the defendant").
[224]   John D. Bessler, *The Public Interest and the Unconstitutionality of Private Prosecutors*, 47 ARK. L. REV. 511, 511–12 (1994) (deciding the case under the Court's supervisory authority).
[225]   *Id.* at 403.
[226]   *Id.* at 409.
[227]   Fairfax at 433.

the very legitimacy of our criminal justice system by treating prosecution as a commodity that can be purchased.[228]

Finally, on a practical level, the animal protection movement's willingness to pursue privately funded prosecutors seems more than a tad myopic. As one journalist has commented on the resurgence of private prosecutions in Britain, "The growing trend for private criminal prosecutions has raised concerns about the prospect of a 'two-tier' justice system, with some cases reaching court only because the victims – often corporations – can afford to pay the substantial costs." Initiating an arms race for the funding of private prosecutors does not seem like a fight that the animal protection movement can ultimately win. It seems unlikely that the movement wants to compete with fur farms, pharmaceuticals, and the food industry in terms of purchasing power. A fund created by Big-Ag – maybe the Tyson Foods Animal Terrorism Prosecution Fund – which would fund FBI agents, undercover sting operations, and prosecutor positions that were devoted entirely to enforcing aggressively trespass or property crimes, animal terrorism laws, Ag-Gag laws, or other crimes against animal protection groups would rightly prompt allegations of impropriety and undue influence. But the animal protection movement must hold itself to the same standard. Presently, the best precedent to establish a privately funded prosecutor that would do the industry's bidding is the animal protection movement's own support for and funding of animal cruelty prosecutions. Agricultural interests are eager to pursue opportunities to privately fund prosecutors aligned with their priorities and goals, with a recent report calling for "vertical prosecution," which means industry-funded and controlled prosecutors, in the realm of agricultural crime.[229] The animal protection movement will not be well-positioned to challenge the propriety and constitutionality of such endeavors given their current entanglements with the prosecutorial function.

In sum, at the cost of the movement's credibility and to the great detriment of the neutrality of our justice system more generally, the animal protection movement is supporting a process that will ultimately protect very few animals. Even for those who believe that the criminal prosecution of individuals is a viable way to improve the status of animals in the law, the privatization of the prosecution function promises relatively few short-term benefits, and massive long-term risks, both in terms of systemic harm and specific risks to the movement.

---

[228] Professor Fairfax asks, "[I]f we can delegate the core prosecution function – including the power to decide whether the sovereign's laws will be enforced – to private hands, what can we not delegate? The delegation of prosecutorial discretion to private actors presents fundamental questions about how we view the sovereign authority to prosecute and punish, whether there is such a thing as an inherently or exclusively governmental function, and how we value the important functional and symbolic role of the modern public prosecutor." *Id.* at 456.

[229] Daniel P. Mears, et. al, *A Process and Impact Evaluation of the Agricultural Crime, Technology, Information, and Operations Network (ACTION) Program*, available at www.ncjrs.gov/pdffiles1/nij/grants/217906.pdf.

5

Race, Mass Criminalization, and Animal Law

President Donald Trump has stoked fears about rampant crime, explaining repeatedly during his campaign that "America is a more dangerous environment than frankly I have ever seen." Given these statements, it is not surprising that the President supports a tough-on-crime approach to criminal justice reform, including longer, harsher sentences and more prosecutions. What is surprising is that the same carceral logic – solving social problems through more incarceration – permeates the animal protection realm. In February 2018, the *New York Times* editorial board lamented that the "rhetoric from the White House and the Justice Department has emboldened some state and local officials to talk tougher, even if just as ignorantly, about crime." Just weeks later, in March 2018, a leading animal protection organization announced to the public that the movement was tirelessly "working to increase the maximum sentencing for felonious cruelty to animals."

Both President Trump and the animal protection movement have vowed to improve society through more and harsher criminal penalties, and incredulously one prominent organization noted in a fundraising email, that "believe it or not, we're fighting entrenched interests that want to stop progress like this." Among these entrenched interests are civil liberties groups, social justice activists, and groups that represent the interests of persons of color – the very groups that are pushing back against Trump's tough-on-crime proposals.

As the animal protection movement is pursuing mandatory minimums, the prosecution of juveniles as adults, more felony prosecutions, offender registries, and similar crime-based animal advocacy, the NAACP recently explained, "rather than provide justice, our criminal justice system and law enforcement has often been the consistent purveyor of injustice." As Emily Gaarder has documented, throughout its history the animal protection movement has been mocked for being "single issue and slow to form coalitions with other progressive social movements."[1] Pursuing convictions on the presumption that such efforts will improve the lives and status of animals is a salient example of this sort of tunnel

---

[1] EMILY GAARDER, WOMEN AND THE ANIMAL RIGHTS MOVEMENT 13 (2011).

vision. The very effort to end one "systematic, institutionalized" form of oppression (mistreatment of animals) by resorting to another (incarcerating humans) would be farcical if it were not taken so seriously by the movement itself.[2]

Race and oppression are highly salient features of the modern criminal justice system in the United States. Race issues also serve as a backdrop to all manner of advocacy and reform efforts that take place in the criminal justice space. Race is never irrelevant when it comes to justice system reforms. Consider first the use of race-based analogies for securing animal rights, such as the groundbreaking work of the Nonhuman Rights Project (NhRP). The NhRP seeks to liberate animals from their confinement by drawing analogies to the role the common law writ of habeas corpus played in helping liberate slaves in Britain in the nineteenth century. NhRP lawyers, led by Steve Wise, point to the writ of habeas corpus – the procedure that William Blackstone referred to as the bulwark against unjust (often criminal) detention – in an effort to obtain the release of animals from cages. Many of the arguments in support of habeas for non-humans resonate with the underpinnings and rationale for the Great Writ – it is not absurd to imagine habeas corpus as a vehicle for helping chimpanzees who are unjustly confined.[3] But notably, many habeas corpus scholars and lawyers have not supported efforts to expand the application of habeas corpus across the species barrier. Some of the hesitation on the part of habeas scholars is that habeas corpus is rarely a meaningful vehicle for reform for *humans* in modern times. There is a sense that if death-sentenced humans are not given a fair shake through habeas corpus, then one ought not take seriously the prospect of the writ applying to non-humans. But the reluctance of leading criminal law and habeas corpus scholars to join the mounting habeas-for-animals call also has to do with the perception of the animal protection movement as pro-incarceration. The movement fails to appreciate that its carceral advocacy does not go unnoticed by leading social reform scholars and activists. The movement is suffering from the isolation that results from a failure to recognize the intersectional connections of race and criminal justice.

When it comes to habeas corpus and understanding the writ in a capacious manner, the animal protection advocates wax poetically[4] about the terrors of unjust confinement and the need for procedural checks on such incarceration. When it comes to habeas corpus, animal protection groups have explicitly connected their advocacy to race-conscious efforts to fight slavery and other injustices. The gravamen of habeas claims for non-humans is the history of former slaves creatively employing habeas corpus; the movement is exploiting the success of former slaves in order to

[2] Lisa Kemmerer, *Introduction* to Sister Species: Women, Animals and Social Justice 1, 2 (Kemmerer ed., 2011).

[3] Justin Marceau & Steven Wise, *Exonerating the Innocent: Habeas for Nonhuman Animals*, in Wrongful Convictions and the DNA Revolution: Twenty-Five Years of Freeing the Innocent 334 (Daniel S. Medwed ed., 2017).

[4] Steven Wise, Though the Heavens May Fall: The Landmark Trial that Led to the End of Human Slavery (2006).

advance the interests of animals. Yet simultaneously and without any sense of irony, the animal protection movement also aligns itself with the carceral state – one of the most racialized spheres in modern America – as an alternative vehicle for pursuing animal protection and claims that all such carceral efforts are race neutral and consistent with combatting oppression. The success of the black slave in obtaining liberation is treated as highly and necessarily relevant to the cause, but the hardship imposed on people of color and their communities by the modern criminal justice system is disregarded as entirely irrelevant to the movement's efforts.

This sort of selective reliance on race, history, and empirical realities is a strong mark against the movement's carceral policies. The movement wants it both ways when it comes to histories of racism – it seeks to analogize to the suffering of black bodies when it is useful, and to ignore it when it is inconvenient. And the relationship between race and incarceration is extremely inconvenient for the movement. But such maneuvering deservedly raises concerns about ethical consistency and the willingness of the animal protection movement to "turn a blind eye to" strategies and campaigns that derive from "political naiveté or insularity."[5] As this chapter seeks to make clear, race is not irrelevant when it comes to policies of incarceration, and nor is it appropriate to selectively rely on histories of racism in order to instrumentally serve the goals of the animal protection. Steve Wise's project is groundbreaking, but his theoretical project is viewed as more fringe than it should be in part because the rest of the movement does not recognize the inextricable connections between oppression and violence against humans and animals.

To be sure, animal protection groups are quick to reassure their base that all advocacy in support of animals, including carceral polices, is "colorblind" and immune from claims of racial discrimination. But this is nothing more than a self-protective reaction, and when pressed, groups often respond defensively in a voice that seems more at home with the alt-right than the progressive left. For example, when pressed on claims that their advocacy may facilitate discrimination, national organizations have accused their detractors (including the NAACP) of "playing the race card." In the context of an important campaign, PETA remarked that the prosecution of a black man was definitively "not a race issue [because] [w]e don't care if he's orange," and then went on to say "[t]his is not a race issue, [a]re you deaf, or just desperate?"[6] It is enough, the movement often assumes, to simply note that it has a *singular* focus on animal protection *without* any conscious thought given to the structural impacts of its advocacy on race and class. It is a focus on animals, they explain, and human issues may be treated as irrelevant. As Emily Gaarder explained, there are segments of the animal protection movement that are comfortable advocating for whatever they perceive to be in the best interest of animals and treating such concerns as trumping any "other concerns, including sexism and racism."[7] But

---

[5] GAARDER at 155.
[6] *Vick at the Office, Part 2*, PETA (Oct. 3, 2007), www.peta.org/blog/vick-office-part-2/.
[7] GAARDER at 117–47.

as Julia Feliz Brueck pointed out in her book *Veganism in an Oppressive World*, advocacy that imagines animal protection as distinct from and even in tension with other anti-oppression efforts is alienating and limiting in the extreme.[8] Some might even say that advocacy divorced from concern about its impacts on racial minorities is itself racist.

Sociologists, for example, have concluded that the very assertion of colorblindness has the effect of leaving systemic forces of discrimination unnoticed and under-appreciated. Eduardo Bonilla-Silva, for example, wrote a book titled *Racism without Racists* examining the problems with so-called colorblindness in the age of "post-civil rights America."[9] In modern times, "except for members of white supremacist organizations, few whites in the United States claim to be racist," according to scholars like Bonilla-Silva. Whereas "Jim Crow racism explained black's social status as the result of their biological and moral inferiority, colorblind racism," by contrast, understands the different social standing of persons of color as a result of "market dynamics" and certain "cultural limitations."[10] In the process, a colorblind approach to the world (or to animal protection) too hastily dismisses systemic forms of discrimination and injustice as coincidence, or worse yet, irrelevant.

One particularly acute area of racial injustice is the modern criminal justice system. In the twenty-first century, any meaningful discussion of the criminal justice system, particularly a conversation about increasing the frequency and severity of its punishments, must include a consideration of racial justice. To put the matter in Paul Butler's plain-spoken terms, "race matters in criminal justice."[11] For many scholars, the operation of the justice system in the United States is inextricably connected to our nation's history of oppression and racism.[12] As Bonilla-Silva explains, "race influences nearly every aspect of incarceration, including arrest rates, conviction rates, the probability of post-incarceration employment, educational opportunities and marriage outcomes."[13] Thus, a reliance on increased criminalization as a means of promoting animal protection is never truly colorblind or race neutral. For many who teach animal law or animal studies, the unique opportunity presented in such a course is the opportunity to allow students to see how, as Michelle R. Loyd-Paige puts it, "their privilege allows them to be unconcerned about issues that they do not

---

[8] Julia Feliz Brueck, Veganism in an Oppressive World: A Vegans-of-Color Community Project 16 (2017).

[9] Eduardo Bonilla-Silva, Racism without Racists: Color-blind Racism and the Persistence of Racial Inequality in America, xiii (5th edn. 2018).

[10] *Id.* at 2.

[11] Paul Butler, *Racially Based Jury Nullification: Black Power in the Criminal Justice System*, 105 Yale L. J. 677, 725 (1995).

[12] Angela Harris has observed that the modern police officer has grown to understand themselves as "law enforcers in a community of savages, as outposts of the law in a jungle." Angela P. Harris, *Gender, Violence, Race, and Criminal Justice*, 52 Stan. L. Rev. 777, 797–8 (2000); *Id.* at 797 n.74 (quoting Angela P. Harris, *Criminal Justice as Environmental Justice*, 1 J. Gender, Race & Just. 1, 17 [1997]) ("criminals as a class" are racialized as non-white, even though, of course, that is not universally true).

[13] Bonilla-Silva at 34.

think pertain to them."[14] Caging more animal abusers for longer periods of time has become just such a blind spot for the movement itself – privilege makes the movement's mainstream leaders view incarceration and crime policy as irrelevant to their members and their cause. But as Loyd-Paige explains, "all social inequities are linked." For a movement looking to expand its reach, the animal protection movement's affinity for criminal punishment solutions smacks of the sort of "colorblind" racial insensitivity that A. Breeze Harper's anthology *Sistah Vegan* so poignantly critiques.

A striking articulation of the concern about the toxic relationship between race and American criminal justice is Michelle Alexander's conclusion that the modern system of criminal justice, with its focus on incarceration and the concomitant loss of voting, housing, and other rights, is properly thought of as the *New Jim Crow*.[15] No less important, Randall Kennedy posited:

> It is entirely plausible that the white-dominated political institutions of America would not tolerate present conditions in jails and prisons if as large a percentage of the white population were incarcerated as is the reality facing the black population. It is surely possible, to many likely, that if the racial shoe were on the other foot, white-dominated political structures would be more responsive than they are now to the terrors of incarceration.[16]

Whether or not animal protection advocates have the background knowledge necessary to fairly comprehend the justice system's negative racial inflection, it is beyond peradventure that among criminal law and race scholars, this is a salient conversation that deserves to be taken seriously. Pursuing carceral policies is the sort of "colorblind" strategy that risks alienating allies and drawing deserved negative attention from civil rights leaders. As a movement looking for greater social acceptance, alienating researchers and activists concerned with the decades-long war on crime is not a promising strategy. And to be clear, the point here is a substantive one, not merely a critique about the messaging of the movement. There is a problem with the priorities and objectives of the movement that is in tension with racial justice. If the goal was simply to improve perceptions or messaging, then as my colleague and critical race scholar Nancy Leong memorably told me, the movement could just engage in racial capitalism by putting up "billboards with black people throwing red paint on people wearing fur."[17] Instead, the carceral policies of the movement are best understood as symptomatic of the movement's failure to take seriously human oppression, and not merely a failure to properly brand the campaigns as sufficiently race-neutral.

[14] MICHELLE R. LOYD-PAIGE, *Thinking and Eating at the Same Time*, in SISTAH VEGAN: BLACK FEMALE VEGANS SPEAK ON FOOD, Identity, Health, and Society 1, 2 (A. Breeze Harper ed., 2010).

[15] MICHELLE ALEXANDER, THE NEW JIM CROW: MASS INCARCERATION IN THE AGE OF COLORBLINDNESS 2 (2010).

[16] RANDALL KENNEDY, RACE, CRIME, AND THE LAW 134 (1997).

[17] Nancy Leong, *Racial Capitalism*, 126 HARV. L. REV. 2151 (2013).

This chapter proceeds by considering two distinct, race-based critiques of the carceral animal law strategy. First, there is something of a guilt-by-association critique: For a movement already stung by accusations of racial insensitivity, being aligned with the mass incarceration ethos is problematic. It cannot be doubted that the animal protection movement is already perceived by many "as a movement solely for privileged white communities, untouched by the realities that affect marginalized peoples."[18] This backdrop combined with a pervasive perception of criminal punishment as enhancing and entrenching race problems in the United States justify viewing the movement's carceral advocacy with greater skepticism. Second, there is anecdotal evidence that even if criminal justice could be considered a race neutral source of solutions (it cannot), the movement's own criminal justice reforms and advocacy are specifically tainted by implicit bias or elements of racism.

5.1 ANIMAL PROTECTION IS PERCEIVED AS A "WHITE THING" AND THAT IS RELEVANT TO CRIME AND PUNISHMENT

Any conversation about increasing the frequency or duration of incarceration has race and class reverberations. There is no truly "race-free space" in which advocacy about animals or other issues arises, and for a movement that is often "dismissed with the phrase, 'That's a white thing,'"[19] to presume that the pursuit of more carceral policies is irrelevant to race is willful blindness. At the very foundation of the carceral impulse in animal law is the sense that animal suffering is so singularly urgent and so neglected that advocates can or must be singly focused on animal protection, even to the point of rejecting or ignoring overlapping oppression and injustice in society. Emily Gaarder, in her study of women in the movement, documented the willingness of some members of the movement to prioritize animal suffering over "any human concern."[20] A popular narrative she documented was the idea that people "should relegate concerns about their own status in society to the back burner for sake for the sake of animals," because the movement does not have the "time or luxury" to address other social justice concerns. As one of the people studied in Gaarder's research framed a critique of advocacy regarding sexual equality within the movement, "All this energy! What about the animals?"[21] The utilitarian calculus of these champions for animal rights is simple – any advocacy or sympathy for a cause other than animal protection detracts from efforts to reduce animal suffering. Concerns about incarceration, registries or privatized prosecutors are written off as irrelevant, or even in tension with the goals of animal protection.

---

[18] BRUECK at 11.
[19] PATTRICE JONES, *Afterword* to SISTAH VEGAN: BLACK FEMALE VEGANS SPEAK ON FOOD, IDENTITY, HEALTH, AND SOCIETY 187, 188 (A. Breeze Harper ed., 2010).
[20] GAARDER at 133–34 (noting the impulse to support potentially sexist campaigns).
[21] *Id.* at 135.

The notion that the oppression of humans must be ignored, and everywhere treated as irrelevant is captured in the "Non-Humans First Declaration," which purports to set out a set of moral rules for people engaged in animal protection.[22] The declaration is certainly not an accepted credo for all individuals interested in animal protection, but its core values are resonant with the idea of pursuing deportations, imprisonments, and other penalties in the name of protecting animals. The Non-Humans First Declaration makes clear, by its very title, that in all instances animal suffering must be prioritized above human rights, and provides that "No one should be excluded from participation in animal rights activities based on their views on human issues."[23] Tolerance for racism or homophobia or sexism as part of the fight against animal subordination is expected; indeed, it is specified that "no tactical idea should be excluded from the discussion based on its conflict with human rights ideology."

A blog post published on the Non-Humans First website in August 2016 featured a letter written as a "parody" of the intersectionalist perspective on animal protection. The letter started with a cartoon illustrating its theme: advocacy that considers the oppression of all beings is politically correct and wrongheaded.

The author, Nicole Huber, addressed the "letter" to all animals in a facetious tone that is intended to denigrate and make light of human suffering and intersectionality:

> [S]top whining, will you? I know you are being tortured and murdered by the trillions, but that doesn't give you the right to try and grab all the attention. No-one of us goes through this life without trauma – and numbers are just a tool of oppression of the white male cis-gendered heteronormative racist sexist misogynist homophobe capitalist patriarchy anyway. . . . But you need to understand that your plight is just a symptom, not the disease. And we all know that it's no good to treat only the symptoms. We need to get rid of the root of the disease – the white male cis-gendered heteronormative racist patriarchy which was established by white men so that each and every single one of them, from the mightiest king to the most destitute beggar, could enjoy white male privilege at the cost of every other being. . . . Believe me, focusing on dismantling the white male cis-gendered heteronormative racist patriarchy is in your best interest as well. It's just inconceivable that you could be free, that we could just leave you the fuck alone, as long as we haven't got rid of any and all human discontent . . . You see, dear non-human animals, we're all in this together . . . There really is no difference. It's all connected, and you simply cannot get rid of one form of oppression without getting rid of all the others first.[24]

As Julia Feliz Brueck puts it, imagine encountering a movement that purports to be interested in engaging diverse perspectives, but that mocks the history and experience of persons of color, and tells them their "own oppression doesn't

---

[22] *Non-Humans First Declaration*, NON-HUMANS FIRST, https://nonhumansfirst.com/ (last visited Feb. 4, 2008).

[23] *Id.* (NON-HUMANS FIRST).

[24] *Id.* (NON-HUMANS FIRST).

matter."[25] Although most animal protection activists would publicly distance themselves from such polarizing rhetoric the practices and advocacy of many activists are
consistent with the ethos espoused in the letter. Indeed, it is not hard to find racist
comments on the blogs and Facebook pages of leading animal protection groups.
In the context of criminal justice policy, groups justify what they are promoting by
saying that it is in the best interest of the animals – deporting or incarcerating a man,
for example. The parody quoted above could find a welcome home in many alt-right
chat rooms, but the willingness of the movement to overlook or encourage subtle as
well as overt racism is not relegated to the fringes of the internet.

On the contrary, the animal protection movement is willing to join forces with the
alt-right and its allies when the outcome would be short-term gains for animal
protection. One example of such an alliance was the work of animal protection
and environmental activists in conjunction with anti-immigration organizations and
individuals in a 2017 campaign to prevent a factory farm for chickens from opening
in a small Nebraska town. The opposition was comprised of an alliance of those who
were morally opposed to the factory farm, and those who were morally opposed to
the immigrant labor that would work at the facility.

Specifically, the opposition to the chicken facility was largely successful because
of the political connections and canvassing of a few local personalities, particularly
a man named Weingart, who was vehemently opposed to immigration, particularly
by Muslims. As Weingart explained to a town hall meeting on the issue, "Being
a Christian, I don't want Somalis in here," elaborating that "They're of Muslim
descent," and noting that if the proposal to allow the facility was passed, "They're
going to live next to you and you and you – and *me*."[26] This form of advocacy
opposing the farm by Weingart was not a surprise to the animal protection movement. When the animal protection movement approached Weingart to form
a coalition, they were not getting a political novice to handle their campaign;
Weingart had previously successfully "led a petition drive to enact a city ordinance
that would bar 'illegals' from renting apartments, buying homes, or holding jobs in
[the neighboring community of] Fremont."[27]

Some would consider the movement's strategy opposing the chicken farm to be an
application of the adage instructing one to keep his enemies close, or at least
a recognition of the importance of coalition building. The activists' work with
avowed (and effective) xenophobes branded them and the movement more generally as racists opposed to immigration. No one leaves a coalition that denigrates
people because of their ethnicity or religious background with clean hands.
The activists tolerated, even facilitated this discourse, because "[l]ogic dictated
that opposition to the plant would only be strengthened by bringing ethnicity and

[25]   BRUECK at 16.
[26]   Ted Genoways, *Compromised*, NEW REPUBLIC (Dec. 6, 2017), https://newrepublic.com/article/145924
       /fighting-toxic-waste-worth-collaborating-islamophobes.
[27]   *Id.*

immigration into the debate," and the end-result was that a champion for their cause was telling the press that when it comes to living in his community, "Even if there's one [Muslim], there's one too many." The movement was not just silent; it was complicit in amplifying a racist message.

Examples like this reinforce the importance of groups like Encompass, which works to build an "inclusive animal protection movement." Encompass posted a story on their website describing "One Person of Color's Experience at the 2017 National Animal Rights Conference."[28] The account details, among other unfortunate events, the fact that a Latina attendee was approached by a white male and "asked in broken Spanish, 'Why don't Latinos care about animal rights?'" The interrogating man went on to say, "you have to bring more Latinos to the conference."[29] Bracketing the essentialism and offensive nature of these comments, might the white advocates who support pro-carceral and anti-immigrant polices, like that discussed immediately above, have a ready hypothesis for the relative dearth of non-white engagement with the movement?

Campaigns like the one in Nebraska likely occur more often than the movement would like to acknowledge – it is small assists to a racist prosecutor, aid given to a zealous ICE Agent, celebrating the work of a violent police officer, or other less high-profile efforts – and they all present an inexcusable dilution of the animal protection movement's moral standing. Some in the movement take comfort in the fact that they are only seeking immigration consequences like deportation, while others find solace in the fact that they only promote criminal prosecutions and stay out of immigration issues. Combining these discrete pockets, however, the sum total of the movement facilitates virulently oppressive strains of social reform.

Moreover, the animal protection movement's alliance with those who oppose human rights and equality is exacerbated by the fact that sometimes overt racism boils out of the movement. For example, in 2007, referring to the animal trade in China, animal rights hero Morrissey suggested that if you examine the way the Chinese treat animals, "You can't help but feel that the Chinese are a sub-species."[30] Comments like Morrissey's are not the norm, and many activists and animal protection scholars are sensitive to racial injustice. But comments like this and alliances (private or public) with racist groups or individuals expose racial insensitivity and even racism within the movement. This is particularly true given that its leadership is overwhelmingly white and male, further exacerbating the movement's

[28] Kassy O, *One Person of Color's Experience at the 2017 Animal Rights Conference*, ENCOMPASS (Aug. 15, 2017), http://encompassmovement.org/one-person-of-colors-experience-at-the-2017-national-animal-rights-conference/.

[29] *Id.* These exchanges call to mind the reflections of Charles Lawrence III, *The Id, the Ego, and Equal Protection: Reckoning with Unconscious Racism*, 39 STAN. L. REV. 317, 318 (1987) (describing analogous exchanges and saying, "Each time my interlocutor was a good, liberal, white person who intended to express feelings of shared humanity.").

[30] *Morrissey Calls Chinese People "a Subspecies,"* VEGANS OF COLOR (Sept. 1, 2010), https://vegansofcolor.wordpress.com/2010/09/07/morrissey-calls-chinese-people-a-subspecies/.

difficulty in relating to the intersectional framing of the problem. As the byline of a blog called "Vegans of Color" puts it, "We don't have the luxury of being single-issue."[31]

On the other hand, it has been aptly noted that to depict animal protection advocates as "a vanguard of the imperialist majority is . . . taking some license with empirical reality."[32] First, the pervasive perception that the animal protection movement is comprised of and caters to affluent whites may be mistaken. There is data suggesting that veganism is just as common among low-income groups, and there are a number of people taking note of the historical, cultural, and anti-colonialist reasons that people of color may prefer plant-based diets. More generally, many of the critiques of the animal protection movement as racist are overstated or unfair. For example, the average member of the public likely equates animal protection with racism because of the movement's advocacy surrounding issues relating to cultural practices, such as indigenous whaling, or the Japanese dolphin hunts, or the consumption of dog meat by certain cultures. But targeting the abuse of animals by any group of persons is not, standing alone, racist. The fact that animal protection advocacy sometimes singles out practices engaged in predominantly by certain ethnic groups does not, as is frequently argued, render the movement racist.[33] To be sure, avoiding an imperialist approach to the advocacy is critical; however, as Claire Jean Kim eloquently points out in discussing regulations of the live animal markets in San Francisco's Chinatown, it would be perverse to argue that:

> [M]inorities' disadvantages earn them a place at the end of the reform queue . . . Unjust disadvantages in one sphere does not earn unjust advantages in another. Having endured racism and colonialism, subjects deserve justice and reparations from their oppressors, but they do not therefore deserve to dominate women, animals, and nature.[34]

Claire Jean Kim goes on to explain in great detail, for example, that it is possible to be against indigenous whaling and "still be anticolonialist," because it is possible to engage in a "[t]houghtful critique of a racially marginalized group."[35] The reflexive branding of some animal protection campaigns as racist, then, is likely unfair, even if the messaging around the campaign is indelicate and imperfect.

Of course, some of the movement's campaigns go well beyond indelicate framing, and leave no room for doubting their racially divisive connotations. PETA has run advertisements and protests in which their members have worn Ku Klux Klan

---

[31] VEGANS OF COLOR, www.vegansofcolor.wordpress.com (last visited Sept. 25, 2018).
[32] CLAIRE JEAN KIM, DANGEROUS CROSSINGS: RACE, SPECIES, AND NATURE IN A MULTICULTURAL AGE 196 (2015).
[33] A Canadian lawyer and public intellectual, Joseph Fearon, for example, has drawn on a few campaigns to conclude that "modern animal advocacy commonly targets isolated practices of already marginalized groups, piggybacking on racism or sexism to try and get the job done . . ."
[34] KIM at 195–96.
[35] *Id.* at 249–50.

costumes to draw attention to the American Kennel Club's obsession with genetic breed purity.[36] The perversity of privileging genetic purity in any species is a deserving topic of protest, but it is hard to fathom how upon seeing a group of white people dressed in KKK attire and talking about animal rights, an African American would be inclined to view the animal protection movement favorably. These types of outreach efforts should not be expected to draw in curious non-whites who might have otherwise wanted to see what was on the handbill being passed out by the activists.[37] Tactless comparisons to slavery or the Holocaust also have the potential to do damage to the movement. As Angela Harris observes, by assuming that "rights struggles are at some level all the same,"[38] in the eyes of some, the comparisons "erase the specificity – and the seriousness – of each rights struggle . . . inflict[ing] a dignitary harm on the group whose struggle is being referenced to support some other struggle."[39]

On this theme, the 2005 PETA campaign called "Are Animals the New Slaves?" warrants mention. The campaign juxtaposed pictures of black people being lynched, sold, and beaten with slaughterhouse images of animals enduring a similar fate. The campaign prompted a backlash from some prominent black public intellectuals, including one local chapter president of the NAACP who said, "Once again, Black people are being pimped. You used us. You have used us enough."[40] Despite the blowback, PETA ran a similar campaign in 2011. For many, the comparison between African Americans and animals is simply never appropriate. As Claire Jeane Kim explained, it was the scientific theories positing a biologically close relation between African Americans and animals that justified slavery and "lynching in the Jim Crow south."[41] As one black queer animal rights activist emphasized,

[W]e're looking at . . . a pattern whereby blackness is used and commodified at different times and by different groups to further an agenda without offering any type of real solidarity on black issues. And if animal rights doesn't address this, our activism will be no different.[42]

[36] *Do PETA's Race-based Tactics Work or Just Alienate?*, VEGANS OF COLOR (Feb. 19, 2008), https://vegansofcolor.wordpress.com/2008/02/19/do-petas-race-based-tactics-work-or-just-alienate/.

[37] *PETA Protests Westminster Dog Show (Klan Hoods and All)*, L.A. TIMES: L.A. UNLEASHED (Feb. 9, 2007), http://latimesblogs.latimes.com/unleashed/2009/02/peta-protests-w.html (showing photographs and documenting that some people believed it was really a KKK rally).

[38] Angela P. Harris, *Should People of Color Support Animal Rights?*, 5 J. ANIMAL L. 15, 25 (2009).

[39] *Id.*

[40] *Another PETA Exhibit Compares Animal Cruelty to Slavery*, BET (July 21, 2011), www.bet.com/news/national/2011/07/21/another-peta-exhibit-compares-animal-cruelty-to-slavery.html.

[41] KIM at 35. *Id.* ("This idea of the Negro as beast waxed and waned and shape-shifted depending on historical and geographical context . . . but it remains part of the fabric of racial meanings in the United States today.") *Id.* at 36 (quoting Thomas Jefferson from *Notes on the State of Virginia*) ("Negro men preferred white women to the same measure that the [orangutans] preferred Negro women, the males of each species reaching up the Chain of Being in their sexual desires.").

[42] Christian Sebastian McJetters, *Animal Rights and the Language of Slavery*, STRIVING WITH SYSTEMS, https://strivingwithsystems.com/2015/12/27/animal-rights-and-the-language-of-slavery/ (last visited Feb. 4, 2008).

Broadly speaking, throughout US history, non-white people have been likened to animals in an effort to justify identity-based exploitation. "To be moved from the human to the nonhuman side of the paper is to be made a being with no moral claims, a being whose body is only flesh, vulnerable to any kind of treatment for any reason, or for no reason," writes Angela Harris in an essay about the relationship between people of color and the animal protection movement.[43] A likeness or closeness to the non-human animal world is a persistent means of stigmatizing and degrading the humanity of a person. Prisoners are belittled for their animalistic behaviors and impulses. Likewise, one who abuses or kills innocent children, or who is considered hypersexual is derided as an "animal." And of course, when an African American is compared to an animal, including former President Obama, one does not have to guess whether it is a compliment or an effort to disparage and demean.[44] Even in athletics, the black body might be described as "a beast" while the white athlete is more likely considered "supernatural." As Angela Harris observed, "[i]n some ways, animals are to people of color – particularly African Americans – as prostitutes . . . are to women."[45] "The existence of the prostitute creates a dynamic in which the woman, to achieve dignity, must always and constantly dissociate herself from that abject figure. She is set up to seek respectability, to make clear, 'I am not that.'"[46] Comparisons between animals and persons of color by white, or predominantly white activists are, for these reasons, not something that should be taken lightly.

To be sure, there are black activists who have been motivated to action by campaigns comparing the horrors of slavery to factory farming, as some of the stories in *Sistah Vegan* vividly illustrate. But there are others who have been repulsed and turned away from the movement. Particularly for a movement whose leadership is overwhelmingly white and privileged, weaponizing the struggle of minorities as a tool for animal protection can seem opportunistic and insensitive to many people of color. And this is especially true if the movement simultaneously appears unconcerned or dismissive about concerns regarding the connection between racism and increased reliance on the criminal justice system. The highlighting of race in contexts where it is useful (habeas and slavery analogies) and the hiding from the relevance of race in the carceral context threaten to make the movement appear disingenuous in its use of racial identity politics.

No off-the-cuff comment by Morrissey and no set of PETA campaigns speaks for the entirety of the movement. As Pattrice Jones put it in *Sistah Vegan*, the movement is neither "as affluent nor all white as it is stereotyped to be, nor as diverse as it ought to be." But high-profile examples of racism, or coalition building with racists, or even just

---

[43] Harris at 22.
[44] *Id.* at 27.
[45] *Id.* (Harris citing an argument of Margaret Baldwin).
[46] *Id.* at 27.

tolerating racism in the service of prioritizing animal rights will deepen the stereotype and the reality of the movement as primarily serving the goals of privileged whites. Such advocacy makes it easy to relegate the movement to the realm of "distinctly unpopular" people who are largely "human-hating, destructive extremists."[47]

The 2015 killing in Zimbabwe of a charismatic lion known as Cecil provides a useful illustration of the problem. Cecil the lion's killing by a wealthy American trophy hunter was senseless, illegal, and apparently prolonged and painful. The killing of the lion was unquestionably an appropriate source of outrage and protest. It is a valid occasion to discuss the problems with trophy hunting and the trade in endangered animals. Unfortunately, the animal protection movement's lack of connections to communities of color left it vulnerable to a wide range of fair (and less fair) critiques when it came to advocacy surrounding Cecil. Specifically, as Cecil the lion protests were capturing headlines nationwide, many communities felt disgust over the attention the lion was receiving because of the daily injustices of discrimination, poverty, and violence that appear to go unnoticed in some communities. Without deep and meaningful connections of shared purpose in the fight against subjugation and abuse, many people viewed the attention heaped on Cecil by the animal protection movement as a slap in the face.

In the case of Cecil the lion, Roxane Gay, a public intellectual and black feminist, played the role of animal protection critic in a *New York Times* op-ed. As Gay wrote, "I'm personally going to start wearing a lion costume when I leave my house so if I get shot, people will care."[48] Gay continued: "A late-night television host did not cry on camera this week for [black] lives that have been lost. He certainly doesn't have to. He did, however, cry for a lion and that's worth thinking about."[49]

Such a critique should give pause to animal protection advocates – it is terrible to be viewed as apathetic to the deaths of young people in the United States. But such a critique would not ring true, or even be published if the animal protection movement had achieved the status of being a far-reaching force in opposing all forms of social injustice and systemic abuse. Rather than excoriating people for sympathizing with Cecil instead of black men, perhaps Cecil could be used to shine a light on the problems with the culture of violence and the insensitivity to the suffering of all animals, human and non-human. It is impossible for the animal protection movement to be fully engaged on all issues of oppression, because as Lisa Kemmerer explained, "[b]y definition, we cannot simultaneously offer an all-out battle against sexism, racism … and the egg industry."[50] But as Kemmerer emphasizes, what is critical is that activists "must not work against one another in their

---

[47] KIM at 73.
[48] Roxane Gay, Opinion, *Of Lions and Men: Mourning Samuel DuBose and Cecil the Lion*, N.Y. TIMES (July 31, 2015), www.nytimes.com/2015/08/01/opinion/of-lions-and-men-mourning-samuel-dubose -and-cecil-the-lion.html.
[49] *Id.*
[50] KEMMERER at 27.

single-minded dedication to one specific cause." It is wise to specialize, but not if the specialization develops "without knowledge of interlocking oppressions, or without the application of that knowledge."[51] Research is needed on this point, but one might speculate that decreasing oppression for all humans will result in meaningful and long-term improvements in the status of animals in society. Perhaps the very animal abuse that the movement seeks to criminalize is largely non-existent in communities with social and economic security and prosperity. It could be that efforts to fight against food oppression, unhealthy living conditions, and even inaccessibility of housing, education, and healthcare could do a lot to raise the tide of animal protection efforts. Comparatively, incarceration reflects a reification of power and structural subordination.

The carceral strategy further entrenches the view of animal protection as divorced from the more general fights against oppression and inequality. When the movement takes up causes that are particularly popular among middle-class whites, even attracting support from the "alt-right" for its advocacy,[52] the movement cannot be surprised that disadvantaged humans, also fighting for civil rights, will remain silent, or even contest the rising tide of animal status. It is no secret that some supporters of animal protection efforts support far-right politicians in the United States, including Donald Trump. Some in the animal protection movement seek to appease an alt-right donor by not speaking out against his politics, out of an interest in appearing neutral, apolitical, or some other variation on the "big tent" theme. And yet, such overtures and alliances will be seen by civil rights groups for what they are – efforts to prioritize animal interests over general civil and human rights. There is a sense that animal protection is the big tent that includes liberals and conservatives (such as Bob Dole and Rick Santorum), but a movement that aligns itself with opponents of civil rights and racial justice will never be taken seriously as a civil rights cause. Likewise, the movement cannot be considered an inclusive, big tent in any meaningful sense if the only images of persons of color on their website are laudatory mugshots depicting animal abusers who are facing imprisonment.

The point is not that animal protection groups must change course so as to prioritize human suffering. One need not call for (and should not call for) a dilution of the intensity or breadth of the protection sought for suffering animals. Yet the failure to recognize inextricable links between human and animal oppression is debilitating for a movement concerned with social justice. Animal protection is at its best – like any social change movement – when it understands and "works against all oppressions."[53] Advocates for LGBTQ+ rights have come to recognize that advancing human rights

[51] *Id.* at 27.
[52] There are a number of white supremacist or alt-right blogs that have commented favorably on issues relating to animal cruelty prosecutions, particularly when the perpetrator is an African American. Indeed, a common theme on these online forums is the notion that African Americans do not have the integrity or self-control needed to treat animals well.
[53] KEMMERER at 28.

positions more generally will often do more good for their movement than advocating for reforms that are directly targeted to benefit their constituency. But incarceration is a form of oppression, one that has ravaged low-income communities and families of color. The movement's reflexive acceptance of incarceration as a quick and easy solution is superficial, and calls to mind the insight from Dr. Martin Luther King, Jr. that a "shallow understanding from people of good will is more frustrating than absolute misunderstanding from people of ill will."[54] Complacency toward the harms of incarceration by social justice movements is more dangerous than support for tough-on-crime policies by conservative lawmakers. To the greatest extent possible, the movement should avoid messaging that appears to promote animal interests at the expense of human interests.[55] Claire Jean Kim calls strategies that focus on shared ideological commitments the "ethic of mutual avowal," and she has rightly called for prioritizing such an approach, because she regards it as critical to the sort of broader, sustainable success the animal protection movement is seeking.[56] On this score alone, a "get tough on crime" approach to animal law fails miserably. Far from mutual avowal, carceral animal law pits the protection of animals against civil rights reforms.

In sum, the proceeding discussion sheds light on two key premises. First, animal law has a problem in how it has addressed race issues in the past; the movement is perceived by many to be racist. Second, the criminal justice system in the United States has a race problem; it is an enterprise viewed by many leading scholars as irredeemably tainted with racism. Two wrongs do not make a right when it comes to problems of race. Instead, the historical perceptions of the movement as insensitive to racial inequality should impose a heightened burden on any policy that would strengthen or reinforce the primacy of criminal justice solutions. As a substantive matter, subjugating other living beings – literally caging them – is unlikely to result in a meaningful path toward animal liberation, and as a pragmatic or utilitarian matter, if the movement seeks to expand its outreach into diverse communities, carceral policies are likely to serve as a barrier. The intersection of criminal law and race is fraught and well-documented, and by treading into these waters the movement exposes itself to the critiques of commentators like A. Breeze Harper, who laments the absence of training and intellectual engagement among animal protection groups in "antiracist and antipoverty praxis."[57] Paul Butler has taught that race is always relevant when it comes to incarceration. If incarceration and tough-on-crime polices are viewed as racist, then the movement's support (and expansion) of these trends is culpable. Or as another commentator put it, "imagine being part of an oppressed group and seeing a movement that claims to be about justice" propping up and justifying the very institutions and people linked to your oppression.[58]

[54] Martin Luther King Jr., Letter from the Birmingham Jail (1963).
[55] Kimberly K. Smith, Governing Animals: Animal Welfare and the Liberal State 151 (2012).
[56] Kim at 20.
[57] Harper at 35.
[58] Brueck at 16.

Animal protection groups sometimes operate as though their advocacy in support of incarceration, deportation, or criminal registration, among other punitive outcomes, are immune from critique because these objectives are pursued in furtherance of animal welfare. But efforts to combat oppression, including animal protection, are "inextricably linked,"[59] and there is not a safe harbor or zone of activism in which race or class are irrelevant to efforts to promote social justice. A true civil rights orientation recognizes the absence of any "sidelines" to social justice; instead, as one scholar has explained, by "our actions or inactions, by our caring or indifference, we are either part of the problem or part of the solution."[60] The deployment and celebration of the criminal justice system makes the animal protection movement part of the problem of social injustice.

5.2 SPECIFIC ISSUES OF RACE IN THE ENFORCEMENT OF ANIMAL CRUELTY LAWS

Beyond the critique that employing carceral policies as a standard-bearer for the movement reflects, at best, an obliviousness to the race and social justice concerns surrounding incarceration generally, there is also a question of whether the carceral policies pursued in the name of animal protection are uniquely problematic from a racial justice standpoint. That is, beyond abstract concerns, might the movement's reliance on criminal prosecution in particular cases raise red flags about race and oppression.

5.2.1 *Historically Racialized Use of Animal-Criminal-Prosecution: DC As a Case-Study*

There is a sense among animal protection groups that animal cruelty prosecutions are fundamentally different. Thus, one might hypothesize that animal cruelty laws do not have the same racially tinged origins or patterns of enforcement as other criminal laws. Unlike the war on drugs, for example, it is conceivable that the war on animal cruelty had origins that were untainted by racism. Such a supposition, however, appears to be false. Although almost no effort has been made to collect or analyze data regarding the racial demographics of individuals historically imprisoned for animal-related crimes, or to study the enforcement of the laws against persons of color, there is at least one notable exception.[61] Paula Tarankow has studied in detail the animal cruelty prosecutions that occurred in Washington, DC in the decades immediately following emancipation.[62] Tarankow studied what she concludes are the most detailed

---

[59] KEMMERER at 1.

[60] LOYD-PAIGE at 2.

[61] Lacy Levitt et al. *Criminal Histories of a Subsample of Animal Cruelty Offenders*, 30 AGGRESSION & VIOLENT BEHAV. (May 2016) (surveying the literature and noting that "sociodemographic characteristics of these offenders, including gender, race, and age have been virtually ignored.").

[62] Paula Tarankow, *Freedom's New Masters: Surveilling and Prosecuting Animal Cruelty in the Nation's Capital* (unpublished dissertation) (on file with author).

prosecution records for animal cruelty in the country during this period, the prosecution records for the Washington Humane Society from 1880 to 1920. Because many cities did not keep records of these prosecutions, Tarankow identifies the Washington, DC statistics as providing critical context for understanding the backstory to the movement's modern proclivities in favor of incarceration.

Tarankow documents that in the post-Civil War nineteenth century, reformers initially continued to employ the longstanding practice of "sentimental" outreach that was aimed at changing hearts and minds about the importance of animal well-being. This was done with educational programs and outreach, particularly in the DC school system. But during the late nineteenth century, the Humane Society also shifted its strategic focus. No longer was sentimental outreach sufficient; instead, incarceration was deemed necessary in order to compel good treatment of animals. This shift in thinking away from empathy-focused outreach corresponded in time, not coincidentally, to the emancipation of the slaves. The recently freed slaves were viewed by society and the animal protection movement as having been rendered "uncivilized" through the brutality of slavery, and thus criminal interventions were necessary to protect animals. Criminal law, Tarankow finds, provided a way for the Humane Society to address the lacking "moral and political capacities" of those recently freed from slavery.[63]

Although Tarankow's account cannot fairly be regarded as a comprehensive origin story for animal cruelty prosecutions, based on the best and most comprehensive data available, she shows that the initial motivations for criminalizing abuse were not lacking in racist underpinnings. Animal cruelty prosecutions were theoretically "colorblind" in the sense that, as is the case today, the crimes applied to all persons. But the motivation for the carceral turn was the fear of the uncivilized behavior of recently emancipated people.[64]

The labor market also conspired with the racist assumptions about recently emancipated people to justify more criminal interventions. Animal protection advocates took note that the poor, recently emancipated African Americans were reliant on cheap, often unhealthy animals for their economic well-being. The livelihood of these individuals often required the exploitation of animals. Unable to afford more expensive, healthier animals, people of color were the subject of disparate criminal attention for animal cruelty. In a telling historical anecdote, Tarankow found a quote from a horse auctioneer in Washington, DC as reported in a newspaper in 1900: "Get some horse sense about you, gentlemen," pleaded the auctioneer as he tried to sell a less decrepit animal, "Buying old skates like you do,

---

[63] *Id.* at 25.

[64] Between 1881 and 1924 the Washington Humane Society convicted 95 percent, or 25,190 of 26,322 persons arrested. This put the District in the category of one of the most aggressive cities in the country in enforcing animal cruelty. Tarankow has not yet carefully parsed the demographics of these arrests and convictions, but her research shows that the shift toward prosecution in the animal protection movement rested on the conclusion that animal cruelty (and all social problems) were a defect in one's "individual nature."

they'll have you arrested for cruelty to dumb animals."[65] The very purchase of an animal necessary for their work was putting persons of color at risk of prosecution.

One of the most reviled classes of persons from an animal welfare standpoint during this time period were the ash cart drivers, who were exclusively people of low status, mostly African American, and who required horses for their job. Ash cart drivers collected the city's "endless heaps of coal ash lying in alleyways and streets," and in the process would subject their horse or mule to loads that averaged more than 2,000 pounds.[66] As one report from the Humane Society in 1903 notes, "to all appearances the driver is in about as poor keep as the horse."[67] Yet the very same report condemns defense lawyers for arguing against cruelty prosecutions and in favor of empathy for the ash cart worker. The Humane Society quoted the defense bar as arguing that the movement's "solicitude for the horse results in cruelty to the owner."[68] It appears that even within the generation immediately following emancipation, the animal protection movement's "sympathies fell decidedly on the side of animals," and created a context where the well-being of recently emancipated slaves was placed in tension with the well-being and protection of animals. The purpose of the cruelty laws even in their earliest iteration was to pit the interests of humans (mostly black men) against those of animals, rather than seeking an intersectional perspective. Thus, the origins of the movement's shift to carceral policies is no more benign than the origins of the war-on-drugs, or the tough-on-crime era.

During this same period, Tarankow documents animal protection advocates engaged in advocacy and outreach about the causes of animal cruelty. The movement itself became known for raising questions about the capacity of blacks in a post-slavery world to "successfully embrace a life of freedom in the age of emancipation."[69] The cruelty of slavery was now being revisited upon the animals. The criminal law, according to the movement, was a necessary means of instilling morality in a community that had been stripped of its humanity. In the decades immediately following emancipation, the animal protection movement gallingly labeled African Americans the new "slave drivers." Because of their "alleged proclivity to commit acts of violence," blacks were suspected of being generally incapable of treating animals properly. It is no wonder that many of the ancestors of the ash cart drivers and other African Americans have come to view the animal protection movement as racist, and singularly interested in animals at the expense of protecting humans from racism.

---

[65] *Id.* at 34.

[66] *Id.* at 36.

[67] *Id.* at 35 ("[M]any impoverished day laborers who bought the horses in various stages of old age and decrepitude ran them into the ground ... oftentimes leaving them to die in deserted alleys.").

[68] *Id.* at 22 (quoting WASH. HUMANE SOC'Y, ANNUAL REPORT 111 [1903]).

[69] *Id.* at 39.

In sum, using Washington, DC as a case study, Tarankow's research supports a hypothesis that the very origin story of animal cruelty prosecutions is one of profound racism. Although there is no evidence that African Americans were actually perpetrating "the majority of violence against animals," the annual reports and the public outreach tended to "highlight violence by African American men"[70] as the root problem and justification for criminal punishment. Some of the examples of animal cruelty that necessitated a criminal response outside of the employment context illustrate that from the very beginning the criminal response often bordered on absurd. For example, in 1903 the Humane Society prosecuted an African American "boy" who was a "recent importation from somewhere down in Virginia" and who had kicked a dog in order to prevent it from "attacking an organ-grinder's monkey."[71] That such an act warranted imprisonment was taken as a given in the years immediately following emancipation. Equally troubling, Tarankow's summary of prosecutions around the turn of the nineteenth century reveals that then, just as now, animal protection groups derided judges or officials who might reduce a jail sentence "on account of poverty" or difficult circumstances. There was zero tolerance for an intersectional approach that looked at slavery, racism, and poverty as forms of oppression that were linked to animal cruelty. Rather, the mantra for animal cruelty prosecutions has always been, it appears, strict prosecution to the maximum extent of the law.

5.2.2 *The Use of Force by Law Enforcement Against People of Color*

The protection of animals through the criminal law introduces the possibility of new sources of tension and potentially violence by law enforcement against people of color. Outside of the animal protection realm, in recent years the shooting of unarmed people by police officers has become a matter of national interest. A *Washington Post* study that does not control for crime rates shows that African Americans are "24 percent of those fatally shot and killed by the police despite being just 13 percent of the U.S. population," and notes that this means "black Americans are 2.5 times as likely as white Americans to be shot and killed by police."[72] For those concerned with civil rights and social justice, these numbers are a cause for serious reflection and critique. Yet as noted above, there is a sense that the fact of police violence against humans does not trigger outrage or empathy from the animal protection community. As Emily Gaarder documented in her study of women in the movement, activists say publicly what some of the leaders in the field think privately: "I do not like humans."[73] The outrage and protests that follow the shooting

---

[70] *Id.* at 46.
[71] *Id.* at 49–50.
[72] Wesley Lowery, *Aren't More White People Than Black People Killed by Police? Yes, but No,* Wash. Post (July 11, 2016), www.washingtonpost.com/news/post-nation/wp/2016/07/11/arent-more-white -people-than-black-people-killed-by-police-yes-but-no/.
[73] Gaarder at 137.

of a lion, or a zoo animal, much less a family pet, simply are not as common when it comes to human victims of police violence.

Even more unsettling, this perception of apathy toward human violence is sometimes overshadowed by outright support for police violence against people in the name of animal protection. Consider one anecdotal but striking example from Hawaii. In 2015, a video was released that showed an indigenous (and according to one account mentally ill)[74] man approaching a monk seal, apparently in order to do a healing ceremony for the seal.[75] The ten-minute-long video is taken from the perspective of onlookers who called the police, concerned that the indigenous man was harassing the seal. At no time did the individual touch the seal, but he approached the animal and remained for several minutes in close proximity, while speaking and gesturing at the animal. The responding police officer was white and he was seeking to enforce a law designed to protect the seal, an endangered animal of which it is believed fewer than 1,000 remain in the wild. The officer's response to the man's non-compliance and disrespect was a vicious use of force. The officer repeatedly applied pepper spray directly to the man's eyes and nose, forcefully clubbed him with his baton nearly a dozen times, and then kicked him while he was already on the ground. The suspect was eventually arrested, treated for broken bones, and pled guilty to harassing the seal.

Even without crediting any exemption from the law to engage in cultural or religious practices, the most striking thing about the entire encounter is the public's reaction to the police officer's use of force. In the face of considerable and excessive force against the man, no one from the group of persons seeking to protect the seal encouraged restraint by the officer, much less intervened to prevent the excessive force. Instead, you can hear people on the video rejoice after the beating took place. As the man lay face down in the sand with broken bones following the assault by the officer, a woman can be heard crying near the recording device saying, "Thank God they got him," and worrying aloud that she had thought the man was going to hurt the seal (who by this time had peaceably returned to the ocean). Tears were shed for the seal who was not harmed, but the battering of the man who was now lying face down on the beach generated what sounds like cathartic relief. The video images of the police officer's use of force against a man of color do not appear to have gained mainstream support from any animal protection group, but neither did any group condemn the assault.

The support for law enforcement violence is a particularly extreme and vivid example of supporting state-sponsored oppression in the name of animal protection.

[74] Ollie Gillman, *Shocking Moment Hawaii Cop Batters Man with Baton and Pepper Sprays Him Because He Was Harassing an Endangered Monk Seal*, DAILY MAIL (Dec. 18, 2015), www.dailymail.co .uk/news/article-3365766/Hawaii-cop-faces-police-brutality-probe-beating-man-harassing-endan gered-monk-seal-throwing-sand-it.html.

[75] Star-Advertiser, *HPD Cop Beats Man Harassing Monk Seal*, YOUTUBE (Dec. 9, 2015), www.youtube .com/watch?v=3GLJqsqnh20.

The comments posted to media stories and the YouTube video of the incident[76] suggest that many other people are willing to publicly agree with the view that the victim of police violence deserved the beating for bothering the seal. Reading these comments, one is left with the inescapable sense that some animal protection advocates would welcome the opportunity to visit physical violence upon a person who harms animals. The visceral support for this police officer is not so far removed from the supposedly highbrow, lawyerly support of increased incarceration or deportation. There is a willingness to tolerate incarceration, deportation, and physical force in the service of protecting animals. The stereotype of the movement as misanthropic is proven correct when people exhibit a willingness to focus on the "situation of animals to the detriment (or outright dismissal) of other social injustices."[77]

5.2.3 Prosecutions and Race

Racial disparity in the justice system is defined as the unequal treatment of similarly situated persons based on race.[78] The causes can be overt, structural, or more subtle and unpredictable. Racial disparity in the justice system is well-documented and not fairly a matter of dispute. African Americans are released on bail at lower rates than whites; they are disproportionately represented in jail and prison populations; they are more likely to receive higher sentences; and they are even more likely to be stopped by police for questioning or searches in the first place.[79]

There appears to be very little quantitative data about the racial demographics of people charged or convicted of animal cruelty, so sweeping conclusions about the presence or absence of racial disparity in the enforcement of animal cruelty laws would be premature. Based on the limited existing data, it appears that, unlike general crime statistics that consistently show that African Americans are three to four times more likely to be convicted of a crime than whites, it is possible that people of color may not be prosecuted for animal cruelty at a disproportionately high rate. For example, one dataset found that African Americans, who make up about 13 percent of the US population, were charged with about 16 percent of animal cruelty crimes.[80] On the other hand, there is some data that would tend to predict a disparate enforcement burden based on class and race. For example, one study suggests that gender (male), race (African American), and lower annual incomes may correlate

[76] GAARDER at 136.

[77] Id.

[78] SENT'G PROJECT, REDUCING RACIAL DISPARITY IN THE CRIMINAL JUSTICE SYSTEM: A MANUAL FOR PRACTITIONERS AND POLICYMAKERS 1 (2nd edn., 2008), www.sentencingproject.org/wp-content /uploads/2016/01/Reducing-Racial-Disparity-in-the-Criminal-Justice-System-A-Manual-for-Practitioners-and-Policymakers.pdf.

[79] Id. at 2.

[80] Lynn A. Addington & Mary Lou Randour, Animal Cruelty Crime Statistics: Findings from a Survey of State Uniform Crime Reporting Programs 15 tbl.2 (2012), https://awionline.org/sites/default/files/pro ducts/ca-12fbireportfinal040312_0.pdf.

with animal cruelty.[81] But other researchers have found that whites are somewhat more likely than non-whites to abuse animals.[82] More data will be available on this question in the coming years, but at the time of this writing the FBI had only started to track and compile data in NIBRS for a single year. For that year (2016), whites were found to be responsible for 60 percent of the animal cruelty offenses, and blacks were responsible for 25 percent. Moreover, 76 percent of those arrested for animal cruelty in 2016 were white and only 20 percent were black. For all "Crimes against society," the rates of offending are similar (70 percent whites and 24 percent blacks), as were the rates of arrest (70 percent whites and 26 percent blacks).

5.2.4 *Overview of the Vick Case: An Exceptionally Aggressive Prosecution*

Notwithstanding the lack of data pointing to a clear pattern of disparate enforcement, it is worth noting that some of the high-profile animal cruelty prosecutions have involved African Americans. There is probably no animal cruelty case more famous than that the 2007 prosecution of Michael Vick. In one sense, the Vick case could be dismissed as aberrational, because there is truly no other example like it in terms of media interest and public outrage. On the other hand, the movement's response to arguably the most high-profile animal cruelty prosecution in US history is telling, and deserving of reflection in its own right.

Vick was an NFL superstar, a quarterback for a leading team, he had a Nike endorsement, a top-selling jersey, and he is African American. Vick was also responsible for a massive dogfighting operation. No less deserving of mention, Vick grew up in a housing project in the part of Newport News, Virginia that was "so depressed that it was called 'Bad News,'" the same name Vick gave to his [dogfighting] kennel."[83] Vick was ultimately charged federally, pled guilty and served two years in federal prison. Contrary to the narrative often told by animal advocates, Vick's prosecution did not predict or portend a new era of federal involvement in the prevention of animal cruelty. Instead, Vick's prosecution stands

[81]   Michael G. Vaughn et al., *Correlates of Animal Cruelty to Animals in the United States: Results from the National Epidemiologic Survey on Alcohol and Related Conditions*, 43 J. Psychiatric Res. 1213 (2009), www.ncbi.nlm.nih.gov/pmc/articles/PMC2792040/ ("Specifically, our investigation found that the prevalence of animal cruelty was higher among males, African Americans and Native Americans/Asians, native born Americans, and individuals with lower levels of income and education.").

[82]   Clifton P. Flynn, *Animal Abuse in Childhood and Later Support for Interpersonal Violence in Families*. 7 Soc'y & Animals: J. Human-Animal Stud. 161 (1999); Holli A. Kendall et. al, *Public Concern with Animal Well-Being: Place, Social Structural Location, and Individual Experience*, 71 Rural Soc. 399 (2006) (finding evidence of an "underdog" phenomena whereby less privileged persons may show more concern for the well-being of non-human animals).

[83]   Heidi J. Nast, *Pit Bulls, Slavery and Whiteness in the Mid- to Late-Nineteenth-Century U.S: Geographical Trajectories*, in Critical Animal Geographies: Politics, Intersections, and Hierarchies in a Multispecies World 127, 141 (Rosemary-Claire Collard & Kathryn Gillespie eds., 2015).

as an anomaly, an example of what criminal law scholars, including former prose-cutors, have described as an "oppressively exceptional" use of prosecutorial discretion,[84] and a prosecution that highlights the role of race in the justice system. The exceptionalism of the prosecution can be understood in multiple ways.

First, the involvement of federal prosecutors in the case is itself notable, because animal cruelty is not even a federal crime. The Animal Welfare Act criminalized dogfighting, but at the time of Vick's arrest it was only a misdemeanor carrying a maximum penalty of a year in jail.[85] By May 2007, shortly after Vick's arrest, Congress had amended the law to make the offense a felony punishable by up to three years.[86] But under the law applicable to Vick's case, dogfighting was a truly petty crime, so the investing of substantial federal resources in the form of federal investigators and prosecutors in the Vick case is itself exceptional.

Secondly, the charging in Vick's case was unusual. Prosecutors ultimately opted to charge Vick not with dogfighting, but with conspiracy to violate the Travel Act, or the "Interstate and Foreign Travel or Transportation in Aid of Racketeering Enterprises" Act.[87] The Travel Act prohibits the use of interstate travel in the service of certain crimes, including illegal gambling. Federal prosecutions for any conduct under the Travel Act, much less for animal cruelty, are exceedingly uncommon. This is particularly so in the aftermath of 9/11, when prosecutorial resources were spread thin on terrorism and immigration-related offenses. In this case, the federal prosecutors bootstrapped a federal felony for dogfighting out of the rarely used Travel Act, simply because Vick engaged in gambling and moved dogs across state lines. As one commentator opined, "[h]ad Vick's Bad Newz Kennels raised all its dogs locally, kept the gambling limited to locals, and only fought the dogs within Virginia, federal jurisdiction for these particular charges would have likely been absent."[88] It is unique to see a defendant prosecuted federally for, at bottom, simply conspiring to violate state gambling laws.[89]

The prosecution of Vick was exceptional as well because of his sentencing. For his role in the gambling ring, Vick pled guilty and was sentenced to twenty-three months in federal prison. The federal sentencing guidelines for the offense appear to dictate a sentence of *no incarceration* based on the offense and Vick's status as a first-time offender.[90] Sentences outside of the guidelines are, by definition, exceptional. As one

---

[84] Adam Harris Kurland, *The Prosecution of Michael Vick: Of Dogfighting, Depravity, Dual Sovereignty, and "A Clockwork Orange,"* 21 MARQ. SPORTS L. REV. 465, 466 (2011) (describing the Vick case as "at best, as an outlier case and, at worst, as a strange example of the misuse of federal power.").

[85] 7 U.S.C. § 2156 (2007).

[86] The ex post facto doctrine prohibited the increased penalty from applying to Vick's case retroactively.

[87] 18 U.S.C. § 1952 (2011).

[88] Kurland at 472.

[89] *Id.* at 475 (noting that the "Virginia gambling offenses [were] the actual state law felony anchor of 'unlawful activity' that made up the Travel Act conspiracy in Vick's indictment."); *Id.* at 516 (noting that had "Vick's federal case gone to trial, all of the animal cruelty evidence concerning the execution of the dogs should have been excluded as either irrelevant or unfairly prejudicial.").

[90] Apparently, in order to arrive at the agreed-upon sentencing range, Vick "agreed to a whopping nine-point upward departure," a concession that is almost unheard of in federal sentencing. *Id.* at 487.

legal scholar summarized the matter, "prosecutors exercised questionable, if not abusive, discretion ... [and] Vick received an unduly harsh federal sentence."[91]

In addition, it is notable that after being convicted and sentenced in federal court, Vick was subsequently prosecuted by the state of Virginia for dogfighting and gambling.[92] While the dual sovereignty doctrine makes it constitutional for both the federal government and a state to prosecute someone for the same offenses, such dual prosecutions are exceedingly rare.

In short, the decision to prosecute and the nature of Vick's prosecution were remarkable. The intensity of emotion surrounding the Vick case and the willingness to engage in unique charging and sentencing mechanisms is due in part to the nature of the harm to the animals, but scholars like Charles Lawrence would no doubt also identify this as a context in which unconscious racism is playing an important role; it is boiling over.[93]

Beyond the actual prosecution, even the investigation of Vick can be viewed as the sort of quintessential case of racialized policing that has drawn public scrutiny in recent years. The case against Vick began with a non-consensual dog sniff of Vick's cousin's car. There is a large body of research documenting the use of racial profiling to stop African Americans who are driving. Scholars have termed the increased risk of being stopped for African Americans the "driving while black" phenomena.[94] As the first African American woman elected as a State Attorney in Florida recently experienced, driving while black is itself often enough to justify a traffic stop.[95] Recent commentators have lamented the expansion of this profiling into what has been called "parking while black," where racial profiling results in people being ordered out of a car, and potentially frisked or searched based on a parking violation or some other trivial offense.[96] The infamous Ferguson report has a paradigmatic example of parking while black to which Paul Butler poignantly called attention:

> Ferguson police charged a man named "Michael" with "Making a False Declaration" because he told them his name was "Mike." Michael had been playing basketball in a public park and went to his car to cool off. The police approached him and, for no apparent reason, accused him of being a pedophile. They requested his consent to search his car and Michael, citing his constitutional rights, declined. At that point, Michael was arrested, reportedly at gunpoint.

---

[91] *Id.* at 514.

[92] Vick ultimately pled guilty in a deal that resulted in no state incarceration. The prosecutor who arranged that deal following Vick's federal sentence of imprisonment was decried as too soft and accused of using the "race card" to excuse Vick's conduct.

[93] Lawrence at 318.

[94] *See, e.g.,* Adero S. Jernigan, *Driving While Black: Racial Profiling in America,* 24 LAW & PSYCHOL. REV. 127, 138 (2000).

[95] Emanuela Grinberg, *Florida State Attorney Pulled Over in Traffic Stop that Goes Nowhere Fast,* CNN (July 13, 2017), www.cnn.com/2017/07/12/us/florida-state-attorney-aramis-ayala-traffic-stop/index.html.

[96] *See* United States v. Johnson, 823 F.3d 408, 412 (7th Cir. 2016) (Hamilton, J., dissenting) (describing pretextual stop for "parking while black").

In addition to "making a false declaration," [about his name] the police charged Michael with seven other minor offenses including not wearing a seatbelt. Michael had been sitting in a parked car.[97]

Vick's entire prosecution grew out of a similar parking-while-black scenario. Vick's cousin, Davon Boddie, was arrested after a police dog smelled marijuana in his parked car, frisked him, and found seventy-nine grams of marijuana on his person. Based on Boddie's arrest, police sought and obtained a search warrant for Boddie's address, which turned out to be Vick's home. While searching Vick's home, authorities located evidence of the dogfighting ring, and based on these observations obtained a federal warrant to search the home.[98] Persons of color face disproportionate rates of prosecution for drug crimes, not because they are more likely to engage in such behavior, but "because these communities are heavily policed." Similarly, Kimberly K. Smith posited that aggressive enforcement of cruelty statutes will likely have the harshest impact on "low-income minority communities ... not because they're more likely to abuse animals but because these communities are heavily policed."[99] Had Vick's cousin been a white man parked in a predominantly white neighborhood, Vick's role in dogfighting might not have ever been exposed.[100]

5.2.5 *Animal Protection's Reaction to the Vick Prosecution: Race As Irrelevant*

The portrayal of Vick by the media and animal protection groups after his federal indictment is also highly relevant to story of race and animal cruelty prosecutions. Vick became a symbol of a particularly demonized form of animal cruelty, dogfighting. Vick's image almost instantly transformed from the epitome of athleticism and leadership to that of a "street thug."[101] It is not unheard of for a celebrity to fall out of favor overnight if he engages in grotesque behavior, but the targeting of Vick was particularly vicious, unforgiving, and long-lasting. Researchers have found that highlighting acts of animal cruelty is a "common way to establish a minority group as barbaric and un-American."[102] And following the media coverage of the Vick case, the

---

[97] Paul Butler, *The System Is Working the Way It Is Supposed To: The Limits of Criminal Justice Reform*, 104 Geo. L.J. 1419, 1421 (2016).

[98] Blacks are almost four times more likely to be prosecuted for marijuana-related offenses, but data shows they are not statistically more likely to be using marijuana.

[99] Smith at 145.

[100] Standing alone, this result may seem problematic from an animal protection standpoint, at least from the perspective of the suffering dogs. But the point is that the system promises arbitrary, not complete enforcement of our laws. White people operating dog rings just as large may still be doing so undetected.

[101] Lawrence Ware, *Leave Michael Vick Alone: The Racism and Misogyny of Football Fans*, Counterpunch (Sept. 3, 2015), www.counterpunch.org/2015/09/03/leave-michael-vick-alone-the -racism-and-misogyny-of-football-fans/.

[102] Smith at 144. It is noteworthy that the infamous Santeria case, Church of the Lukumi Babalu Aye v. City of Hialeah, 508 U.S. 520 (1993), which pitted religious liberties against animal protection efforts, grew out of a larger national effort by animal advocates to denounce Santeria as demonic and

media frenzy fed a public narrative of non-whites, particularly urban black men, as uncivilized savages. Indeed, the case is credited with creating the urban myth that black men are the primary participants in dogfighting – there is an ahistorical narrative that the black man is holding back moral progress with his obsession for the blood sport of dogfighting.[103] As one author framed the reaction to dogfighting post-Vick:

> The Humane Society quickly sniffed dollars in the fable of the ghetto dogfighting pandemic. One society official branded it a growing nightmare and solemnly declared that there were more than 40,000 professional dogfighting rings in the country and that there were probably dozens more that stage fights in back alleys and abandoned tenements in black neighborhoods. [Others] claimed that thousands of young black gang members and potential gangsters were lathering the streets with blood and gore from wounded, injured and beat up dogs in dog gladiator contests.[104]

In reality, there is probably no more credibility to the moral panic around dogfighting (created by the movement) than there is to the moral panic surrounding animal rights activists as "terrorists" (created or perpetuated by prosecutors and law enforcement). There is very little data to support claims that dogfighting is a prolific practice in black communities. As one commentator has explained, "[t]his race tinged fable just as other fables is long on anecdote, rumor and sensationalism and short, very short, on hard evidence."[105] Evidence suggests, in fact, that dogfighting may be on the rise among white working-class southerners, and the practice's popularity in this country has its origins in white communities, particularly slave-holders and people emulating the aristocratic European practice.

Animal protection groups were very active in framing the narrative around the prosecution of Vick; leading organizations took the almost unheard-of step of filing an amicus briefs with the trial court in a criminal case. Notably missing from the move-ment's discussion of the Vick case, even to this day, is any acknowledgment of the underlying race issues. Their advocacy, they continue to claim, was entirely colorblind and divorced from racial politics. Indeed, the movement defensively characterized race as irrelevant to their calls for maximum sentences. Illustrative was PETA's claim that "We don't care if he is orange. This is not a race issue. White people who fight dogs need to fry."[106] But society's relationship with racism, much less the animal protection move-ment's relationship with race, is far too complex for such a facile statement.[107] By making

---

pass laws across the country that would impose six months imprisonment for any ritual animal sacrifice. SMITH at 130.

[103] Earl Ofari Hutchinson, *Ghetto Dog Fighting: The Latest Urban Myth*, HUFFINGTON POST (Sept. 5, 2007), www.huffingtonpost.com/earl-ofari-hutchinson/ghetto-dog-fightingthe-la_b_63143.html.

[104] *Id.*

[105] *Id.* (noting that some jurisdictions would support claims of surging dogfights with a single case).

[106] *Id.* at 144 (quoting a contemporaneous PETA blog post).

[107] As Melissa Harris-Perry has explained, "[f]or many observers, the decision to demonize Vick seems motivated by something more pernicious than concern for animal welfare. It seems to be about race." Melissa Harris-Perry, *Michael Vick, Racial History, and Animal Rights*, THE NATION (Dec. 30, 2010), www.thenation.com/article/michael-vick-racial-history-and-animal-rights/.

analogies to slavery for one campaign, and then invoking the idea of colorblindness for another, the movement is unwittingly snared in a trap that Thurgood Marshall described when he said that colorblindness was "several centuries too late and at least a generation too early."[108]

Contrary to the movement's claims that prosecuting a black man for dogfighting was the epitome of colorblind justice, the history of dogs and African Americans in general, and Vick in particular make race particularly relevant in this case. As Kimberly K. Smith explained, "African Americans have a long and difficult history with dogs."[109] Both before and after emancipation, dogs were used to hunt down and brutalize African Americans. Pit bulls like those raised by Vick, in particular, were used to apprehend runaway slaves. More generally, "dogs and dog fighting were instrumental in asserting the racial truths and consequences of white supremacy."[110] More generally, the history of dogfighting shows a relationship between the "sport" and demonstrating cultural status.[111] From the ancient Romans to the monarchs of England, dogfighting was celebrated as a "sport" associated with the upper class.[112] The tradition and its associated status emigrated to America, particularly with many of the Scottish and Irish. The role of dogfighting as a status symbol in early America is further reinforced by the conclusion of Heidi Nast that the training of fighting dogs "would have been the preserve of slaves."[113] To put this in context, just a few generations before Vick's Virginia estate was raided for hosting a dogfighting enterprise, blacks were being forced to train fighting dogs, and dogfighting was used as one of the markers of white privilege and status.[114]

Not only was dogfighting historically a symbol of status and one that was lorded over the slaves, but the notion of dogfighting as honorable continued well into the postbellum years, when African Americans "began tenuously to enter the formerly whites-only fighting fray."[115] Like other areas of social society during the Jim Crow era, it was commonplace for the role of blacks in dogfighting be ridiculed and made to look foolish. Although emancipated men could engage in dogfighting if they had the money to do so, an important claim of white superiority became the supposed deficiency of African Americans in training and disciplining a dog as required for the sport of dog fighting. Post-Emancipation, it was commonplace to find lithographs for leading newspapers denigrating blacks and mocking them as hopelessly inferior, and one scholar, Heidi Nast, has focused on a series of lithographs using dogfighting as

---

[108]   Deborah L. Rhode, *Letting the Law Catch Up*, 44 STAN. L. REV. 1259, 1263 (1992).

[109]   SMITH at 146.

[110]   Nast at 128 (compiling research showing the ways in which dogfighting was used as an indicator of status and cultural superiority by white people).

[111]   SMITH at 146.

[112]   KENNETH N. ROBINSON, FROM VICK-TIM TO VICK-TORY: THE FALL AND RISE OF MICHAEL VICK 27 (2013).

[113]   Nast at 133.

[114]   ROBINSON at 32.

[115]   Nast at 133.

the indicator of black incompetence.[116] The images showed African Americans as utter failures when it came to dogfighting. And this is a matter some importance, because in the dogfighting world, scholars have observed that it is common for people to say "I only expect a dog to be as good as the man behind him."[117] The lithographs studied by Nast make clear that as a historical matter, "[d]ogfighting is a decidedly white masculine endeavor at which African Americans are bound to fail."[118] Successfully breeding and fighting dogs was the domain of people of class and wealth, not people of color. This history is not irrelevant to Vick's actions and prosecution.

By the time of Vick's arrest, the sport of "aristocrats" had become a "felony in all fifty states."[119] But Vick's own unique life experience is also highly relevant. Vick was raised in a culture that taught him to understand dogfighting as appropriate, and part of a loving relationship with an animal. Being exposed to his first brutal dogfighting exhibition when he was only seven, and growing up in low-income housing, he learned that one could somehow love dogs and treat them inhumanely.[120] These facts and others that might have been relevant to Vick's prosecution were entirely ignored by the animal protection movement, and yet "it is almost certainly true that our judgments about cruelty are strongly culturally inflected ... [and] [t]his means that the concern about cruelty can easily become (and has often been) a vehicle for ethnocentrism."[121] The point here is not that animal protection groups or scholars are not free to criticize and seek to prevent *any and all* inhumane or abusive uses of animals – there will always be human interests, be they religious, cultural, or financial, in support of abuse. But pretending that race is irrelevant in the criminal prosecution space is not an option.[122]

Understanding that dogfighting was held up as one of the markers that divided the races and separated whites from the "fundamentally inferior,"[123] one can appreciate that the movement's portrayal of Vick as anathema to the moral underpinnings of this country is more than a touch ironic. Dogfighting and Vick are part of this nation's cultural fabric. It is notable that the most high-profile animal cruelty prosecution in decades turns on the prosecution of an African American for the very practice that was flaunted as a symbol of his racial inferiority during his grandparents' lives.

---

[116] *Id.*
[117] Kim at 259.
[118] *Id.* at 259.
[119] *Id.* at 257.
[120] Smith at 148.
[121] Kim at 82–83.
[122] For Claire Jean Kim and others, "there is no race-free space" where scholars or activists can speak "without racial implications." *Id.* at 185.
[123] *Id.*

5.2.6 *Animal Protection and Empathy. Vick's Post-Incarceration Attempts at Redemption*

Animal protection advocates frequently invoke empathy as the cornerstone of the movement, and yet one of the most striking features of the Michael Vick saga is the reaction to Vick after he had served nearly two full years in federal prison. Vick completed his above-guidelines federal prison sentence in 2009, but animal protection groups callously treated the notion that Vick might be permitted to return to gainful employment in his profession as tantamount to allowing him "to get away with murder."[124] After Vick's incarceration, he issued public apologies, paid nearly a million dollars for the rehabilitation of the dogs he injured, partnered with animal advocacy groups to speak out against dogfighting, and participated in empathy workshops.[125] It was Vick's lack of empathy, the movement gushed, that caused his criminal abuse of animals.

Yet there was a sense among the public, and certainly the animal protection community that Vick himself was entirely undeserving of empathy. Theorists and activists alike agreed that he should never be able to resume a normal life, much less a well-paid career as a football star.[126] Indeed, Vick frequently received death threats and had community events he attended, such as fundraisers for children, protested by animal rights groups for several years after he had been released from prison.[127] Giving voice to the feelings of many dog lovers, and the notion that animal protection is a bipartisan concern, conservative TV commentator Tucker Carlson called for Vick's execution *after his release from prison*: "I'm a Christian, I've made mistakes myself, I believe fervently in second chances . . . But Michael Vick killed dogs, and he did it in a heartless and cruel way. And I think, personally, he should've been executed for that."[128] It would generally be irresponsible to credit a rightwing pundit with speaking for the animal protection movement. And yet, Carlson's comments are not far off the mark from those made by some of the foremost leaders of the animal protection movement.

[124] Richard Cohen, *Michael Vick's Sordid Behavior – And the NFL's*, Wash. Post (Aug. 11, 2009), www .washingtonpost.com/wp-dyn/content/article/2009/08/10/AR2009081002454.html.

[125] *The Day I Spent with Michael Vick*, PETA (Jan. 22, 2009), www.peta.org/blog/day-spent-michael-vick /; *Michael Vick and the HSUS's Work to End Dogfighting*, Humane Soc'y U.S., www.humanesociety .org/issues/dogfighting/qa/vick_faq.html (last visited Feb. 4, 2008).

[126] Vick is certainly not the only example of a high-profile athlete committing a crime of violence: data suggests that the rate of domestic violence among NFL athletes is "extremely high." As one researcher put it, "relative to the income level (top 1 percent) and poverty rate (0 percent) of NFL players, the domestic violence arrest rate is downright extraordinary." Benjamin Morris, *The Rate of Domestic Violence Arrests Among NFL Players* (July 31, 2014), https://fivethirtyeight.com/datalab/the-rate-of -domestic-violence-arrests-among-nfl-players/.

[127] Robert Klemko, *Michael Vick Fires Back at Animal Activists*, USA Today: Sports (Mar. 16, 2013), www.usatoday.com/story/sports/nfl/2013/03/16/michael-vick-responds-to-animal-activists/1992935/.

[128] Michael David Smith, *Tucker Carlson: Michael Vick Should Have Been Executed*, NBC: Sports (Dec. 29, 2010), http://profootballtalk.nbcsports.com/2010/12/29/tucker-carlson-michael-vick -executed/.

Joyce Tischler, the mild-mannered, modest woman whose title as the "mother of animal law" understates her charisma and accomplishments, formed a leading animal protection non-profit based on the idea that empathy must not be limited to conventional, easy boundaries.[129] Her group litigates and advocates for rats, mice, pigs, and all animals relegated to the status of vermin or food by mainstream society. Yet Tischler wrote multiple public pieces condemning Vick, even after he had served his entire sentence. Tischler, for example, ridiculed as the "hollow rhetoric of second chance" Vick's opportunity to return to work and society.[130] People heralding empathy for all living beings as a core value apparently could not conceive of allowing a black man who had completed his sentence to return to work. And it must be noted that comments on ALDF's website in response to Tischler's posts on Vick include racist rants that have not been removed in the more than half-decade since they were posted. One commentator applauded Tischler's criticism of President Obama for supporting Vick's efforts to rejoin society by writing:

> Obama needs his Brain Cat Scanned if he thinks this mungrel [sic] deserves a second chance. What the hell is he on???? I say put the dogfighting mungrel [sic] in the ring with Mike Tyson and let Mikes teeth do the talking!!'[131]

This is worth a moment of reflection. A leading animal protection organization's website includes within its coverage of the Vick case a comment arguing that the proper response to a black man who engages in dogfighting is to force him to engage in a human cage fight against another black man. Other comments on other postings by animal protection groups are similarly jarring and racialized.

Moreover, the head of the criminal justice program for ALDF at the time, Scott Heiser,[132] typed a blog post that remains on the website in which he invoked a racial trope and referred to Vick as an incorrigible "thug" (reminiscent of the racist term "superpredator"). Heiser even mocked efforts by the NAACP and others who were calling for "empathy" for Vick.[133] Indeed, Heiser derided efforts to contextualize the Vick case with information about Vick's childhood poverty and exposure to dog-fighting by calling them "ridiculous," and Heiser said he would feel sorry for anyone who would sympathize with such factors.[134] Heiser scolded persons who thought less than a maximum sentence was necessary: "Classic: minimize the conduct and attempt to induce empathy for the defendant." Heiser explained that Vick's

---

[129]   Tischler regularly speaks about the need for empathy, compassion, and more peaceful interactions in the world. She is a coveted speaker on topics relating to the need for the animal protection movement to be inclusive and not divisive.

[130]   Joyce Tischler, *Obama Supports Michael Vick's Second Chance*, ANIMAL LEGAL DEF. FUND (Dec. 30, 2010), http://aldf.org/blog/obama-supports-michael-vicks-second-chance/.

[131]   *Id.*

[132]   Scott Heiser, who was the director of the criminal justice program at the time, has since left ALDF.

[133]   Scott Heiser, *What the Hell Are They Thinking?*, ANIMAL LEGAL DEF. FUND (Sept. 10, 2007), http://aldf .org/blog/what-the-hell-are-they-thinking/.

[134]   *Id.*

defendeis point to his childhood and upbringing as relevant to his sentence, and Heiser responded that "[l]abeling this logic as offensive and insulting is being way too generous."

The animal protection movement insisted that its advocacy for maximalist sentencing and its support for severe collateral consequences for Vick were entirely race neutral. But the reality, particularly when it comes to incarcerating black men, is that "there is no standpoint of racial innocence from which to make" claims of a "race-free-space."[135] Indeed, the movement's defense of its own language and tactics has become, in the words of a leading black vegan commentator, "defensive and downright hostile."[136] Illustrative of the movement's defensiveness, Tischler went so far as to write an open letter to the president of the Atlanta Chapter of the NAACP excoriating his call for restraint by the media and the movement with regard to Vick. That the animal protection movement thought it was wise to condemn the NAACP's position on an issue of race and criminal justice is itself striking. Tischler rebuked the NAACP, saying their "active embrace of Vick appears to be a classic case of the *good old boys* circling the wagons to protect one of their own." To many such a comment would be a stunning shot across the bow of intersectional efforts. The founder of a major animal protection organization referred to the conduct of the NAACP in advocating for compassion with regard to the prosecution of a black man as tantamount to a "good old boys'" club, a phrase that is associated with white men, particularly southern white men who bestow undeserved privilege on their kind.[137] It is unlikely that the irony of this poor word choice was missed on the NAACP. As A. Breeze Harper has observed, even in the context of fighting for social justice, institutionalized racism has become invisible to members of the animal protection movement.[138] Persons who have dedicated their lives to social justice may be "convinced that they are exempt from" racism, and thus they may ignore subconscious or structural forms of racial oppression. The animal protection movement goes to great lengths to avoid infighting within its own ranks, and yet when the question of carceral animal law is up for debate, many members of the movement showed no restraint in attacking civil rights organizations, including the NAACP. Tucker Carlson may be the easiest target, but the calls for Vick to be placed in his own fighting pit, neutered, caged, or killed were coming from (or condoned by) a movement that trades on the need for compassion, understanding, and empathy.[139]

---

[135]   KIM at 196.
[136]   A. BREEZE HARPER, *Connections: Speciesism, Racism, and Whiteness as the Norm*, in SISTER SPECIES at 76–77.
[137]   *See* Merriam-Webster Dictionary, www.merriam-webster.com/dictionary/good%20old%20boy ("[A] usually white Southerner who conforms to the values, culture, or behavior of his peers").
[138]   HARPER, *Connections* at 77.
[139]   At the federal courthouse some people identified by the media as animal rights protesters held signs with slogans like "Neuter Vick." Mike Kulick, *Vick's Mixed Welcome*, RICHMOND.COM (July 27, 2007), www2.richmond.com/news/2007/jul/27/vicks-mixed-welcome-ar-593919/ (quoted in Kurland at 471 n.24).

Even if animal protection groups truly believed that any limited defense of Vick was normatively intolerable, it should give any intersectionally aware movement pause that the polling at the time of the Vick case showed that more than 50 percent of African Americans believed that the press coverage of Vick was unfair, while only 12 percent of whites felt similarly. Only a movement that speciously believes that Vick's defenders were themselves racist, or playing the race card, could ignore such figures.

The reason for such ferocious advocacy by the movement when it came to Vick was that the Vick prosecution created a media frenzy for animal protection groups. There was a sense, as with many high-profile prosecutions, that groups could benefit from the "massive short-term publicity."[140] Many organizations joined the team so that they could take part of the credit. The Humane Society and other groups "helped build the case against Vick."[141] One company created a Michael Vick figurine chew toy for dogs – evoking images of the vicious dogs that once chewed on fugitive slaves – and animal protection groups gratefully accepted the proceeds from its sales.[142] Presumably because of the popularity of the cause among donors, even five years after Vick's prison sentence was completed, activists continued to circulate petitions and organize protests calling for Vick to be banned from the NFL. Tischler opined that President Obama's support for Vick's efforts to rejoin society and the NFL "trivialized" the atrocities committed by Vick. As a petition from another organization put it, "We MUST send the message that we won't be party to the torture of animals by conveniently forgetting what he has done."[143] But it is unclear what the movement expected – would they have been satisfied if Vick was playing football for six figures in a foreign football league instead of making millions in the NFL? Would they have been okay with him working as a sports broadcaster? Or would justice only have been served if Vick was forced to return to the low-income, subsidized housing of his childhood? It is difficult to read the calls to cage Michael Vick by members of the movement – unspeakable as his animal abuse was – without questioning whether its carceral tendencies have corrupted or blinded the movement's general humanity when it comes to animal cruelty. Raw emotion more than reason was certainly at play in the movement's advocacy in the Vick case. Or as scholars like Charles Lawrence would explain, the Vick case was an example in which the unconscious racism of our society boiled up to the surface.[144]

Ultimately the Vick case and the accompanying media coverage gave rise to a victory for the carceral animal law movement. In the wake of the Vick prosecution,

[140]   Kurland at 469.

[141]   SMITH at 144.

[142]   Charlie White, *Michael Vick Dog Chew Toy: Payback's a Bitch*, GIZMODO (Aug. 8, 2007), http://gizmodo.com/287220/michael-vick-dog-chew-toy-paybacks-a-bitch.

[143]   Mike Chiari, *Petition Calls for Michael Vick to Be Banned from Jets Training Camp Site*, BLEACHER REP. (Apr. 8, 2014), http://bleacherreport.com/articles/2021327-petition-calls-for-michael-vick-to-be-banned-from-jets-training-camp-site.

[144]   Charles Lawrence III, *Unconscious Racism Revisited: Reflections on the Impact and Origins of "The Id, the Ego, and Equal Protection,"* 40 CONN. L. REV. 931 (2008).

several states increased penalties for dogfighting, and Congress made dogfighting a felony as opposed to a misdemeanor.[145] Nonetheless, history is unlikely to judge the movement's involvement in the Vick case favorably. As one scholar put it, the animal protection movement's reaction to and handling of the Vick case demonstrated that the movement was "ill equipped to appreciate the racial dimension of animal welfare policy."[146] Rather than dismissing the NAACP (and a majority of African Americans) when concerns are raised relating the treatment of a black man, and instead of insisting that carceral animal law strategies are thoroughly colorblind, Claire Jean Kim has explained that "we should instead understand race as constituting the very cultural frame through which the story came to be read."[147] Kim concludes that any organization that believes it is *above* or outside of race and power dynamics defeats any claim by that organization to be considered an advocate for social justice.[148]

5.2.7 *Beyond Vick: Racialized Crimes and Racism in the Implementation of Criminal Animal Law*

5.2.7.1 Racialized Crimes

The above discussion raises the question of whether, beyond the Vick case, there may be signs that criminalization in the animal law realm is racially inflected. In several instances, the answer appears to be a resounding yes.

As for dogfighting, Heidi Nast has explained that it was during the recession of the 1980s that dogfighting first became more commonplace among African Americans, with the dogs being used to "protect drug dealers." During this same period, as dogfighting became increasingly associated with drug dealers and minorities, the practice evolved to be regarded as barbaric, rather than aristocratic.

Crimes and penalties for dogfighting became popular when the practice moved from the upper class to the lower class, and largely across the racial divide. Few would disagree – because of anecdote or cultural conditioning – that dogfighting is often associated with black men, particularly urban black men. Indeed, in some of the research regarding the link between human violence and animal abuse, researchers have treated dogfighting as a confounding variable that may skew rates of animal abuse, because of varying societal standards around dogfighting. In particular, one set of researchers found that in their dataset the only incidences of animal cruelty by non-violent inmates were dogfighting by African Americans,

---

[145] Kurland at 469.
[146] Smith at 148.
[147] Kim at 254–55 (explaining the explosiveness of the Vick case because Vick was the "most animal of humans [the Black man]" and the victim "was the most human of animals [the dog]").
[148] *Id.* at 276.

and thus they worried that varying degrees of social acceptability surrounding dogfighting along class or race lines could skew their data.[149]

In light of such racial inflections, it is notable that to this day Congress has *only* criminalized one form of animal cruelty at the federal level: the racially charged and publicly recognized practices of animal fighting (both dog and cockfighting).[150]

Cockfighting, the only other federally criminalized form of animal cruelty, also has strong race and class inflections. As historian Jeff Forret has discovered, during the antebellum years in particular, unlike horse racing and similar events that were limited to the "gentry," "cockfighting in particular attracted men from all ranks of society," and slaves and poor whites participated in these events together.[151] More recently, as one sheriff's deputy explained the popularity of the practice in modern America, "I think as more Hispanics come from Mexico, Cuba, the Dominican Republic – places where their heritage teaches cockfighting as a national pastime – it's growing."[152] Indeed, in Mexico and some Latin American countries cockfighting is still legal, and an encyclopedia of "Latina Folklore" explains that "Cockfighting has a special place in the culture of Mexican Americans."[153] According to at least one commentator, "Anglo American culture tends to depict cockfighting in a negative or absurd light, Mexican Culture exalts it."[154] It would be a serious mistake to essentialize and assume that cockfighting is important to all persons of Mexican or Latin American culture, but it cannot be doubted that cockfighting has a certain cultural valence that is intertwined predominantly with non-white cultures. Academic essays defend the practice on cultural terms, and there have even been petitions gathering thousands of signatures in support of legalizing the practice based on the perceived need to protect non-white cultural autonomy.[155]

In contrast to these animal-fighting crimes that are now associated primarily with non-whites and punished federally, are the range of abusive uses of animals for entertainment that go largely unnoticed. For example, the practice of fox and coyote penning, another form of "entertainment" that has remarkable similarities to dog fighting, remains legal in several states and under federal law. Penning involves enclosing a fox or coyote in a pen while several dogs compete to chase and brutally tear apart the cornered and outnumbered animal. It is literally a fight to the death

[149] Linda Merz-Perez et al., Childhood Cruelty to Animals and Subsequent Violence Against Humans, 45 Int'l J. Offender Therapy & Comp. Criminology 556, 563 (2001).
[150] Federal law criminalizes both dogfighting and cockfighting, both of which are strongly associated with non-white traditions in modern society.
[151] Jeff Forret, Race Relations at the Margins: Slaves and Poor Whites in Antebellum Southern Countryside 61 (2006).
[152] Kevin Smetana, Culture, Law Clash in Cockfighting, St. Petersburg Times (Mar. 15, 2009) 1B.
[153] Christopher Gonzalez, Pelea de Gallos (Cockfighting), in Celebrating Latino FolkLore: An Encyclopedia of Cultural Traditions 898–900 (Maria Herrera-Sobek ed., vol. 3, 2012).
[154] Id. at 899.
[155] Petition to Legalize Cockfighting in the U.S., United Nations of Cockfighting, https://unofc.wordpress.com/signature-petition/petition-to-legalize-cockfighting-in-the-u-s/ (last visited Feb. 4, 2018).

(albeit a rigged one) between canines. But unlike dogfighting, penning has received very little public attention or legislation, and anecdotal evidence suggests the practice occurs overwhelming in white communities.[156]

Similarly, in response to the movement's effort to ban fox hunting in the United Kingdom, an impassioned cultural defense emerged. Fox-hunting aristocrats, Prince Charles worried, were being persecuted: "I would not dare attack an ethnic minority in the way that supporters of fox hunting [were] being persecuted."[157] Hunting advocates piggybacked on the Prince's statements, declaring that the anti-fox hunting crusade had "nothing to do with animal rights – it is a class issue . . . Any other minority would have their rights respected."[158] Closely related to the defense of fox hunting are the passionate legal efforts that are undertaken to protect all manner of hunting in the United States. The killing of innocent wild animals, unlike dogfighting, is deemed worthy of constitutional protection in many states, and statutes criminalize efforts to interfere with hunting in other states. Unlike animal fighting, hunting is overwhelmingly associated with white men; data shows that 86 percent of fisherman are white while 7 percent are African American, 94 percent of hunters are white and 3 percent are African American.[159] Most hunting is not for sustenance or survival, but rather is legally sanctioned animal killing for sport.

Numerous other examples of harming animals for entertainment – from animal racing, to rodeos, to fur farms – further illustrate the point that animal cruelty, especially at the federal level, takes a quite specialized – some might say racialized – approach to what should be criminalized. Bruce Friedrich is one of the few people in the animal protection movement to have called attention to this incongruity:

> Dogfighting is justifiably illegal in all fifty states and under federal law, but it is not the worst abuse of animals happening in the United States . . . Compare Vick's crime to the opening line of a front page story in the Washington Post: "Nearly 1 million chickens and turkeys are unintentionally boiled alive each year in U.S. slaughterhouses."[160]

While trips to Sea World, the circus, and horse races are celebrated as venerable family entertainment, the practices with the greatest connections to people of color – dog and cock fighting – represent the sole federal animal cruelty crimes. Many of the non-criminalized forms of animal entertainment traditions are predominantly

[156] PROJECT COYOTE, INDIANA COYOTE "PENNING": AN INSIDE LOOK AT ANIMAL ABUSE AND CRUELTY, www
     .projectcoyote.org/documents/IN_Penning_Report_PC_ALDF_AWI_Final_low_res.pdf.
[157] *Prince: I'll Leave Britain over Fox Hunt Ban*, SCOTSMAN (Sept. 22, 2002), www.scotsman.com/news
     /politics/prince-i-ll-leave-britain-over-fox-hunt-ban-1-1377082.
[158] *Id.* Ben Johnson, Fox Hunting in Britain, HISTORIC UK, www.historic-uk.com/CultureUK/Fox
     -Hunting-in-Britain/ (last visited Feb. 4, 2018); *Foxhunting*, ENCYCLOPAEDIA BRITANNICA, www
     .britannica.com/sports/foxhunting (last visited Feb. 4, 2018) (noting that the practice was banned in
     2005).
[159] U.S. FISH AND WILDLIFE SERV., 2011 National Survey of Fishing, Hunting, and Wildlife-Associated
     Recreation 28, 31 (rev. 2014), www.census.gov/prod/2012pubs/fhw11-nat.pdf.
[160] Bruce Friedrich, *Still in the Jungle: Poultry* Slaughter *and* the USDA, 23 N.Y.U. ENVTL. L.J. 247, 250
     (2015).

enjoyed by wealthier, white people. Describing the Kentucky Derby, one African American writer said, "I've always been fully aware that the elite and lily-white sporting event isn't really for me – for *us*."[161]

Moreover, as a quantitative matter, the crime of dogfighting potentially raises the same problematic issues of racially disparate impact that infect the justice system more broadly. While data about race in the context of animal cruelty more generally is very limited, there is data pointing to disparate racial impacts in the context of dogfighting prosecutions. For example, in the five years following the Vick case, blacks accounted for 74 percent of all arrests for dogfighting, a nineteen-percent increase over the five years prior.[162] The actual number of blacks arrested for dogfighting tripled from 64 to 306 within this same time period, and out of all the racial groups, blacks were the only group to have experienced an increase in dogfighting arrests in the five years following Vick's conviction.[163]

5.2.7.2 Race and Carceral Animal Law More Generally

While the crime of dogfighting and Vick's case in particular provide a useful platform for discussing the unsettling intersection of animal cruelty, race, and the law, these are not isolated examples.

The case of Andre Robinson, although less prominent, is another helpful illustration of the way race has come up in the context of animal cruelty prosecutions.[164] In 2014, Robinson was caught on video luring a stray cat toward himself, and then kicking the animal nearly twenty feet through the air.[165] While acknowledging the depravity of kicking a cat, defense lawyers and lawyers for Legal Aid were caught off-guard by the intensity of animal protection advocates' calls for Robinson's incarceration. "The nature of the crime should not automatically mandate a jail sentence if a person is found guilty," noted a Legal Aid attorney who is skeptical of any reflexive calls for a carceral solution to social problems.[166] Anthony Cheeseboro, a professor at

---

[161] Andrea Arterbery, *A Black Fashion Journalist Went to the Kentucky Derby and Here's What Happened*, ESSENCE (May 9, 2016), www.essence.com/2016/05/09/black-fashion-journalist-kentucky -derby.

[162] ROBINSON at 8–9. Data obtained by examining over 643 criminal arrests for "fighting" between 2002–12 from an animal cruelty conviction database, www.pet-abuse.com.

[163] *Id.*

[164] Tatiana Schlossberg, *Should a Cat-Kicker Go to Jail? Readers Respond*, N.Y. TIMES: CITY ROOM (Sept. 30, 2014), https://cityroom.blogs.nytimes.com/2014/09/30/should-a-cat-kicker-go-to-jail-readers -respond/ ("However, several commenters focused on the racial dimensions of this particular case – that imprisonment disproportionately affects black men and that the problem of mass incarceration is not helped by putting those convicted of misdemeanors in jail.").

[165] Stephanie Clifford, *He Kicked a Stray Cat, and Activists Growled*, N.Y. TIMES (Sept. 29, 2014), www.nytimes.com/2014/09/30/nyregion/animal-abuse-gains-traction-as-a-serious-crime-with-jail -more-often-the-result.html.

[166] ROY WALMSLEY, INT'L CTR. FOR PRISON STUD., WORLD PRISON POPULATION LIST (10th edn., 2013), www.prisonstudies.org/sites/default/files/resources/downloads/wppl_10.pdf (noting that data is not available for China and North Korea).

Southern Illinois University, went further and described the racial dimension in the Robinson case as obvious based on the photograph that accompanied the New York Times story.

The picture accompanying the story, Professor Cheeseboro explained, "showed Mr. Robinson in the foreground, with animal rights activists – three white women – standing behind him" with looks of condemnation.[167] He claims that upon looking at these grimacing middle-class white women, many African Americans will think, "They probably care less about a young black man being killed by police than they do about this cat."[168]

This insight conveys the failure of the movement to understand the way that a criminal justice focus derails intersectional efforts. Cheeseboro is right: the image of disapproving white persons advocating for maximalist sentencing against young black men sends a signal that will not be missed by civil rights leaders, much less people of color considering joining the movement. Advocating for increased incarceration – particularly for the most over-represented demographic in our society, young black men – for a first offense is not an act that can be viewed as race-neutral in the twenty-first century. This sort of advocacy signals what so many people have come to believe, that animal protection advocates appear to be hypocrites – they are not against all forms of oppression, just non-human oppression. The movement does not, they will argue, regard all injustices as inextricably linked, but rather prioritizes the suffering of animals over that of humans.

The substantive concern here is that by employing a racially tainted criminal justice system to cases like those of Robinson and Vick, the movement is part of the country's story of injustice and oppression. Changing the oppressive and violent conditions that characterize society's treatment of animals is not as simple as pursuing supposedly "colorblind" pro-incarceration policies. A predominantly white movement seeking comfort (not true reform) from what is called the *New Jim Crow* reflects a deliberate ignorance about the connectivity between human and animal violence. Animal protection advocates cannot ask of mainstream Americans (with regard to animals) what they are not willing to do themselves (with regard to humans): to reject subordination and oppression. The suggestion here is not that such people should be categorically exempted from criminal prosecution for such acts. But these cases illustrate that, as A. Breeze Harper has posited, those "who are privileged must give way so that others" and other strategies can bring "new social justice concerns and methods to the activist table."[169] The fight for animal protection, leading theorists have noted, is a fight against "subordination, domination and oppression."[170] Just as the movement regards people who, for example, consume animals as intolerably self-justifying their behavior through "loopholes," (such as "humane meat"), so too

---

[167] Schlossberg.
[168] *Id.*
[169] KEMMERER at 29.
[170] *Id.* at 32.

does the movement look for an exception to anti-subordination and anti-oppression principles when it comes to incarceration. As A. Breeze Harper notes, in reflecting on the collective naiveté of the animal protection movement when it comes to racism, how can the movement exempt itself from the sort of "emotionally difficult self-analysis[171] that we demand from speciesists?"

A final category of race and animal cruelty concerns comes up in the context of factory farms. Not infrequently during my work on this project, people remarked "What about abuse on factory farms?" To be sure, the focus of the critique on carceral animal law as a tool of racial or other oppression has focused on prosecutions based on rogue acts of abuse – kicking a cat, harassing a seal, or fighting dogs. One might reasonably conclude that if the criminal law's focus was redirected away from these discrete acts of abuse and toward the sort of systemic suffering inflicted at factory farms, then concerns about perpetuating oppression would dissipate. The reality, however, is more complicated. Although prosecutions inside the factory farm are rare, those that do occur highlight an unmistakable element of race and class that permeates these prosecutions.

Factory farms are one of the most dangerous workplaces in America. The workers endure horrible working conditions, are desensitized to violence, and paid very little. Each day they perform dangerous, labor-intensive tasks and are forced to reach quotas that mandate a speed of production that many argue is impossible to sustain humanely and safely.[172] Studies have found that the working conditions in factory farms may actually make people more violent.[173] As Upton Sinclair observed, "men who have to crack the heads of animals all day seem to get into the habit, and to practice on their friends, and even on their families, between times."[174] These facilities may very well be creating a class of animal (and human) abusers by desensitizing the workers and subjecting them to terribly violent and unsafe working conditions.

Of course, these desensitizing and dehumanizing impacts are not borne equally across class and race. The vast majority of farmworkers in the United States are non-white, with 75 percent of them being Latina or Latino.[175] This means that the run-of-

---

[171] Harper at 77.

[172] U.S. Dep't of Labor, Findings from the National Agricultural Workers Survey 2013–2014: A Demographic and Employment Profile of United States Farmworkers (2016), www.doleta .gov/naws/pages/research/docs/NAWS_Research_Report_12.pdf (2013–14 report stating that 62 percent of farmworkers self-identified as non-white).

[173] See, e.g., Amy J. Fitzgerald et al., *Slaughterhouses and Increased Crime Rates: An Empirical Analysis of the Spillover from "The Jungle" into the Surrounding Community*, 22 Organization & Enviroment 158, 158 (2009).

[174] Upton Sinclair, The Jungle 18–19 (1946) [1905]; See also Immanuel Kant, Lectures on Ethics at 213 (Peter Heath & J. B. Schneewind eds., 1997) (noting that "in England, no butcher, surgeon, or doctor serves on the twelve-man jury, because they are already inured to death.").

[175] It is estimated that 76 percent of all agricultural workers are Latino, and some sources suggest that as much as 70 percent of the agricultural work force is undocumented. Farmworker Justice, Selected Statistics on Farmworkers 2 (2014), www.farmworkerjustice.org/sites/default/files/NAWS%20data %20factsht%201-13-15FINAL.pdf.

the-mine prosecution from a factory farm pits the resources of the state and main-stream society against some of the most disadvantaged people in our society, many of whom are people of color. Political scientist Timothy Pachirat has provided a compelling exposé of work in a slaughterhouse that kills between 2,200 and 2,500 cows per day, noting that the slaughterhouse employed "close to 800 nonunionized workers of which the vast majority were immigrants and refugees from Central and South America, Southeast Asia, and East Africa."[176] It is these low-level employees, if any, that are likely to face prosecutions for animal abuse in a factory farm, and yet it is the "front office," where an all-white team of sales staff, receptionists, and upper management work to ensure the rate of killing in the slaughterhouse is sufficiently high. The front office is divided from the rest of the slaughterhouse by a "metal wall."

> This wall both demarcates and enables the volatile combinations of citizenship, race, class, and education that separate the industrialized slaughterhouse's zones of privilege from its zones of production. The wall divides categories as well as physical space: front office versus back room; task-conceiving versus task-executing; creative versus rote; managerial versus subordinate; north versus south; white versus brown, yellow, and black; clean versus dirty; "civilized" versus "barbarian."[177]

The metal wall also demarcates the boundaries of prosecution for animal abuse. In the rare instances when slaughterhouse employees are held criminally liable for animal cruelty, those residing in the air-conditioned, sterile comfort of the "front office" are almost never implicated.[178] But even to say that the front office staff and executives escape criminal liability is to understate the problems of race and class endemic to this system. The division of labor allows the executives to affirmatively blame and scapegoat the low-income workers for the mistreatment of animals. The people working for poverty wages are denigrated as "bad apples" when a whistleblower reveals animal suffering, and through this process upper-level management is absolved of any responsibility. By pointing the finger at the low-level, often non-white employee the company avoids any concerns about structural or systemic abuses, or what Philip Zimbardo might describe as the "rotten barrel" that corrupts the apples within.[179]

Illustrative is the high-profile investigation at the Bettencourt Dairy farm in Idaho, which revealed abuse to the cows that led to protests and calls for product boycotts.

---

[176] Timothy Pachirat, Every Twelve Seconds: Industrialized Slaughter and the Politics of Sight 17–27 (2011).

[177] *Id.* at 27.

[178] Snejana Farberov, *Nine Arrested for Animal Cruelty at Wyoming Pig Farm Where Workers Were Caught on Video Brutally Punching Sows and Flipping Piglets in the Air*, Daily Mail (Dec. 26, 2012), www.dailymail.co.uk/news/article-2253325/Nine-arrested-animal-cruelty-Wyoming-pig-farm-workers -caught-video-brutally-punching-sows-flipping-piglets-air.html (noting the prosecutions of nine pig farm workers); *Farm Workers in Undercover Video Charged with Animal Abuse*, NBC News (Feb. 13, 2014), www.nbcnews.com/news/investigations/farm-workers-undercover-video-charged-animal -abuse-n29541 (noting the prosecutions of four dairy farm workers).

[179] Philip Zimbardo, The Lucifer Effect: How Good People Turn Evil (2008).

Almost immediately after the investigation video was publicized, the executive team for the dairy lamented the abuse as "devastating" and vowed to cooperate with local prosecutors. Cooperation in this sense meant ensuring the successful prosecution and deportation of the low-level employees. No managers or executives for Bettencourt Dairy were prosecuted, but three low-level employees, Jesus Garza, Jose Acensio, and Javier Victor Rojas Loayza, were all convicted of animal abuse. Indeed, legislators in the state affirmatively complimented the owners of the dairy for taking steps to aid with the prosecution of these men. Legislators lamented as unfair to the dairy industry the negative media attention that continued *even after* the prosecution of these men. In the end, then, the executives were treated as heroes by the leaders of their state.

Many other investigations and prosecutions have followed a similar pattern – purported shock and disavowal by the executives, and prosecution of the low-level employees who are oftentimes recent immigrants, or people of color. The prosecutions allow for a collective sense of relief at our social rejection of abuse, and a tacit acknowledgment that it is savage, low-income individuals, often people of color, who are causing harm to animals. These prosecutions, perhaps no less than those of Vick, entrench oppression and scapegoat people of color as the instigators of animal suffering. Consuming meat produced at a factory farm is not a moral problem; the issue, we are taught, is the lack of morals among the immigrant workers at these slaughterhouses.

Another striking example of corporate (and racial) scapegoating in this context is the Hallmark Meat investigation. In 2008, two men, Daniel Ugarte Navarro and Rafael Sanchez Herrera, pled guilty to animal abuse charges stemming from an undercover investigation of the Hallmark Meat Company.[180] Navarro was sentenced to nine months in jail, while Herrera (who has two American children) was sentenced to six months incarceration and ordered to be deported from the country.[181] The company's CEO, Steve Mendell, released a statement shortly after the investigation which expressed his disbelief over the brutal behavior of his workers: "Words cannot accurately describe how shocked and horrified I was at the depictions contained on that video ... We have taken swift action regarding the two employees identified on the video and have implemented aggressive measures ..."[182]

One can imagine that sensationalized news coverage would focus on the immigration status of the offending laborers, and again celebrate the courage of the executive who is willing to condemn his entirely expendable labor force. More generally, as political scientists have explained, "characterizing a group as barbaric and uncivilized

---

[180]   *Former California Slaughterhouse Worker Sentenced in Cow Abuse Case*, L.A. TIMES: L.A. UNLEASHED (Sept. 25, 2008), http://latimesblogs.latimes.com/unleashed/2008/09/california-slau .html.

[181]   *Id.*; Associated Press, *Sentence in Cow Cruelty*, L.A. TIMES (Mar. 23, 2008), http://articles.latimes.com /2008/mar/23/local/me-beef23.

[182]   Steve Mendell, Statement (Feb. 3, 2008) (on file with author).

because of its treatment of animals – is a common trope in American culture, constituting a chief means of distinguishing 'real' Americans from racial or ethnic outsiders."[183] But the Hallmark example is particularly striking because a subsequent civil suit brought by the DOJ (as an intervener) under the False Claims Act resulted in a settlement of nearly $500 million dollars against the Hallmark company.[184] The company was in fact responsible for unsavory practices – the shock and horror the executives expressed was not genuine, but was all part of an elaborate effort to scapegoat people of color for prosecution. The men prosecuted and deported were just the tip of iceberg, better thought of as canaries in the coal mine rather than the monsters who were truly responsible. Punishing the low-level slaughterhouse worker facilitates the very sort of race and class stigmas that have existed throughout America's history. Thus, even as applied to factory farms, the carceral animal law strategy has negative racial inflections that are at war with a true civil rights orientation.

***

Race is an under-examined problem in the animal protection movement, particularly in the movement's strident support of prosecutions. The movement frequently draws on analogies to slavery and emancipation when discussing the plight of modern non-humans, but advocates are also very quick to announce that each of their campaigns are colorblind, and beyond racialization. But the reality is never so simple. It is not possible to engage in a campaign that lacks any racial context or significance; indeed, that is why the analogies to the suffering of humans who were treated as animals can be so powerful. The point is certainly not that animal abuse should be tolerated. However, a movement cannot credibly claim a place under the civil rights umbrella if it fails to confront its relationship with issues of class and racial injustice. Decisions to seek the deportation or incarceration of people accused of animal abuse perpetuate an entrenched system of racial disadvantage.

Alternatively, even for members of the movement who do not want to address race problems for their own sake, carceral animal law is still a problem. If nothing else, even the most Machiavellian approach to animal protection should recognize the instrumental value in having the movement perceived as inclusive and interested in alliances with other social justice movements. Such an instrumentalist approach to race is shameful, and prioritizes messaging above true reform – something the movement would never accept for non-human animals (consider the rejection of

---

[183] SMITH at 135. Similarly, A. Breeze Harper noted that actress Brigitte Bardot expressed displeasure at the killing by Muslims of non-human animals, but did not make any comments about "nonhuman animals slaughtered for traditional white French cuisine," and instead, as in many contexts, the mistreatment of animals is strategically deployed to "racialize an immigrant group as barbaric." Harper, *Connections* at 74.

[184] Helena Bottemiller, *Landmark Settlement Reached in Westland-Hallmark Meat Case*, FOOD SAFETY NEWS (Nov. 18, 2012), www.foodsafetynews.com/2012/11/landmark-settlement-reached-in -westlandhallmark-meat-case/#.WneKfpM-eCR.

labeling such as "humane" meat), but even a message of inclusivity is arguably better than a blithe assertion of colorblindness.

More substantively, in recent years the view that the modern American prison system is simply irredeemably racist, and broken, has become mainstream.[185] Glen Loury described the modern justice system as a "monstrous social machine" that grinds up the mentally ill and the underclass, and he describes punishment as "state violence" meted out because of the criminogenic conditions that characterize low-income, minority life.[186] For Loury and others, there is a need for a Rawlsian reflection: how severe would the justice system be if you could not know where in society's rigid class system you would be, if you could not anticipate being born poor, black, or otherwise disadvantaged; then might you support a more individualized, less brutal criminal justice system?[187] Paul Butler is an even better known advocate of what has been called the "moral case against our current crime policies."[188] From Butler's vantage point as a black man and former successful federal prosecutor (he describes himself as a "recovering prosecutor"),[189] there is a need to completely abolish prisons and prosecution and to reinvent the system anew. In a characteristically unapologetic and biting tone, Butler once wrote, "If it took the white majority more than two hundred years to understand that slavery was wrong, and approximately one hundred years to realize that segregation was wrong (and still many don't understand), how long will it take them to perceive that American criminal justice is evil?"[190] Is the animal protection movement really prepared to treat the social insights of scholars like Paul Butler as entirely irrelevant to their movement; is incarceration such a cornerstone of animal protection that reforms are off the table? The "ethics of captivity"[191] and the pursuit of felony convictions, particularly as these goals intersect with race and class, is something the animal protection movement needs to reflect upon more seriously,[192] because the view of increased felony prosecutions and longer sentences as an entirely race- and class-neutral strategy is unacceptably trite and detached from reality.

---

[185] Butler, *The System Is Working the Way It Is Supposed To* at 1427, 1478 (considering whether the vast range of racial disparities in our justice system cannot be "fixed through legal reform" and explaining that the system is actually working exactly the way "it is supposed to" when it applies in a way that is unfair to minorities and poor people).

[186] Glen C. Loury, Race, Incarceration, and American Values 27–28 (2008).

[187] James Forman, Jr., *Why Care About Mass Incarceration*, 108 Mich. L. Rev. 993 (2009) (reviewing Paul Butler, Let's Get Free: A Hip-Hop Theory of Justice [2009]) (quoting Loury's work).

[188] *Id.*

[189] Paul Butler, Let's Get Free: A Hip-Hop Theory of Justice 18 (2009).

[190] Forman at 998 (quoting Paul Butler, *Brotherman: Reflections of a Reformed Prosecutor, in* The Darden Dilemma: 12 Black Writers on Justice, Race, and Conflicting Loyalties 1, 16 [Ellis Cose ed., 1997]).

[191] Ethics of Captivity (Lori Gruen ed., 2014).

[192] This section has focused primarily on the racial dimension of animal protection advocacy in the context of African Americans. Much more could be said if one expands the range of discussion to indigenous persons, Asians, and Latinos.

6

Animal Protection and the "Link" Between Animal Abuse and Human Violence

The presumed connection or "LINK"[1] between human and animal violence is probably the single most significant explanation for the modern enthusiasm for a carceral approach to animal law. The link is the theory that violence begets violence, and thus that violence against animals is predictive of violence against humans. The movement relies on this hypothesis to support the claim that aggressive punishment will protect humans. As an animal advocate explained in his legislative testimony in favor of a felony cruelty law, "scientific studies have shown a link between animal cruelty" and subsequent violent human behavior – "the *next strike* is often toward a child, a spouse, or another innocent human being."[2] Because it speaks to the public's desire to be safe from violence, the link serves as the last best defense for a carceral system, and thus as a critical roadblock to reforms seeking to move beyond cages.

But the movement's reliance on the link is overstated and badly flawed. Heather Piper has observed that, although the link hypothesis is poorly supported by data and "highly contested," the movement refers to the link as an absolute truism.[3] The link provides an illusion of "mathematical certainty" and scientific fact that the movement exploits in support of its carceral policies. In reality, the link research is best understood as a microcosm of the problems underlying the entire carceral animal law project; it is an effort to appeal to the masses with overly "simple explanations and solutions to complex problems."[4] Concerns about poverty or racism, which may correlate strongly with animal abuse and human violence, are eschewed by the movement as irrelevant and intractable, and instead we are told with an almost religious zeal that incarcerating animal abusers will make society safer. More

---

[1]   The term "LINK" is actually trademarked by the Animal Welfare Institute, and is often written in all caps. For purposes of this project, the use of the lower-case word "link" means the same thing as the broadly used "LINK" typology.

[2]   *Advocates of Animal Cruelty Speak Out*, PARAGOULD DAILY NEWS, Sept. 5, 2002.

[3]   Heather Piper & Debbie Cordingley, 1 POWER AND EDUC., 345, 351 (2009).

[4]   *Id.* at 346.

aggressive cruelty prosecutions, the public is told, will result in fewer mass shootings, less serial killers, and an overall drop in violence.

The temptation to embrace a strong narrative about the predictive power of animal abuse is particularly strong for the animal protection movement given that the deployment of this "highly questionable evidence and data" has afforded organizations a mainstream soapbox from which to opine about animal protection, and a "capacity to punch well beyond their weight."[5] Portraying the link as a basic truth allows the movement to treat as clearly established scientific fact that people who harm animals progress to harming humans, *and* that incarceration will cure this cycle of violence. It turns out that both of these premises are a product of sloppy link-think, and are in considerable tension with empirical realities. Much of the link advocacy and research, as scholars such as Piper observe, resembles a motivational speech or the proselytizing of a missionary, much more than academic research. The starting point for many papers and talks is the presumption of a link without any reasoned discussion about whether it really exists. In this way the research may have something in common with the discredited forensic sciences used to convict countless people of crimes.[6] It is a passion for punishment more than it is a tailored response to research that drives the movement's reliance on the link. This chapter does not claim that a link between human violence and animal abuse is implausible, or that such a link never exists, but argues instead that the advocacy in support of a more carceral orientation based on the link is misguided.

Ecofeminist author Pattrice Jones said that "integrity may be the central problem of our time," because we "live in a social world defined by divisive lies" and exaggerations that isolate us from reality. The weaponizing of the link as a pressing reason to support incarceration is unseemly because the use of the research is at best misinformed or greatly oversimplified, and it runs the distinct risk of appearing deliberately false.

6.1 AN OVERVIEW OF THE LINK AS A JUSTIFICATION AND EXPLANATION FOR CARCERAL POLICIES

Animal law's enthusiasm for criminal punishment is easy to understand in the abstract. Criminal law and its willingness to impose penalties on the mistreatment of animals provides a ready rhetorical response to those who might want to characterize animals as nothing more than property. In many states, the criminal code serves as the primary or exclusive statutory basis for describing animals as something

---

[5] *Id.* at 346.

[6] A Presidential Council issued a report in 2016 finding that several types of forensic evidence that are commonly used to secure convictions are based on discredited science, or a misapplication of existing science. Press Release, The White House, *PCAST Releases Report on Forensic Science in Criminal Courts* (Sept. 20, 2016), https://obamawhitehouse.archives.gov/blog/2016/09/20/pcast-releases-report -forensic-science-criminal-courts.

clearly other than property. Punishing people who hurt animals, then, has emerged as an important way for animal protection groups to demonstrate the value of animal lives. Underlying this symbolic victory for animal status in the law is an important irony. The legislative and judicial advocacy in support of more robust criminal laws and more rigorous enforcement of these laws is often predicated on the need to keep humans safe. The status of animals as more than property in the eyes of the criminal law is actually propped up by advocacy that links animal cruelty to human safety and well-being. Human safety, we are made to believe, turns on the protection of animals. A New York court's discussion is emblematic of the thinking on this point: "[M]an's inhumanity to man often begins with inhumanity to those creatures that have formed particularly close relationships with mankind."[7]

These comments echo the supposedly neutral research that is being generated and perpetuated by experts within the field. For example, Randall Lockwood, an esteemed social scientist who works for the ASPCA, has repeatedly trained social workers and educators to recognize that "abuse and neglect is a true warning sign" of future dangerousness.[8] When the researchers are making such categorical claims, it is hardly surprising that leaders in the movement, repeat these claims in press releases and fundraising materials. In a 2018 fundraising email Steven Wells nearly quoted Lockwood when he explained that, "Animal cruelty is a clear predictor of future violence [against people], so why are perpetrators merely slapped on the wrist?"[9]

According to the dominant understanding of the link among policy-makers and advocates, abusing an animal may predict or affirmatively cause later interpersonal violence by desensitizing a person to suffering, or in the words of Immanuel Kant, by "hardening their hearts." Each time someone kills people in a high-profile manner and turns out to have abused animals in the past, like Devin Kelley, who killed twenty-six people in 2017 at a church in Texas, the animal protection movement seizes the moment to re-emphasize the need for criminal interventions in order to keep society safe. Some researchers have dubbed this view of the link the "graduation thesis" – that is, animal cruelty temporally precedes, generally predicts, and may even cause interpersonal violence.

As discussed in this chapter, the link's presumed ability to reliably predict human violence provides a clear-cut, publicly popular justification for criminally punishing harm to animals; it is treated as an obvious win-win across species lines. As one group

---

7   People v. Garcia, 812 N.Y.S.2d 66, 71 (N.Y. App. Div. 2006) (explaining that animal cruelty as a crime "was established in recognition of the correlation between violence against animals and subsequent violence against humans" and noting that liability turns not on the suffering of the animal, but on the "state of mind of the perpetrator").

8   Heather Piper & Debbie Cordingley, 1 *Power and Education*, 3 345, 353 (2009).

9   Stephen Wells, *Animal Cruelty Is a Clear Predictor of Future Violence, So Why Are Perpetrators Merely Slapped on the Wrist?*, ALTERNET (Jan. 15, 2018), https://www.alternet.org/animal-rights/animal-cruelty-clear-predictor-future-violence-so-why-are-perpetrators-merely-slapped ("We need stronger animal cruelty laws to protect both animals and people.").

of law professors wrote in an amicus brief to the Supreme Court, "[f]or more than a century, American courts have recognized that preventing animal cruelty ultimately serves human interests."[10] The head of a leading police chiefs' association echoed this sentiment and pointed to harsher sentencing as a necessary means of preventing "future domestic violence,"[11] while the national prosecutors' association trains prosecutors and law enforcement to treat animal abuse as a reliable method for the "early identification of violent perpetrators."[12] Thus, as the story is commonly told, the link research provides a space for recognizing a convergence of interests between humans and animals – animals are given status in the law through the enactment and enforcement of criminal penalties, and human interests in preventing human violence are simultaneously served.

This chapter critiques the tidiness of this oft-told story – that humans are protected by punishing more, and more severely, humans who abuse animals. The evidence of a strong correlation between animal abuse and human violence, much less evidence of animal abuse's capacity to predict future crime, has been characterized by some of the leading researchers in the field as plagued by "[w]orrisome evidentiary weaknesses."[13] For some, the claimed power of animal abuse to predict other crimes or to establish reliable profiles for criminals are not just flawed, but "unethical and unjust."[14] Recognizing the current link research as "weak or inconsistent," some researchers have sought to dramatically limit the claims being made about the correlative or predictive power of animal abuse by, for example, focusing only on the most extreme, hands-on cruelty as a possible "red flag" for human violence.[15] Still others strongly disagree even with this much more modest hypothesis. Instead, researchers have argued that animal abuse may well be pervasive among violent offenders, but even extreme cruelty is "not necessarily predictive" of violence.[16] Two of the leading researchers in this field summarized the some of the shortcomings of the link data:

---

[10]   Brief for a Group of American Law Professors as Amicus Curiae in Support of Neither Party at 11, United States v. Stevens, 533 F.3d 18 (3d Cir. 2008) (No. 08–769), 2009 WL1681459, at *11 [hereinafter U.S. v. Stevens Amicus Brief].

[11]   Int'l Ass'n of Chiefs of Police, Inc., *Cruelty to Animals and Family Violence Training Key, reprinted in* Creating Safer Communities for Older Adults and Companion Animals 70 (2003).

[12]   Allie Phillips, *The Dynamics Between Animal Abuse, Domestic Violence and Child Abuse: How Pets Can Help Abused Children*, 38 Prosecutor 22, 22–23 (2004) (quoting a district attorney from Ohio).

[13]   Piers Beirne, *From Animal Abuse to Inhuman Violence?: A Critical Review of the Progression Thesis*, 12 Soc. & Animals 39, 52 (2004) (noting that the combination of flaws in the research dictate "that current generalizations about a progression from animal abuse to interhuman violence are, at best, premature."); *Id.* at 46 ("Even if it is true that youthful animal abusers tend to have more psychosocial health problems than do nonabusers and also to engage in other antisocial acts, these facts alone shed no light on the question of whether they are more likely subsequently to engage in interhuman violence."); *Id.* at 47 (providing a detailed summary of the critiques surrounding the link's focus on incarcerated persons).

[14]   Piper & Cordingley at 345.

[15]   Jack Levin & Arnold Arluke, *Reducing the Link's False Positive Problem*, in The Link Between Animal Abuse and Human Violence 163, 169 (Andrew Linzey ed., 2009).

[16]   *Id.*

It could still be argued that any attempt to predict human violence from animal abuse is bound to fail, even if each and every killer can be shown to have tortured animals. The false positive problem is not reduced by showing a strong relationship between animal abuse and human violence because there are apparently millions of normal people who have committed animal cruelty.[17]

One recurring problem with the current reliance on the link as strongly indicative of interpersonal violence (before or after the animal abuse) is that studies have repeatedly documented extremely high rates of animal abuse across society.[18] One study even found that a majority of adults studied in a population of social workers and animal welfare workers admitted to harming animals in the past.[19] For this reason, Hal Herzog noted that even if every "school shooter had a history of animal abuse, we could not conclude that most animal abusers, including those of the up close and personal variety, are likely to" engage in acts of violence.

Researchers have identified other serious methodological flaws with the seminal link research as well. For example, Heather Piper and Steve Myers have observed that "researching a limited and extreme [criminal] population to produce what is presented as a broadly applicable generalization is obviously problematic."[20] Moreover, though many studies tend to show that violent offenders have abused animals at a higher rate than nonviolent offenders (sometimes at a much higher rate), the critical and oft-overlooked common denominator in these studies is that they consistently show that most people who commit crimes of violence *do not have a history of animal abuse.*[21] As another scholarly paper concludes, though there is no

---

[17] Arnold Arluke & Eric Madfis, *Animal Abuse as a Warning Sign of School Massacres: A Critique and Refinement*, 18 HOMICIDE STUD., 7, 7–22 (2014). These researchers argue, however, that the "false positive problem can be substantially reduced by limiting the range of *predictive* acts of animal abuse to those in which dogs and cats are tortured in a hands-on manner." If there are any meaningful correlations or predictions that can be observed, they conclude, it is with the most brutal, prolonged, and sadistic torture of the most socially valued animals. Others disagree that their small dataset and methodology even allows for this much more limited articulation of the link. More importantly, it appears that this research still tends to find that *most* violent people *had not abused* an animal – that is, it is more likely that a violent mass shooter, for example, will *not* have any history of animal abuse.

[18] Piers Beirne has observed disparity in the research attempting to calculate out how common animal abuse is among non-criminals, but the rates are all quite high: "Miller and Knutson (1997, p. 77) found that 20.5% of a sample of 308 Iowan undergraduate psychology students (with a slight overrepresentation of females) reported that they actually had engaged in one or more acts of animal cruelty. However, from a sample of undergraduate psychology and sociology students at a southeastern university in the United States, Flynn (1999, pp. 165, 166) found that 34.5% of males and 9.3% of females admitted that they had abused animals during childhood. Moreover, much higher rates of animal abuse than these have been reported by Baldry (2003). In her study of animal abuse and exposure to interparental violence among Italian youth aged 9 to 17, Baldry (p. 272) found that 50.8% of the 1,392 youth in her study had abused animals at least once; 66.5% were boys." Beirne at 43.

[19] Heather Piper & Steve Myers, *Forging the Links: (De)Constructing Chains of Behaviours*, CHILD ABUSE REVIEW VOL. 15: 178, 180 (2006).

[20] *Id.* at 183.

[21] Emily Patterson-Kane, *The Relation of Animal Maltreatment to Aggression*, in ANIMAL MALTREATMENT: FORENSIC MENTAL HEALTH ISSUES AND EVALUATIONS 140, 140–58 (Lacey Levill et. al eds., 2016).

reason to contend that "there is never a link between violent behaviors," the existing data does not "provide secure foundations for generalized arguments, predictions or policies that can safely or ethically be applied to the mass of the population."[22]

In short, the veracity of using animal abuse as a measure of likely human violence has been rather dramatically called into question, and the research on this point is summarized in detail below. However, it is worth pausing to presage the second, and perhaps even more important contribution of this chapter: Even assuming for the sake of argument that the research could establish that animal cruelty was a reliable red flag for human violence, then the critical question is what should be done with this information. This chapter argues that animal law scholars and advocates grievously err when they assume that a more punitive, carceral approach to animal cruelty will reduce future interpersonal violence. There is no research suggesting that incarceration will break the alleged cycle of violence and make our communities safer.[23] The underlying assumption is as bizarre as it is unfounded: A more carceral response to animal abuse will somehow undo the desensitization that occurred when a person abused an animal. Research in the criminology field suggests that the opposite may be true – the punished offender may be more stigmatized, and even further desensitized by incarceration. In short, the link research does not provide a solid evidentiary basis for many of the claims animal protection groups attribute to it, and even if it did, relying on prosecutions to break the cycle of violence is a radical assumption that lacks empirical support.

The remainder of this chapter provides a blueprint for re-envisioning the conversation about the link between animal mistreatment and human violence. The first part discusses the heavy reliance on link-based data by animal protection advocates, and increasingly lawmakers, and examines the conclusions these advocates and policy-makers attribute to the research. The next part provides a detailed overview of the key link research, examining what conclusions the data actually supports and where future research in this field appears to be trending. And the remaining sections discuss the conceptual and empirical problems associated with the current use of link data by animal protection groups. The conclusion is not that the link definitively does not exist, or that the research has no place within the world of animal protection advocacy. Rather, this chapter is a call for scholars and advocates to take a more careful look at the disconnect between the evidence and the advocacy surrounding the link. If the link is to provide the defining rationale for more incarceration, then the data needs to be exceedingly strong, it needs to be applied in a faithful and rigorous manner, and other, more complicated factors bearing on violence such as socioeconomics must also be considered.

---

[22] Piper & Cordingley at 353.

[23] Presumably, incapacitation has some relevance for the period of time while the abuser is actually incarcerated, but once the person is eventually released there is no data to suggest that they will be less desensitized or more emotionally connected with their community.

6.1.1 *How the Link Data Is Used by Animal Protection Advocates*

There has always been disagreement about the proper justification for animal cruelty prohibitions. The laws are viewed by some as a freestanding protection of animals, by others as a protection of our moral purity,[24] and by still others as a more tangible protection of humans from violence.[25] There is no doubt that among modern legislators, prosecutors, and animal advocates, the latter rationale predominates. The salience and cultural acceptance of this point is no coincidence, but rather the product of a concerted, long-term public relations campaign by a variety of organizations interested in the well-being of animals. First, there are organizations whose sole purpose is to spread awareness and advocacy relating to the link.[26] For example, the National Link Coalition was formed to raise awareness and provide interdisciplinary resources on the relationship between animal abuse and human violence.[27] According to the National Link Coalition's homepage as of 2017, "animal abuse [is] a sentinel indicator . . . the tip of the iceberg, and often the *first sign* of other family and community violence."[28] Phil Arkow, the coordinator for the Link Coalition, attempted to distill the research down to its essence for public consumption, explaining that "Family violence often *begins* with pet abuse."[29] Randall Lockwood has conducted trainings during which he reported that those who abuse an animal "for no obvious reason are budding psychopaths."[30]

---

[24] MODEL PENAL CODE § 250.11 cmt. 1 (Am. Law Inst., 1980) ("the object of [anticruelty] statutes seems to have been to prevent outrage to the sensibilities of the community.").

[25] *See e.g., Tracking Animal Cruelty: FBI Collecting Data on Crimes Against Animals*, FBI (Feb. 1, 2016), www.fbi.gov/news/stories/-tracking-animal-cruelty. ("The National Sheriffs' Association's John Thompson urged people to shed the mindset that animal cruelty is a crime only against animals. 'It's a crime against society.'"); *Id.* ("If somebody is harming an animal, there is a good chance they also are hurting a human.")

[26] For example, there is the National Link Coalition, *What Is the Link*, NAT'L LINK COAL., http://national linkcoalition.org/what-is-the-link (last visited Apr. 23, 2016), and many state link programs as well. *See, e.g., Colorado Link Project*, COLO. LINK PROJECT, http://coloradolinkproject.com/ (last visited Apr. 23, 2016); Allie Phillips, *Understanding the Link Between Violence to Animals and People*, NAT'L DIST. ATTYS ASS'N (2014), www.ndaa.org/pdf/The%20Link%20Monograph-2014.pdf; Alison Knezevich, *FBI to Start Tracking Animal Cruelty in 2016*, BALT. SUN, Nov. 27, 2015, www.baltimoresun.com/news/maryland/bs-md-fbi-animal-cruelty-20151126-story.html (noting that the FBI started in 2015 tracking animal abuse in its national statistics because of the link between human and animal violence). The American Humane Association even went so far as to trademark "The Link" to help promote the idea. *The Link*, U.S. TRADEMARK AND PAT. OFF., http://tmsearch.uspto.gov/bin/showfield?f=doc&state=4806:28m702.2.89 (last visited, Apr. 23, 2016); *The Link®*, AM. HUMANE ASS'N, www.americanhumane.org/interaction/professional-resources/the-link/ (last visited Apr. 23, 2016).

[27] NAT'L LINK COAL.

[28] *Id.*

[29] Susan I. Finkelstein, *Canary in a Coal Mine: The Connection Between Animal Abuse and Human Violence*, 58 BELLWEATHER MAG. 10 (2003), http://repository.upenn.edu/cgi/viewcontent.cgi?article=3651&context=bellwether.

[30] Piper & Cordingley at 345, 353.

Other organizations have followed the lead of these principal actors in the field and provided similarly clear-cut interpretations of the link data. A national therapy animals group explained, "today, we know that what is called 'The Link' is real and that animal abuse often indicates *and predicts* other forms of family and community violence."[31] A veterinary science journal summarized the link data by saying that "it is well known in the criminology field that people who perpetrate acts of cruelty on animals, frequently *escalate* to torturing humans, usually the young and helpless."[32]

Likewise, animal protection groups fuel and reinforce this narrative of the predictive power of animal abuse. In the wake of high-profile human violence, any past act of animal abuse by the suspect is exploited by the movement as evidence that more aggressive animal cruelty prosecutions would better protect the public. The movement regards animal cruelty as predictive of human violence, and it unflinchingly assumes that incarceration is the only way to prevent this predicted harm. For example, in the weeks immediately following a mass shooting in 2017 at a Texas church, the animal protection movement focused considerable attention on the fact that the perpetrator had a previous conviction for animal abuse. Making the case that longer sentences and more prosecutions might have prevented this shooting, groups argued that "[f]elony penalties allow prosecutors to better prosecute offenders."[33] And on this score, it is notable that the talking points are nearly identical for government officials and animal protection groups. For example, as noted above, the executive director of one of the leading animal law organizations in the country recently explained that "animal cruelty is a clear predictor of future violence." The National District Attorneys Association parroted this same explanation in its published handbook: "violence to animals is a predictor that the abuser may become violent to people."[34]

The message across nearly all animal protection groups appears uniform – animal abuse is a predictor of future harm to humans. One organization publicly celebrated the increased sentencing ranges for animal abuse by noting "abusive acts toward animals are unacceptable, and all too often can lead to violence toward people."[35] Similarly, Cathy Kangas, a board member of the HSUS, explained that animal abuse

[31] *Animal Abuse and Human Violence*, ANIMAL THERAPY, http://animaltherapy.net/animal-abuse-human -violence/ (last visited Feb. 4, 2018).

[32] Gail S. & Niki R. Huitson, *Myiasis in Pet Animals in British Columbia: The Potential of Forensic Entomology for Determining Duration of Possible Neglect*, 45 CANADIAN VETERINARY J. 993, 996 (2004).

[33] *Animal Cruelty and Domestic Violence*, ANIMAL LEGAL DEF. FUND, http://aldf.org/resources/when-your -companion-animal-has-been-harmed/animal-cruelty-and-domestic-violence/ (last visited Feb. 4, 2018).

[34] PHILLIPS.

[35] *Massachusetts Legislature Stiffens Penalties for Animal Cruelty*, ANIMAL RESCUE LEAGUE (Sept. 8, 2014), www.arlboston.org/massachusetts-legislature-stiffens-penalties-animal-cruelty/; see Editorial Board, *Abuse Preventative: Stiffer Penalties Would Curb Harm to Animals*, PITTSBURGH POST-GAZETTE (Oct. 21, 2015), www.post-gazette.com/opinion/editorials/2015/10/21/Abuse-preventative-Stiffer-penalties -would-curb-harm-to-animals/stories/201510310019 ("In his sponsorship memorandum for the bill, Mr. Costa said the measure is necessary for the protection of animals, but he also points to studies linking animal cruelty and domestic violence, as well as other attacks on people.").

is "not an animal rights issue. It is a way to identify and help those who may one day become a danger to the community at large."[36] Or as PETA's website explains, "[r]esearch in psychology and criminology shows that people who commit acts of cruelty to animals don't stop there – many of them move on to their fellow humans."[37] If animal abuse is not punished "aggressively," according to PETA, society is essentially facilitating the detonation of a "ticking time bomb."[38] One leading animal protection group took the link research to an extreme and argued in a recent brief that the link research justified trying a fourteen-year-old child as an adult. Cruelty to animals, the brief argues, "is an ominous *predictor* of brutality toward humans in the future. . . . as established in numerous academic studies."[39] Children should be caged as adults, according to this brief, despite clear science about differences in brain function and development, because of the dubious predictive power of the link. Many other animal protection groups have made similarly forceful claims.[40]

The legal scholarship discussing the link has also accepted and propagated the theory that animal abuse will necessarily lead to interpersonal violence.[41] A leading animal law textbook makes the point laconically, explaining that the "idea that criminalizing animal cruelty can also prevent abuse of humans has been proven to be valid."[42] The Animal Legal and History Center informs the public that animal abuse "endangers everyone" in the community and requires a penal response in order to

---

[36]   Cathy Kangas, *Animal Cruelty and Human Violence*, HUFFPOST: THE BLOG (Jan. 18, 2013), www .huffingtonpost.com/cathy-kangas/animal-cruelty-and-human-_b_2507551.html.

[37]   *Animal Abuse and Human Abuse: Partners in Crime*, PETA, www.peta.org/issues/companion-animal -issues/companion-animals-factsheets/animal-abuse-human-abuse-partners-crime/ (last visited Feb. 4, 2018); *see also The Animal Abuse-Human Violence Connection*, PAWS.ORG, www.paws.org/get-involved/take-action/explore-the-issues/animal-abuse-connection/ (last visited Feb. 4, 2018) ("[P]eople who abuse animals rarely stop there.").

[38]   *Id.*

[39]   Comm. v. a Juvenile, SJC 12277, Amicus Brief of ALDF at 19 (filed in the Massachusetts Supreme Court on Aug. 18, 2017).

[40]   Stacy Wolf, Esq., Senior Vice President of the ASPCA's Anti Cruelty Group, for example said, "Aggressive prosecution of crimes against animals is critical to ensuring the safety of New York City residents, both human and animal." Press Release, Queens County DA, *Queens District Attorney Richard A. Brown Establishes Animal Cruelty Prosecutions Unit* (Jan. 11, 2016), www.queensda.org /newpressreleases/2016/JAN%202016/animal%20cruelty%20unit_01_2016.pdf. *See also Texas Governor Signs Animal Cruelty Bill!*, TEX. HUMANE LEGIS. NETWORK (June 10, 2017), www.thln.org /texas_governor_signs_cruelty_bill (quoting Texas Humane Legislation Network's Executive Director, Laura Donahue, stating, "The link between animal cruelty and domestic violence is well documented . . . When animals are safe from harm, communities are safer.").

[41]   There are some notable exceptions. Margit Livingston, for example, has noted that recent research shows that animal abuse is "not necessarily a precursor to criminal behavior because the animal abuse was as likely to occur after the criminal offense as before it." Margit Livingston, *Desecrating the Ark: Animal Abuse and the Law's Role in Prevention*, 87 IOWA L. REV. 1, 56 (2001). Livingston is one of the few academics writing in the field who have recognized a value in the well-being of the human offender as well. *Id.* at 73 (calling for "reforms" that could allow the law to "function more as a therapeutic agent and by so doing to increase the psychological well-being both of humans and animals in society."); *id.* at 62 (calling for "treatment for youthful offenders").

[42]   SONIA S. WAISMAN ET AL., ANIMAL LAW: CASES AND MATERIALS 72 (5th edn. 2014).

help with the "prevention of violence." A leading animal law scholar posited that the prosecution of "animal cruelty can prevent future violence towards human victims, since animal cruelty is often the first step towards violence against humans."[43] Another insightful scholar observed that "the mainstream belief with regard to animal cruelty statutes is that they are enacted as a way of identifying and neutralizing presumptively dangerous individuals before they engage in acts that are harmful to human beings."[44] Yet another commentator identified animal cruelty prosecutions as an important "weapon" in the fight against domestic violence, and explained that the cruelty "laws have been enacted to prevent humans from acting cruelly towards other humans."[45] Gary Francione, a leading animal law intellectual, remarked that the justification for animal cruelty laws is the overriding notion that cruelty "toward animals" leads to "cruel treatment toward humans."[46] The legal commentary by academics, then, largely accepts without modification the talking points advanced by national animal protection groups; it accepts that animal abuse can be used to "predict other forms of abuse."[47]

There is now a relative consensus among the media, prosecutors, policy-makers, and animal protection advocates that animal violence is an early warning or "canary in the coal mine" for interpersonal violence.[48] One news media outlet recently ran a story about the link with the headline "[i]f you want to stop violence against people, stop violence against animals."[49] Animal abuse is treated as the predictor par excellence of human violence; indeed, many lawmakers and prosecutors now posit "a direct *causal link* between animal cruelty and subsequent violent offending."[50] Policy-makers often treat the prompt and severe punishment of animal

43 Joan E. Schaffner, *Laws and Policy to Address the Link of Family Violence*, in THE LINK BETWEEN ANIMAL ABUSE AND HUMAN VIOLENCE at 230.
44 Luis E. Chiesa, *Why Is It a Crime to Stomp on a Goldfish? – Harm, Victimhood and the Structure of Anti-Cruelty Offenses*, 78 MISS. L.J. 1, 31 (2008).
45 Charlotte A. Lacroix, *Another Weapon for Combating Family Violence: Prevention of Animal Abuse*, 4 ANIMAL L. 1, 4 (1998).
46 Gary L. Francione, *Animals, Property and Legal Welfarism: "Unnecessary" Suffering and the "Humane" Treatment of Animals*, 46 RUTGERS L. REV. 721, 753 (1994). *See also* Rebecca L. Bucchieri, *Bridging the Gap: The Connection Between Violence Against Animals and Violence Against Humans*, 11 J. ANIMAL & NAT. RESOURCE L. 115, 115 (2015) (positing the existence of "a robust legal and scientific discourse firmly establish[ing]" animal abuse as a "predictor" of future human violence).
47 Angela Campbell, Note, *The Admissibility of Evidence of Animal Abuse in Criminal Trials for Child and Domestic Abuse*, 43 B.C. L. REV. 463, 465 (2002).
48 Finkelstein at 465.
49 Lynne Peeples, *If You Want to Stop Violence Against People, Stop Violence Against Animals*, HUFFINGTON POST (Oct. 8, 2015), www.huffingtonpost.com/entry/animal-abuse-human-violence -link_us_560f2269e4boaf3706eofd5b (quoting an animal control officer regarding a horrible act of animal abuse as saying, "Any person capable of doing this to an animal is also capable of doing it to a human.").
50 Glenn D. Walters, *Testing the Specificity Postulate of the Violence Graduation Hypothesis: Meta-Analyses of the Animal Cruelty-Offending Relationship*, 18 AGGRESSION & VIOLENT BEHAV. 797 (2013).

abuse as a key means of protecting society from interpersonal violence. The mayor of Baltimore, for example, recently said on the occasion of signing into law a suite of legislation enhancing animal cruelty penalties, "[i]f you improve animal welfare in a community, you improve public safety for everyone."[51] A Mississippi legislator who introduced a more serious felony animal abuse bill in the state legislature explained, "[i]t's mind boggling when you look at the numbers. . . . It's like a great predictor . . . Jeffrey Dahmer, the Boston strangler, it just goes on and on."[52] Or as a New York State Senator said in support of a 2017 package of increased penalties for animal cruelty, "those who would be so dastardly as to torture a defenseless animal would not hesitate to inflict extreme pain on another person."[53] And as one commentator put it, animal abuse is "an excellent predictor of violent and abusive behavior."[54]

While serving as the director of the National Center for Prosecution of Animal Abuse, a program affiliated with the National District Attorneys Association, Allie Phillips incorporated these exaggerated claims into her training, ostensibly as a means of encouraging law enforcement to take animal cruelty more seriously:

> You always hear police, prosecutors and judges say that they have more important, bigger cases to work on . . . So I tell them, "Hey, wouldn't it have been nice to stop that [sexual abuser or murderer] before they did that?"[55]

Allie Phillips's assessment of the literature is the mainstream view – that animal cruelty predicts future violent offending. As an Ohio district attorney's office put it, "If you stop animal cruelty in its tracks, you very well may be minimizing future domestic violence."[56] Urging the adoption of a felony cruelty provision in Colorado, the district attorney for Denver (and subsequently the governor) explained that "[t]he evidence is clear that violence directed toward animals is a reliable precursor for

[51] Ed Sayres, *Baltimore Mayor Signs Anti-Animal Abuse Advisory Commission into Law*, HUFFINGTON POST (Nov. 5, 2011), www.huffingtonpost.com/ed-sayres/aspcas-ann-church-speaks-_b_778950.html (noting the focus on increased policing and prosecution).

[52] Sarah Fowler, *MS Legislator Pushing Animal Cruelty Bill*, DES MOINES REG., Jan. 1, 2017, www .desmoinesregister.com/story/news/politics/2017/01/01/ms-legislator-pushing-animal-cruelty-bill /96046492/ (emphasizing as well the sponsor's irritation with the "rumor" that the bill would apply to farm animals and quoting her as saying, "The bill is strictly limited to domestic pets, dogs and cats.").

[53] James Tedisco, *NYS Senate Today Passes Three Tedisco Bills*, N.Y. ST. SENATE (June 6, 2017), www .nysenate.gov/newsroom/press-releases/james-tedisco/nys-senate-today-passes-three-tedisco-bills.

[54] Heather D. Winters, Comment, *Updating Ohio's Animal Cruelty Statute: How Human Interests Are Advanced*, 29 CAP. U. L. REV. 857, 858 (2002).

[55] Peeples.

[56] Sheila McLaughlin, *Animal, Domestic Abuse Linked: Prosecutor Says New Policy May Help Prevent Violence*, CINCINNATI ENQUIRER, June 11, 2008. Similarly, the Honolulu Prosecuting Attorney, Keith Kaneshiro, participating in a town hall meeting with the Hawaii Humane Society on September 19, 2012 said, "What we found is people who are cruel to animals are usually cruel to people and that's why it goes to the heart of public safety making sure we protect the community." *Keith Kaneshiro Talks About Animal Cruelty*, KEITHKANESHIRO.COM (Sept. 19, 2012), http://keithkaneshiroprosecutor .com/keith-kaneshiro-talks-about-animal-cruelty/.

other forms of violence."[57] He also quoted with approval the lay observation of a citizen, "animal torture today, child abuse/serial killer tonight."[58] The International Association of Chiefs of Police urged that "[c]omplaints of animal cruelty should be taken seriously as they often provide an opportunity for early identification with violent perpetrators."[59] The National Association of District Attorneys reported that "prosecuting animal abuse is critical because animal abuse is a strong predictor and indicator that additional animal and human victims may be next."[60] The head of the FBI's investigative support unit likewise explained that the research shows that violence falls along a "continuum" such that those who harm animals may progress farther along the continuum toward humans.[61]

These characterizations of the link research are dramatically overstated, if not outright inconsistent with the data. For leading social scientists, the animal protection movement's tendency to definitively ascribe to animal abuse an ability to predict future interpersonal violence is stupefying. Scholars have openly questioned why there is a persistent mischaracterization of the data. No doubt a partial explanation for this narrative can be found in the success such characterizations yield for the movement – legislative and legal victories are hard to come by in the animal protection realm, so overplaying or misstating the link research has become a staple of effective legislative reform.[62] Or perhaps at this point, the leaders of the movement are simply repeating the conventional wisdom without actually reading the relevant studies. Future qualitative research should include interviews with leaders in the field on their views about why the link is an important part of animal protection advocacy. What is the explanation for the consistent mischaracterization of the data by key players in the field?

Regardless of the underlying reason for characterizing the connection between human and animal violence as an important part of animal advocacy, the success on

---

[57] A. William Ritter, Jr., *The Cycle of Violence Often Begins with Violence Toward Animals*, PROSECUTOR 31, 32 (1996) (relying on anecdote, and explaining that "evidence of this connection has been documented in the media").

[58] *Id.*

[59] Int'l Ass'n of Chiefs of Police, Inc. at 79.

[60] Allie Phillips & Randall Lockwood, *Investigating and Prosecuting Animal Abuse: A Guidebook on Safer Communities, Safer Families and Being an Effective Voice for Animal Victims* 20, 22 (2013), www .ncdsv.org/images/NDAA_Investigating-and-prosecuting-animal-abuse_2013.pdf ("[B]rushing off an animal abuse case as 'unimportant' is a mistake because a proper response can reduce recidivism.").

[61] Randall Lockwood & Ann Church, *Deadly Serious: An FBI Perspective on Animal Cruelty*, in CRUELTY TO ANIMALS AND INTERPERSONAL VIOLENCE: READINGS IN RESEARCH AND APPLICATIONS 241, 262 (Randall Lockwood & Frank R. Ascione eds., 1998) ("You can look at cruelty to animals and cruelty to humans as a continuum."). *See also* U.S. v. Stevens Amicus Brief at 19 (quoting the same sources). *See* Arnold Arluke, Jack Levin, Carter Luke & Frank Ascione, *The Relationship of Animal Abuse to Violence and Other Forms of Antisocial Behavior*, 14 J. INTERPERSONAL VIOLENCE 963, 971 (1999) (criticizing as simplistic this sort of "phylogenetic reasoning" regarding the link).

[62] Arluke, Levin, Luke & Ascione at 970 (asking "why" a graduation or progression thesis persists without any "consistent empirical support" and positing that part of the explanation is the value that such advocacy has for animal protection advocates in raising their profile).

this front cannot be gainsaid. Indeed, every state has criminalized animal cruelty, and even more recently all fifty states have adopted a felony animal abuse statute. Prosecutors now pursue more animal abuse prosecutions and higher sentences in these cases. Legislators are contemplating animal abuse registries, and the FBI recently announced that it will track statistics for animal abuse, just as it does with other serious crimes.[63] All of these reforms are endorsed by the animal protection community, and each of them have traction in no small part because the link provides a human-centric basis for explaining animal protection prosecutions. To animal lovers and governing officials alike, it seems like an easy win-win – protecting animals to protect humans.

In reality, however, the reliance on the link to support a wave of efforts to make animal protection efforts more carceral is empirically and conceptually problematic, and in the eyes of some researchers unethical. First, current link-based advocacy as summarized in Section 6.2 is out of touch with the actual link research: Whether animal cruelty is a reliable predictor, much less the best, of future interpersonal violence, is far from settled. In the words of some of the most preeminent thinkers on this point: "[T]here must be a moratorium on painting a broad stroke of violence over most cases of abuse," because deceptively treating abuse as a "magic bullet" or the indicator of violence par excellence will only undermine the credibility of animal advocacy and "hurt the cause."[64] Or as another research paper lamented, despite the fact that the link "hypothesis is highly contested, it has nevertheless acquired the status of a truism."[65]

Second, even if the research confirmed, as animal protection groups claim, that animal violence is a reliable predictor of subsequent interpersonal violence, there is no data suggesting that criminal punishment is the best, or even a viable means of preventing the violence predicted by link research. There is likely "some truth" to the link – some violence is undoubtedly connected across time, place, and manner. But even accepting for the sake of argument the strongest version of the link – the notion that animal abuse is a clear predictor or early warning sign of future human violence – research does not support the hypothesis that incarceration will break this cycle of violence.

6.2 OVERVIEW OF THE LINK RESEARCH IN THE SOCIAL SCIENCES

6.2.1 Origins of the Link – Speculation, Urban Legends, and Intuition

The link, sometimes called the graduation theory, graduation hypothesis, violence graduation hypothesis, or progression thesis, has existed as speculation for centuries. At its core, the theory is that animal abuse is strongly predictive, if not causally linked to human violence. As far back as 500 BC, Pythagoras philosophized about kindness to

---

[63] *Tracking Animal Cruelty*, FBI.
[64] Arluke, Levin, Luke & Ascione at 973.
[65] Piper & Cordingley at 346.

animals and how killing an animal could fairly be compared to the killing of a human.[66] In the late 1600s, John Locke encouraged parents to teach their children about being kind to animals, as children "who delight in the suffering and destruction of inferior creatures, will not be apt to be very compassionate or benign to those of their own kind."[67] Other leading intellectuals such as Immanuel Kant in the 1700s,[68] Phillipe Pinel in the 1800s,[69] and Sigmund Freud in the 1900s[70] also suggested that animal cruelty was a precursor to violence toward humans. None of these theorists moved beyond anecdote and speculation, or attempted to gather empirical support for their beliefs, but the narrative has a long history. A famous British artist, William Hogarth, even engraved *The Four Stages of Cruelty* in 1751, depicting a young boy abusing an animal, then becoming a stage coach driver and abusing horses, then murdering his pregnant lover, and finally being hung and publicly dissected.[71]

The speculated connection between human and animal violence was first studied in 1961 and 1963. Dr. John Macdonald, a prominent psychiatrist, studied a group of one hundred patients, all of whom had threatened to kill someone, at the Colorado Psychopathic Hospital in Denver and concluded that there was a triad of symptoms that could be used as potential predictors of a child's propensity to commit violent crime as an adult.[72] This triad – often referred to as the Macdonald Triad – was comprised of firesetting, bed-wetting, and animal cruelty.[73] Macdonald believed that a child who showed either an individual symptom or a combination of the triad would be more likely to commit violent crime later in life.[74] Macdonald's triad resonated with other researchers and the public; it continues to be referenced today and included in crime shows such as *Law and Order*, and is common in reporting on serial killers.[75]

---

[66] ELEONORA GULLONE, ANIMAL CRUELTY, ANTISOCIAL BEHAVIOR, AND AGGRESSION: MORE THAN A LINK 5 (2012); *see* Mary Ann Violin, *Pythagoras – The First Animal Rights Philosopher*, 6 BETWEEN THE SPECIES 122, 123 (1990) ("If souls of humans enter into bodies of animals, all creatures must be viewed as king. Eating animal flesh becomes cannibalism, and killing animals becomes murder, incurring the same bloodguilt as slaying a human.").

[67] JOHN LOCKE, SOME THOUGHTS CONCERNING EDUCATION, *in* 9 THE WORKS OF JOHN LOCKE IN TEN VOLUMES 112 (11th edn. 1812 [1693]).

[68] GULLONE, ANIMAL CRUELTY, ANTISOCIAL BEHAVIOR, AND AGGRESSION, at 5 ("If he is not to stifle his human feelings, he must practice kindness towards animals, for he who is cruel to animals becomes hard in his dealings with men.").

[69] *See* PHILIPE PINEL, A TREATISE ON INSANITY 150–56 (D. D. Davis trans., 1962 [1806]).

[70] *See* Sigmund Freud, *Three Contributions to the Theory of Sex* (1905), *in* BASIC WRITINGS OF SIGMUND FREUD 593–94 (A. A. Brill ed., 1938).

[71] *The Four Stages of Cruelty*, TATE, www.tate.org.uk/whats-on/tate-britain/exhibition/hogarth/hogarth -hogarths-modern-moral-series/hogarth-hogarths-4 (last visited Feb. 5, 2018); *see* GULLONE, ANIMAL CRUELTY, ANTISOCIAL BEHAVIOR, AND AGGRESSION, at 6.

[72] JOHN M. MACDONALD & STUART BOYD, THE MURDERER AND HIS VICTIM 205, 299 (1961); John M. Macdonald, *The Threat to Kill*, 120 AM. J. PSYCH. 125, 125–30 (1963).

[73] Macdonald, *The Threat to Kill* at 125–30; *see* GULLONE, ANIMAL CRUELTY, ANTISOCIAL BEHAVIOR, AND AGGRESSION at 7.

[74] Macdonald, *The Threat to Kill* at 125–30.

[75] Roxanne Palmer, *Can You Spot a Serial Killer Before He Kills?*, INT'L BUS. TIMES (Oct. 12, 2012), www .ibtimes.com/can-you-spot-serial-killer-he-kills-847435.

The triad, however, is borne more out of intuition or speculation than hard science and research.[76] More recent studies have suggested that the triad is more "urban myth" than scientific discovery, and in fact pointed to these factors as most likely indicators of childhood victimization. Macdonald himself largely discredited his thesis in his later book, *Homicidal Threats*, in which he noted that he could not find any "statistically significant association between homicide perpetrators" and the triad, including cruelty to animals.[77] The research suggested that the triad simply cannot be identified as a reliable predictor of criminality. According to one scholar, the continued saliency of the triad in popular culture and in practice has dangerous consequences, because children who exhibit one or more of the symptoms might "be falsely labeled as potentially dangerous," and targeted by police.[78]

The Macdonald triad, then, is emblematic of the theme of this chapter – the claims sounds plausible in theory, but are not borne out by research and hard data. As early as 1985 researchers came to regard it as a "psychiatric mistake."[79] As one scholar summarized the current state of research on this point, "[t]ogether or alone, the triad behaviors can indicate a stressed child with poor coping mechanisms or a developmental disability; such a child needs guidance and attention." However, they are not reliable indicators of future dangerousness, and the media and public should stop reporting results to the contrary.[80] Indeed, rather than a marker of criminality, research demonstrates that the presence of one or more of the triad factors is perhaps best used as a marker of an "abusive home life" such that the "triad may be a reaction to abuse before and during adolescence."[81] And yet the view of the triad theory as a prediction of violence persists, and in important ways serves as the parent or predecessor theory for the "link," which makes similar claims, but isolates animal abuse alone as sufficiently predictive of future violence to justify criminal justice interventions. Posing a question

---

[76] *See id.*

[77] Karen Franklin, *Homicidal Triad: Predictor of Violence or Urban Myth?*, PSYCHOL. TODAY (May 2, 2012), www.psychologytoday.com/blog/witness/201205/homicidal-triad-predictor-violence-or-urban -myth.

[78] Kori Ryan, *The Macdonald Triad: Predictor of Violence or Urban Myth?* AMERICAN SOCIETY OF CRIMINOLOGY (May 2009) (unpublished MS thesis, California State University, Fresno) (available at http://cdmweb.lib.csufresno.edu/cdm/ref/collection/thes/id/37222). It is worth noting that if the form of intervention was not incarceration, but treatment and interventions, then an overinclusive risk factor for antisocial behavior could be a positive thing. *See* Jack Levin & Arnold Arluke, *Reducing the Link's False Positive Problem*, in THE LINK BETWEEN ANIMAL VIOLENCE AND HUMAN VIOLENCE at 169. It is the risk of associating one with criminality and brutality at a young age based on overinclusive data that is concerning.

[79] JACK LEVIN & JAMES ALAN FOX, MASS MURDER: AMERICA'S GROWING MENACE 27 (1985).

[80] Katherine Ramsland, *Triad of Evil: Do Three Simple Behaviors Predict the Murder-Prone Child?*, PSYCHOL. TODAY (Mar. 16, 2012), www.psychologytoday.com/blog/shadow-boxing/201203/triad-evil (explaining the flaws with the published data purporting to confirm the triad by noting, for example, that they made "no effort to work within a randomized scientific design, [and] they gathered information from just 36 convicted murderers ... All had voluntarily agreed to talk. Once more, the sample was too problematic to draw significant conclusions.").

[81] Llian Alys et. al, *Developmental Animal Cruelty and its Correlates in Sexual Homicide Offenders and Sex Offenders*, in THE LINK BETWEEN ANIMAL VIOLENCE AND HUMAN VIOLENCE at 147–48.

that might be similarly apt with regard to the link relied on by animal protection groups, one researcher asks why the triad has persevered without evidence and speculates that "urban myths ... are difficult to eradicate," positing that the triad has maintained its "status as a truth largely because of its retelling."[82]

In addition to Macdonald, the work of Margaret Mead could also fairly be considered among the intellectual projects that spurred the current interest in the relationship between animal abuse and human violence. Mead published an article in 1964 in which she summarized psychological studies of murderers and other violent adults.[83] Her review of the literature suggested that killing animals was a common theme among violent individuals, and she posited that inconsistent parental teaching about when it is okay to kill animals, how animals should be killed, and what animals should be killed, may lead children to harm animals in their youths.[84] Dr. Mead also suggested that if children are neither caught nor punished for inappropriately killing, they may grow up to be more hostile, which may lead to aggressiveness in adulthood.[85] She concluded that schools should follow "a more carefully planned" curriculum based on "handling of behavior toward living creatures" and that child therapists should be alert for any reports of children killing living things, as it "could prove a diagnostic sign, and that such children, diagnosed early, could be helped instead of being allowed to embark on a long career of episodic violence and murder."[86]

Ultimately, Mead's conclusions on this point are rather modest; the article is simply her observations made in the course of reviewing studies and speaking to other psychologists and psychiatrists. Nonetheless, Macdonald's symptom triad and Mead's paper, both from the same time period, are credited with playing a critical role in directing attention toward animal cruelty as a precursor and predictor of violence.[87] Macdonald's speculative and debunked triad and Mead's article are in no small part the background and inspiration for contemporary link research.

6.2.2 *Empirical Research Regarding the Link*

Following centuries of conjecture about a connection between animal abuse and human violence, over the last several decades researchers have set out to empirically

---

[82] Ryan at 60, 66 ("[W]ithout further research, the use of the Macdonald triad to predict future violent behavior is not warranted.").

[83] Margaret Mead, *Cultural Factors in the Cause and Prevention of Pathological Homicide*, 28 Bull. Menninger Clinic 11, 11–13 (1964).

[84] *Id.* at 21.

[85] *Id.* at 22.

[86] *Id.*

[87] *See, e.g.*, Gullone, Animal Cruelty, Antisocial Behavior, and Aggression, at 6–7 (discussing Dr. Macdonald and Dr. Mead and how, in the early 1960s, "cruelty to animals as an important sign of other problematic behavior had caught people's attention"); Arluke, Levin, Luke & Ascione at 964 (crediting Macdonald's triad as the beginning of researchers' interest in "the relation between animal abuse and interpersonal violence").

prove the existence of a "link" between human violence and animal abuse.[88] In the view of the animal protection movement, the research has succeeded in confirming the link between animal and human violence. In 2018, leaders in the animal protection movement declared that animal abuse is a clear and unequivocal "predictor of future violence." Such a view of the link has unquestionably shaped the way that police, prosecutors, and lawmakers think about and respond to animal abuse. As the literature review that comprises the remainder of this section reveals, however, the research does not support the "clear predictor" of violence thesis, and in fact does not support many of the dominant characterizations of the literature employed by the animal protection movement.

There is simply not a reliable body of research showing that animal abuse will predict human abuse. Animal abuse appears to be widespread among violent offenders, but not particularly predictive of such violence. In fact, although many studies show that a history of animal abuse is more common among people who commit violence against humans, the data is clear that *most people* who commit violent crimes *do not* have a history of animal abuse. Thus, the first error of link-think is the assumption that most people who commit animal abuse will move on or graduate to interpersonal violence. In addition, there is a second and potentially even more powerful quantitative critique that has been ignored to date: Even assuming the existence of a clear link between human violence and animal violence, there is no support for the commonplace claim that incarceration would negate the violent tendencies of one who abuses an animal so as to make the community safer, as promised by link advocates. Accepting the truth of the link as predictive of violence (which has not been proven), the question still arises of what to do with this information. Before elaborating on these critiques, this section provides an overview of the seminal link research conducted after the publication of Macdonald's triad theory. The studies discussed below are those that are most frequently cited by other scholars and those that have been specifically identified as producing important findings. As a group, they demonstrate that many violent criminals have abused animals, but the body of research offers almost nothing to support the repeated claim that animal cruelty is a "clear predictor" of future human violence. This analysis of the seminal research in this field exposes, as Heather Piper has explained, that the movement has let its "prejudices get in the way" of fairly interpreting and extrapolating from the available data – the version of the link presented to the public is more a "gut feeling" shrouded in a façade of scientific inquiry than it is a true representation of the research.

---

[88] *See e.g.*, Melissa Trollinger, *The Link Among Animal Abuse, Child Abuse, and Domestic Violence*, 30-SEP COLO. LAW. 29, 30 (2001) ("It is likely that if an animal is being abused, a child or partner in the household also is being abused. This link originates with the fact that women, children, and animals have shared similar histories and characteristics – all three were considered property in the past.").

6.2.2.1 Felthouse and Yudowitz (1977)

In 1977, Dr. Alan Felthouse and Dr. Bernard Yudowitz conducted the first seminal study of the link. They evaluated thirty-one female prisoners in the Massachusetts Correctional Institution at Framingham, and nineteen male prisoners in the Middlesex County House of Correction.[89] The evaluations consisted "of a multiple choice questionnaire, a psychiatric interview, and review of the subject's record."[90] The multiple choice questionnaire consisted of thirty-eight questions, eleven of which were demographic and twenty-seven which "were hypothetically related to assaultive behavior."[91] Twenty-seven questions asked about childhood psychopathology, with each question having an answer range that the evaluators determined were nondeviant and an answer range that was deviant. For example, one question asked about bedwetting and provided four answers: "under 6, 6 to 9, 10 to 14, and 15 or older." If a participant selected "under 6," the answer was in the nondeviant category, while if a participant selected any other answer, she was considered deviant.[92]

The evaluators then separated the female participant group into "assaultive and nonassaultive" groups.[93] Felthouse and Yudowitz found that 36 percent of assaultive females reported a history of animal cruelty, while none of the nonassaultive females reported a history of animal cruelty.[94] The researchers argued that this was consistent with Macdonald's "familiar symptom-triad" of bedwetting, "firesetting, and cruelty to animals." However, Felthouse and Yudowitz were quick to acknowledge that cruelty to animals is not specifically indicative "of assaultive potential in females." Indeed, the findings are that other factors, including abusive parental punishment, are more strongly correlative with future violence. And the data confirms that people who commit violent felonies are more likely than not to have no history of animal abuse.

---

[89]   Alan R. Felthouse & Bernard Yudowitz, *Approaching a Comparative Typology of Assaultive Female Offenders*, 40 PSYCHIATRY 270, 271 (1977).

[90]   *Id.*

[91]   *Id.*

[92]   *Id.*

[93]   *Id.* The evaluators placed women with "a conviction of a crime of personal violence (assault and battery, assault with a deadly weapon, manslaughter or murder)" in the assaultive group. Women who did not have any known charges involving personal violence were placed in the nonassaultive group. Interestingly, seven of the thirty-nine women were not placed because of legal "ambiguities" regarding whether to classify a particular crime as a crime of violence. Some of these ambiguities threaten to undermine the soundness of the researchers' approach because they reflect a tenuous grasp of the legal realities of criminal law. For example, the researchers did not include within their study of violent women those women whose conviction was for armed robbery, on the theory that such women might have had as their primary objective "acquiring money." It is legally specious to treat one's conviction as somehow more or less violent depending on their motive rather than their intent to cause harm. The apparent conclusion that any conviction for an assaultive behavior would have been motivated primarily or solely by a desire to harm, instead of perhaps out of a desire to gain a financial or personal advantage, is untenable.

[94]   *Id.* at 273.

Further, even the limited correlation demonstrated by the research in this study is doubtful given a number of deficiencies with the study design.[95] Beyond the very small number of research participants, more recent research has documented problems associated with relying on inmate populations for this type of study.[96] Specifically, when using inmate populations, a substantial rate of inmates (usually well more than half) refuse to participate in the study. The ones who do participate "may have a psychological vested interest in presenting mean and aggressive personae ... they might be expected to exaggerate, or even to fabricate, in discussing the violent side of their personalities."[97] And there is even reason to believe that prison population studies will under-report the rate of animal abuse among non-violent offenders, because it should not be surprising, researchers have explained, "that inmates who are willing to disclose their aggressive activities toward humans would also be willing to disclose their aggressive activities toward animals."[98]

Moreover, insofar as the study is cited as support for the proposition that people who abuse animals often move on to interpersonal violence, the complete failure of the study to consider any acts of interpersonal violence that preceded a participant's conviction for a violent crime is highly relevant. The study cannot demonstrate a graduation-theory type of link because the offender may have engaged in regular acts of violence before ever being convicted. For example, a participant could have been involved in school fights prior to ever committing animal cruelty. More recent research has in fact shown that animal abuse frequently does not precede human violence, and in some cases children start "by abusing people and then later graduate to animals." Without a clear timeline for when the human violence and when the animal violence began, it is impossible to know whether one graduated from human violence to animal violence, or vice versa.

Despite its methodological shortcomings and the limited nature of the findings, the study is frequently invoked by scholars as an important source of scientific support for a connection between human violence and prior animal abuse. Even more troubling, the reliance on this study has frequently been misleading. In discussing the results, activists and researchers have focused on the "symptom-triad" (of bedwetting, animal abuse, and firesetting), but it is striking that those three symptoms were not the "items

---

[95] First, the study relies on a very small sample size and is entirely retrospective in nature, meaning that it is nearly impossible to meaningfully conclude that animal abuse in the past caused subsequent human violence. *See, e.g.*, Clifton P. Flynn, *Examining the Links Between Animal Abuse and Human Violence*, 55 CRIME L. & SOC. CHANGE 453, 460 (2011) (summarizing the critiques of research claiming to show the link); Eleonora Gullone, *An Evaluative Review of Theories Related to Animal Cruelty*, 4 J. ANIMAL ETHICS 37 (2014). In addition, the data relies on the participants honestly and accurately reporting what happened in their past, sometimes distant past.

[96] Arluke, Levin, Luke & Ascione at 965–66. Because the participants were all prisoners, it is not clear whether the findings translate to individuals who are not part of the criminal justice system but who are also violent. Flynn at 460 ("In most cases, the samples comprise groups who are not representative of the population as a whole – typically, incarcerated criminals.").

[97] Flynn at 460.

[98] *Id.*

of highest" incidence among the group of violent offenders. For example, 70 percent of assaultive females and 31 percent of nonassaultive females reported parental alcoholism.[99] Additionally, 56 percent of assaultive females and 8 percent of non-assaultive females reported injurious parental punishments.[100] Childhood headaches, parental abandonment, poor peer relations, and neglectful or brutal paternal discipline all correlated more strongly among offenders than animal abuse.[101] Indeed, of all the factors singled out for study by the researchers, only "injurious maternal punishments" correlated less than animal cruelty with violent crime (33 to 36 percent).[102]

This research, then, might well be cited for the very general proposition that a wide range of conditions, including social and family relationships as well as medical conditions, may correlate with future violence. Animal abuse is not uniquely important or predictive, and instead is less likely to predict future violence than many other factors based on this data.

6.2.2.2 Kellert and Felthous (1985)

Recognizing the limitations of research based on studies of only inmates, in 1985 Dr. Felthous continued his research along with Dr. Stephen Kellert in a study entitled *Childhood Cruelty Toward Animals Among Criminals and Noncriminals*.[103] In this study, the evaluators gathered 152 participants, including 102 male federal prisoners and 50 random male non-inmates in Connecticut and Kansas.[104] The evaluators interviewed each participant for one to two hours using a standardized interview that included closed- and open-ended questions. These questions focused on the participant's demographics, "childhood family relationships, childhood behavior patterns, relationships to animals in childhood, adult behavior patterns, and a closed-ended survey on attitudes toward animals and human aggression." Prison counselors, rather than the evaluators, rated inmates on a scale of 1–10 for aggressiveness based on their observations of the inmates during incarceration.[105] Additionally, the evaluators formed their own ratings based on their interviews with the inmates. Based on those ratings, inmate participants were separated into aggressive (32 inmate participants), moderately aggressive (18 inmate participants), and nonaggressive (52 inmate participants) groups. Most strikingly, Kellert and Felthous found that 68.7 percent of aggressive inmates, 44.4 percent of moderately aggressive inmates, 48.1 percent of nonaggressive inmates, and a whopping 72 percent of non-inmates had committed at least one act of animal cruelty. This data is consistent with other research that has

---

[99]   Felthouse & Yudowitz at 273.
[100]   *Id.* at 273.
[101]   *Id.* at 273.
[102]   *Id.* at 275.
[103]   Stephen R. Kellert & Alan R. Felthous, *Childhood Cruelty Toward Animals Among Criminals and Noncriminals*, 38 Hum. Rel. 1113 (1985) [hereinafter Kellert & Felthouse 1985].
[104]   *Id.* at 1117.
[105]   *Id.* at 1116–17.

TABLE 6.1 *Frequency of Childhood Animal Cruelties Among Criminals and Noncriminals in Kansas and Connecticut*

	Number of animal cruelties				
	0	1–2	3–4	5 +	N
Aggressive criminals					
N	10	9	5	8	32
Percent	31.2	28.1	15.6	25	
χ^2	.63	1.26	.56	11.83	
Moderately aggressive criminals					
N	10	5	2	1	18
Percent	55.6	27.7	11.1	5.6	
χ^2	1.07	.75	.00	.12	
Nonaggressive criminals					
N	27	20	2	3	52
Percent	51.9	38.5	3.8	5.8	
χ^2	1.8	.07	2.5	.30	
Noncriminals					
N	14	28	8	0	50
Percent	28	56	16	0	
χ^2	1.84	2.84	1.04	3.95	
Totals					
N	61	62	17	12	152
%	40.1	40.8	11.2	7.9	
$\chi^2 = 30.56, df = 9, p = < .005$					

[a] This category includes inmates at Leavenworth prison only.

found a surprisingly high rate of animal abuse among all persons, and that find other "links" that are more predictive of future violence or crime than animal abuse.

It would come as a big surprise to many who have relied on the Felthous study as a foundationally critical piece of link research that this very study finds that noncriminals committed animal abuse at a higher rate than all offenders, including those deemed particularly aggressive or violent.

To account for this discrepancy, Kellert and Felthous also developed "1–5 severity ratings" for the various types of reported animal cruelty.[106] Using this 1–5 severity scale, Kellert and Felthous concluded that the aggressive inmates scored significantly higher than the other groups.[107] The most violent animal abuse, they conclude, is committed by the most violent offenders. But Kellert and Felthous do not elaborate on how this scale was created, or which acts fall into which rating. Their subjective assessments are

[106]   *Id.* at 1120.
[107]   *Id.* at 1121.

based in part on the "social acceptability" of the practice, but this is a slippery metric leading them, for example, to conclude that dogfighting is an act of cruelty, but cockfighting is less clearly so.[108] Such a subjective metric is susceptible to implicit bias along race or class lines. In addition, by using their sense of social acceptability, Kellert and Felthous unilaterally limited their study to harms on the most charismatic or statused animals in the most socially disapproved contexts. Such a framework is at odds with recognizing that the deliberate killing of an animal can occur in a variety of socially acceptable contexts, including hunting, food production, and research. These socially acceptable killings may in some (or many) instances be less sadistic and more "normalized," but it is not clear that such killing would necessarily do less to desensitize people to the suffering of others than socially unacceptable killing.[109] Animal abuse of a form that is more socially disapproved may be a better indicator of deviance, but if the theory is that harming animals strips one of empathy or hardens their heart, there is no reason that this could not happen in socially acceptable settings as well. Of course, it may be the case that injuring certain animals of particular social value is more predictive of interpersonal violence, but this is something that should be studied, and not simply assumed away.[110] Research from the agricultural setting suggests that such assumptions may not be true, and instead points to the dehumanizing effects of slaughterhouse work. And some practices that are socially acceptable, such as hunting, are still limited to a very small percentage of the population (less than 6 percent of Americans), and may be viewed as socially unacceptable by many people in spite of the legality of the practice.

Another feature of their findings that the researchers never directly confront is that the data shows that the most "aggressive" offenders had a higher rate of zero violence toward animals than the non-offenders. It is striking that only 28 percent of non-criminals had never abused an animal, as compared to roughly 31 percent of aggressive offenders and 55 percent of moderately aggressive offenders. The complete absence of animal abuse in one's past, in other words, is a very poor predictor of whether one will become violent or not – people who had never abused animals were *more* likely to be violent or moderately violent offenders.

Similarly, Kellert and Felthous do not necessarily find that animal abuse is the best predictor of subsequent human violence. They explored the family dynamics of each participant, including their childhood aggressiveness toward humans.[111] They found that aggressive inmates had significantly higher childhood aggressiveness

---

[108] *Id.* at 1119.

[109] That is not to suggest that a person who engages in socially acceptable research or slaughter practices is not engaging in acts that are distinguishable from a diagnostic or psychological standpoint from the person who gratuitously abuses a puppy. But more research is needed as to what predictive role systemic acts of animal violence can play, if any, in assessing the likelihood of human violence.

[110] Some research has indeed found that aggressive, sadistic violence, particularly of a repeated nature, is the most likely form of animal abuse to predict subsequent interpersonal violence. Levin & Arluke at 169.

[111] Kellert & Felthouse 1985 at 1125.

scores toward humans than the other groups.[112] Kellert and Felthous also found that aggressive inmates had a high rate of fighting as a child (61.1 percent), a high rate of domestic violence within their families (75.5 percent), and a high rate of parental alcohol or drug abuse (49 percent).[113] Kellert and Felthous conclude that "aggression among adult criminals may be strongly correlated with a history of family abuse and childhood cruelty toward animals."[114] They conclude that society needs to be more attuned to the "importance of childhood animal cruelty as a potential indicator of *disturbed family relationships* and future antisocial and aggressive behavior."[115] Animal cruelty may be predictive of violent crime, the researchers find, but perhaps no more so than problematic family relationships, and ultimately people who are not violent offenders were found to be more likely than violent criminals to have committed animal abuse.

Such findings bear almost no resemblance to the public advocacy surrounding the link discussed above. Moreover, this study, like the 1975 study, is plagued by a relatively small sample size and its entirely retrospective nature.[116] As the researchers concede, "[a]ny retrospective study of an adult's childhood is fraught with methodological problems associated with the reliability and validity of recall information," and such problems are "compounded when collecting information from a population of prison inmates who are influenced by institutional" context.[117] Kellert and Felthous attempted to use additional methods to validate the results, such as cross-referencing criminal history and contacting a family member of another "significant and important figure in the subject's childhood," but those methods failed and were ultimately not used in the study.[118] And like the research discussed in Section 6.2.1, the absence of a timeline indicating that the individuals who harmed animals did so *before* moving on to harm humans precludes any attempt to prove a progression or graduation thesis from this data. The most generous reading of the data is that those people who at some point demonstrated extreme aggressiveness to animals also showed a propensity to harm people.

6.2.2.3 Felthous and Kellert (1987)

In 1987, Felthous and Kellert provided what appears to be the first compressive literature review of the research examining the so-called link.[119] Felthous and

---

[112] *Id.* at 1125.
[113] *Id.* at 1126–27.
[114] *Id.* at 1127.
[115] *Id.* at 1127–28.
[116] Levin & Fox at 35 ("The problem with generalizing the traits observed in specific mass killers to larger groups is demonstrated in the predictive limitations of elements in the Macdonald triad.").
[117] Kellert & Felthouse 1985 at 1117–18.
[118] *Id.* at 1118.
[119] Alan R. Felthous & Stephen R. Kellert, *Childhood Cruelty to Animals and Later Aggression Against People: A Review*, 144 Am. J. Psychiatry 710 (1987) [hereinafter Felthouse & Kellert 1987]. In 1979,

Kellert aimed to determine "whether the scientific literature support[ed] an association between a pattern of repeated, substantial cruelty to animals in childhood and later violence against people that is serious and recurrent."[120] Felthous and Kellert identified ten studies conducted between 1968 and 1984 that found no relationship between cruelty to animals and violence against humans,[121] and they identified four studies during the same period which found some relationship. That is, more than 70 percent of the studies at that point found no connection or correlation whatsoever, and three of the four that found some relationship were conducted by Felthous.[122]

Felthous and Kellert attempt to explain why some studies find a relationship, while others do not.[123] A principle critique of the research that did not find a relationship was what they considered to be the absence of a standardized definition of animal cruelty. When the definition of cruelty is left "vague" or no definition is provided, Kellert and Felthous argued that people might include activities such as "swatting at house flies or disciplining a pet dog with a gentle slap," which "are presumably common" and "may not be particularly symptomatic of abnormal aggression."[124] It is unclear why these researchers conclude, without citation, that people would be inclined to include such acts within their definition of animal cruelty. It seems unlikely in the extreme that many of the prisoners, for example, who reported engaging in animal cruelty in the past were referencing acts of insect control.

Most significantly, however, as they critique the studies finding no "link," Felthous and Kellert's review of the existing research leads them to conclude that predicting a prior act of animal cruelty based on a violent act toward a human "would be risky indeed." The data simply cannot support such a conclusion. Ultimately they argue that more "serious and recurrent" acts of human violence, but not one-off acts of violence against humans, would be expected to correlate with animal abuse. Felthous and Kellert note that, applying the "serious and recurrent" standard, all but one of the studies found a relationship between such human violence and animal cruelty. In their view, then, the best available data suggests that if there is a connection between human violence and animal violence, it exists

---

Dr. Alasdair J. MacDonald, a psychiatrist, published a literature review of research pertaining to the relationship between children and companion animals. Alasdair J. MacDonald, *Review: Children and Companion Animals*, 5 CHILD: CARE, HEALTH & DEVELOPMENT 347 (1979). This review focused on the general relationship between children and companion animals, and whether companion animals may aid children during psychotherapy. *Id.* at 347–48. Within his review, Dr. MacDonald discussed some of the research relating to cruelty to animals. *Id.* at 352–55. He noted that "the scientific literature is scanty and in large part anecdotal." *Id.* at 352. Dr. MacDonald briefly discussed three studies that showed a relationship between Macdonald's symptom triad and violence. *Id.* at 353–54. Only one of those studies, Macdonald's 1963 study discussed above, attempted to link animal cruelty as a child to later adult violence. *Id.*

[120]   Felthous & Kellert 1987 at 710.
[121]   *Id.* at 711–13.
[122]   *Id.* at 713–15.
[123]   *Id.* at 715.
[124]   *Id.*

primarily in instances where a person repeatedly engages in serious violent offenses. Their proposal based on these findings is a modest one: They urge "clinicians, jurists, school teachers, parents, and others who work and play with children" to "be alert to the potentially ominous significance of [animal cruelty] in childhood and the advisability of concerned, helpful intervention."

In sum, the classic, foundational research in the field does not support the conclusion that one who commits abuse to an animal will likely graduate to human violence.

6.2.3 *The Most Recent Studies*

6.2.3.1 Merz-Perez, Heide, and Silverman (2001)

In 2001, Linda Merz-Perez, Dr. Kathleen M. Heide, and Dr. Ira J. Silverman conducted a study "designed to investigate whether the phenomenon of cruelty to animals might serve as an early warning sign of predictable future violence against humans."[125] This study evaluated ninety participants, forty-five violent inmates and forty-five nonviolent inmates incarcerated in a maximum-security prison in Florida.[126] The participants were randomly selected by prison staff members based on the current offense each person was serving time for. Evaluators then looked at the nonviolent inmates' criminal histories, and if one had a violent offense, that individual was removed from the participant pool.[127] Then, evaluators looked at the most serious offense committed by each inmate. The violent group contained inmates with convictions for: murder (33 percent); attempted murder (2 percent); sex offenses (30 percent); assault and/or battery or resisting a law enforcement officer with violence (21 percent); burglary of an occupied dwelling and armed burglary (9 percent); and robbery with a dangerous weapon or firearm (5 percent).[128] The nonviolent group contained inmates with convictions for: burglary of unoccupied structures (40 percent); drug offenses (35 percent); property crimes (23 percent); and possession of a firearm (2 percent).[129] Demographically, the two groups were very similar in terms of age, race, education, and marital status.[130]

Evaluators then used the Children and Animals Assessment Instrument, developed by Dr. Frank R. Ascione, "to gather data with respect to the participants' experience with animals, including cruelty to animals either committed or observed by the study participants."[131] Evaluators interviewed each participant face-to-face

---

[125] Linda Merz-Perez et al., *Childhood Cruelty to Animals and Subsequent Violence Against Humans*, 45 INT'L J. OFFENDER THERAPY & COMP. CRIMINOLOGY 556, 557 (2001).

[126] *Id.* at 558.

[127] *Id.*

[128] *Id.*

[129] *Id.*

[130] *Id.* at 558–59.

[131] *Id.* at 559.

and looked through documents provided by the prison, including "police reports; charging, conviction, and sentencing materials; presentence investigations; and correctional assessment forms."[132]

Merz-Perez et al. found that 56 percent of violent inmates had committed past acts of animal cruelty, compared to 20 percent of nonviolent inmates.[133] Broken down further, 29 percent of violent inmates had committed animal cruelty to wild animals, compared to 13 percent of nonviolent inmates; 14 percent of violent inmates had committed cruelty to farm animals compared to 2 percent of nonviolent inmates; 26 percent of violent inmates had committed cruelty to pet animals compared to 7 percent of nonviolent inmates; and 11 percent of violent inmates had committed cruelty to stray animals compared to 0 percent of nonviolent inmates.[134] The differences in wild and farm animals were not statistically significant.[135]

Merz-Perez et al. conclude that "offenders who committed violent crimes as adults were significantly more likely than adult nonviolent offenders to have committed acts of cruelty against animals in general and pet and stray animals in particular."[136] The data is indeed striking and shows a strong correlation between pet and stray animal abuse and violent offending. Yet even as to pets and strays, the most predictive forms of animal abuse, somewhere between 75 and 89 percent of violent offenders had not engaged in such abuse. Conceding that predictions about deviant behavior, even among people who abuse the most beloved animals, are nearly impossible, the researchers conclude by noting the need for more research:

> Is aggression against animals committed as children predictive of subsequent adult aggression against human beings? Our results underscore the need for a longitudinal study of children through their adult years to see to what extent violence toward specific types of animals as children is causally connected to adult violence against humans.[137]

Given the complexity of the topic, the number of factors that are relevant in considering why a person behaves violently, and the lack of a longitudinal study, they caution that when a child commits an act of cruelty against an animal, it "should be investigated as a specific act committed by a specific individual against a specific animal."[138] They

[132] *Id.* This study suffers from many of the same methodical flaws as those that came before it. It uses a small sample size of ninety participants. It is also entirely retrospective, and while the evaluators also had some documents to verify the participants' claims, Merz-Perez et al. note that some of the violent inmates were inconsistent in what they told evaluators. *Id.* at 561–63 ("Furthermore, in the case of violent offenders, contradictory information had been sometimes reported.").
[133] *Id.* at 561–62.
[134] *Id.* at 562.
[135] *Id.* In discussing the differences in cruelty toward pets, Merz-Perez et al. note that the only incidences of cruelty toward pets by nonviolent inmates were dog fighting. *Id.* at 563. The three nonviolent inmates who reported a history of dogfighting were all black. *Id.* Merz-Perez et al. suggest that dogfighting may be a confounding variable because of varying societal standards around the practice.
[136] *Id.* at 570.
[137] *Id.*
[138] *Id.*

rebuke the temptation to make sweeping, general conclusions about the predictive power of past animal abuse as unsupportable by existing research, including their own. The research does not prove that a significant percentage of animal abusers become violent offenders; indeed, it is more likely that animal abusers will not commit violent offenses than that they will, and the best available data does not lend itself to anything approaching a predictive conclusion.[139] Of course, an individualistic, holistic assessment of children engaged in animal abuse may lead mental health experts to identify participants who are in need of intervention, so animal abuse should not be written off as irrelevant, just as bullying, self-confidence issues, and family abuse should all be recognized as having *links* (emphasis on the plural) to deviant behavior, including interpersonal violence. According to these researchers, animal abuse is not uniquely linked to human violence, but rather it is one of many links to human violence. Moreover, subsequent research has even questioned the reliability of the limited conclusions announced by Merez-Perez et al.[140]

6.2.3.2 Piper (2003)

Writing from the perspective of a relatively new academic who had a substantial career as a social worker, Heather Piper wrote a provocative research paper questioning whether the conventional wisdom regarding the link wrongly maligned the children she had been working with as a professional. Can children who commit animal abuse, she wondered, be the "sheep in wolf's clothing"?[141] Piper details her impressions from a review of the existing literature, and her summary calls to mind the critiques of overstated or bogus forensic evidence that have been exposed as resulting in wrongful convictions in the Unites States. Piper concludes that much of the research regarding the link "has a quasi-scientific expert quality to it, even when the data fail to warrant it," and she criticizes the misleadingly "seductive power of numbers." She claims that too much of the research and too many of the conclusions from the research start from the assumption of a link, and suffer from a "self-fulfilling tendency."[142] Piper laments that many academic papers and advocacy groups have rejected the subtle and nuanced nature of the research, and instead have perpetuated a view of human behavior that is a "myth or legend."

As an experienced social worker, Piper laments what she refers to as the "snowballing potential of research" that all starts from the assumption that the dominant discourse regarding the link is valid. She notes that the research simply does not

---

[139]   *Id.* at 571 (conceding that animal cruelty "is but one expression of violence" among the many forms that may be indicative of future or past violence of another form).

[140]   Levin & Arluke at 163–71.

[141]   Heather Piper, *The Linkage of Animal Abuse with Interpersonal Violence*, 3 J. Soc. Work 161 (2003).

[142]   Among the defects Piper identifies is the logical fallacy of assuming that because a handful of infamous killers have admitted to abusing animals, one should assume that all animal abusers are potential serial killers. *Id.* at 165–66 (quoting a research paper identifying a "definite cycle of abuse that starts with animals and leads to humans").

support the claims made by leaders in the field, such as Phil Arkow, who has written that animal cruelty is a clear predictor of future human violence. Piper even expresses skepticism for what is treated as an obvious intervention in cases of potential animal abuse, the need for cross-reporting across agencies. To Piper, the data simply does not support suggesting that, for example, a veterinarian should be in the position of predicting based on injuries to a pet, either that a child was abused, or that he will grow into an abuser. The problem of the link's practical application, as she puts it, is that "a great deal is extrapolated from very little."[143] She finds that the expert opinions by animal protection advocates on the topic of the link tread into the realm of the disingenuous, and credits them with giving the link a sensationalized "life of its own" that is largely divorced from reliable research.

Piper's main contribution, then, is a compilation of the critiques of the link studies up through 2004. These critiques, she observes, do not get as much attention, but they are also far from a "minority quirk," and instead reflect a more thoughtful approach to understanding human behavior.[144] Piper's earnest call to avoid a moral panic, and to avoid rigid quantitative formulas for detecting violence (or deviancy), is an important piece of the link literature. She calls for a significant corrective in the form of avoiding absolutist rhetoric with regard to animal abuse, and instead provides an "endorsement of the need for more qualitative and practice-related" understandings of individuals. Piper's work is a call to social workers to engage in more holistic inquiries rather than focusing on the provided "abusing profile," because the use of such profiles, she concludes, will ultimately not "assist in preventing abuse," but rather will attach a "negative label" to children that "once applied is unlikely to ever leave them." The point is not that "links never exist"; instead, the focus on links and the use of such language "narrows options and therefore limits knowledge and understanding" by excluding "more challenging explanations." In the end, Piper offers a particularly cynical take on the link research: "[I]t is often impossible to know for sure whether a given problem is or is not caused by another particular problem."[145]

6.2.3.3 Tallichet and Hensley (2004)

In 2004, Dr. Suzanne E. Tallichet and Dr. Christopher Hensley sought "to establish whether a link between recurrent acts of childhood and adolescent animal cruelty and later repeated acts of interpersonal violence toward humans exist[ed] in

---

[143] *Id.* at 168 (finding fault with the methods and conclusions in Ascione's seminal study finding that over half of the women in domestic violence shelters had experienced animal abuse in their homes).

[144] *Id.* One set of critiques relates to the general framing of the link research. As a product in modern times of medical and legal thinkers, Piper identifies a critique based on the inherently conservative approach of these fields that regards those who cause harm as "either bad (or evil) and requir[ing] punishment, or mad (or criminally insane) and [in] need of being locked up."

[145] *Id.* at 174 (observing that it is better to solve the "actual complaint rather than the presumed underlying problems") (quoting FURMAN & AHOLA, SOLUTION TALK: HOSTING THERAPEUTIC CONVERSATIONS 192).

a sample of violent and nonviolent offenders known to have committed a variety of crimes."[146] The authors distributed 39-item questionnaires to male inmates in two medium-security prisons and one maximum-security prison.[147] Out of 2,093 inmates, 261 participated in the study.[148] The problem of self-selection for participation and the study of an inmate-only population are acknowledged by the authors. The authors also acknowledge that the pace and robustness of the academic studies of the link have not kept up with the media narrative and public confidence that animal cruelty is a predictor of human violence.

The survey asked inmates whether they had been convicted of a violent crime, such as murder, attempted murder, rape, or aggravated assault. The inmates were also asked how many times they had been convicted for those offenses. On top of demographic information, such as race, education level, residence, marital status, number of siblings, and whether the inmates were sent to a juvenile detention facility, they were asked "[h]ow many times have you ever hurt or killed animals, other than for hunting?" Out of the multitude of factors studied by Tallichet and Hensley, two were found to have a statistically significant relationship with crimes of violence. They found that the number of siblings the inmate had and the number of times the inmate committed animal cruelty correlated with violence as an adult. The researchers do not posit an explanation for why there was a relationship between family size and later adult violence, and thus play into Piper's narrative above about the self-fulfilling nature of this research by focusing exclusively on their finding that "animal cruelty may be a predictor of later adult violence."[149]

Like other researchers in the field, however, Tallichet and Hensley are cognizant of the limitations on their data. Their data-gathering instrument, for example, may not accurately categorize people as violent or nonviolent. The questionnaire only asked inmates whether they had been convicted of violent crimes, but convictions do not necessarily reflect the reality of one's prior crimes; for example, an inmate may have committed a violent act, but never been caught, or as frequently happens, the inmate may have pleaded guilty to a nonviolent charge in exchange for the more serious, violent charges being dismissed.[150] It is also the case that people are wrongfully convicted of both violent and nonviolent offenses.[151] The authors also recognize that in light of the "very low" response rate of only 12.5 percent, it is doubtful whether the results could be generalized "to the larger population of inmates across the

---

[146]   Suzanne E. Tallichet & Christopher Hensley, *Exploring the Link Between Recurrent Acts of Childhood and Adolescent Animal Cruelty and Subsequent Violent Crime*, 29 CRIM. J. REV. 304, 309 (2004).

[147]   *Id.*

[148]   *Id.*

[149]   *Id.* at 313.

[150]   *Id.* at 313–14.

[151]   *See generally* WRONGFUL CONVICTIONS AND THE DNA REVOLUTION: TWENTY-FIVE YEARS OF FREEING THE INNOCENT (Daniel S. Medwed ed., 2017). More generally, problems have been identified with studying only prison populations for this sort of research. The currently available data, then, does not truly allow one to isolate differences between those who commit crimes and those who do not. *Id.*

U.S.," let alone the general public.[152] Also, like the studies that preceded it, Tallichet and Hensley's work focuses on the predictive power of animal cruelty, but it does not consider whether other interpersonal violence preceded (and predicted) the first acts of animal abuse.[153] Was the child or adolescent getting into fights and confrontations at school long before mistreating an animal, and if so, should this sort of antisocial behavior be treated as the real miner's canary?

Ultimately, their data might support an intuition that violence against animals is connected to subsequent human violence, but there is a great deal of speculation baked into such a conclusion. As the authors note,

> [T]his question can only be addressed by examining the outcome of a large cohort of youth who have committed animal cruelty, to determine whether these behaviors are truly predictive and, if so, to what degree.[154]

Although the researchers acknowledge that there are simply too many variables, too many unknowns to be able to say with confidence that animal abuse is predictive of future interpersonal violence, they note that animal protection groups have been stressing the utility of animal abuse as "a symptom of human violence."

6.2.3.4 Levin and Arluke (2009) and Arluke and Madifs (2014)

Arnold Arluke and Jack Levin published a series of papers, culminating in a book chapter in 2009, examining what they perceive as some of the glaring problems with prior link research. One problem identified by these researchers was the inflexible adherence to the assumption that animal violence by people, particularly kids or adolescents, will predict future human violence. Arluke and Levin, along with two other researchers, published a paper in 1999 that noted the "failure of previous studies" to demonstrate a consistent link between animal cruelty and human violence, and they posited that the data is better viewed as supporting a generalized "deviance model."[155] Piper and others have criticized these conclusions as indicative of the sort of cultural scripting that is overly deterministic and preoccupied with finding a *singular* cause for behavior, rather than recognizing the multifaceted nature of links that make reliable predictions based on one set of behaviors impossible. Nonetheless, it was a groundbreaking moment of introspection when some of the leading researchers in the field challenged, and undermined the assumption that dominates the animal protection narrative about the link – that animal abuse is a predictor of future violence. Arluke et al. critiqued this sort of link-

---

[152]   Tallichet & Hensley at 313–14.
[153]   *See* Arluke, Levin, Luke & Ascione at 964 (noting that researchers have been overly "simplistic" and failed to recognize that violence toward humans might occur prior to violence to animals).
[154]   Tallichet & Hensley at 314.
[155]   Arnold Arluke, et. al, *The Relationship of Animal Abuse to Violence and Other Forms of Antisocial Behavior*, 14 J. INTERPERSONAL VIOLENCE 963 (1999).

think as an overly simplistic characterization of human deviance, and as unsupported by existing research.

In 2009, Arluke and Levin confronted a discrete concern regarding the link data, the pervasive "false positive" problem.[156] Research has consistently shown that a surprisingly large percentage of people have abused animals during childhood, but most of them do not go on to commit crimes of violence. Even in the most prominent studies finding a statistically significant correlation between animal abuse and human violence, more often than not the animal abuser does not grow up to abuse humans. This is because "many ordinary people – those who presumably would never commit a serious act of human aggression – perpetrate acts of animal cruelty."

Seeking to address the false positive problem in link research, Arluke and Levin conducted two very limited studies. First, they administered a questionnaire about childhood animal abuse to a large undergraduate sociology class at Northeastern University. As with prior research, they found a very large number of participants who admitted to being abusive to an animal (28 percent), and they also found that a large number of the students (13 percent) admitted to up-close-and-personal methods of abuse such as bludgeoning or strangulation. But the researchers noticed that only 5 percent of students admitted to intentionally inflicting pain and suffering (what the researchers called "torture") on a dog or cat, and only about 1 percent admitted to intentionally inflicting torture on a dog or cat in a hands-on, up-close-and-personal manner. With regard to this latter category, then, the researchers speculate that the subset is sufficiently small as to minimize or eliminate any false positive problems regarding the predictive capacity of animal abuse.

As part of the same research, Arluke and Levin also the examined the criminal histories for those serial killers for whom there were "true-crime books," and who had tortured their human victims. So, the dataset (forty-four people) was limited to serial killers who had tortured their victims and had a book written about their lives. The conclusions are important insofar as they represent some of the more sanguine views about the predictive power of link data in modern research. Levin and Arluke found that thirty-two of the forty-four torturer-serial-killers, or 73 percent, "had reportedly also injured or killed animals."[157]

This figure warrants attention and further study. But there are a variety of reasons to believe that this data is too limited to make any generalizing statements. First, it must be noted that this study focuses on forty-four very violent offenders spread across decades, to the exclusion of studying the thousands of violent crimes that occur each year. This was a deliberate choice, but the smallness of this dataset makes it very hard to draw general conclusions about the many people each day who abuse animals across the United States. A dataset of that size is so small, and so underrepresentative of the class of criminals who violently abuse people, as to look more

[156] Levin & Arluke, *Reducing the Link's False Positive Problem, in* THE LINK BETWEEN ANIMAL ABUSE AND HUMAN VIOLENCE at 163–71.
[157] *Id.*

like anecdote than empirical research. Moreover, even if 100 percent of the forty-four torturer-serial-killers had abused animals, that says very little about the hundreds of thousands or millions of people who abused animals when they were children. If all of the serial killers had (or had not) graduated from college, would researchers use that as a reliable predictor of becoming serial killer? The serial killer study, in short, does not address the false positive problem.

Arluke and Levin, however, attempt to use the undergraduate questionnaire to overcome the false positive dilemma with their serial killer study. Sure, they acknowledge, many people admit to abusing animals, but very few admit to abusing dogs or cats, much less torturing dogs or cats in a hands-on, intimate way. In other words, Arluke and Levin attempt to combine their findings from true-crime books about serial killers with their findings about undergraduates to create a net showing that particularly egregious animal abuse does correlate with particularly egregious human violence. But this step is tenuous on multiple levels. First, is it fair to compare students with some degree of privilege and social status, given their matriculation into a major national university, with the worst serial killers in the nation's history? More critically, the researchers seem to elide a key problem with combining these two distinct datasets. The rate at which the college students admitted to hands-on torture of dogs and cats was only about 1 percent, which appears to limit the false positive substantially; however, just over 50 percent of the forty-four serial killers studied tortured any animals (not just dogs and cats). This means that even among the most heinous serial killers, it is about as likely that they tortured animals as it is that they did not torture animals. The figures are much higher for any abuse (including non-torture) to an animal by these killers (73 percent, or thirty-two of the forty-four), but so too are the rates of abuse found by Arluke and Levin among students – they found that a shocking 28 percent of the undergraduates admitted to having been abusive to animals.

It is interesting that a high percentage of the killers who tortured and have books written about them abused animals, and it is also deserving of note that they found very few of their college students had engaged in intimate, up-close torture of a dog or cat. But these two datasets don't work together in a way that ameliorates their respective shortcomings. On the one hand, they found that most serial killers had abused animals, but they also found that 28 percent of Americans, or more than 80 million people, have abused animals. Roughly the same percentage of Americans (30%) are estimated to own guns as the researchers found abuse animals. If tens of millions of people have abused animals, this group of forty-four serial killers who also abused animals seems like a rather paltry and quite unrevealing subset. If millions of people are abusing animals, then we can safely assume that most of them are not going to become serial killers. On the other hand, they found that comparatively few people tortured dogs and cats (about 1 percent), but notably only about half of the serial killers had tortured animals, thus making torturing dogs and cats a relatively poor predictor of serial killers too. There may be relatively few persons who torture dogs and cats (thus addressing false-positive concerns), but it turns out that persons who do torture dogs or cats are not particularly likely to become serial killers.

Levin and Arluke concede that animal abuse is "not necessarily predictive of subsequent violence against humans."[158] But Arluke and Levin seem to believe that extreme animal cruelty can be a useful prognosticator or red flag about one's future behavior. Yet for the reasons discussed immediately above, this predictor hypothesis looks to be more speculation than hard fact. Reasonable people could differ about how to read their very limited dataset, and some who have studied it strongly disagree with their conclusion that extreme violence is a red flag for human violence. For example, Heather Piper called this sort of conclusion the product of "gut feelings" obscured through the reporting of numbers that provide a "quasi-scientific" feel to the conclusion. As Arluke and Levin recognize, even as to the small subset of aggravated up-close animal abuse that they think is most predictive, it "may turn out to be an important, but hardly exclusive, pivotal point for certain children who later become repeat killers."

A second effort to narrow, and in the process rehabilitate, the overstated and overhyped claims about a link between human and animal violence was published by Arluke and Eric Madfis in 2014. Arluke and Madfis set out to study whether animal abuse was a reliable warning sign for identifying people at risk for committing a mass shooting or school massacre.[159] The authors framed this paper as a response to the well-founded critiques of the link research by scholars like Heather Piper. Piper and others rebuked as unfounded, for example, the statement published by the HSUS in 2008 asserting that "serial killers and school shooters almost invariably have histories of abusing animals." Agreeing to an extent with Piper, these authors noted that the link was often perpetuated "as fact without much, if any, scientific evidence," and it had become more an "ideology" than a serious area of study.

Hoping to add a layer of empirical rigor to the discussion of school shooters, the authors researched twenty-three school shootings between 1998 and 2012 where two or more people were killed. The researchers recognized that measuring the incidence of animal cruelty among school shooters based on the offenders' own reports risked overstating the amount of cruelty, as these individuals may have been "boasting ... as a way of showing their dangerousness" to their friends. But even based on data derived from such boasting, the researchers found that only ten of the twenty-three school shooters had abused an animal. Following a school shooting in 2018, the authors wrote an op-ed in the *Washington Post* describing animal abuse, particularly hands-on abuse of dogs and cats, as a "red flag" that someone may turn into a mass shooter. But this notion that animal cruelty can serve as useful red flag is arguably at war with their own data. The data produced by Arluke and Madfis show that if one suspects a person of being a mass shooter based on prior acts of animal abuse, *more often than not* that prediction will be wrong. They emphasize the fact

---

[158] *Id.*
[159] Arnold Arluke & Eric Madfis, *Animal Abuse As a Warning Sign of School Massacres: A Critique and Refinement*, 18 HOMICIDE STUD. 7 (2014).

that 90 percent of the "animal abusing school shooters" used up-close and personal styles of abuse, but that does not change the fact that only 43 percent of the shooters abused an animal at all. That less than half of the school shooters abused animals is particularly striking when it is noted that the researchers also documented that nearly 20 percent of the school shooters "displayed empathy for an attachment" to non-human animals. Nearly one out of five school shooters in this data had empathy for animals, one even claiming to be an "ethical vegan," and others taking dramatic steps to show kindness to animals.

Arluke and Madfis acknowledge that their findings call into question the "link's robustness as a warning sign," even in cases of "extreme violence." It is true that most of the animal abusers who moved on to school shootings engaged in particularly intense, up-close abuse, but nonetheless, most of the school shooters they studied did not harm animals at all. Thus, they acknowledge that their research tends to support the critiques of using "checklists and profiles to identify youth at risk of violence." Torturous animal abuse may be the *best* predictor of mass shooting among the various categories of animal abuse, but still only nine out of the twenty-three shooters they studied had engaged in such torture. Other research shows much stronger correlations or links between mass shooting or murder and things like a fascination with guns, an interest in violent media, and bullying, among many others. There may be a "link" between animal abuse and human violence, but it is not the strongest link, nor the most predictive or useful.

6.2.3.5 Patterson-Kane (2014)

One of the most recent comprehensive examinations of the link data was authored by Emily Patterson-Kane, who conducted a meta-analysis of the existing research in 2014.[160] Patterson-Kane notes the extensive interest in proving a relation between aggression against animals and violence, and she cautions that merely showing that a "greater proportion of persons with crimes against people have animal abuse histories does not answer this question." Her research, then, sets out to explain why this is so, and examines existing data for proof of a meaningful link.

First, Patterson-Kane synthesized the datasets for thirteen studies in order to estimate the prevalence of animal abuse among "non-violent or ostensibly normal control populations (e.g., students, community members)." Her findings are rather remarkable in this regard. Across all thirteen studies, the data shows the average incidence of one or more acts of animal cruelty was 27 percent. Patterson-Kane notes a number of factors, including the varying definitions of animal cruelty, that may account for this high figure, and she suggests caution with regard to treating this figure as definitively correct. But similar figures have been observed in some of the seminal studies noted above, including Kellert and Felthouse (1985). Based on this

---

[160]   Emily Patterson-Kane at 140–58.

rate of animal abuse, Patterson-Kane acknowledges the disturbing conclusion reached in prior studies that "some participation in animal abuse may be considered normative among American males."[161] Any rate of animal abuse above a few percent would suggest that millions, or tens of millions of Americans have abused animals, thus illuminating the false positive problem with link research.

Second, Patterson-Kane conducted a meta-analysis on fifteen link studies and found that, as prior researchers had reported, "people with a history of violence against people were significantly more likely to have a history of animal abuse than matched groups with no history of violence." Specifically, her analysis found that 34 percent of violent offenders had abused animals, whereas only 21 percent of non-violent offenders had done so, and thus recognized that there is a measure of validity in concluding that violent offenders are more likely to have abused animals. However, she is quick to note what is perhaps the more salient finding, "a majority of individuals with a history of violence against humans" do not have a history of abuse against animals. Accordingly, if animal abuse raised suspicions about future violence, then based on the most comprehensive research to date, "these suspicions would be wrong more often than they are right." In addition, Patterson-Kane pithily summarizes the false positive problem, explaining that "the rate at which violent offenders have committed animal abuse provides no valuable information about the rate at which animal abusers will go on to be violent offenders, as it does not allow us to know how many animal abusers do not take this path." To put this in even simpler terms, many murderers have a conviction for a prior nonviolent offense, but this does not make prior nonviolent crimes a good predictor of future murderers.[162]

Patterson-Kane recognizes that with regard to reoccurring and particularly severe acts of animal abuse, "it remains possible" that there is a more reliable link to future offending. But she cautions that any "prediction of dangerousness must be recognized as an exceedingly difficult task with serious consequences for society and the individual."[163] In sum, according to Patterson-Kane's effort to synthesize the existing empirical data, the research is much less conclusive, much more anecdotal, and much more nascent than the conventional public narrative about the link suggests. Moreover, particularly when the criminal justice system is involved, the construction of a child or adolescent as a "moral monster" carries the possibility of potentially lifelong negative effects.

6.3 CRITIQUE OF THE LINK AS THE TALISMAN AND SHIBBOLETH OF CARCERAL ANIMAL LAW

The presumed connection between animal abuse and subsequent human violence has emerged as a salient, often preeminent feature in the animal protection

[161] *Id.* at 143.
[162] *Id.* at 146 (drawing a similar analogy).
[163] *Id.* at 149, 152.

FIGURE 6.1 The logo for the National Link Coalition

movement's public advocacy for harsher criminal law interventions. It is the link, we are told, that justifies new felony laws, it is the link that warrants the aggressive lobbying of prosecutors, and it is the link that necessitates measures like felony registries. In justifying lobbying efforts to make New York's felony cruelty laws harsher in 2018, a leader in the animal protection movement said the decision was simple because "animal cruelty is a clear predictor of future violence." But this framing of the link as a clear warning sign of future violence is a shibboleth, as is the unfounded belief that punishing animal abusers more severely will make society safer.

Among animal protection advocates, the link has emerged as something of a talisman, or "magic bullet."[164] The sensationalized accounts of the link generate reliable and high-profile press opportunities for the movement, and the link offers the promise that one can help animals by protecting humans. The public accepts as common sense the intuition that animal abuse will rapidly and "inevitably escalate," and at every opportunity, experts from nearly every major animal protection movement have (unwittingly or otherwise) reinforced this narrative and dressed it up in an appearance of scientific fact.[165] Often presentations and trainings on the link include a PowerPoint slide, like the one that appears on the homepage for the National Link Coalition, presented in figure 6.1. The use of the Venn Diagram creates "an impression of mathematical certainty" and suggests that the link has been "scientifically proven."[166]

At this point, the media and the public have become so intoxicated with the sensational reports of animal-abusing children growing into the next Ted Bundy, that a strong conception of the link and its predictive capacity has emerged as a near truism within state legislatures and prosecutors' offices. Among the movement itself, the link has an ideological quality to it – it is almost heretical to suggest that perhaps the aggressive prosecution of animal abusers does very little, if anything, to protect humans or animals.[167] Summing up the movement's own ideology on the issue, Stacy Wolf, the Senior Vice President of the ASPCA's Anti-Cruelty Group

[164] Arluke, Levin, Luke & Ascione at 971 (noting the willingness of groups to treat animal abuse as a "single magic bullet" that would help with intervention strategies to decrease human violence).

[165] Patterson-Kane at 141.

[166] Piper & Cordingley at 351.

[167] One article has posited that because the link has obtained such a degree of social acceptance, it has even become difficult to "publish academic papers suggesting otherwise." Piper & Cordingley at 347.

explained, "Aggressive prosecution of crimes against animals is critical to ensuring the safety of New York City residents, both human and animal."[168]

This section laments this hyperenthusiasm for the link by critiquing the movement's use of the research as overly simplified, if not outright misleading, and by calling attention to the shortcomings of the movement's link-predicated reforms. In a nutshell, the actual data does not support the *conclusions asserted* or the *criminal reforms pursued* in the name of the link. In part, this is because, quite simply, the link research often fails to "uncover significant differences [in the rate of animal abuse] between violent and non-violent criminals."[169] Recent studies described above note that the evidence of a connection or predictive link is "weak or inconsistent."[170] Increasingly, the claim that animal abuse is a "clear predictor of future violence" is understood as more of an urban myth that has been "perpetuated as fact without much, if any, scientific evidence to support it."[171] The link has become a convenient cultural script, because a discourse about "breaking cycles is much easier and safer" than a far-reaching discourse about the need to address the oppressive "structure of social relations."[172] It is easier for the movement to imagine that aggressive abuse prosecutions will make the world safer than to contemplate how reducing poverty, oppression, or other variables that might correlate more strongly with violence could be achieved. Even the most modest link-based claims, that animal abuse serves as a red flag or important warning sign, seem overly simplistic and misleading in light of the fact that the data consistently shows that *most* violent offenders, even in the case of mass murderers, have never abused or mistreated an animal. As elaborated below, rather than a predictor of future violence against others, animal abuse by a child or adolescent is more likely to reveal domestic violence and/or poverty in that person's home.[173]

First, however, it warrants mentioning that, at least to the eye of someone familiar with the criminal justice system, the anecdotal and intuitive appeal of the link as a predictor of crime parallels the wave of overstated forensic methods, such as bitemark evidence, firearm identification, and microscopic hair comparisons, that a presidential commission recently concluded lack reliable scientific support. Like animal cruelty, the media and popular culture, including TV shows like *CSI*, have popularized the myth of forensic science as infallible. Emily Patterson-Kane cautions that in the rush for certainty and in the name of safety, there is a willingness to cling to "unreliable warning signs" as evidence or predictors of criminality. In the context of forensic science, the presidential commission's report in 2016 served as a much-needed wake-up call regarding the fallibility of quasi-science that had

[168] Press Release, Queens County DA.
[169] Levin & Arluke at 164.
[170] *Id.* at 169.
[171] Arluke & Madfis at 9.
[172] Piper at 174.
[173] Elizabeth DeViney, Jeffery Dickert & Randall Lockwood, *The Care of Pets Within Child Abusing Families*, 4 INT'L J. STUDY ANIMAL PROBS. 321 (1983) (finding that pet abuse was present in 88 percent of homes studied where there was physical child abuse).

obtained a revered status among the public. The report observed that faulty forensic evidence had been relied on in about *half* of criminal cases in which DNA subsequently resulted in an exoneration.[174] Similarly, as noted above, people convicted of violent offenses have committed prior acts of animal cruelty less than *half* of the time. It turns out that neither animal cruelty nor a number of entrenched forensic approaches are good indicators of criminality. A variety of forensic sciences have come to be pejoratively called "junk science" because of their poor ability to accurately identify criminals, but the link's similarly tenuous predictive power is celebrated as the primary justification for more aggressive policing and prosecution in the animal cruelty realm. In the forensic sciences, scholars are increasingly placing scrutiny on once-sacrosanct practices that are now understand to be unreliable predictors of guilt; it is time for a similar move away from reflexive link-think, and toward individualized assessments. All too often the movement and the media perpetuate the myth of a clear-cut link "without much, if any, scientific evidence to support it."[175]

One of the first studies to rebuke superficial link-think, and call attention to the myopic focus of many link studies – often using human violence as the exclusive dependent variable – was a 1999 article by Arnold Arluke, Jack Levin, Carter Luke, and Frank Ascione.[176] Arluke et al. found that animal abusers were significantly more likely than the control group (their neighbors) to commit crimes; 70 percent of people who committed animal cruelty had also committed at least one criminal offense, compared to 22 percent of people who had not committed cruelty to an animal. In addition, they found that animal abusers were 5.3 times more likely to commit a violent crime against a person (37 versus 7 percent). At least superficially, this data seems to support the general conclusion that animal abusers are likely to graduate to human violence – that human violence can be predicted by a prior act of animal abuse. However, interpersonal violence was not uniquely associated with animal abuse. In fact, they found that the percentage of animal abusers who engaged in property, drug, or other crimes was just as high or higher than the percentage of animal abusers who engaged in violent crimes. An animal abuser was most likely, according to their data, to commit a property crime.

According to the conventional or what the authors call the "simplistic" understanding of the link, "the five year old who abuses an animal is on the way to become an elementary school bully, aggressive adolescent, and adult violent offender."[177] But as Arluke et al. show, among all classes of criminals studied, more often than not

---

[174] Harry T. Edwards & Jennifer L. Mnookin, Opinion, *A Wake-Up Call on the Junk Science Infesting our Courtrooms*, WASH. POST (Sept. 20, 2016), www.washingtonpost.com/opinions/a-wake-up-call-on-the-junk-science-infesting-our-courtrooms/2016/09/19/85b6eb22-7e90-11e6-8d13-d7c704ef9fd9_story.html?utm_term=.3b6c73cdcf35 (summarizing the presidential report).

[175] Arluke and Madfis at 10.

[176] Arluke, Levin, Luke & Ascione at 965–66.

[177] *Id.* at 964.

TABLE 6.2 *Abusers and Controls Who Committed Various Offenses (Arluke et al)*

	Abusers		Controls	
	N	Percentage	N	Percentage
Violence	57	(37)	11	(7)
Property	67	(44)	17	(11)
Drug	57	(37)	17	(11)
Disorder	57	(37)	18	(12)

the prisoner had not abused animals. Moreover, the researchers found that, contrary to the graduation thesis, "animal abuse was no more likely to precede than follow either violent offenses, or non-violent offenses."[178] Specifically, in about 40 percent of both violent and nonviolent crimes animal abuse preceded the crime, and in about 60 percent of all violent or nonviolent crimes the animal abuse came after the other crime.[179] "[O]verall, only 16% of the abusers studied graduated to subsequent violent crime." Only one out of every six people who abused an animal graduated to human violence.

Based on these findings, Arluke et al. conclude that it was time for an outright "moratorium on painting a broad stroke of violence over most cases of abuse."[180] The conventional wisdom that animal abuse is a "magic bullet" for predicting human violence is simply incorrect. The researchers went on to express concern over the fact that, despite a persistent lack of strong evidence, the "graduation hypothesis" had been consistently "espoused by concerned lay people and research-ers alike" as a reason for stronger animal cruelty laws. In a shot across the bow of the animal protection movement, they asked "Why does this thinking persist when it does not have strong and consistent empirical support?" and posited that animal protection advocates are deliberately providing a misleading narrative about the strength of the link data in order to motivate the public and government officials to "take animal abuse more seriously."[181] They criticize as overly simplistic the "com-monsensical" view that people graduate from animals to humans, and note that their findings showed that a graduation in violence "does not happen." They posit that the continuing mischaracterizations of the data by advocates will ultimately undermine the animal protection movement's credibility, and thus ultimately "hurt the cause of those who genuinely champion the protection of animals."

[178] *Id.* at 969–70.
[179] Specifically, in 42 percent of violent crimes, abuse preceded the crime, while in 58 percent it followed the crime. For nonviolent crimes, 39 percent were proceeded by animal abuse, while 61 percent were followed by animal abuse.
[180] *Id.* at 973.
[181] *Id.* at 970–71.

Arluke et al. state that the only definitive way to test the graduation hypothesis is to conduct a longitudinal study focusing on children and determining what happens among those who abuse animals prior to any other antisocial behavior. But in their view, there is currently no reliable evidence that animal abuse precedes, much less predicts interpersonal violence. As Emily Patterson-Kane summarized the data in 2016, "the graduation hypothesis" or the notion of animal abuse as a "sentinel crime" is simply "not supported."[182]

Five years after Arluke et al.'s attempt to narrow the scope of rhetoric surrounding the link by unequivocally rebuking the theory that animal abusers "inevitably graduate to interpersonal violence,"[183] Piers Beirne, a leading criminologist,[184] conducted an extensive review of the literature that was purported by the movement to support the view of animal abuse as a clear predictor of human violence. Beirne also laments that "longitudinal analysis never has been applied to [the link]" and describes the current body of research as instead being "generated in a hodge-podge" uncritical manner. The notion of people "trying out" violence on animals or "graduating" to human victims has such intuitive or visceral appeal that much of the research, he concludes, is less rigorous than would be ideal. The link-think has become more an ideological value than a scientific fact, or as another commentator has put it, an affirmation of our "gut feelings" and visceral impulses "even when the data fail to warrant it."[185] Beirne draws attention to the multitude of *different links* in the life of one who becomes violent and dangerous – drug use, family violence, other crimes, for example – and he criticizes the narrative about the link that is pushed by animal protection groups on the public. The existing studies, he notes, "cannot be regarded, even generously, as a functional, if lesser, equivalent of the would-be findings of longitudinal studies," and cautions that for sensible, fair-minded advocates "it is prudent not to rely too much" on current predictive claims about animal abuse. This is similar to the pathmarking work of Heather Piper, who sounded the alarm on "over-reliance on the analysis of risk factors" (of any sort) in predicting violence, and instead emphasized the need for more qualitative information about individuals. Dr. Beirne concludes his summary of the existing research as follows:

> [A]lthough the several forms of family violence undoubtedly are strongly associated, existing knowledge of how, and how often, companion animal abuse exists with other forms of family violence tends neither to confirm nor to disconfirm [the link]. Crucially, it is not known whether animal abuse precedes and signifies other forms of violence or whether it follows them. Whichever the case, we need additionally to know under what circumstances it is so, and why. What currently is known about

[182] Patterson-Kane at 150.
[183] Id.
[184] Beirne is the recipient of a lifetime achievement award from the American Society of Criminology.
[185] Piper at 163.

their futures actually sheds little light on the likelihood that assaultive children subsequently will engage in interhuman violence.[186]

Reaching similar conclusions, a meta-analysis of research on the link led another criminologist to observe that "animal cruelty correlated as well with non-violent offending as it did with violent offending"; indeed, among men "animal cruelty correlated slightly better with non-violent offending."[187] The absence of support for the movement's claim that animal abuse is a clear predictor of interpersonal violence is the reason some scholars have endorsed a lesser-link-theory known as the Deviance Generalization Hypothesis, which treats animal cruelty as one anti-social behavior among many.[188] Under the deviance hypothesis, researchers suggest that without studying the particulars of a situation, one could simply never know "whether animal cruelty is an origin of subsequent interpersonal violence, or simply *one of many markers of general deviance.*"[189] One leading study on the Deviance Generalization Hypothesis was published in 2011, by Dr. Clifton P. Flynn.[190] Among his review of the research, he observed that of those "participants who engaged in animal abuse, a majority (62.2%) had also experienced child maltreatment or exposure to domestic violence." Further, committing animal cruelty was "signifi-cantly correlated with a history of witnessing animal abuse." He found that 67.6 percent of those who committed acts of animal cruelty had witnessed animal cruelty, compared to 19.4 percent of those who did not report committing animal cruelty. Flynn also notes that studies have demonstrated that "[t]he leading antecedents of children's animal cruelty [are] a) being a victim of physical or sexual abuse, b) witnessing violence between one's parents, and c) witnessing parents or peers harm animals."[191] Flynn concludes that "some homes may be prone to generalized physical violence – with lines blurred between victims and perpetrators." In the words of Flynn, "There are multiple pathways that lead to and from and through animal abuse.... . Most who abuse animals don't go on to be violent toward humans," so overemphasizing this relationship may lead authorities to falsely label and stigmatize children as potential abusers or worse, resulting in greater deviance, not less.

---

[186] *Id.* at 52. Dr. Beirne also urges a study of the link, if any, that might emerge from "institutionalized social practices where animal abuse is routine, widespread, and often defined as socially acceptable" such as slaughterhouses. *Id.* at 54.

[187] Walters at 798–802. *Id.* at 800 (noting though that it may be "premature" based on the limited data to dismiss the graduation hypothesis among females).

[188] *See, e.g.,* Flynn at 458–60 (discussing how generalized deviance posits that animal cruelty and human violence are associated as antisocial behaviors, but does not specify a time-order); GULLONE, ANIMAL CRUELTY, ANTISOCIAL BEHAVIOR, AND AGGRESSION, at 4–8, 14–15 (discussing the differences between the two theories).

[189] Walters at 802.

[190] Flynn at 453.

[191] *Id.* at 455.

Such a view is consistent with Arluke et al.'s 1999 renunciation of the link, discussed above, as predictive of future violence or crime. Arluke et al. offered a considerably more diluted (deviance) version of the link as a vehicle for continuing to emphasize animal cruelty as a potential red flag: "[r]ather than being a predictor or a distinct step in the development of increasingly criminal or violent behavior," as animal protection groups claim, "animal abuse … is one of many antisocial behaviors committed by individuals in society, ranging from property to personal crimes." On the one hand, the "general deviance" view – the notion that animal abuse is just one of many antisocial behaviors that a person may carry out if they are following a deviant or criminal path – is hardly surprising given the social stigma associated with animal cruelty. It is not surprising that one who chooses to commit one crime might commit other crimes. On the other hand, it may be reckless to read too much into this notion of general deviance, because "deviant behavior generalizes in a relatively idiosyncratic manner," and animal abuse does not meaningfully predict any "*specific* kind of co-occurring or future offending."[192]

Accepting the generalized deviance view of the link is a bit like acknowledging that animal cruelty, like multitudes of other deviant behavior, tends to predict or occur in conjunction with other deviant behavior. Such an abstraction is hardly profound, much less cause for a characterization of cruelty as uniquely indicative of one as a "moral monster." There does not appear to be any evidence that of the many crimes committed in society, animal abuse is better at predicting recidivism or repeat offending; animal cruelty is "simply one of many criminal acts associated with criminal lives characterized by similar rates of recidivism."[193] Thus, the deviance theory has little to offer animal protection advocates seeking to use the link as leverage to obtain criminal law reforms.

Emily Patterson-Kane put it best when she observed that, even in the context of a generalized deviance theory, "group-level predictions remain suggestive but unreliable."[194] Our gut reaction and urban legends tell us that animal abusers are uniquely dangerous – this would no doubt prompt many people to refuse, for example, to hire a past animal abuser as a child care provider. And some of these people who committed animal abuse in the past may well persist or progress in their patterns of violence, or commit other crimes. After all, the "chance of this hypothesis (of any crime) being confirmed is undoubtedly higher than in a non-abusing control subject."[195] Thus for some, a continued emphasis on some version of the link is still warranted. But at the very least, it is clear that the current narrative surrounding the link ("clear predictor of violence") is incorrect, and further, as Flynn posited, "[r]esearch on the link has been *overly psychological in nature*, assuming the animal abuse is pathological." The link discussion "ignore[s] the numerous social and

---

[192] Patterson-Kane at 150.
[193] Piper at 173.
[194] Patterson-Kane at 150.
[195] *Id.*

cultural factors that contribute to the perpetration of violence against animals," even as the research is clear that "individual factors are insufficient in explaining" the occurrence of crime or violence.[196] There are many cultural factors or links to crime, and only through personalized individualized analysis can the "extent and meaning of" deviant behavior be explored.[197] And it must not be assumed that raising red flags in an overly indiscriminate manner is simply harmless error. As Patterson-Kane put it, "If we overestimate their dangerousness, we may be reacting in ways that are unfair and increase the likelihood of the person's aggression, such as through custodial" responses. There are "damaging effects that may result from labelling the perpetrator a moral monster."

To put the matter plainly, it is impossible to reconcile the research regarding a connection between animal abuse and human violence with the claims of inevitability and certainty that comprise the narrative espoused by animal protection advocates. If the movement wants to be taken seriously and regarded as credible, it needs to stop using the link as a justification for a harsher criminal justice response to animal cruelty; the movement needs to acknowledge "animal cruelty as being neither a necessary precursor to other forms of deviance, nor a direct cause of violent interpersonal behavior."[198] Contrary to the claims of those advocating for ever more carceral responses to animal abuse, most people who exhibit the presumed symptom (of harming an animal), the research shows, "do not get the disease."[199] Indeed, as one researcher concluded, animal abuse may be "barely [better] than chance in predicting offending behaviors."[200]

***

In the eighteenth century, the English artist William Hogarth created a provocative series of four prints called *The Four Stages of Cruelty*. These prints are frequently reproduced during trainings and lectures on the link, because they sequentially tell the story of a boy who starts his life abusing small animals and progresses to violent abuse against his pregnant wife. As Beirne puts it, these prints have "achieved canonical status in ... the animal rights movement ... and in sociological criminology as an influential milestone in the study of the link between childhood animal cruelty and subsequent violence between one human and another."[201] Beirne

---

[196] Flynn at 460.
[197] Patterson-Kane at 150.
[198] Flynn at 460.
[199] Arluke, Levin, Luke & Ascione at 972.
[200] Walters at 801. *See also* Alys et al. at 156 (finding that "animal cruelty may be widespread and not a causal factor predictive of sexual homicide"); *Id.* at 157 (noting limited support for the graduation hypothesis because more sexual homicide offenders have committed animal abuse, but noting that "in keeping with the serial killer literature ... the numbers of offenders who are known to have abused animals in childhood are not as robust as one might expect."). Alys et al. also caution against discarding any theory yet, including graduation, even though there are very likely many "better predictors" of violent crime. *Id.* at 159.
[201] Piers Beirne, Hogarth's Art of Animal Cruelty: Satire, Suffering and Pictorial Propaganda 2 (2015).

describes the prints as propaganda for the time, aimed at fueling interest in animal rights.[202] Of course, if the prints were originally conceived of as propaganda in support of a hunch, their continued use by the modern animal protection movement is apt. As one scholar framed the modern campaigns, the popular discourse about "the relationship between animal abuse and interhuman violence [is] ... more the brittle product of sloganeering than of hard evidence and logic."[203] One might fairly conclude that, in the name of animal protection, we are entering the third century of overstating and propagandizing the link.

It would be nearly impossible to find an animal protection organization in recent years whose public statements about the link reflect the actual consensus among researchers. The idea that animal abuse is not clearly predictive of future human violence is not even contemplated; instead, belief in the link has taken on ideological, almost religious importance to adherents of animal protection – a failure to believe that animal-abusing children grow into violent monsters and mass shooters is a rejection of a central tenant of animal protection. "Espoused by its holders at a high level of abstraction and disseminated in the mantra-like catchphrase 'The Link,'" the predictive power of animal abuse is not regarded as fairly in dispute.[204] But as discussed above, the data is, at best, inconsistent and uncertain. Heather Piper noted that the idea of a single link as a predictor of human violence is a myth, but a myth grounded in "stories in the Bible, statements by philosophers, poetry, novels, and folklore," and perpetuated by the mass media, who quote "experts to back up the rumors," and thus create a self-fulfilling and validating process.[205] In the end, a movement committed to truth over myth and scientific fact over speculation should distance itself from the unfounded hyperbole and recognize the "desperate need for longitudinal studies" if claims about the link are to be taken seriously.[206] It is time to stop perpetuating as science our "gut feelings" cloaked in the "seductive power of numbers."[207]

6.4 PRISON IS NOT THE ANSWER: THE LINK DATA DOES NOT SUPPORT A CARCERAL SOLUTION

The research summarized in Section 6.3 makes a strong case for discounting altogether the predictive version of the link, which treats animal abuse as an early warning sign for interpersonal violence. Contrary to the oft-repeated claims of theorists and advocates alike, animal abuse is not a sentinel crime or a clear predictor

---

[202] *Id.* at 100 (noting that the prints were attempts to trigger emotional reactions of "disgust and pity" in the hopes of stirring action in the direction of animal rights).

[203] *Id.* at 52.

[204] Piers Beirne, *From Animal Abuse to Inhuman Violence?: A Critical Review of the Progression Thesis*, 12 Soc. & Animals 39, 52.

[205] Piper at 166.

[206] Flynn at 461.

[207] Piper at 163.

of future criminality. But what if the link was a perfect, or at least very reliable predictor of future human violence? What should we do with the knowledge that the vast majority of pet abusers, or up-close-and-personal animal abusers, graduate to human violence? Is incarceration a necessary or even logical response to such data? A prominent textbook in the field proclaims that incarceration for animal cruelty will "prevent abuse of humans."[208]

This section rejects this generalization as unsupported, and argues that *even accepting the link as valid* in predicting violence or deviance, the movement's emphasis on the link as a justification for more aggressive criminal interventions is still a grievous mistake. Simply put, there is no reason to believe that prosecution will break the presumed cycle of violence that the link is believed to predict.

The National District Attorneys Association responded predictably to the link evidence, stating that "prosecuting animal abuse is critical because" it keeps the community safe from would-be violent offenders.[209] Accepting the predictive power of the link, anti-cruelty laws allow police to "identify dangerous individuals before they decide to harm a human being."[210] One commentator summarized the need for a highly punitive approach by noting that it allows "law enforcement personnel [to] nip serious psychological problems in the bud before these criminals graduate to exercising their rage and morbid curiosities out on human victims."[211] The HSUS website exemplifies similar thinking: "Reporting, investigating, and prosecuting animal cruelty can help take dangerous criminals off the streets.... Acts of animal cruelty are linked to a variety of other crimes, including violence against people, property crimes, and drug or disorderly conduct offenses."[212]

At first blush, such calls for aggressive enforcement of cruelty laws appear well-founded; if one assumes that animal abuse is strongly predictive of future violence, then perhaps through severe punishment the community can prevent interpersonal violence. But the reality is more complicated. Even assuming for the sake of argument that the data shows (or will show) exactly what the advocates claim regarding the predictive power of the link, such findings nonetheless do not support the conclusion that either humans or animals will be safer under a more incarceration-based approach to animal cruelty. As set forth in more detail below, the assumption that more criminal justice interventions will reduce crime is at war with the criminology research documenting the criminogenic consequences of incarceration. Increasing criminal punishments is unlikely to have a meaningful impact on deterrence (specific or general), and it could actually risk increasing

---

[208]   WAISMAN at 72.
[209]   PHILLIPS & LOCKWOOD at 20, 22 ("[B]rushing off an animal abuse case as 'unimportant' is a mistake because a proper response can reduce recidivism.").
[210]   Chiesa at 33.
[211]   Jessica Bond, *Some Thoughts for Animal Lovers (and First Amendment Aficionados) in the Wake of United States v. Stevens*, 90 U. DET. MERCY L. REV. 59, 84 (2012).
[212]   *Animal Cruelty and Human Violence*, THE HUMANE SOCIETY OF THE UNITED STATES, www.humanesociety .org/issues/abuse_neglect/qa/cruelty_violence_connection_faq.html (last visited May 20, 2018).

recidivism rates. A leading criminal law textbook observes that increasingly researchers are finding that increases in the severity of a punishment may "have the opposite
of their intended effect."[213]

First, there is a growing body of research showing that incarceration has
a desensitizing or hardening effect.[214] Of course, proponents of the link research
have identified the hardening of one's heart, and the desensitization of individuals
that occurs when they abuse animals, as a central explanation for why people
graduate from animal abuse to human violence. By abusing an animal, so the
reasoning goes, one becomes more callous and more capable of committing other
crimes of violence. The act of abuse diminishes one's empathy. But the idea that two
hardening or desensitizing events – incarceration and animal abuse – will somehow
produce a net positive outcome such that the offender will de-escalate and break
their cycle of violence is untenable. The notion that an animal abuser will depart
from their predicted path toward interpersonal violence because of incarceration
goes well beyond speculation, and approaches incoherence. In fact, sociologists
have documented what they call empathetic inurement, or the diminishment of
empathy among incarcerated men. Researchers have shown that one's empathy
"dampens" during incarceration as they adopt what has been called a "prison mask"
that suppresses emotion and sensitivity, and data suggests that many offenders are
unable to remove the "mask" and its resulting diminution of empathy when they
leave prison.[215] Coping with prison may require one to shed their empathy. Yet the
animal protection movement imagines that in this more callous, post-incarceration
state, past animal abusers will present themselves as less violent and more sensitive to
the suffering of humans and animals. Thus, if one accepts that the link proves that
animal abuse causes a loss of empathy (and thus predicts future violence), then
incarceration is more of the same medicine. It induces more callousness rather than
curing a deficiency in empathy.

More generally, there is no data to support the notion that incarceration will
render a person who is predicted (via the link) to be violent any less violent or less
antisocial. Quite the contrary, researchers are just beginning to fully "understand the
extent to which prison behavior and violence is a product of the carceral system, not
an explanation for its need."[216] Ironically, researchers studying this phenomenon

---

[213]   KADISH, SCHULHOFER & BARKOW at 120. *See also* Neal Kumar Katyal, *Deterrence's Difficulty*, 95 MICH.
        L. REV. 2385 (1997).

[214]   Dorothy E. Roberts, *The Social and Moral Cost of Mass Incarceration in African American
        Communities*, 56 STAN. L. REV. 1271, 1297 (2004) (compiling research showing the criminogenic or
        reciprocal effects of incarceration); *Id.* ("These findings demolish deterrence-based rationales for
        harsh sentencing policies.")

[215]   Tony N. Brown, Mary Laske Bell & Evelyn J. Patterson, *Imprisoned by Empathy: Familial
        Incarceration and Psychological Distress Among African American Men in the National Survey of
        American Life*, 57 J. HEALTH & SOC. BEHAV, 240, 240–56 (2016).

[216]   K. M. Morin, *Wildspace: The Cage, The Supermax, and the Zoo*, in CRITICAL ANIMAL GEOGRAPHIES:
        POLITICS, INTERSECTIONS, AND HIERARCHIES IN A MULTISPECIES WORLD 73, 87 (Rosemary-Claire
        Collard & Kathryn Gillespie eds., 2015).

have noted the "animalistic" effects of incarceration on humans.[217] Robert Weisberg sagely summarized the research showing that criminal punishment, particularly incarceration, tends to produce, not negate criminogenic consequences:

> [W]e must attend to … the possibility of punishment, especially incarceration, increasing recidivism…. [W]e can imagine, and find at least unsystematic evidence of, at least two mechanisms for this effect. One is the old idea of prison as a school for crime, perhaps traceable back to the early twentieth century notion of new inmates being tutored in the logistics of specific crimes by more experienced inmates… The other mechanism is the degradation of social skills and other forms of human capital from the time spent in prison. For offenders who already lacked social skills, or who were prone to antisocial behavior, or who were disinclined or unable to undertake productive labor, or who were seriously mentally ill before incarceration, the time spent on the inside is as likely to exacerbate as to mitigate these deficits.[218]

The animal protection movement's call for imprisonment as a cure for animal abuse, much less human violence, is rooted in a faith that if we punish more people, more severely, there will be less animal abuse and less human violence. A lengthy term of imprisonment for an animal abuser may sound good, and it may even signal that animal abuse is a serious matter, but there is no data-driven reason to believe that it will break the presumed causal chain between animal abuse and human violence, and there is data suggesting exactly the opposite.

An additional reason for rejecting as unfounded the notion that a link between animal abuse and human violence justifies a dramatically heightened criminal justice response is that increased penalties can lead to a reduction in the rate at which the crime is reported to authorities. Many studies demonstrate that witnesses "become less willing to report crime or to cooperate in prosecution," and prosecutors may even "become reluctant to file the highest charges, and juries hesitate to convict" when penalties are increased.[219] Scholars studying the context of domestic violence crimes have recognized this reality, noting that increases in criminal penalties for domestic violence have likely resulted in a decrease in the rate at which that crime is reported by the public. As Margit Livingson recognized, "if the crimes carry with them a relatively severe punishment, juries will be reluctant to find guilt and *citizens will be disinclined to assist law enforcement authorities* in their efforts to find and convict perpetrators of these crimes."[220] No one can be sure, without data, whether diminished reporting issues will follow increased penalties for animal cruelty, but nor is there a clear reason to predict that animal cruelty would be an outlier in this regard.

---

[217] *Id.*

[218] Robert Weisberg, *Meanings and Measures of Recidivism*, 87 S. Cal. L. Rev. 785, 793–94 (2014).

[219] SANDFORD H. KADISH, STEPHEN J. SCHULHOFER & RACHEL E. BARKOW, CRIMINAL LAW AND ITS PROCESSES: CASES AND MATERIALS 120 (10th edn. 2016).

[220] Livingston at 60.

Although complete decriminalization of animal cruelty would be expected to result in increased rates of cruelty, there is no data to support the conclusion that incarceration, much less marginal increases in the punishment for abuse, will result in reduced rates of animal abuse. Leading spokespeople for animal protection efforts, such as Allie Phillips and Randall Lockwood, have repeatedly assured policymakers and the public that higher penalties for animal cruelty will reduce recidivism. But generally speaking, more severe punishments do not reduce recidivism.[221] As the National Research Council found in 2014, significant incarceration does not produce improved deterrence.[222] Among some of the highlights in the Council's report are findings that a unique federal program called "Project Exile in Richmond, Virginia" that imposed heightened penalties for firearm offenses in order to reduce that crime (and crimes predicted by firearm violations) was found to have "no apparent deterrent effect."[223] The report of the National Research Council concludes that existing research "demonstrates that lengthy prison sentences are ineffective as a crime control measure."[224]

Indeed, even the infamous "three-strikes" laws, which are said to provide the "ideal" vehicle for testing the ability of harsher sentences to increase deterrence, have been deemed to demonstrate the opposite effect.[225] Researchers have documented a precipitous decline in violent and nonviolent crime in non-three-strike states relative to three-strike states.[226] Even more striking is the conclusion of a recent survey of the relevant academic literature:

> Can we conclude that variation in the severity of sentences would have differential (general) deterrent effects? Our reply is a resounding no. We could find no conclusive evidence that supports the hypothesis that harsher sentences reduce crime through the mechanism of general deterrence. Particularly given the significant body of literature from which this conclusion is based, the consistency of the findings over time and space, and the multiple measures and methods employed in the research conducted, we would suggest that a stronger conclusion is warranted.

[221] *See* David A. Anderson, *The Deterrence Hypothesis and Picking Pockets at the Pickpocket's Hanging*, 4 Am. L. & Econ. Rev. 295 (2002).

[222] NAT'L RES. COUNCIL, THE GROWTH OF INCARCERATION IN THE UNITED STATES: EXPLORING CAUSES AND CONCERNS 137 (Jeremy Travis et al. eds., 2014), www.nap.edu/read/18613/chapter/1.

[223] *Id.* at 137 ("Perpetrators of gun crimes, especially those with a felony record, were the targets of federal prosecution, which provided for far more severe sanctions for weapon use than those imposed by Virginia state law.").

[224] *Id.* at 155 (NAT'L RES. COUNCIL) ("Specifically, the incremental deterrent effect of increases in lengthy prison sentences is modest at best. Also, because recidivism rates decline markedly with age and prisoners necessarily age as they serve their prison sentence, lengthy prison sentences are an inefficient approach to preventing crime by incapacitation.").

[225] Anthony Doob, *Sentencing Severity and Crime: Accepting the Null Hypothesis*, 30 CRIME & JUST. 143, 173–74 (2003).

[226] *Id.* at 175 (citing research showing "[f]rom 1994–1995, violent crime in non-three-strikes states fell nearly three times more rapidly than in three-strikes states. In non-three-strikes states, violent crime fell by 4.6 percent. In states which have passed three-strikes laws, crime fell by only 1.7 percent."); *Id.* at 177 (discussing research on California three-strike legislation).

More specifically, the null hypothesis that variation in sentence severity does not cause variation in crime rates should be conditionally accepted.[227]

The finding that variations in sentencing severity do not correlate with fluctuations in crime rates is fundamentally irreconcilable with the calls for increased penalties for animal cruelty that are predicated on the presumed ability of incarceration to reduce future crime.[228]

Similarly, the presumption that one will be specifically deterred from engaging in future antisocial conduct is without empirical support. Specific deterrence and recidivism are not easy things to measure or predict, and research has shown that recidivism rates vary dramatically depending on the type of crime at issue.[229] But as a general matter, the National Institute of Justice reports that within five years of release, "about three-quarters, 76.6 percent of released prisoners are rearrested."[230] As the National Justice Institute summarized the research: Some policymakers and practitioners believe that increasing the severity of the prison experience enhances the "chastening" effect, thereby making individuals convicted of an offense less likely to recidivate. In fact, however, researchers have found no evidence of the chastening effect; instead, prisons may exacerbate recidivism.[231] "[C]ompared to non-custodial sanctions, incarceration has a null or mildly criminogenic impact on future criminal involvement."[232] There is no link-specific data indicating that harsh criminal punishment for animal abuse would produce lower rates of recidivism, or that heightened penalties in this realm would not have criminogenic consequences – punishment for animal abuse is unlikely to outperform other categories of crime in its ability to produce specific deterrence and prevent an offender from recidivating.[233] Accordingly, even if one accepts that animal abuse reliably predicts

---

[227] *Id.* at 187.

[228] A congressional task force recently found that there is "broad, bipartisan agreement that the costs of incarceration have outweighed their benefits." Charles Colson Task Force on Fed. Corrections, Transforming Prisons, Restoring Lives: *Final Recommendations of the Charles Colson Task Force on Federal Corrections* ix (2016), www.urban.org/sites/default/files/publication/77101/2000589 -Transforming-Prisons-Restoring-Lives.pdf (calling for a more "data-based" approach to criminal justice problems).

[229] Weisberg at 789 ("Robbers, car thieves, and burglars are very prone to recidivism, with rates measured in the 70 percent range. At the other end of the spectrum, murderers often have very low recidivism rates.").

[230] *National Statistics on Recidivism*, NAT'L INST. OF JUST. (June 17, 2014), www.nij.gov/topics/correc tions/recidivism/Pages/welcome.aspx (reporting an 82.1 percent rate of rearrest for property crimes and a 71.3 percent rearrest rate for violent crimes).

[231] *Five Things About Deterrence*, NAT'L INST. OF JUST., https://nij.gov/five-things/pages/deterrence.aspx #addenda (last visited Sept. 5, 2017).

[232] *Id.*

[233] As the National Research Council found based on a review of the recidivism research, "there is no credible evidence of a specific deterrent effect of the experience of incarceration." National Research Council, *The Growth of Incarceration in the United States: Exploring Causes and Consequences* at 156 (Jeremy Travis, Bruce Western & Steve Redburn eds., 2014), www.nap.edu/read/18613/chapter /7#155.

future violence, there is no reason to believe that incarceration will meaningfully reduce the rate of predicted interpersonal violence by these offenders in the future.[234]

There is a body of criminology research showing that the certainty and imminence of punishment are much more effective at deterring future crime than more serious penalties. According to some of these studies, increased spending on the law enforcement side had a fourfold-greater deterrent effect than equal amounts of increased spending on incarceration.[235] The National Research Council, noting these facts, highlighted the success of Project HOPE from Hawaii.[236] Project HOPE was an effort to tackle recidivism among drug offenders and others with a particularly high rate of recidivism. Under the program, people on probation faced nearly certain and swift punishment, but the punishment was very minimal (a day or two of incarceration) for any violations of probation. Notably, people on probation for drug offenses under the program failed drug tests at a much lower rate than those who were not in the program (and faced considerably greater, but less likely punishments). The program has been heralded as proof that reducing crime does not require more severe penalties; instead, what is needed are penalties that are swift and predictable. At this point, Project HOPE remains relatively unique, but its results in reducing recidivism "in a population in which deterrence has previously been ineffective in averting crime makes the finding potentially very important."[237]

Similarly, the conclusion of leading criminology researchers is that harsher criminal penalties are not successful in reducing levels of crime.[238] Compiling research on this point, Anthony Doob and Cheryl Webster recently explained that

> sentencing policies currently in place in many jurisdictions are still based on the
> assumption that harsh sentences deter, [but there is] no plausible body of evidence

---

[234] Of course, any truly prolonged sentence will have the benefit of incapacitation. But these offenders will eventually be released, thus begging the question of how long should one be imprisoned for animal abuse. Would animal protection groups tolerate a sentence of decades because of the incapacitation effect? As the National Research Council has reported, "because recidivism rates decline markedly with age and prisoners necessarily age as they serve their prison sentence, lengthy prison sentences are an inefficient approach to preventing crime by incapacitation." *Id.* at 155. Chapter 7 contains a more detailed discussion of incapacitation as a justification more severe animal cruelty penalties.

[235] Council of Econ. Advisors, *Economic Perspectives on Incarceration and the Criminal Justice System* 6 (2016), https://obamawhitehouse.archives.gov/sites/whitehouse.gov/files/documents/CEA%2BCriminal%2BJustice%2BReport.pdf.

[236] Doob at 137 n.8 ("Its strong evaluation design – a randomized experiment – puts its findings on a sound scientific footing and is among the reasons why its results are highlighted in this report."). *See also* Sandra D. Jordan, *Have We Come Full Circle? Judicial Sentencing Discretion Revived in Booker and Fanfan*, 33 PEPP. L. REV. 615, 651 (2006) ("It is now evident that the increased criminalization effort has failed to produce the desired results in decreasing the amount of crime, especially as related to the war on drugs which has been a documented failure.").

[237] *Id.* at 138; *see also id.* at 136–37 (compiling other similar research examples finding that certainty rather than severity of punishment improves deterrence).

[238] *Id.* ("sentence severity has no effect on the level of crime").

that supports policies based on this premise. On the contrary, standard social scientific norms governing the acceptance of the null hypothesis justify the present (always rebuttable) conclusion that sentence severity does not affect levels of crime.[239]

Yet the rationale behind the reform efforts sought by many animal protection groups is that more severe animal cruelty punishments are necessary in order to protect humans. In the wake of recent school shootings, commentators, newspapers, and animal protection groups proclaimed that if we are serious about stopping murderers, then we should punish animal cruelty more seriously. These claims are based on speculation and knee-jerk understandings of criminology, and are not borne out by data.

To be sure, data specific to animal cruelty has been hard to come by in the past. The FBI's recent decision to track animal abusers in its national crime database marks an important shift in this regard; it will hopefully provide a wealth of new data for future research.[240] Presently, however, good data about the predictive value of animal abuse, much less the beneficial impact of criminal punishment in this arena, does not exist. If the primary goal of increased cruelty enforcement – higher sentences and increased criminalization – is human protection (or even animal protection), then the success of criminal punishment in achieving these goals is an empirical question, and animal protection groups should ensure that the incarceration they are advocating for is actually producing the results they are expecting. If the rate of animal cruelty crimes is not going down, for example, as states enact ever more punitive animal cruelty systems and prosecute more cases, then advocates should reassess their actual goals and motivations. And most importantly, animal protection advocates should not fall into the circular path of reasoning that inevitably vindicates the conclusion that incarceration works. As David Downes explained, the push for ever more incarceration is "an experiment that cannot fail – if crime goes down, prisons gain the credit; but if it goes up, we clearly need more of the same medicine whatever the cost."[241] For many people who rightfully

---

[239] *Id.* at 146 (recognizing, however, that increased attention to a crime may lead to more police enforcement, and thus a higher "certainty" of punishment, which could impact deterrence). It is also the case that, although harsher sentences appear not to have any general deterrent benefit, the existence of the "overall system" of justice does have some deterrent effect. *Id.* at 144 (expecting that a system that criminalizes a crime will likely reduce the quantity of that crime).

[240] Quantitative data about the rates of animal abuse prosecutions, much less rates of animal abuse, does not appear to be available. Beirne at 41 ("Indeed, no technologically advanced society has generated large-scale, police-based data on the incidence and prevalence of animal abuse. There are no large-scale self-report studies on animal abuse, no household victimization surveys."); *see Along With Assault and Arson, FBI Starts to Track Animal Abuse*, NATIONAL PUBLIC RADIO (Jan. 16, 2016), www.npr.org/2016/01/16/463094761/along-with-assault-and-arson-fbi-starts-to-track-animal-abuse ("This could help save more animals – and, perhaps, people: Research has shown that animal abuse is often a precursor to other acts of violence.").

[241] David Downes, *The Macho Penal Economy: Mass Incarceration in the United States – A European Perspective, in* MASS IMPRISONMENT: SOCIAL CAUSES AND CONSEQUENCES 51, 57 (David Garland ed., 2001).

detest animal abuse, this sort of thinking has corrupted the advocacy surrounding the presumed link between animal cruelty and human violence.

A final, more conceptual, and less empirical point on the topic of severe punishment as a response to the link is warranted. Punishing animal cruelty more severely *because* of the presumed connection between animal violence and human violence fits somewhat uncomfortably within our system of criminal justice. As the President of the National Association of Criminal Defense Lawyers remarked, "[w]e don't punish individuals for alleged future misconduct they might at some point in the future engage in, but have not" because "[t]o do so would be to punish a person for a 'crime' that has not occurred and was not committed."[242] Calibrating levels of punishment to predictions of future violence is not unheard of in criminal law, but as scholars like Christopher Slobogin have documented, it is quite controversial.[243] Under such a framework, one is punished for crimes that have not occurred, and more likely than not are never going to occur. If the link, then, is being used to justify punishment for speculative future harms, would animal protection supporters adhere to the same logic and, for example, support lengthy terms of incarceration for children who shoplift, so long as the data showed that juvenile shoplifters are more likely than others to engage in other property crimes and eventually violent crimes as well? If shoplifting correlated with future animal abuse, would the leaders of the movement support sentences of five or ten years (or more) for juvenile shoplifting? And if the logic applies to shoplifters, why not to child abuse victims as well? Assume that research shows that being the victim of child abuse is a "clear predictor" of future violence or antisocial behavior. Should a child abuse victim, because they are statistically more likely to commit a violent offense against humans or animals in the future, be civilly confined or committed? Do animal protection advocates believe that policy-makers should seek out all individuals who are statistically more likely to engage in crimes in the future, and impose upon them a criminal sanction or punishment commensurate with their likelihood to commit future crimes? Notably, things like being bullied or suffering from depression or social isolation are all factors that at least some researchers have found correlate more strongly than animal abuse with future human violence, such as mass shootings.

6.5   TREATMENT AS OPPOSED TO INCARCERATION?

Andrew Linzey said, "[o]ne of the saddest features of abuse literature, concerning both humans and animals, is reading accounts of how those who abuse have

---

[242]   Stephanie Clifford, *He Kicked a Stray Cat, and Activists Growled*, N.Y. TIMES (Sept. 29, 2014), www .nytimes.com/2014/09/30/nyregion/animal-abuse-gains-traction-as-a-serious-crime-with-jail-more -often-the-result.html.

[243]   Christopher Slobogin, *The Civilization of the Criminal Law*, 58 VAND. L. REV. at 154 (2005).

themselves been abused. The pattern is now so familiar to welfare agencies that it almost passes without comment."[244]

Recognition of the interconnectedness of many different "links" or risk factors for abuse or being abused might suggest that social work interventions and counselling, as opposed to incarceration, would be preferable. If punishing for animal abuse is not merely an exercise in collective revenge or symbolic scapegoating, but rather an effort to reduce all forms of victimhood, then creative solutions focused on treatment and prevention as opposed to prosecution might better serve the twin goals of protecting humans and animals from violence.[245]

There is a body of social science research suggesting that animal abuse is a "potentially significant symptom of psychological dysfunction associated with child maltreatment and exposure to domestic violence."[246] People who abuse animals, particularly younger people who abuse animals, are often victims themselves.[247] "Children with a history of sexual abuse [are] significantly ... more likely to [be] cruel to animals," and children who live in homes where there is domestic violence (whether that violence includes the pets) are likely to "express the pain of their own victimization by abusing vulnerable family pets," and even boys subjected to corporal punishment are much more likely to have abused an animal than other men.[248] There is presumably a high false positive rate in using child abuse as a predictor of animal abuse, but one study found animal abuse rates as high as 88 percent among people subjected to physical child abuse,[249] and other research has consistently linked paternal alcoholism and physical abuse by a parent with animal abuse.[250] Thus, it seems that for many, perhaps most youthful animal abusers, like the animals they abuse, these people have often experienced powerlessness and been voiceless in the face of human aggression.[251] Perhaps the best use

---

[244] Andrew Linzey, *Introduction* to THE LINK BETWEEN ANIMAL ABUSE AND HUMAN VIOLENCE at 5.

[245] One could argue that treating those who abuse animals is also a superficial response to the problem of human violence. Interpersonal violence is a complex problem and it likely requires a solution that considers all forms of oppression, including poverty and racism. The animal protection movement should fund research examining the correlation between poverty and animal abuse, and if the research supports it, commit resources to alleviating poverty and increasing education as a way of meaningfully reducing animal cruelty.

[246] Frank R. Ascione, et al., *Cruelty to Animals in Normative, Sexually Abused, and Outpatient Psychiatric Samples of 6–12 Year Old Children*, 16 ANTHROZOOS 194, 195 (2003) (finding that among Italian adolescents who committed an act of animal abuse "almost all" of them had been exposed to domestic and animal violence).

[247] *Id.* at 208 ("The data add to our understanding of cruelty to animals, suggesting that it is more frequent in children who have experienced physical abuse themselves.").

[248] *Id.*

[249] DeViney, Dickert & Lockwood at 327.

[250] Alys et al. at 158 (noting "some evidence" in their research for the hypothesis that "paternal alcoholism predicts child abuse, and that child abuse in turn ... predicts animal cruelty.").

[251] Bill C. Henry, *The Relationship Between Animal Cruelty, Delinquency, and Attitudes Toward the Treatment of Animals*, 12 SOC'Y & ANIMALS 185 (2004) (finding "that observation of animal cruelty is more critical than participation in animal cruelty for the development of concern toward animals.").

of the link data is to demonstrate that animal abuse is highly relevant as a clue "that families are in need of intervention and support services."[252]

Particularly in light of these cycles of victimhood, a movement focused on expanding the bounds of compassion might use the link data to promote criminal interventions. Stated differently, if the interventions are other than prosecutions, perhaps the link's relatively crude and imprecise ability to predict future violence can be better deployed as a vehicle for encouraging policy-makers to invest more heavily in social work interventions. If evidence of animal abuse by a child led not to demonization and detention, but rather pro-social outreach and opportunities for interventions that, in the words of Heather Piper, are "inclusive and non-prejudicial ," then society would be taking seriously risks to humans and animals and the connectivity of these issues. In this way, animal abuse is not treated as unimportant or irrelevant, but rather "group level predictions" about a child's Ted Bundy-like propensities are avoided in favor of a "functional analysis of the individual."[253] In the past, some states prohibited mandatory psychological counselling for people convicted of animal abuse,[254] but thoughtful reformers might pursue something closer to a mandatory system of counselling and treatment for those who abuse animals, particularly the youthful offender.

Of course, the range of available treatments as opposed to punishments for animal abusers is in great need of further investigation and elaboration. One of the best things incarceration as a response to cruelty has going for it is that the research on effective counselling and interventions for animal cruelty is nascent and inconsistent. But thoughtful research in this field is underway, and the movement should support efforts to better understand what sort of approaches are effective. The movement should be open to the possibility of creative, non-penal solutions. For example, as counterintuitive as it initially sounds, treating animal abusers with animal therapy may produce favorable social outcomes. Under closely controlled circumstances, some researchers are coming to conclude that animal-assisted therapy may provide a path for an animal abuser to better integrate with society and learn to empathize.[255] Just as a person with an antisocial disorder who harms other people would not likely be effectively treated by forcing him to avoid all human contact,

[252] *Id.* at 367; Frank A. Ascione, Children and Animals: Exploring the Roots of Kindness and Cruelty (2004) (cataloguing examples where there was a failure of intervention by neighbors or professionals when there was knowledge of animal abuse). On the other hand, scholars such as Heather Piper have urged caution even when it comes to cross-reporting, given the dangers of wrongfully stigmatizing a family by placing them in the crosshairs of the social services or criminal justice system. For this reason, she has described certain systems of cross-reporting that have a criminal backdrop as "worrying."

[253] Patterson-Kane at 150.

[254] Deborah J. Challener, *Protecting Cats and Dogs in Order to Protect Humans: Making the Case for a Felony Companion Animal Statute in Mississippi*, 29 Miss. C. L. Rev. 499 (2010) ("Under Mississippi's animal cruelty laws, the sentencing judge could not order Bradford to have a psychological evaluation or seek counseling.").

[255] Alys et al. at 394.

some social workers and researchers are tentatively concluding that animal abusers are not necessarily well-served by being kept away from all animals. The research here is still emerging, but it is possible that animal-assisted therapy could provide a means of protecting humans and animals by establishing a meaningful human–animal connection among past animal abusers. Animal-assisted therapy may ultimately play a pivotal role in reducing human and animal violence by individuals who have harmed animals in the past.[256]

By and large, the modern focus of the animal protection movement has been a focus on prosecutions, rather than treatment. Although there was considerable celebration around the fact that all fifty states enacted felony animal cruelty laws, there has been no concerted legislative push for a requirement of mandatory treatment or cross-reporting. There is not a single state that mandates "two-way reporting."[257] Researchers in the mental health field have already shifted toward an understanding of animal abuse as an important symptom of conduct disorder or a personality disorder, warranting treatment that is consistent with these conditions.[258] And while there are dangers in overly emphasizing negative diagnoses and stigmatizing offenders, these risks likely pale in comparison to the harms flowing from incarceration. Moreover, many supporters of a carceral response to animal abuse argue that a criminal intervention gets the individual in the system and creates a "permanent record so in the future law enforcement officials know this is somebody who has these dangerous tendencies."[259] But a robust system of intervention and tracking without incarceration would not be inconsistent with this aspiration. Indeed, without more funding, the goal of stopping abusers or even serial killers by

---

[256] *Id.* at 389 (discussing the interest in this form of therapy for animal abusers and noting that "there appears to be a good potential of reaching individuals with a history of conduct problems and antisocial behavior; on the other hand, we have a responsibility never to place an animal in a situation that could result in intentional abuse or harm"); *Id.* at 394 (recognizing that "abuse behaviors are found pathologically embedded with other human cruelty problems [and explaining that] [t]he new generation of social workers must recognize both sides of the human/animal connection, protecting both people and animals but also see the potential to utilize animals in therapeutic settings and channel these interventions to help our clients connect with themselves, each other, and the world at large.").

[257] Schaffner (noting that regular communication between adult services and child protective services is rare). Non-mandatory cross-reporting is permitted in many states. *How Do I Report Suspected Abuse?*, NAT'L LINK COAL. http://nationallinkcoalition.org/how-do-i-report-suspected-abuse (last visited May 20, 2018).

[258] Frank A. Ascione, *Animal Abuse and Developmental Psychopathology*, in HANDBOOK ON ANIMAL-ASSISTED THERAPY: THEORETICAL FOUNDATIONS AND GUIDELINES 362 (Aubrey H. Fine ed., 3rd edn. 2010) ("These developments now make it more likely that clinicians and other mental health professionals will attend to this symptom during assessment and diagnostic work. Although research has not specifically addressed how often animal abuse is one of the symptoms present in diagnoses of conduct disorder, one estimate suggests that animal abuse may be present in 25% of conduct disorder cases.").

[259] *No Boundaries for Abusers: The Link Between Cruelty to Animals and Violence Toward Humans*, ANIMAL LEGAL DEF. FUND, http://aldf.org/resources/when-your-companion-animal-has-been-harmed/no-boundaries-for-abusers-the-link-between-cruelty-to-animals-and-violence-toward-humans/ (last visited Apr. 23, 2016).

expecting greater police monitoring of people with a history of animal abuse is beyond aspirational. After all, law enforcement is incapable of vigilantly monitoring even the terrorist watchlists, so it is unlikely that they would engage in some sort of close monitoring of everyone convicted or suspected of past acts of animal abuse. Social work interventions are far from perfect, and considerably more research is needed on effective methods, but incarceration as a means of enhancing empathy and encouraging nonviolent behavior is a proven failure.

6.6 FINAL THOUGHTS ON THE LINK: CRITIQUING THE LINK AS ENTRENCHING THE HUMAN/ANIMAL DIVIDE

In substantial part, the carceral animal law strategy adopted by animal protection organizations is underwritten by the link. Tabling concerns about the link data as insufficient to justify the predictive power that is prescribed to it, and overlooking the mismatch between incarceration and a desire to instill greater empathy in animal abusers, the strategy of employing the link as the cornerstone of the carceral strategy warrants interrogation on its own terms. Overreliance on the link as a means of protecting animals undermines a central feature of modern animal protection efforts – that is, the notion that animals warrant protection for their own sake. The bottom line for many animal advocates pushing for a more punitive response to animal abuse is that such a response is necessary in order to protect people. The link strategy is the embodiment of anthropocentric advocacy and law reform.

By the logic of the link's most strident public spokespeople, society can reduce child abuse and prevent domestic violence by aggressively deploying the criminal justice system against animal abusers. A law enforcement officer's explanation of how he conducts training for prosecutors on the importance of enforcing animal abuse crimes is emblematic, "You have to sell it to them in such a way that it's not a Fluffy-Muffy issue," but rather that animal abuse is "part of a larger nexus of crimes and the psyche behind them."[260] It is not, at bottom, about the animal at all. The link provides a justification for taking animal abuse seriously that is centered on improving the lives of humans, and at best protecting animals as a secondary or collateral benefit. The protection of animals is sometimes even omitted as a peripheral concern. As one leading link commentator, Allie Phillips, straightfor-wardly explained the matter in a training manual published for prosecutors: "Why is it important to take animal abuse seriously: 'the Link' to human violence."[261] The same clarity was expressed by the HSUS's Director of Animal Cruelty: because

---

[260] Charles Siebert, *The Animal-Cruelty Syndrome*, N.Y. Times, June 11, 2010, at MM42.
[261] Phillips & Lockwood at 15.

"animal abuse is a strong indicator of future violence, it is imperative for law enforcement agencies to" take it seriously.[262]

The animal protection groups employ the same narrative, and they do so precisely because it has traction with politicians whose constituents care about crime reduction. James Tedisco, the New York State Senate sponsor in 2018 for two bills increasing penalties for violating animal abuse laws, discussed the relevance of the link to animal protection with particular candor: "These measures aren't about protecting our pets, they're about keeping all members of our family safe from violence."[263] Given the agricultural exemptions that most states have carved out, it has long been clear that animal cruelty is not about farm animal protection. The link makes it clear that the prosecutions are not even about the "pets."

For race scholars, such an approach might superficially call to mind Derek Bell's interest convergence theory advanced in his famous law review article from 1980.[264] Bell posited what he called a "sober assessment of reality" wherein whites will adopt laws and pursue reforms that benefit blacks only when there is a "convergence of black and white interests." Analogizing to this framework, one could certainly regard it as plausible, even laudable to believe that the interests of animals will only be pursued by humans when animal protection efforts serve the interests of the human population. There is certainly truth to the insight that the "interests of animals are vulnerable to domination by the interests of humans as long as the two are perceived to be in competition."[265] If increased criminalization allows us to catch would-be serial killers before they kill, and to prevent mass shooters, then one can appreciate the sentiment that "at least in animal abuse, animal and human interests converge."[266] Of course, as discussed throughout this book, it is facile to assume that a more robust criminal justice apparatus – a larger prison industrial complex – is truly in the interest of all human communities. More incarceration is fundamentally bad for many people and communities, and not just those who are incarcerated.

Moreover, some critical race scholars have argued that Bell's model may actually impede civil rights development by constraining the options for reform that people will pursue: "[T]he assertion that black people receive favorable judicial decisions only when their interests converge with those of whites invites proponents of racial equality to limit the menu of possible remedial strategies for seeking black advancement."[267] Animal protection would be untenably limited if all reforms

---

[262] *Implications and Risks of Animal Cruelty, and How the Criminal Justice Community Can Help*, Off. Just. Programs Diagnostic Ctr. (July 3, 2013), www.ojpdiagnosticcenter.org/blog/implications-and -risks-animal-cruelty-and-how-criminal-justice-community-can-help.

[263] Senate Passes Three Bills to Protect Pets & People, https://www.nysenate.gov/newsroom/press -releases/ (last visited November 2, 2018).

[264] Derrick A. Bell, Jr., Comment, *Brown v. Board of Education and the Interest-Convergence Dilemma*, 93 Harv. L. Rev. 518, 523 (1980).

[265] Elizabeth Clawson, *The New Canaries in the Mine: The Priority of Human Welfare in Animal Abuse Prosecution*, in The Link Between Animal Violence and Human Violence at 95–96.

[266] *Id.* at 96.

[267] Justin Driver, *Rethinking the Interest-Convergence Thesis*, 105 Nw. U. L. Rev. 149, 189 (2011).

had to pass a litmus test of interest convergence. It may also be supposed that the pursuit of reforms at the point of convergence between animal interests and human values may serve to ensconce and calcify the hierarchical species status quo, at least if framed in a manner that precludes anti-oppression efforts potentially in tension with capitalism and profiteering from animal exploitation. At best, criminal punishment for animal abuse is a means of correcting a wrong perpetrated against a single animal (or set of animals), "but as a tool of long-term status change it falls short."[268]

At bottom, pursuing reforms because of the presumed link raises questions about the rationale and scope of animal protection efforts. As one moral philosopher posed the question, "what makes abusing animals immoral? Is it that the injury to the animal may lead to interpersonal violence, or is the immorality primarily a function of the negative effects that the abuse has on the animal herself?"[269] Is animal abuse inherently wrong, or only instrumentally so? The link-focused advocacy, certainly as applied on the ground, is a quintessential example of treating animal abuse as instrumentally wrong. Recall the quip from Allie Phillips, "Why do we care about animal abuse: the link."[270] The reality is that cruelty laws don't "care" about most animal abuse; instead, animal cruelty codes reflect the social consensus that certain things ought to be taboo, and injuring high-status animals, particularly because such abuse may lead to harm to humans, is in that category. The cruelty laws, with their sweeping exemptions, protect primarily the charismatic, high-status animals against abuse, and the laws are predicated on a desire to keep humans, not animals, safe.

These conclusions do not dictate that animal cruelty should be legalized, but rather that the link-based advocacy affords primacy to human interests. In the eyes of some scholars, any such anthropocentric approach is fundamentally stifling to long-term animal protection efforts. It is not inconceivable that link advocacy pursued by animal protection groups actually entrenches the status of animals as inherently lesser beings whose suffering should be avoided *or* sought in ways that maximize human well-being and enjoyment. It is the calculus of minimizing harm and suffering to humans that is actually prioritized by link reforms. These concerns about the rationale for pursuing incarceration make the interspecies dilemma about the "ethics of captivity" all the more salient.[271]

---

[268] Clawson at 98 (arguing that the speciest nature of the criminal code perpetuated a double standard that actually "devalues animals").

[269] Mark H. Bernstein, *Responding Ethically to Animal Abuse*, in THE LINK BETWEEN ANIMAL VIOLENCE AND HUMAN VIOLENCE at 85. *Id.* ("Compare this to a second kind of view that primarily, if not exclusively, situates the moral wrongness of animal abuse not in the harm done to the animal, per se, but instead in harm done to other beings.")

[270] Phillips & Lockwood at 15.

[271] *See generally* THE ETHICS OF CAPTIVITY, Lori Gruen ed. (2014).

7

Anticipating Challenges to the Critique of Carceral Animal Law

Pioneering animal rights leader Nathan Runkle published a biography in 2017, in which he describes the context for his decision to create an animal protection organization, Mercy For Animals, while he was still in high school. Detailing the organization's ascension from a local Ohio coalition of friends to an international non-profit, Runkle credits the organization's success to, among other things, the fact they devised a plan for getting animal law issues into the court system. As Runkle explains it, undercover investigations have produced "an extremely important ... blueprint for litigating" factory farm abuses.[1] The blueprint that Runkle is referring to is the criminal prosecution, incarceration, and deportation of factory farm abusers based on undercover footage. The litigation strategy is simple: Mercy For Animals conducts an undercover investigation, and then uses its video footage as leverage to pressure for a prosecution. Investigations weaponize transparency in favor of prosecutions.

The litigation championed by Runkle and the movement measures its success in terms of incarceration of low-level farm workers, almost invariably people of color, who are already vulnerable because of their immigration and socioeconomic statuses.[2] The notion of criminal prosecution as advancing animal rights is not limited to insiders within the movement. One of the preeminent legal scholars of our time, Cass Sunstein, characterized prosecution as a form of animal rights: "[I]t is entirely clear that animals have legal rights, at least of a certain kind. Even those who seem most antagonistic to animal rights are likely to favor animal rights of certain sorts (for example, protection against gratuitous cruelty)."[3]

Incarcerating the poor men and women who are forced through personal circumstances to work in our nation's factory farms should not be celebrated as social change lawyering. Rather, such litigation should be denigrated as social reform escapism. The pursuit of maximalist sentences against these people will not reduce

---

[1] NATHAN RUNKLE, MERCY FOR ANIMALS 96 (2017).
[2] The US agricultural workforce is more than 90 percent Latina/Latino.
[3] Cass R. Sunstein, *Standing for Animals (with Notes on Animal Rights)*, 47 UCLA L. REV. 1333, 1335 (2000).

crime generally, nor prevent animal suffering. Instead, the prosecution provides a distraction from the arduous and seemingly impossible task of slowing the rate of animal suffering. The low-level employee becomes the sacrificial lamb offered up by the industry as proof of their commitment to animal welfare standards, and by the animal protection groups as evidence of their success in liberating animals from cruelty. There is a shameful parity between the animal protection movement and the agricultural industry in their treatment of low-level agricultural employees as expendable and as deserving targets of blame. For the movement, no less than for the industry, targeting low-level abuse for vilification is a way of vindicating social norms in favor of respecting animal well-being.

Yet, the movement's resort to criminal law as the ideal blueprint for litigation is not as confounding as it might seem at first blush. It may be ineffectual for the reasons already discussed, but an interest in carceral policies is not surprising. This chapter briefly anticipates the major critiques to the central claims of this book.

7.1 THE ABSENCE OF ALTERNATIVES

The preoccupation with criminal prosecution as a means of advancing the status of animals in the law is often explained, as a historical matter, as a reflection of the absence of other litigation or legal options. This framing of the criminal prosecution focus of many animal protection advocates as a necessary evil would likely ring true for many people within the movement. But as a wider range of litigation successes are achieved, as victories are measured in terms of habitats protected, animals released from roadside zoos, or needless killings or abuse enjoined, the notion that criminal punishment is the only, *much less the best* means of legal intervention is less clear. Increasingly, animal protection movements are working effectively to protect animals in spite of prosecutors, not because of them. PETA's first notable legal intervention was its involvement in the criminal prosecution of a cruel primate researcher in Silver Springs, Maryland, but today its legal efforts are considerably more far-reaching and creative. Like their involvement in prosecutions, including the Silver Springs case, not every effort results in a total vindication of their theory in court. But the litigation raises social consciousness about issues of animal mistreatment, and starts new dialogues.

In light of the actual successes and publicity associated with a new wave of civil litigation and reform efforts, at least in private, there is an increasing number of animal protection advocates who are willing to acknowledge that the carceral strategy of animal law is not an unmitigated good for society, or perhaps even individual animals. Nonetheless, many such people who might express skepticism about the long-term benefits of incarcerating humans to advance the status of animals would be quick to suggest that criminal prosecutions remain a critical form of intervention. Even in light of more promising civil litigation opportunities, prosecution is regarded as a necessary evil, because it promises state involvement with a person who presents a danger to animals; it is a way of intervening in a volatile situation for the protection of both the human and the animal. On this view, through prosecution, animal abusers will gain the formal attention of authorities, through registries and criminal records. Moreover, it is posited that the criminal law can play the role of ensuring that people who are disposed toward animal abuse will get treatment.

But as a means to these laudable ends, criminal prosecution promises both too much and too little. First, as a means of social intervention, criminal prosecution is like choosing the proverbial sledgehammer when a scalpel would do much better. Criminal prosecution as an intervention is harsh medicine, threatening to impose lifelong disabilities on the person prosecuted. One scholar astutely observed that a conviction is "not merely" an intervention:

> It gives rise to a legal status making convicted persons subject to restrictions on freedom, benefits, and rights. . . . Every conviction implies a permanent change, because these disabilities will "carry through life." A convicted criminal may be disenfranchised, lose the right to hold federal or state office, be barred from entering certain professions, be subject to impeachment when testifying as a witness, be disqualified from serving as a juror, and may be subject to divorce. To this ever-increasing list may be added the loss of the right to keep and bear arms. For noncitizens, conviction may result in deportation. . . . Conviction potentially affects many aspects of family relations, including, for example, the ability to adopt, be a foster parent, or retain custody of one's own children. Conviction can make one ineligible for public employment, such as in the military and law enforcement. It can preclude private employment, including working in regulated industries, with government contractors, or in fields requiring a security clearance. Conviction can also restrict one's ability to hold a government contract, to obtain government licenses and permits, or to collect a vested public pension. Those convicted of certain crimes may lose the right to drive a car.[4]

In light of these consequences, it borders on the absurd for the animal protection movement to treat criminal prosecutions as mere helpful interventions designed to safeguard the well-being of a person accused of animal abuse. Criminal punishment is deemed necessary in order to keep people safe. But intervention is a term that calls to mind carefully tailored efforts to improve one's health or well-being, whereas criminal prosecutions are oftentimes permanently debilitating, and may actually lead to more crime or violence.[5]

The Even if prosecutions are not beneficial for defendants themselves, many would argue that a criminal justice response is necesary for human safety. This rationale for

---

[4] Gabriel J. Chin, *The New Civil Death: Rethinking Punishment in the Era of Mass Conviction*, 160 U. PA. L. REV. 1789, 1799–801 (2012).

[5] If the protection of an animal is the intervention that is truly desired, civil forfeiture laws, animal treatment and adoption programs, and other programs keyed to the well-being of the animal would seem better suited to the task than incarceration. People who are creative enough to imagine a society in which animals are not regarded as property should be able to conceive of an intervention or set of interventions other than incarceration.

criminal punishment often derives from the movement's contorted reliance on the link research, discussed in detail in Chapter 6, but it is worth reiterating a couple of important themes on this point. Given the presumed link between human violence and animal abuse, so the argument goes, criminal punishment is essential.

To make this point, a leading animal law textbook reproduces a list of eight notorious serial killers (including Ted Bundy and Jeffrey Dahmer) who are believed to have killed or tortured animals in order to demonstrate that the connection between violence to humans and animal violence is, in the words of the authors, more than "anecdotal."[6] Of course, such a list is the very definition of anecdote, and the argumentation it represents is a classic logical fallacy. The fallacy of the converse is the logical fallacy of assuming that because all "A" are "B," therefore all "B" are also "A." Although all dogs are mammals, it is not true that all mammals are dogs. Thus, even assuming that all serial killers had abused animals, it would be a fallacy to assert that all (or most) animal abusers will become serial killers. The reality is that nearly all people convicted of murder have a prior criminal history, but the fact of a prior criminal history is not predictive of one becoming a murderer. And the data about serial killers is actually much more complicated. Studies have shown that a surprisingly large number of people engage in some form of animal cruelty during their youth or adolescence, but the majority of these people do not grow into adults who are violent toward humans or animals. Summarizing recent research on this point, Hal Herzog explained that "[t]here is a surprisingly weak relationship between animal cruelty and human-directed violence."[7] Contrary to the narrative espoused by the animal protection movement, "most people who commit violent crimes against humans do not have a history of violence directed at animals."

Emily Patterson-Kane directly critiqued this reliance on the most infamous Bundy-like criminals who abused animals by noting that people who "do not fit that pattern are rarely cited," and there are some notable examples. She notes that serial killer Carl Panzram was sorry for two things, "I am sorry that I have mistreated some few animals in my life-time and I am sorry that I am unable to murder the whole damed [sic] human race."[8] Patterson-Kane explains that if the claims are based on anecdote, then one can find examples linking animal killing or animal compassion to violence.

Recent mass shootings have also provided an opportunity to posit the need for more aggressive animal cruelty prosecutions in order to provide early "interventions." For example, Nikolaz Cruz killed seventeen people at a high school in February 2017, and Devin Kelley killed twenty-six in a church in Texas just a few months earlier. These

---

[6] Bruce A. Wagman et al., Animal Law: Cases and Materials 181 (4th edn. 2010).

[7] Hal Herzog, *Animal Cruelty Does Not Predict Who Will Be a School Shooter*, Psychol. Today (Feb. 21, 2018), www.psychologytoday.com/us/blog/animals-and-us/201802/animal-cruelty-does-not-predict -who-will-be-school-shooter.

[8] Emily Patterson-Kane, *The Relation of Animal Maltreatment to Aggression*, in Animal Maltreatment: Forensic Mental Health Issues and Evaluations 140, 143–44 (Lacey Levill et. al eds., 2016).

cases attracted the attention of animal protection advocates because both of the shooters had a history of animal maltreatment. Kelley had apparently beaten a dog in his backyard, and Cruz had shot a pellet gun at squirrels and birds, poked sticks into rabbit holes, and killed toads. Using these cases as examples, animal protection groups argue that society could prevent mass shootings if it responded more reliably and aggressively to animal abuse. Animal cruelty requires a robust criminal response, it is argued, because is a reliable predictor of mass shootings. But here too the reality is more complicated.

First, as noted in Chapter 6, most people who engage in violence toward humans, including most mass shooters, *have not* abused animals. According to Dr. Emily Patterson-Kane's 2016 meta-analysis of fifteen separate link studies, only 34 percent of all violent offenders had a history of animal abuse. Most mass shooters had no history of animal abuse. As two leading researchers found, 57 percent of school shooters did not have a history of prior animal abuse.[9] Research by the Secret Service and the Department of Education found that only five out of thirty-seven school shooters had a history of animal abuse, and studies have consistently shown that other factors – such as bullying, depression, or mental illness – correlate much more closely with school shooting. Ignored in the movement's narrative about the need for a criminal response to abuse is the data showing that some of the worst mass shooters of the modern era had a demonstrated and unique level of empathy and care for animals. Moreover, it is difficult to take seriously the notion that a six-month stint in a juvenile detention facility for Cruz after he killed a toad or shot a squirrel would have positively altered the course of his life and made him less dangerous. Even bracketing the fact that hunting is legal, and so is merely killing animals for sport with no intention of consuming or using the flesh, including animal-killing contests with assault rifles, it is inconsistent with existing data about the often criminogenic consequences of incarceration to conclude that the prosecution of someone like Cruz would have "cured" him so as to prevent future violence.

To put the matter plainly, the claim that criminal punishment is a necessary intervention is overstated and misleading. In reality, there are a multitude of reasons that criminal prosecutions have failed to trigger successful rehabilitation. First, it must be noted that in the rush to prosecute people associated with animal abuse, very few resources have been devoted to funding the creation of evidence-based treatment programs for abusers. It seems to go without saying that animal abusers should receive treatment, but the result of a conviction is all too often a conviction (and collateral consequences) that make one's life harder, without *any* meaningful

---

[9]   Arnold Arluke & Eric Madfis, *Animal Abuse as a Warning Sign of School Massacres: A Critique and Refinement*, 18 HOMICIDE STUD. 7, 7–22 (2014) (finding that of the 43 percent of mass shooters who had committed animal abuse, the abuse was usually "up close" or hands-on abuse of a particularly egregious nature). *Id.* (noting that "torturing animals in an up-close and personal way, especially animals like dogs and cats that have been heavily anthropomorphized in our culture" may be a red flag or predictor of persons who may resort to inter-human violence).

treatment to deal with the prior conditions or stressors that resulted in animal abuse, much less the new stressors present after incarceration. Many social workers lament the absence of meaningful frameworks for even studying, much less implementing data-based treatment for animal abusers. But the absence of data-based approaches to treating the conditions that make animal abuse more likely has been, to date, ignored by the animal protection movement. Funding research regarding the proper treatment of such individuals would be a far better use of resources than incarceration, if the goal of the intervention is really to make society safer.

In this way, criminal law as an intervention also promises too little intervention. When it comes to the mismatch between existing treatment options and the enthusiasm for criminal interventions, Colorado is a notable example. The state's cruelty laws provide that a judge must evaluate all animal abuse offenders to assess the appropriateness of treatment, and the courts are required to order treatment for anyone whose evaluation results in a recommendation of treatment, as well as for all individuals convicted of second or subsequent animal cruelty offenses.[10] Yet there is an open acknowledgment that the statutorily mandated evaluations are rare in the extreme, and even when they are conducted there is very little consensus about the appropriate methodologies. For related reasons, treatment is also rarely ordered or completed.

Even in the face of a clear statutory mandate of treatment for animal abusers, such treatment is rarely ordered by judges, giving lie to the claim that prosecution is a reliable way of ensuring treatment that will ensure the safety of society. Intervention may be necessary and appropriate, but the criminal justice system is oftentimes either uninterested or incapable of providing meaningful, often costly treatment. Instead, the criminal prosecution of an animal abuser keeps society safer in only one sense: the abuser is locked up for a period of time. But Cruz was never going to be sentenced to life in prison for killing toads, nor was he even going to spend decades in prison for such an offense. So, a mature justice system and animal protection movement must consider that the risks to animals and people *may be exaggerated* by incarceration. For the animal abuser sentenced to months or years in prison without data-based treatment procedures, there is good reason to believe that their violent tendencies will be exacerbated, not improved, upon their release. As discussed above, incarceration has been documented by some to increase the risk of re-offending, or future criminality.

Even if there is no hope of treating violent offenders and curing them of their violent tendencies, many in the animal protection movement argue that criminal prosecutions serve as an intervention that puts the person on the radar of law enforcement and society. Assuming, contrary to the data, that animal cruelty is a reliable predictor of mass shootings, for example, then maybe the risk of violence from these people should be made known to the public. So understood, prosecution provides a sort of early response to future violence. The headline to a column that

[10]   Colo. Rev. Stat. Ann. § 18–9-202 (West 2017).

ran in the days after the Cruz shootings is emblematic of this view: "Nikolas Cruz may have never killed if society took more action on link between animal abuse and mass murderers."[11] Such claims sound good in the heat of the moment following a tragic shooting, but what would "more" criminal action mean? The author of the piece chides the outmoded view of kids being kids because it is "just a squirrel, [or] just a toad." The idea that a more criminal response would help reduce violence appears to be hyperbole, and presumably most people would not posit that a toad-killing teen or pre-teen should face years of incarceration as a means of protecting society from his future self. Probably, incarceration is not appropriate in such circumstances. If, instead of incarceration, the import of prosecution is an interest in alerting society to Cruz's dangerousness, then what form should that heightened awareness take? Would we tolerate some sort of scarlet letter for life on all animal-harming kids? Does it matter that some data show that nearly one in three people admit to some level of animal abuse prior to college? More importantly, what role would such a system of heightened readiness play in preventing mass shootings? In this regard, Nikolas Cruz is a great example of someone who was able to carry out a horrific mass shooting in spite of the fact that he was on the radar of state and federal law enforcement. Cruz was well known to law enforcement, not because he had killed toads and squirrels, but because they had received explicit reports of a desire by him to engage in a mass shooting. Cruz had previously threatened members of the school community with violence, and the FBI had received at least two tips about Cruz and his interest in a school shooting. Local law enforcement was contacted about Cruz at least twenty times in the years leading up to the shooting. In light of such overt warnings, it strains credulity to imagine that it was the lack of an animal cruelty registry or prosecution that resulted in Cruz flying under the radar. It is impossible to imagine that an early childhood act of animal maltreatment would be of more interest to the FBI or local law enforcement than social media posts threatening actual violence, and repeated tips suggesting the individual is planning to engage in a mass shooting.

It is tempting to assume that more aggressive criminal protections for animals would have stopped someone like Cruz by making him a person of interest to law enforcement. But the reality is that mass shooters often present warning signs well beyond and more significant than animal abuse. As in the case of Cruz, his own expressed interest in becoming a "professional school shooter" would seem to have been the strongest possible warning sign, and yet it did not result in a mass shooting being averted. Violence in America is common, and school shootings occur more than once per month on average. Thus, although one can appreciate the pressure on animal protection organizations to look favorably on criminal prosecutions given the limited number of litigation alternatives, and in view of the public support for such

[11]   Jessica Scott-Reid, *Nikolas Cruz May Have Never Killed If Society Took More Action on Link Between Animal Abuse and Mass Murderers*, DAILY NEWS (Feb. 17, 2018), www.nydailynews.com/opinion/animal-abuse-scrutiny-stop-killers-nikolas-cruz-article-1.3826671.

prosecutions, the reality is that there is no data or logical supposition that supports the notion that convictions promise the best intervention for protecting humans or animals.

7.2 THE POWER OF CRIMINAL LAW IN SHAPING NORMS AND MAINSTREAM SUPPORT FOR PROSECUTIONS

Many animal protection advocates view severe criminal sanctions for abuse as a necessary piece of the symbolic or theoretical war being waged on behalf of animals. A laudably simplistic syllogism implicitly undergirds the entire theory: The law should value animal welfare; permitting animal abuse to go unpunished does not reflect legal value for animal welfare; therefore, animal abuse must not go unpunished. That is, if abusing an animal is treated as a de minimus crime – like jaywalking or littering – then the message that the law values the lives and well-being of animals is undermined.[12]

On the other hand, the symbolic or norm-shifting benefits expected from robust criminal enforcement may be drastically overstated. For one thing, psychology research has shown that humans employ motivated cognition when it comes to animal welfare[13] – that is, we disregard relevant information that would create a moral dilemma for us personally. Support for criminal prosecutions for rogue, non-institutionalized abuse is entirely consistent with and reinforces these patterns of motivated cognitions. Americans have a remarkable interest in information about the well-being of animals, unless the information they are obtaining conflicts with their preexisting moral beliefs or dietary habits. The mistreatment of a service dog or a therapy goat is a momentous scandal,[14] but the daily horrors of a slaughterhouse are beyond society's comfort zone for discussion. A focus on othering and prosecuting a handful of bad actors makes animal protection seem comfortable and mainstream to Americans.

---

[12] As the Supreme Court has observed, the line between necessary and gratuitous animal suffering is often opaque. Church of the Lukumi Babalu Aye, Inc. v. City of Hialeah, 508 U.S. 520, 537–38 (1993) (questioning the distinction between deeming sacrificing animals for religious reasons as unnecessary, but deeming "hunting, slaughter of animals for food, eradication of insects and pests, and euthanasia as necessary").

[13] Jared Piazza & Steve Loughan, *When Meat Gets Personal, Animal Minds Matter Less: Motivated Use of Intelligence Information in Judgments of Moral Standing*, 7 Soc. Psychol. & Personality Sci., 867, 867–74 (2016) (demonstrating through original studies that people find animal intelligence highly relevant to their moral status, but also showing that evidence of intelligence is disregarded when it relates to one's own eating habits).

[14] Nick Caloway, *Man with Goat at Davidson County Court Now Investigated for Animal Cruelty*, WKRN.com (Feb. 3, 2017), http://wkrn.com/2017/02/03/man-with-goat-at-davidson-county-court-now-investigated-for-animal-cruelty/; see also *Special Set of Wheels Sends Injured Spring Grove Goat on Road to Recovery*, WLWT5 (June 7, 2017), www.wlwt.com/article/special-set-of-wheels-sends-injured-spring-grove-goat-on-road-to-recovery/3566395 (documenting community outrage over an attack on a local goat used to eat weeds in a community space).

But being mainstream when it comes to animal protection is not particularly good for the animals. By making animal protection seem mainstream and easy, and largely about the bad actions of others, the carceral focus presents risks to the animal protection movement. Even assuming a utilitarian sacrifice of human liberty in pursuit of symbolic victories for animals is morally palatable, the prosecution policies pursued by animal protection groups are actually distorting the message of the movement. The focus on appearing mainstream distracts attention away from the greatest suffering of animals, and directs it instead toward a handful of particularly gruesome injuries, oftentimes to the most charismatic (non-food) animals.[15] The reality is that most people consume animal products from factory farms, and are complicit in animal suffering on a massive scale. The trend of increased incarceration is likewise laser-focused on people who engage in non-institutionalized cruelty, and the prosecutions often involve injuries to dogs or cats. The animal cruelty prosecutions, then, are concentrated on the sort of psychopath that is commonplace in horror movies.

But even the most prolific, serial animal abuser cannot compete in volume with the sheer amount of suffering caused by large-scale industrialized meat and dairy production,[16] which, as already explained, is almost entirely exempted from criminal prosecution by the very cruelty statutes celebrated by animal protectionists. Take Colorado's cruelty provision.[17] The law explicitly exempts from its coverage cruelty associated with the creation of "agricultural products," the racing of animals, the hunting or trapping of animals, the use of animals in research, the use of animals in rodeos, and the treatment of any undefined "wildlife nuisances." With more than a half-dozen exemptions, the moral priorities of the criminal law are clear. The act of beating a dog or a pig with a shovel would presumably be a felony, but doing so to discipline a racing dog, or as a form of "nuisance" control, or potentially to train an animal for hunting, or as an accepted agricultural practice, might be entirely legal. Once one is fully aware of the far-reaching exemptions from cruelty laws,

---

[15]   David J. Wolfson, *Beyond the Law: Agribusiness and the Systemic Abuse of Animals Raised for Food or Food Production*, 2 Animal L. 123, 131 (1996) (noting that animal cruelty "enforcement is largely directed at dogs, cats, and horses rather than animals raised for food or food production"). For a helpful analogy, *see* G. Kristian Miccio, *A House Divided: Mandatory Arrest, Domestic Violence, and the Conservatization of the Battered Women's Movement*, 42 Hous. L. Rev. 237, 243 (2005) ("Mandatory arrest is merely the vehicle in understanding how the Protagonists, perhaps unwittingly, have conservatized a movement and distorted a feminist politic.").

[16]   For the reader unfamiliar with the field of animal law, the assertion that meat and dairy production are sources of extreme violence to animals may seem pejorative. But a quick review of the leading literature in this field leaves no doubt. Quoting a veterinary textbook, some scholars have noted that "one of the best things modern animal agriculture has going for it is that most people in the developed countries are several generations removed from the farm and haven't a clue how animals are raised and processed." Peter Singer & Jim Mason, The Ethics of What We Eat: Why Our Food Choices Matter 11 (2007) (quoting Peter R. Cheeke, Contemporary Issues in Animal Agriculture [2003]); *see generally* Singer & Mason at 29 (describing a day's work at a bird processing facility); Ted Connover, *The Way of All Flesh*, Harpers Mag. (May 2013), http://harpers.org/archive/2013/05/the-way-of-all-flesh/ (detailing the author's experience working undercover as a meat inspector).

[17]   § 18–9-202.

exemptions that effectively swallow the rule, the emphasis on the enforcement of these laws as a standard-bearer for the movement is disorienting. The effect of the movement's focus on the narrow reach of criminal cruelty is to create scapegoats and demons out of a few animal abusers, almost as a way of ignoring or de-prioritizing the large-scale suffering of animals that is, very much, a mainstream American practice.

Many animal protection advocates might be inclined to conclude that the limited scope of potential animal cruelty prosecutions is regrettable, but largely irrelevant to the progression of the animal protection movement more generally. On this view, one could posit that, all other things being equal, while it would be better if more animal abuse was illegal, it is not a zero-sum game. By focusing on the protection of dogs and cats from particularly macabre, if rare, abuse that captures media headlines and public interest, the law is still being used to produce messaging favorable to the status of animals. The assumption behind such logic seems to be that a focus on these prosecutions will generate a rising tide of respect for all animals. But the reality is not quite this simple.

There are high-profile examples in which animal cruelty prosecutions have served to fossilize animal rights, or impede the development of the field. The existence of animal cruelty laws has provided a basis for courts to refuse to extend the most basic rights of autonomy and liberty to other species. For example, in the context of denying the existence of a right for elephants and chimpanzees not to be isolated in solitary cages, judges have pointed out that such legal rights need not be recognized, because if the living conditions become too torturous for the animals, the cruelty laws may serve as a stopgap. A Connecticut trial court ruling in cases filed by the Nonhuman Rights Project explicitly pointed to that state's cruelty to animals statutes "as a potential alternative method of ensuring the well-being of any animal," and a New York appellate court noted that "[o]ur rejection of a rights paradigm for animals does not, however, leave them defenseless, for existing statutes state they can't be tortured, unjustifiably killed, abandoned in a public place, or transported in cruel or inhumane ways."[18] The fact of cruelty prosecutions, then, provides a ready-made excuse for refusing to take seriously claims made on behalf of animals that seek more than merely to avoid torture or abject cruelty. The more felonies, the higher the sentences, and the more prosecutions, the less inclined courts are to take seriously other forms of more sweeping efforts at litigation-based reform. Carceral animal law has played a direct role in undermining litigation seeking rights for animals. Far from showing that animals have rights, the criminal law can be used to show that they do not need rights.

Moreover, prosecuting the owner of a neglected collie,[19] but not the owner of a massive pig processing plant, sends a message about the methods and goals of the

[18] Nonhuman Rights Project *ex rel.* Beulah, Minnie & Karen v. R.W. Commerford & Sons, Inc. 12 (Conn. Super. Ct. 2017); People *ex rel.* Nonhuman Rights Project, Inc. v. Lavery, 124 A.D.3d 148, 152–153 (N.Y. App. Div. 2014), *leave to appeal denied*, 26 N.Y.3d 902 (N.Y. 2015).

[19] P. Christine Smith, *Collie Abusers Plead, Get Tougher Sentences*, Whidbey News-Times (June 19, 2002 12:00 AM), www.whidbeynewstimes.com/news/22092619.html.

animal protection movement. Any movement that wants to be taken seriously should be very concerned about allegations of internal inconsistency or hypocrisy. But the use of criminal prosecution as a tool to advance the status of non-humans presents many ironies and inconsistencies. As Professor Sherry Colb aptly noted,

> If the law endorses animal cruelty, as it does, in so many zones, and if most of the population funds animal cruelty, as it does, then who are we, "the people," to be prosecuting and locking up those individuals who happen to violate a law that identifies and stigmatizes some small sphere of animal cruelty which society has arbitrarily decided it will not tolerate.[20]

The very popularity of animal abuse laws and prosecutions is a reflection of the "rarity of the practice targeted by the law[s]," and focusing on such laws actually has the effect of distorting the message that all animal suffering matters, by instead reinforcing society's abiding view of itself as compassionate to animals.[21] Cruelty prosecutions may actually produce complacency insofar as the incarceration and othering of a deviant (or a group perceived as deviant, such as the Santeria), provide a "warm and fuzzy" sense of superiority that enables folks to help them "feel good about their sensitivity to nonhuman animals."[22] In a world that causes so much pain to animals, these warm and fuzzy feelings may come at a cost. Professor Colb summarized the public support for criminal prosecutions of animal cruelty by noting that it is only "when we have no personal investment of habit to defend that we are best able to see the true cruelty and violence involved in a practice in which others are still participating."[23] This conclusion is consistent with the research on motivated cognition discussed earlier in this section, and is unquestionably related to the reason that so many people vigorously support anti-animal cruelty legislation.

Writing from his jail cell, Martin Luther King, Jr. noted that, although laws are supposed to facilitate justice, when laws fail in this purpose they "become dangerously structured dams that block the flow of social progress." The animal cruelty laws, and the movement's obsession with them present such an impediment to progress. For example, social science research on framing suggests that a focus on discrete acts of animal cruelty may actually impede the development of animals'

[20] *See e.g.*, Sherry F. Colb, *Whether or Not to Prosecute Animal Cruelty*, DORF ON LAW (Jan. 21, 2015), www.dorfonlaw.org/2015/01/whether-or-not-to-prosecute-animal.html (explaining the symbolic nature of the animal cruelty prosecutions, specifically which type of animal abuse do we prosecute and which types do we not, and ultimately concluding that there may be symbolic reasons to continue such prosecutions in some instances).

[21] *Id.; see e.g.*, Colb ("in a particular case, the person who goes to dog fights [and who] is also consuming a strictly plant-based diet …might therefore be responsible for far less violence against animals than the non-vegan who prosecutes him (or the society that urges his prosecution.").

[22] Colb.

[23] Sherry F. Colb, *New York State Bans Tattoos of Companion Animals*, JUSTIA https://verdict.justia.com /2015/01/21/new-york-state-bans-tattoos-companion-animals

status in the law.[24] Specifically, the social science literature on framing teaches that animal cruelty prosecutions may tend to facilitate inertia regarding what issues are relevant in the debate over the status of animals in the law.[25] Framing teaches that the way a group articulates and pursues its objectives will have a critical defining and reinforcing effect. For example, social scientists have discovered that "framing processes have come to be regarded, alongside resource mobilization and political opportunity processes, as a central dynamic in understanding the character and course of social movement."[26] As one leading article on the topic explained:

> Social movement actors choose which frames to employ and guide the public to become proponents of their cause ... From this perspective, social movements are not viewed merely as carriers of extant ideas and meanings that grow automatically out of structural arrangements, unanticipated events, or existing ideologies. Rather, movement actors are viewed as signifying agents actively engaged in the production and maintenance of meaning for constituents, antagonists, and bystanders or observers.[27]

Simply put, it must be acknowledged that focusing considerable resources and acclaim on prosecutions will have an impact on how society understands animal well-being, and animal protection efforts more generally. A heavy reliance on animal cruelty prosecutions for outreach and publicity will have the effect of framing animal protection efforts as either tolerating blindness to the suffering of other animals, or suggesting that it is less important. Of course, the movement can and does employ multiple framing devices simultaneously, but the point is to note that advocacy in support of certain prosecutions does not occur in a vacuum; it impacts the very perception and reality of animal protection efforts. If the animal protection movement is serious about social change, it needs to recognize what Aya Gruber identified as the critical difference between being part of the mainstream, "socially conservative tough-on-crime ideology," and being part of the historical

---

[24] The salient influence of Professor Gary Francione's thinking on my research must be acknowledged. *See* Gary L. Francione, *We Are All Michael Vick*, PHILLY.COM (Aug. 14, 2009), http://articles.philly .com/2009-08-14/news/24986151_1_atlanta-falcons-quarterback-vick-illegal-dog-dog-fights ("Michael Vick may enjoy watching dogs fight. Someone else may find that repulsive but see nothing wrong with eating an animal who has had a life as full of pain and suffering as the lives of the fighting dogs. It's strange that we regard the latter as morally different from, and superior to, the former ... We are all Michael Vick.").

[25] For an overview of the concept of framing as it is studied in the social sciences, *see, e.g.*, Robert D Benford & David A. Snow, *Framing Processes and Social Movements: An Overview and Assessment*, 26 ANN. REV. OF SOC. 611–39 (2000); Robert D. Benford, *Frame Disputes Within the Nuclear Disarmament Movement*, 71 SOC. FORCES 677, 677–701 (1993); Holly J. McCammon et al., *Movement Framing and Discursive Opportunity Structures: The Political Successes of the U.S. Women's Jury Movements* 72 AM. SOC. REV. 725, 725–49 (2007); David A. Snow et al., *Frame Alignment Processes, Micromobilization, and Movement Participation*, 51 AM. SOC. REV. 464, 464–81 (1986).

[26] Benford & Snow at 612.

[27] *Id.* at 613.

"movement[s] of resistance against the power elite."[28] Using a tough-on-crime framing, even if it is just one of many frames, will have lasting impacts on the way the public perceives the movement, and on the way the movement understands itself.

Finally, it is worth noting that seminal criminology research tends to confirm the view that aggressive enforcement of existing criminal cruelty laws will not provide a meaningful symbolic benefit for animals. Rather than improving the legal status of all animals, prosecutions through a system that exempts the worst and most abundant forms of animal suffering tend to demonstrate the low status of most animals. In this way, the paradigm of cruelty prosecutions in this country tends simply to confirm a long-standing criminology insight: defendants who harm higher-status victims will be dealt with more severely than defendants who commit crimes against low-status victims. In the realm of human victims, this is a well-documented sociological phenomenon.[29] Donald Black famously found that the variation in the severity and frequency of punishment for crimes can oftentimes be explained based on the status of the victim and the status of the offender. When a low-status offender harms a high-status victim, punishment is more likely, and more likely to be severe.[30] Black expends considerable effort defining the contours of social status; he considers wealth, social integration, reputation, and a variety of other factors. But defining the social hierarchy among domestic animals is a much simpler task. Pets in the United States are the paradigmatic example of a high-status victim; the animals, for which the cruelty laws are most aggressively enforced, are viewed as part of the family, often enjoy access to healthcare that is greater than many people across the globe, and some even have considerable wealth, because the law has developed so as to permit them to inherit wealth. Of course, when it comes to animals raised for consumption or research (or other human purposes besides companionship), the same is not true. These animals do not inherit money, receive adequate healthcare, and they are viewed as commodities for sale, not as members of the family. That is to say, farm animals are the quintessential low-status victim.

Just as Black's theory would predict, the modern criminal justice system functions such that far more punishment is imposed on individuals (mostly low-status persons) who victimize high-status animals. The animal cruelty system thus reflects the same sort of class biases among animals that exist in the justice system more generally. Rather than serving as a symbol of the rising status of animals in society, the carceral animal system reifies the clear dividing line that exists between beloved high-status animals, and the out of sight, low-status animals that live and die on factory farms. There is no doubt that "farmed animals are at the very bottom of the contemporary,

---

[28]   Aya Gruber, *The Feminist War on Crime*, 92 Iowa L. Rev. 741, 763–64 (2007).
[29]   Scott Phillips, *Status Disparities in the Capital of Capital Punishment* 43 Law & Soc'y Rev. 807 (2009).
[30]   Donald Black, The Behavior of Law (1976).

Western hierarchy of beings."[31] What is true of humans is true of animals: "Some victims matter more than others."[32] The presumed symbolic value of prosecuting animal abusers may, be having an effect that is quite the opposite of what was intended because they confirm the social norms that recognize a strict dichotomy between high-value and low-value animals.

7.3 REVENGE OR RETRIBUTION AND ANIMAL PROTECTION

It is quite likely that many leaders in the movement would support a ten-year prison sentence for the violent abuser of a dog, even if the movement knew that this sentence would not make the abused animal happier, would not improve the status or reduce the suffering of animals in society more generally, and would not meaningfully deter acts of violence against animals or persons. For many, the punishment would be viewed as desirable for its own sake, and worthy of celebration. It is worth considering why the movement would treat as laudable punishment that did not serve any utilitarian goals.

It has long been posited that aggression can result in positive feelings, or even cathartic pleasure.[33] But modern research supports the hypothesis that the pursuit of more punishment for animal abusers may serve a satiating role in the lives of animal advocates. It turns out that revenge really can be sweet. A growing body of work finds that simply by imagining revenge against another person, one may activate pleasurable responses in the brain.[34] Researchers are positing that "social rejection," among other factors, can contribute to negative emotions that are partially repaired or rendered more positive by revenge.[35] The greater the social rejection, or sense of being outside of mainstream values and society, the stronger the motivation to seek revenge out and receive a degree of sadistic pleasure.[36] These researchers have found that most people will seek revenge if an opportunity is presented, that, statistically speaking, people will feel happier if revenge is in fact exacted, and that this is particularly true among those who feel a degree of mainstream social rejection.[37] When many Americans learned of the death of Osama Bin Laden, they greeted the news with patriotic chants and celebrations. Others – even those morally opposed to the death penalty – might find themselves rooting for the death of a child abuser. Perhaps the impulse to celebrate or seek death is motivated in part by a sense of relief in knowing that the person could not harm another innocent child or orchestrate

[31] Lisa Kemmerer, *Introduction* to SISTER SPECIES: WOMEN, ANIMALS AND SOCIAL JUSTICE 1, 19 (Lisa Kemmerer ed., 2011).
[32] *Id.*
[33] Joseph W. Slap, *Freud's View on Pleasure and Aggression*, J. AM. PSYCHOANALYTIC ASS'N., 370 (1967).
[34] David S. Chester & C. Nathan DeWall, *Combating the Sting of Rejection with the Pleasure of Revenge: A New Look at How Emotion Shapes Aggression*, 112 J. PERSONALITY & SOC. PSYCH. 3 (2017).
[35] *Id.*
[36] *Id.*
[37] *Id.*

another terrorist attack. But a body of scientific research is developing that shows that our brains may actually provide a pleasure response to revenge.[38] Magnetic resonance imaging (MRI) scans show that one's thoughts about revenge can actually trigger a dopamine response in the brain that produces a sensation that could be analogized to the consumption of "sweet foods or even drugs."[39]

There is a sense among social scientists that we are hardwired to seek revenge and to take pleasure in the suffering caused by such vengeance.[40] Indeed, the research suggests that "[n]ot only can revenge give people pleasure, but people seek it precisely because of the anticipation it will do so."[41] For many philosophers, revenge is the unseemly combination of "hatred and pleasure,"[42] and some have gone so far as to say that revenge is "as closely related to thirst for justice as lust is to erotic love."[43] For those animal advocates who have relatively few legal victories, the thirst to punish an animal abuser is often too great to resist. Those who love animals share a visceral reaction to abuse, a hatred for people who harm animals. Perhaps there is a bit of pleasure or schadenfreude in seeing the animal abuser suffer. And perhaps such punishment (and "even the idea of seeking it"), as research in other contexts suggests, actually improves the mood of the animal advocates.

In this way, occasional acts of criminal punishment may provide a sadistic, but palliative, pleasure to the movement's members. Perhaps the effect of seeking revenge is a recurring source of pleasure and comradery among the movement. Punishment may be accomplishing exactly what members of the movement desire. Any effort to explain the punitive focus of modern animal law that failed to account for the strong, visceral (and masculine)[44] impulse for punishment among the general public would be lacking.

---

[38]   Katherine Harmon, *Does Revenge Serve an Evolutionary Purpose?*, Sci. Am. (May 4, 2011), www .scientificamerican.com/article/revenge-evolution; Monica M. Gerber & Jonathan Jackson, *Retribution as Revenge and Retribution as Just Deserts*, 26 Soc. Just. Res. 61, 63 (2013).

[39]   *Id.*

[40]   *Id.* "When Chester and DeWall used MRI scans to study the brains of those who did not succumb to the temptation to seek revenge, they found particularized brain activity in the lateral pre-frontal cortex, which is associated with impulse control." Melissa Hogenboom, *The Hidden Upsides of Revenge*, BBC (Apr. 3, 2017), www.bbc.com/future/story/20170403-the-hidden-upsides-of-revenge.

[41]   *Id.* (interviewing the authors of recent studies on the topic and observing that "while rejection initially feels painful, it can quickly be masked by pleasure when presented with the opportunity to get revenge – it even activates the brain's known reward circuit, the nucleus accumbens. People who are provoked behave aggressively precisely because it can be 'hedonically rewarding.'")

[42]   *See, e.g.*, Jonathan Glover, Responsibility 145 (1970). For this reason, a great deal of effort has been spent distinguishing revenge from retribution. *See* Corinna Barrett Lain, *The Highs and Lows of Wild Justice*, 50 Tulsa L. Rev. 503, 515–16 (2015) ("[R]etribution and revenge are just two sides of the same coin; what the state does as retribution, the victim experiences as revenge."). Susan Jacoby, From Metaphysics to Ethics 28 (1983).

[43]   *Id.* at 28.

[44]   Research has found that men may derive more pleasure than women from acts of revenge. Tania Singer et al., *Empathic Neural Responses Are Modulated by the Perceived Fairness of Others*, 26 Nature 439 (2006). Yet the majority of animal rights activists are female. Emily Gaarder, *Where the Boys Aren't: The Predominance of Women in Animal Rights Activism*, 23 Feminist Formations 54, 55 (2011) ("One of the most striking characteristics of the animal rights movement is that the majority of its activists are women. They have been at the forefront of animal rights activism in the United States

Of course, this sort of punishment-lust is not an image the movement should be proud of. Punishment detached from any social objective other than hedonistic pleasure is at odds with any serious philosophy of empathy or anti-oppression. As one scholar disparagingly remarked, "perhaps some PETA members enjoy the same sense of bonding and group solidarity when facing off against dogfighters that dogfighters enjoy when watching a fight."[45]

7.4 WHY DO ANIMAL CRIMES HAVE TO BE THE PROVERBIAL GUINEA PIG FOR SENTENCING REFORM?

Another foreseeable objection to the criticism directed at the animal protection movement's commitment to aggressive criminal responses to animal cruelty is that the movement is certainly not alone in pursuing a more carceral approach to the issues they care most about. Advocates and scholars in the field insist that increased criminalization is a mark of the rising status of animals. Felony anti-cruelty provisions are championed as necessary in order to "bring America's laws in line with the humane values of the 21st Century."[46] Of course, it says something rather profound about our society that an increase in the number of felonies is a step toward a more humane society. Expanding felony provisions was viewed as an essential step toward promoting a "peaceful world for humans [and] animals."[47] And yet, the argument that something only matters when it is a felony is not devoid of all merit. After all, so many seemingly trivial infractions are treated as felonies at this point in history that punishing animal abuse lightly risks making it one of the very few crimes that is so trivial as to warrant no serious penalty. Animal cruelty would be a notable exception if such a crime could not be a felony.

Commentary by one of the preeminent federal sentencing experts in the country is illustrative of the current paradox underlying the relationship between criminal law and animal punishment. Professor Douglas Berman wrote insightfully about the six-month sentence for criminal abuse – largely in the form of horrible neglect – that was issued against a man who had recently been divorced, diagnosed with kidney disease, and was suicidal.[48] As Professor Berman notes, hundreds of people attended

and Great Britain since the 1800s, and current studies show that women constitute 68–80 percent of the animal rights movement.").

[45] KIMBERLY K. SMITH, GOVERNING ANIMALS: ANIMAL WELFARE AND THE LIBERAL STATE 145 (2012).

[46] "We congratulate South Dakota and local grass roots organizations like South Dakotans Fighting Animal Cruelty Together for helping bring America's laws in line with the humane values of the 21st century." Chris Berry, Animal Legal Def. Fund, Statement, *South Dakotans Fighting Animal Cruelty Together*, Mar. 2013, available at www.all-creatures.org/articles/ar-all-50-states-cruelty.html.

[47] *Id.*

[48] Douglas A. Berman, *What Message Does Six-Month Prison Sentence in High-Profile NJ Animal Cruelty Case Really Send?* (Nov. 19, 2013), http://sentencing.typepad.com/sentencing_law_and_policy/2013/11/what-message-does-six-month-prison-sentence-in-high-profile-nj-animal-cruelty-case-really-send.html; Carissa Byrne Hessick & Douglas A. Berman, *Towards A Theory of Mitigation*, 96 B. U. L. REV. 161, 183 (2016).

hearings for the case, wore buttons advocating for the maximum sentence, threatened the defendant, and otherwise made their presence known by gleefully cheering the sick man's substantial sentence of incarceration.[49] Professor Berman describes himself as an animal lover, but noted his unease with both the sentence and the advocacy surrounding it. Berman stressed that the defendant did not appear to pose any future risk to the public, and noted that the maximalist sentence for a fellow human being who was so obviously in distress and physical suffering reflected the "reality that many folks view incarceration as the only serious and meaningful" answer to crime.[50] Professor Berman pondered how society could ever achieve humanity in our sentencing system if it is impossible in a case like this one.

The response from advocates who sought an even harsher sentence for the man is easy to anticipate. Animal protection advocates would explain that animals should not be the vanguard for experimenting with more progressive and lenient sentencing reforms. Some might even concede the need for systemic criminal justice reform, but would argue that such reforms should not start with lighter sentencing for those who abuse animals. To put the matter more plainly, why should animal-victims be the guinea pigs for testing out sentencing reforms? Or to use Donald Black's vocabulary, why should animals be treated as the ultimate low-status victim? To start sentencing reform with animal abuse cases, skeptics might say, reinforces the view that animal abuse is the least important class of crime. According to this logic, animals are entitled to a status in the law that is equal to or better than the run-of-the-mill property crime, and the reality is that this often means that more (not less) incarceration is justified. Frequently persons will rationalize a criminal response to animal cruelty by noting that kids go to jail for crimes as trivial as graffiti.

This is a well-founded objection. There is something unfair, even speciest,[51] about designating animal abuse as the front lines for more lenient, or creative sentencing. Incarcerating virtually every other type of offender, but reserving treatment and community service for animal abusers, appears to be a clear slight to the animal victims. On the other hand, defending severe carceral responses to animal abuse because of the existence of harsh criminal penalties in other contexts is ultimately a race to the bottom.[52] By this logic, if drug sentences were to be even further enhanced, then animal advocates would be denying animals justice if they failed to seek correspondingly higher sentences. Animal advocates are in some sort of maximalist sentencing arms race against property crimes, children crimes, and any other crime *du jour*, such as revenge porn, that happens to spark an interest in greater criminalization and incarceration.

---

[49]   *Id.*
[50]   *Id.*
[51]   Peter Singer coined the term "speciest" in PETER SINGER, ANIMAL LIBERATION 6 (1975).
[52]   Rachel E. Barkow, *The Political Market for Criminal Justice*, 104 MICH. L. REV. 1713, 1720 (2006) (noting the "race to the bottom, in which states overspend on criminal-justice resources and produce sentences that are harsher than necessary.").

The movement champions cruelty as a felony in an effort to delineate acts of animal abuse as uniquely bad and depraved. But the concept of a felony in modern times is so broad as to be devoid of moral content. As Alice Ristroph explained, "[o]nce upon a time, felony seemed to be a discrete and relatively small category," but today the "category reaches everything that seems even a little bit wrongful or harmful, and much that does not."[53] More felonies and longer sentences do not have the signaling effect the movement intends. It is also worth noting that measuring the status of animals in the law based on the severity of the sentences available for animal cruelty creates a classic limiting principle problem for the animal protection movement. If the animal protection movement is faithful to its foundational orientation in opposing systems that give priority to the suffering of humans over the suffering of animals – that is, if the movement rejects speciesism – what, then, are the limits on punishment for animal abuse? Is one who needlessly tortures or kills an animal culpable to a similar degree as one who tortures or kills a human? If cruelty to animals rivals cruelty to humans in seriousness, does the movement's logic make it duty-bound to seek more punishment through higher sentences, more crimes, more charges, separate counts, and maybe even mandatory minimums and offender registries? But would a mandatory minimum sentence of twelve months for cruelty shock the conscience? What about a mandatory minimum of five years for the negligent killing of a dog or a cat? Should mandatory, accelerated deportation for any non-citizen who abuses an animal be pursued more frequently?

And if the movement is willing to pursue parity in punishment for cruelty to animals and cruelty to humans, is it also willing to accept that the current criminal justice system is not overly punitive or inhumane? Would the movement object to life without parole sentences in cases of particularly egregious animal abuse, or even the death penalty for a serial animal abuser? Perhaps these seem like far-off, impossible hypotheticals. But if the movement has a coherent theory for seeking increased criminal punishment, it should also be able to identify the logical boundaries or limiting principles applicable to its carceral policies. To make the point more starkly, if criminal punishment serves merely as a symbolic lever that can be yielded in the service of improving the status of animals in the law, is it obvious that the blueprint for expanding criminal sanctions in this realm would preclude the pursuit of the death penalty for particularly egregious cases of animal abuse that result in death? Presently, the Eighth Amendment effectively precludes the imposition of a death sentence for crimes that do not involve deceased victims.[54] It is conceivable that animal lawyers would argue that this Eighth Amendment limit on executions should be read as inapplicable to animal abusers who kill an animal insofar as there is a deceased *victim*. The animal protection movement has made it a priority to have animals designated as "victims" in criminal cases. Would the animal

---

[53] Alice Ristroph, *Farewell to the Felonry*, HARV. C.R.-C.L. L. REV. 1, 21 (2019).
[54] Kennedy v. Louisiana, 554 U.S. 945 (2008) (apparently exempting crimes against the state such as treason).

protection movement file amicus briefs arguing for a death sentence for the human, and urging that animals must be considered victims in the same sense as people? After all, a decisive victory on that Eighth Amendment issue – that the killing of animals is among the worst of the worst crimes – would represent an ultimate expression of the sort of significant symbolic victory that seems to be coveted by the carceral animal law adherents. If the carceral priorities include law reforms that allow for greater punishment because animals are victims, there could be few greater victories for the movement.

If the movement realizes that it would not have any principled basis for opposing legislation proposing death sentences or life imprisonment, or solitary confinement for animal abuse so long as the punitive measures are justified as necessary in order to demonstrate the significance and import of animal victim-hood then the movement needs to reconsider its first principles. Such reforms are not consistent with an agenda that wishes to be considered a civil rights movement. Yet it appears that the movement would not recognize any conclusive limit on the amount of punishment that should be imposed for animal cruelty, and instead the "serpent windings of utilitarianism," as Immanuel Kant described it, would permit any punishment so long as the calculated the benefits of such a carceral approach could be presumed to outweigh the burdens of it. If animal protection does not want to be the guinea pig or vanguard for less aggressive sentencing policies, and anti-oppression efforts more generally, because of a fear that such a stance would effect a symbolic harm on the status of animals, why should the movement oppose being at the vanguard of aggressive punishment if it holds out the promise of increasing the social stigma associated with mistreating animals? This realization should be deeply troubling to people involved in the animal protection movement. The absence of an obvious limiting principle (other than political power) that would constrain the instrumental use of punishment against humans guilty of animal abuse should, serve as a strong cautionary note about carceral animal law.

One of the preeminent criminal law scholars of modern times, William Stuntz, recognized that the competition for heightened criminal penalties among various victims' groups presents a dangerous "one-way ratchet."[55] This sort of race to the bottom cannot be the path forward for a movement seeking recognition as a social justice movement. More punishment, more jails, more cages is not more justice. It cannot be that the world will come to have more empathy for the pain of animals only if animal advocates jealously ensure that humans are punished more severely. Likewise, if animal protection efforts are primarily directed at exposing and critiquing state-sanctioned violence against powerless, forgotten creatures, the movement would do well to look at the criminology literature regarding the impacts and demographics of incarceration. As Professor Aya Gruber explained in the context of another civil rights

---

[55] William J. Stuntz, *The Pathological Politics of Criminal Law*, 100 MICH. L. REV. 505, 509 (2001).

movement, "feminists should not be channeling their efforts into helping the government find new, better, and easier ways to incarcerate people, most likely minority people."[56] Prosecution will not undo the problems of injustice and social status that plague disempowered groups in society, it will exacerbate them.

7.5 INCAPACITATION AS THE LAST-BEST DEFENSE OF CARCERAL ANIMAL LAW

Perhaps the most straightforward response to the variety of critiques lodged against the carceral animal law project's inability to shape moral norms or even behavior is incapacitation.[57] Defenders of an ever more punitive criminal law regime in the animal law realm could applaud increased punishment, because, if nothing else, incarceration removes the dangerous person from society. As the so-called Wattenberg's law puts it: "A thug in prison can't shoot your sister."[58] By the same logic, animal abusers who are locked up are not able to harm animals. This alone, the movement might argue, justifies more aggressive animal cruelty prosecutions. As one research paper endorsing harsher penalties based on the link posits, if offenders had "received more stringent penalties," they would have been deprived of the opportunity to "reoffend so quickly."[59]

Justifying severe punishments on incapacitation grounds appears to have the benefit of defusing, or rendering irrelevant, all of the data presented in prior chapters about the limited utility of increased sentences in reducing recidivism or promoting deterrence. But it is important to recognize that people convicted of animal cruelty will eventually be released.[60] Barring success in obtaining life sentences for animal abusers, one has to anticipate the offender's eventual return to society, and this makes directly relevant the data correlating the length of one's sentence and the difficulty one experiences in reentering society.[61] Such data may be particularly

---

[56] Gruber at 824.

[57] Writing in 1995, noted criminologists Franklin Zimring and Gordon Hawkins argued that "[o]f all the justifications for criminal punishment, the desire to incapacitate is the least complicated, the least studied, and often the most important." FRANKLIN E. ZIMRING & GORDON HAWKINS, INCAPACITATION: PENAL CONFINEMENT & THE RESTRAINT OF CRIME 1 (1995).

[58] The term Wattenberg's law was coined by Professor John Dilulio in discussing the benefits of incarceration in the 1990s. Recent commentary have identified this quote as a "sort of anthem for the get tough movement." Todd R. Clear, Policy Essay, *Downsizing Prisons: "A Thug in Prison Can't Shoot your Sister,"* 15 CRIMINOLOGY & PUB. POL'Y 343–47 (2016).

[59] Lacey Levitt et al., *Criminal Histories of a Subsample of Animal Cruelty Offenders,* 30 AGGRESSION & VIOLENT BEHAV. 48, 56 (2016) (finding that violent crimes like assault against persons were more common *before* animal abuse, as opposed to *after* it).

[60] Even "incapacitation theorists have rejected indefinite incapacitation." Hessick & Berman at 183.

[61] Alex R. Piquero & Alfred Blumstein, *Does Incapacitation Reduce Crime,* 23 J. QUANT. CRIMINOLOGY 267, 268 (2007) ("[I]t is still uncertain how much [incapacitation] affects the crime rate and how it is distributed among individual offenders.").

relevant in the animal abuse context because some research has found that animal abusers, as a group, are more likely to be older at the time of their offense.[62]

Recent research finds that for each additional year of incarceration, there is an increased risk of re-offending of four to seven percentage points. Such figures make the decision about whether to incapacitate an individual for five years, as opposed to three months, considerably more complicated from the perspective of net crime reduction and animal protection. Even if incarceration presents the front-end promise of protecting animals, it risks increased rates of crime when the individual is released. Indeed, some researchers actually blame lengthy rates of incarceration for *slowing* the decline of crime in the United States.[63] According to Martin H. Pritikin, data supports the conclusion that "incapacitative punishments may possess additional criminogenic properties that are not present in other deterrent sanctions," by "stigmatiz[ing] and induc[ing] reactance."[64] Consistent with this view, Paul Butler argued that everyone should be concerned with mass incarceration because our own self-interest in safety is reduced, not enhanced, by longer terms of incarceration.[65]

Over-reliance on incapacitation as a primary justification for carceral animal law policies also presents yet another area in which the animal protection movement risks looking detached from, or disinterested in, broader social reform initiatives. Scholars have raised a number of serious challenges to a justice system that is justified primarily on incapacitation grounds.[66] As Paul Robinson and John Darley have explained, "the most severe criticism of an incapacitation-based sentencing system is that it requires a distribution of liability very different from what the community regards as just punishment for the offense committed, [because] ... it assigns sentences of very different lengths ... where one is predicted to be a repeat offender."[67] The blameworthiness of the offender in a retributive sense is irrelevant, and the punishment of an offender could be as long as necessary to prevent future crimes. The failure of incapacitation as a justification for punishment, then, is that it

---

[62] Levitt et al. at 54 (noting that the mean age of animal abusers in the study was thirty-seven, which contrasts sharply with general crime data showing that only 30 percent of violent offenders [outside of the domestic violence context] are over thirty years old).

[63] Oliver Roeder et al., *What Caused the Crime Decline?*, Columbia Business School Research Paper No. 15–28 (Feb. 12, 2015), http://dx.doi.org/10.2139/ssrn.2566965.

[64] Martin H. Pritikin, *Is Prison Increasing Crime?*, 2008 Wis. L. Rev. 1049, 1098 (2008) ("According to the theory of psychological reactance, people may perceive attempts to control their conduct as a threat to their freedom, which they react against either consciously or subconsciously.").

[65] *See also* James Forman, Jr., *Why Care About Mass Incarceration?*, 108 Mich. L. Rev. 993, 999 (2010).

[66] This is not to suggest that no leading scholars accept incapacitation as a legitimate justification for punishment. *See, e.g.*, Hessick & Berman at 183 (discussing incapacitation theory's goal of crime reduction); James Q. Wilson, *Selective Incapacitation*, in Principled Sentencing: Readings on Theory and Policy (Andrew Ashworth & Andreas Von Hirsch eds., 2nd edn. 1998); Marijke Malsch & Marius Duker, *Introduction* to Incapacitation: Trends and New Perspectives 1, 7 (Marijke Malsch & Marius Duker eds., 2012).

[67] Paul H. Robinson & John M. Darley, *The Utility of Desert*, 91 Nw. U. L. Rev. 453, 467–68 (1997).

"presupposes that past offenders are uniquely dangerous individuals who are destined to offend and re-offend regardless of social context."[68]

Likewise, commentators note the incongruity of incapacitation with our basic concepts of due process and fairness, insofar as incapacitation turns on future risks of crime such that the "offender is being punished for an action that he has not yet done, or perhaps even thought of."[69] Yet another critique of incapacitation as a justification for punishment relates to the inability of courts to accurately predict who will re-offend. Scholars have identified a high false positive rate (greater than 60 percent) among efforts to predict future criminality.[70] Such findings are particularly striking in the animal protection context in light of the conclusions among leading researchers on the "link" that there is a high false positive problem associated with predicting future interpersonal crime based on acts of animal cruelty.

In short, incapacitation's simplicity is also its downfall. The seemingly obvious conclusion that society is always better off if someone deemed dangerous is locked up is complicated by the difficulty in making such predictions, as well as the criminogenic consequences of increased incarceration. If animal protection rests its appetite for incarceration on incapacitation rationales, it will be aligning itself with a theory that is faulted as both ineffectual and immoral. In the conclusion of two highly regarded legal scholars, "an incapacitation-based sentencing system undercuts the moral credibility of the criminal law."[71] For a movement seeking moral authority among social justice lawyers, it would be a mistake to wed carceral aspirations to such an ethically murky justification for punishment.

---

[68]   Guyora Binder & Ben Notterman, *Penal Incapacitation: A Situationist Critique*, 54 AM. CRIM. L. REV. 1, 3 (2016).

[69]   *Id.* at 3.

[70]   SANDFORD H. KADISH, STEPHEN J. SCHULHOFER & RACHEL E. BARKOW, CRIMINAL LAW AND Its Processes: Cases and Materials 130 (10th edn. 2016) (compiling sources).

[71]   Robinson & Darley at 467–68 (1997). For its part the Supreme Court has never rejected incapacitation as a justification for punishment. Ewing v. California, 538 U.S. 11, 30 (2003) (upholding California's three-strikes law).

8

Conclusion: Toward a New Research and Advocacy Agenda for Animal Protection

We, as a country, are confused about what we are trying to achieve with the criminal justice system. The public needs to be moved away from the idea that the criminal justice system can provide "the" answer to crime. Indeed, our responses to crime often exacerbate the problem.[1]

I. Matthew Campbell, former Assistant State's Attorney

Oliver Wendall Holmes concluded that "[t]he law is the witness and external deposit of our moral life. Its history is the history of the moral development of the race."[2] The litigation and legislative work pursued in the name of animal protection will tell the movement's history to future generations. Lawyers and advocates associated with the movement must be mindful about creating a history that facilitates rather than impedes the movement's status as a social justice movement. The central question in this book is what role criminal law plays in advancing the status of the animal protection movement. Pursuing greater sentences, more prosecutions, and other forms of criminal intervention is not, as the preceding chapters have shown, an unmitigated good for animals or for people. Incarceration enjoys a visceral appeal, but at bottom it is a form of oppression, and in pressing carceral solutions – more cages for humans – "activists and theorists adopt the sort of exclusionary theorizing they ostensibly reject."[3]

There is a sense among many advocates that success in the form of greater prosecution is the gateway to mobilizing grand social change when it comes to animal protection. A belief that animal abusers should go to jail, preferably for a very long time, is perceived as the low-hanging fruit, or the lowest common denominator of social agreement when it comes to improving the status of animals in the law. If

[1] *Reducing Racial Disparity in the Criminal Justice System: A Manual for Practitioners and Policymakers* iii, SENT'G PROJECT (2nd edn., 2008), www.sentencingproject.org/wp-content/uploads/2016/01/Reducing-Racial-Disparity-in-the-Criminal-Justice-System-A-Manual-for-Practitioners-and-Policymakers.pdf.
[2] Oliver Wendall Holmes, Jr., *The Path of Law*, 10 HARVARD L. REV. 457 (1897).
[3] Lisa Kemmerer, *Introduction* to SISTER SPECIES: WOMEN, ANIMALS AND SOCIAL JUSTICE 20 (Lisa Kemmerer ed., 2011) (discussing the presence of "exclusionary theorizing" among people who fail to treat the suffering of animals as morally relevant).

the rogue cat or dog abuser can't be punished, so the argument goes, then society will never get to a point where the status of animals more generally is a matter of social and legal concern. But such thinking is not just unsupported by data, it is at odds with the very notion that improving the status of animals will require a fundamental rethinking of our relationships with non-humans. The punishment of dog and cat abusers is palatable precisely because it does not challenge social norms, or accepted practices, but rather entrenches dominant practices that separate animals into high- and low-status categories. The carceral project reifies the view that the suffering of certain high-status animals is of the utmost concern and ignores the plight of low-status animals. The criminal project has a satiating effect on people by allowing them to feel happy with their civilized treatment of animals, and to rest easy knowing their donations are supporting the prosecution and incarceration of moral monsters. These feelings of moral superiority are convenient and might even be indulged over a steak dinner or a hamburger. More generally, the project of demeaning certain humans based on their treatment of high-status animals is consistent with a centuries-old practice of creating outsiders to dominant American racial and moral norms. Projects directed at identifying true American values and culture are never free from negative racial and class-based impacts.

To be fair, standing alone, there is probably no single reform achieved by the carceral animal law movement that fundamentally reworks the criminal justice system. In the aggregate, however, the reforms are striking in their breadth and their callousness. If a jurisdiction adopted all of the reforms advocated for by the carceral animal law movement, a person who became ill and neglected his dog could face mandatory arrest, would be charged by a movement-funded prosecutor, would face felony liability, would be sentenced to an increasingly long maximum term of imprisonment, and would have to be listed on a publicly available abuse registry. The sum is greater than the component parts of this carceral project.

One need not conclude that all investment in criminal prosecution should be abandoned. But criminal interventions have existed as an unchallenged centerpiece of the movement for too long. Presently, many scholars and activists view criminal justice as one of the most important, if not the most important, form of legal and political advocacy within the animal protection sphere. Criminal punishment, according to one of the leaders in the field, is the "cornerstone of American animal protection."[4] The slogans surrounding criminal justice focus on blame and guilt (like the slogan "Our clients are the only ones on earth who are always innocent"), and when it comes to criminal punishment the logic is similarly binary: more is always better. One could imagine a very different allocation of resources and set of alliances if the animal protection scholars thought critically about how to position

---

[4] Joyce Tischler, *A Brief History of Animal Law, Part II* (1985 – 2011), 5 STAN. J. ANIMAL L. & POL'Y 27, 57 (2012).

the movement first and foremost as a civil justice movement, and at most, secondarily, as a reluctant abider of the need to incarcerate and punish.

Claire Jean Kim has thoroughly rebuked the notion that long-term progress for the protection of animals will come through campaigns that place human and animal interests in avoiding subordination and oppression in competition. Any zero-sum game framework – either humans must suffer more in prison, or animals will never see improved status – is short-sighted and misconceived. Yet, unflinchingly aggressive criminal prosecutions in the name of animal protection create exactly this dynamic. As Kimberly K. Smith explained, animal mistreatment is "morally objectionable, but the punitive approach to ending [it] can have negative consequences for civil liberties and racial and class equality."[5] Taking it one step further, this book advances the argument that the movement's purported race neutrality or color-blindness in the realm of social advocacy, and its carceral obsession in particular, threaten to disqualify animal protection efforts as a member of the civil rights family. In 2018, any movement that supports criminal justice solutions to social problems and purports to be acting in an entirely race-neutral manner has a tenuous, if not entirely obscured understanding of social justice more generally.[6]

The call is not for decriminalization, but rather for a more careful and searching inquiry into reducing animal suffering without endorsing the system of over-criminalization. There is a stereotype of people concerned with protecting animals as misanthropes. Many of those who critique animal protection efforts decry the tactics and rhetoric as evincing concern for all species except the Homo Sapiens. Fairly or not, this view of the animal lover as a human hater takes on added credibility when seen in light of the carceral animal law project. One scholar recently compiled an exhaustive list of the movement's views regarding the shortcomings of animal cruelty prosecutions, and he was only able to identify factors that the movement identifies as generating too little, not too much punishment. This calls to mind the work of the nineteenth-century English judge James Fitzjames Stephens, a famous advocate for harsh criminal penalties as a means of expressing social vengeance, who explained that the value of punishment is that its infliction "gives definite expression and solemn ratification and justification to the hatred which is excited by the commission of the offence."[7] For a movement that implores trans-species compassion and treats insufficient empathy as the root cause of animal suffering, it is beyond paradoxical to reify an image of hatred toward criminals as a long-term solution. If animal protection scholars and activists are interested in true change, a general emphasis on what Claire Jean Kim calls "mutual avowal," as opposed to subordination of humans in the service of animals, is necessary. It is not enough to argue only for

---

[5]   KIMBERLY K. SMITH, GOVERNING ANIMALS: ANIMAL WELFARE AND THE LIBERAL STATE 145 (2012).
[6]   CLAIRE JEAN KIM, DANGEROUS CROSSINGS: RACE, SPECIES, AND NATURE IN A MULTICULTURAL AGE 276 (2015).
[7]   JAMES FITZJAMES STEPHENS, A HISTORY OF THE CRIMINAL LAW OF ENGLAND 81–82 (1883).

the protection of animals, or the punishment of humans who harm animals. The movement needs to find ways to conceive of their struggle as part of and intertwined with the struggles of low-income people and people of color. The fight against subordination is not unique to animals, and the movement needs to build alliances that recognize this overlap.

More generally, if the animal protection movement is serious about aligning itself with the substantive goals of justice and equality, then its advocates should look for ways to align animal protection with other movements, such as racial justice – that is, seek out an interest convergence. There are several areas where more investment, attention, and research from the animal protection community has the potential to make a difference in the lives of animals and humans. Research to identify examples of convergence should be pursued in future scholarly projects, but some seemingly straightforward examples in this arena would include taking up the issues of food oppression that have been elucidated in Andrea Freeman's work.[8] Making a healthy, plant-based diet more accessible in low-income, urban neighborhoods could be a tremendous boon to animal protection efforts. Alternatively, animal protection advocates might invest in programs to help redefine the role of police more generally. There is a line of legal scholarship that argues, in essence, that police should be less involved, and less ready to use force. One need not go to the extreme of calling for the abolishment of police, as some scholars do, to recognize that investments in a less force-oriented form of policing would result in fewer people and fewer animals being killed by law enforcement. One could imagine that the number of animals killed by law enforcement, which some have estimated to be about twenty-five per day, may rival or even exceed the incidence of animal cruelty, and probably greatly exceeds the amount of cruelty that is prevented by a carceral solution.

Other seemingly gainful paths for future research on convergence might include gun culture and the valorization of guns and machismo in culture. There is research linking, for example, an obsession with guns and school shootings. Likewise, efforts to combat environmental degradation or climate change have direct and near-term impacts on animals and humans. Even immigration-related issues present promise for animal protection advocates. Rather than seeking opportunities to support governmental efforts to deport people who are forced to work in our factory farms (either by endorsing immigration raids, or rhetoric about the harms flowing from immigrants residing in our communities), animal protection scholars and organizations should search for ways to illustrate the intersections of subordination that harm non-humans and immigrants. In this way, the movement's litigation against President Trump's promised wall along the border with Mexico is a useful, if only symbolic olive branch. Animals and humans will be harmed by the wall, research shows, thus litigation and activism in this arena have mutually reinforcing roles.

---

[8]   *See, e.g.,* Andrea Freeman, *Fast Food: Oppression Through Poor Nutrition,* 95 CAL. L. REV. 2221 (2007); Andrea Freeman, *The 2014 Farm Bill: Farm Subsidies and Food Oppression,* 38 SEATTLE U. L. REV. 1271 (2015).

More generally, innovations in the legal system would likely also strike a convergent tone with many members of the public. For example, litigation and advocacy seeking to expand on the modern trend of laws that permit people to rescue animals from hot cars without the owner's consent would seem to be a logical doctrinal foothold. As would exploiting creative ways to deploy the laws in some states that provide for a right to provide emergency care to animals in danger of dying.

None of these proposed strategies are particularly novel. The claim is not that these suggestions have never been considered by leading animal protection thinkers. Rather, the point is a much more modest one. There is a need for research and resources to be devoted to campaigns that would help reduce the suffering of animals and bring their plight into the public eye without resorting to prosecution. The notion that there may be important overlaps between the goals of the animal protection movement and other social justice causes is consistent with a well-established social science literature. For example, Harvard psychologist Steven Pinker observed that as attention to civil rights has increased over time, so too has interest in animal rights.[9] The fact that an interest in animal protection tends to correlate with diminished interpersonal violence and increased concern about civil rights is a fact worth being more fully internalized and explored by the animal protection movement. Likewise, leading LGBTQ+ rights policy and lawyering organizations have recognized that securing civil rights for all disadvantaged people is not infrequently the best method for advancing the cause of gays and lesbians. Their research shows that increasing the economic and housing security of an entire community could very well do more to increase the living conditions of a particular minority group than targeting that minority group for benefit. For example, the Williams Institute, the pathmarking institute that is housed at UCLA and has served as an intellectual engine for the LGBT movement, has published research showing that the best way to improve the status of gays and lesbians in the work force is *not* to target the LGBT pay gap, but rather to pursue increases in the minimum wage and to target the gender pay gap. The animal protection movement would do well to explore ways to capitalize on the accepted wisdom that sometimes the best way to advance one's social movement is to contribute to advocacy and policy changes that take on issues of overriding humanitarian concern.

Instead, an irony presently underlies the animal protection movement's push for greater use of the criminal law. The rationale for pursuing a punitive approach to animal cruelty is, in part, that such legal actions will signal the improving status of animals in our social and legal community. But underlying the pursuit of felony laws and more prosecutions is a justice system that recognizes large swaths of people as "unfit for full membership in the political community with complete legal rights."[10] Criminal prosecution as a vehicle for advancing the legal status of animals rests on the

---

[9] STEVEN PINKER, THE BETTER ANGELS OF OUR NATURE: WHY VIOLENCE HAS DECLINED 380 (2012).

[10] Alice Ristroph, *Farewell to the Felonry*, HARV. C.R.-C.L. L. REV. 1, 46 (2019).

assumption that we need to strip certain individuals of the legal status that makes them fully part of the human social and political community. In a word, society needs to recognize these violent humans as "animals" deserving of a degraded status. Making certain people less human in the eyes of the law is, according to the carceral vision of animal protection, a viable means of enhancing the legal personhood of animals. The value of animals is reflected by the diminishment of individual humans.

However, just as the point of this project is not so simple as to call for complete decriminalization, so too is it undesirable and impractical to pedantically insist that there is a single set of approved forms of social change strategies. As scholars like Doug Nejaime,[11] Scott Cummings, and Alan Chen have made clear, no one has the clairvoyance or vision to be able to predict what will truly advance lasting social change goals. But there is an unexamined tension in the assumption that prosecutors and prisons will do more to promote animal protection than those engaged in criminal civil disobedience. The hostile reception by the animal protection movement of the California-based organization DxE (Direct Action Everywhere) is illustrative. DxE's campaigns frequently include civil disobedience, including overtly illegal actions such as trespass. For a movement that seeks mainstream credibility, brash illegal campaigns such as rescuing animals from factory farms are understandably viewed as too radical, and therefore unpalatable. On the other hand, the rescuing of baby piglets who were, as covered in the *New York Times*, wallowing in their own blood, suffering, and facing an imminent death, is arguably of at least peripheral concern to any organization dedicated to alleviating animal suffering. Of course, civil disobedience and direct action are not for everyone; Martin Luther King, Jr., and other icons of the civil rights movement recognized as much. Indeed, not every vehement opponent of slavery was willing to risk going to jail by violating, for example, the fugitive slave laws that made criminals of those who tried to rescue enslaved people through the underground railroad. Not everyone is willing or able to risk incarceration. It is, however, significant that every major animal protection organization takes a hard line condemning direct actions, including those of DxE. Prosecution is preferred to civil disobedience.

One does not have to agree with civil disobedience in general, nor with the specific philosophy or leadership of groups like DxE, to see the symbolic value of defending activists facing criminal charges for rescuing abused animals. If the movement can find symbolic value in incarcerating an abuser, it is hard to believe that there is no room for symbolism or sympathy for a (criminal) animal rescuer. And yet, animal protection organizations staffed with experienced lawyers and dedicated to the protection of animals have fervently rejected all overtures to be involved in the legal defense of such civil disobedience in recent decades. It is not difficult to imagine that cozy relationships with prosecutors have influenced the movement's position on this point. After spending years trying to ingratiate itself to prosecutors,

---

[11] Doug Nejaime, *Winning Through Losing*, 96 IOWA L. REV. 941 (2010).

and to appear "mainstream," it is probably not surprising that the movement's willingness to tolerate, much less assist in the defense of civil disobedience is effectively non-existent.

The movement might do well to reflect on the advice of civil rights icon William Kunstler, who believed that "the primary role of a progressive lawyer was to protect the rights of those in society who were trying to cause a paradigm shift in thinking."[12] The movement's blind faith in prosecutors as agents of social change, when juxtaposed with the deep skepticism for civil disobedience, is deserving of the sort of reflection and conversation that this book is designed to initiate.

More generally, looking back throughout American history, it is difficult to come up with examples where prosecutors have been among the early adopters of a rising tide of civil rights change. They enforce the law as is, the status quo, and do not advocate for sweeping legal reforms or normative changes. It is cold comfort to recognize that prosecutors are willing to enforce animal cruelty laws. After all, during the same period when the movement was pursuing felony cruelty legislation so as to enshrine the movement's values through prosecutions, prosecutors across the country were still enforcing sodomy laws. Prosecutors famously sought to enforce criminal prohibitions on the use or distribution of birth control in the 1970s. Even today prosecutors are pursuing prosecutions for the possession and use of marijuana despite mounting research regarding its effectiveness as a medicinal or palliative treatment. At the same time, in July 2017, a prosecutor responded to an undercover investigation by the Humane Society of the United States that revealed horrific animal abuse on a factory farm by sending a letter to HSUS explaining that he would prefer to prosecute the undercover investigator than the factory farm: "We do not appreciate the moral busybodies of the Humane Society taking advantage of a lifelong farmer, whose small business may forever be ruined by the actions of your videographer. If you choose to conduct another such expose, it is my sincere wish that you do it somewhere else."[13] The loyalty of the prosecutor for animal protection is not very broad or very deep; it is as facile and superficial as the tough-on-crime façade more generally.

The point is not that prosecutors are evil or that the justice system should be abandoned. Again, the point is more modest. It is a call for more tempered enthusiasm for prosecution and for something approaching a cost-benefit examination of the long-term outcomes likely to flow from alliances with prosecutors. The reality of a carceral approach in modern America is that it falls somewhere between being merely antiquated, and entirely anathema to virtually every major civil rights movement.[14] If a burgeoning civil rights movement like animal protection invests heavily

---

[12]   Gary L. Francione, *Reflections on Animals, Property, and the Law and Rain Without Thunder*, 70 LAW & CONTEMP. PROBS. 9 (2007) (quoting Kunstler).

[13]   Wayne Ford, *Madison County D.A. Lambastes Humane Society for Video That Cost Farmer Contract*, ATHENS BANNER-HERLAD (July 4, 2017), http://onlineathens.com/local-news/2017–07-04/madison -county-da-lambastes-humane-society-video-cost-farmer-contract.

[14]   The "commonality of treatment provides the opportunity for a symbiotic relationship between the animal protectionist and civil rights communities. It provides an opportunity for each to borrow from

in schemes that run contrary to general civil rights goals and agendas, animal advocates cannot expect that the civil rights community will rush to their aid when the need arises. To be sure, the animal rights causes have sometimes been treated as the pariahs of the civil rights world. The ACLU infamously refused to protect the civil liberties of animal protection advocates when it did not oppose a sweeping expansion of federal domestic terrorism laws targeting animal protection advocates in the early 2000s.[15] But times are changing, and mainstream civil rights organizations, including the ACLU, now provide critical assistance to the animal rights cause. The ACLU devotes considerable resources to lobbying and litigating threats to the civil liberties of animal protection advocates.[16] Likewise, the Center for Constitutional Rights has taken up the animal rights cause in several key cases recently, including challenges to the Animal Enterprise Terrorism Act,[17] and the National Lawyers Guild is increasingly hospitable to the animal rights movement.[18] To jeopardize the nascent support and trust of civil rights groups would be a high price to pay for the perceived benefits of insisting on an uncompromising approach to prosecution when it comes to animal cruelty. Civil rights leaders and advocates are rightly making the end of mass incarceration and over-criminalization a top priority,[19] and for a social justice group to promote more and longer terms of

the lessons and experiences of the other." Joseph Lubinski, *Screw the Whales, Save Me! The Endangered Species Act, Animal Protection, and Civil Rights*, 4 J. L. Soc'y 377, 378 (2003).

[15] Will Potter, *Where Was the ACLU When Green Scare Legislation Passed Congress?*, Green Is the New Red (Nov. 28, 2006), www.greenisthenewred.com/blog/where-was-the-aclu/165; *see also* Will Potter, *The Green Scare*, 33 Vt. L. Rev. 671, 682 (2009) ("[T]his time around, the silence of the ACLU spoke volumes, essentially giving the Green Scare the green light."). Analyzing why the ACLU would not oppose such legislation, one commentator has observed: "Perhaps because there are so many other civil-liberties issues competing for critical attention. Perhaps because corporate scare-mongering and green baiting has turned animal-rights activists into political lepers. Or perhaps history repeats itself. The ACLU has a long, venerable history of defending the civil liberties of even the most unsavory characters, including the KKK. Yet during the Red Scare of the 1940s and 1950s, the ACLU formally barred communists from leadership or staff positions." Potter, *The Green Scare*.

[16] *See Animal Legal Def. Fund* 44 F. Supp. 3d at 1199.

[17] Blum v. Holder 744 F.3d 790, 791–93 (1st Cir. 2014); *see also* United States v. Buddenberg, No. CR-09-00263 RMW, 2009 WL 3485937 (N.D. Cal. 2009) (challenging AETA's constitutionality as a defense to prosecution); United States v. Buddenberg, Ctr. for Const. Rights, http://ccrjustice.org/home /what-we-do/our-cases/united-states-v-buddenberg (last visited Apr. 24, 2016) (discussing CCR's defense of four individuals indicted under AETA).

[18] *See e.g., Animal Rights Activism Committee*, Natl. Law. Guild, www.nlg.org/committees/animal rights (last visited Apr. 24, 2016) ("The committee engages Guild members to advocate for changes in the law to recognize the rights of non-human animals, and to provide legal support and resources to animal rights activists."); *Amicus Curiae*, Natl. Law. Guild, www.nlg.org/publications/amicus-curiae (last visited Apr. 24, 2016) (discussing amicus briefs the Guild has submitted, including three in cases related to animal rights).

[19] To be fair, leading progressives and conservatives are both championing this cause. Both President Obama and the Koch brothers have called for reforms to mass incarceration. Tim Mak, *Koch Bros to Bankroll Prison Reform*, Daily Beast (Jan. 13, 2015), www.thedailybeast.com/articles/2015/01/13/koch -bros-to-bankroll-prison-reform.html; Leon Neyfakh, *Obama Wants to End Mass Incarceration*, Slate (July 15, 2015), www.slate.com/articles/news_and_politics/crime/2015/07/obama_and_mass_incarcer

incarceration is to buck one of the most important and widespread civil rights trends of this era.

The preceding chapters have made the case that few things are harming minority communities more,[20] causing more financial, familial, and community strain for Americans, or producing fewer evidence-based positive results than criminal convictions.[21] The research simply does not support the view that the carceral animal law campaigns will do more good than harm. Even if animal protection groups do not care about the loss of fidelity with other disadvantaged groups, or the alienation they risk among other social justice causes, it is very likely that the carceral orientation of the movement will limit civil litigation opportunities by unnecessarily making appeasement of the prosecuting state a litigation and advocacy consideration. Lawyers and activists will choose different cases, different priorities, and sometimes an altogether different framing of issues when they have as a goal appeasing and impressing prosecutors. Conflicts between civil rights litigators in the animal law field and prosecutor-sympathizing advocates are inevitable, and they are having an unacknowledged impact on the day-to-day activism within the movement.

Overzealous prosecutions, deportations, and a general lack of empathy are the hallmarks of the aggressive turn to criminal justice by the animal protection movement. This book is meant as a wake-up call for scholars and policy leaders who support regressive, failed criminal justice policies as a means of propping up the animal protection agenda. The ultimate resolution of this dilemma will be left for future works, but the maturation of the movement dictates that the time has come to talk candidly about its allegiance to the incarcerating state. The animal rights movement has partnered with law enforcement and prosecutors in ways that is foreign territory for civil rights movements in this country. Such a state of affairs is long overdue for critique. Punishment may remain a necessary evil in some instances, but it should not be sought out as a good in itself, an opportunity for celebration, or as a keystone of animal protection efforts. At the very least, animal protection advocates must make a clear-eyed decision to pursue incarceration as an important piece of the movement's agenda.

Rather than framing the findings of this book exclusively in the negative (as a call for limiting prosecutions), it is useful as well to understand the positive framing of this research – that is, there is an unrealized harmony between core civil rights issues and animal protection. Civil rights advocates bemoan the increasing use of

---

ation_how_much_power_does_the_federal_government.html. Indeed, calls for increased incarceration seem misplaced, or outdated relics from a bygone era.

[20] *See generally* MICHELLE ALEXANDER, THE NEW JIM CROW: MASS INCARCERATION IN THE AGE OF COLORBLINDNESS (2012); BRYAN STEVENSON, JUST MERCY: A STORY OF JUSTICE AND REDEMPTION (2015).

[21] *See, e.g.*, Dena M. Gromet & John M. Darley, *Punishment and Beyond: Achieving Justice Through the Satisfaction of Multiple Goals*, 43 LAW & SOC'Y REV. 1, 31 (2009) ("If there is only a prison sentence available for the repairing of the number of different harms that crime causes, then people are likely to favor lengthy prison sentences in an attempt to satisfy a number of goals.").

incarceration and supermax prisons, and animal protection advocates are quick to condemn the domination and caging of non-human animals. Both animal advocates and critics of prisons have noted that caged subjects suffer from symptoms, including "depression, despair, lethargy, stress, fear, shame and eventually anger."[22] Researchers in both fields, including Dale Jamieson, note that confinement "produces anxiety, sadness, neurotic behavior, poor hygiene, and suffering." Yet those who have examined the sensory deprivation and loneliness that is inflicted upon confined animals have been missing from the calls to rethink imprisonment as a solution to social problems. Indeed, as discussed throughout this book, the animal protection movement stands uniquely situated as a movement that seeks civil rights through ever more carceral policies. Likewise, those who are advocating for prison reform or abolition (for violent offenders) do not lend their voices to calls to extend compassion to (entirely innocent) non-human animals. It is time for these conceptual barriers to be broken down. Those who care about the harshness of incarcerating humans would do well to reflect more on the suffering of non-human animals, and those who work toward the goal of ending animal suffering must not ignore human suffering.

✻✻✻

For centuries, animals and even inanimate property were subjected to trials and punished if they caused injury to a human being.[23] One book describing the history of prosecuting animals for crimes notes the frequency with which pigs were singled out as the culprits of some social harm. Because a pig was often afforded a trial where evidence was presented, for example, in support of charges that the pig ate and murdered an infant, some have suggested animals were afforded greater legal status in the 1500s than they are today. Recognizing animals as legal persons warranting attention and punishment in our justice system might be regarded as the high-water mark for animal status in the law. But such reasoning is too simplistic. In fact, the punishment of animals for harming humans is best understood as a "primal" instinct designed to "atone for the taking of life in accordance with certain crude conceptions of retribution."[24] Of course, it made no sense to believe that either human life or that of a deity were honored by punishing an animal. All that was achieved was animal suffering (perhaps with the satiating effect of vengeance). Far from redeeming society, these trials are probably best described as "ritualistic animal abuse."[25] This book asks whether the human instinct in favor of punishing, and punishing severely, animal abusers is any less primordial, or any more capable of improving the

[22] K. M. Morin, *Wildspace: The Cage, The Supermax, and The Zoo, in* Critical Animal Geographies: Politics, Intersections, and Hierarchies in a Multispecies World 73, 76–77 (Rosemary-Claire Collard & Kathryn Gillespie eds., 2015).

[23] E.P. Evans, The Criminal Prosecution and Capital Punishment of Animals (1906).

[24] Evans at 190.

[25] Katie Sykes, *Human Drama, Animal Trials: What the Medieval Animal Trials Can Teach Us About Justice for Animals,* 17 Animal L. 273, 292 (2011).

status of animals in the law. Our desire for atonement or revenge is palpable, but burning a pig at the stake is unlikely to have made society safer in the 1500s, and increasing prosecutions for animal abuse is unlikely to ensure that either animals or humans are safer today. As E. P. Evans wrote in 1906, the system of punishing animals was "the product of a social state in which dense ignorance was governed by brute force."[26] It is unlikely that the modern obsession with punishing animal abusers enjoys a refinement much beyond "brute force."

The problem of mass incarceration and over-criminalization is a vexing one that calls to mind a quote from Thomas Jefferson: "We have the wolf by the ear, and we can neither hold him, nor safely let him go. Justice is in one scale, and self-preservation in the other."[27] When referencing the wolf's ear, Jefferson was not talking about incarceration, but rather slavery and the fear that abolishing the institution would bring great violence against white slaveholders. In reality, the emancipation of the slaves did not lead to a "wave of violence by blacks against their former masters."[28] Instead, the violence seemed to run in the opposite direction.[29] This book makes the case that animal protection advocates should loosen their grip on their own metaphorical wolf's ear – criminal punishment – and focus instead on other means of protecting humans and animals. Meaningful social change requires integrity, or "actions that are consistent with beliefs."[30] The social project of un-caging and protecting animals is discordant and sits uncomfortably with the pursuit of more incarceration. More cages do not beget more empathy or less systemic violence. It is time to look Beyond the Cage, and to engage efforts to combat all oppression and inequity. The movement needs to scrutinize its tough-on tough-on-crime mentality, because, as noted by Audre Lourde, "there is no such thing as a single issue struggle."

[26] EVANS at 41.
[27] WILLIAM STUNTZ, THE COLLAPSE OF AMERICAN CRIMINAL JUSTICE 41 (2011) (quoting Thomas Jefferson, Letter to John Holmes [Apr. 22, 1820]).
[28] *Id.* at 43.
[29] *Id.* (discussing homicide rates by whites against blacks during the post civil-war era).
[30] PATTRICE JONES, *Afterword* to SISTAH VEGAN: BLACK FEMALE VEGANS SPEAK ON FOOD, IDENTITY, HEALTH, AND SOCIETY 187, 191 (A. Breeze Harper ed., 2010).

Index

Abramovsky, Aviva, 147
abuse. *See animal abuse*
Acensio, Jose, 190
ACLU. *See American Civil Liberties Union*
adoption programs, 253
advocacy. *See animal advocacy*
affirmative abuse, of animals, 51
African Americans
  comparisons to animals, 162
  incarceration rates for, 41–42
  prosecution rates of, 171–172
Agan, Amanda, 130, 132–133
Ag-Gag laws, 15, 48
agricultural practices exemption, 98–110
  for animals used for food, 99
  AVMA on, 101
  for customary farming practices, 104
  dates of enactment of, 102
  felony cruelty laws and, 102–110
  states without, 104
ALDF. *See Animal Legal Defense Fund*
Alexander, Michelle, 40–41, 155, 187
alt-right, animal protection movement and,
    158–159, 164
American Bar Association, 144
American Civil Liberties Union (ACLU), 117, 280
American Society for the Prevention of Cruelty to
    Animals (ASPCA), 7, 54
  carceral animal law and, 53–54
American Veterinary Medical Association
    (AVMA), 101
animal abuse
  in childhood, 213
  decriminalization of, 8–9
  failures in prosecution of, 7–8
  mass shooters and, 255
  non-criminals and, 197
  public awareness of, 19

  serial killers and, 254, 255
  social science perspective on, 13
animal abuse registries, 126–135
  as deterrence strategy, 130–132
  establishment of, 126
  goals and purpose of, 127
  as legislative priority, 126
  mandatory registration for, 134
  non-public, 134
  PETA support for, 129–130
  racial profile imbalances in, 127
  recidivism rates and, 135
  sex offender registries as template for, 128–129
    as legislative necessity, 128
    recidivism rates in, 128–129
  state bills for, 127, 128
  status of animals in law through, 127
animal advocacy, 78–83, 273–283
  guardian ad litem context for, 81–82
  lack of resources for, 82–83
  lack of training for, 82–83
animal cruelty laws. *See also* carceral animal law;
    felony cruelty laws
  agricultural practices exemption, 98–110
    for animals used for food, 99
    AVMA on, 101
    for customary farming practices, 104
    dates of enactment of, 102
    felony cruelty laws and, 102–110
    states without, 104
  Animal Legal Defense Fund and, 86–87
  anti-cruelty laws, 55–62
  cockfighting under, 184
  in Colorado, 54, 71, 203–204, 256, 259–260
  as crime against nature, 58
  exemption laws, 108
  felony cruelty laws
    agricultural practices exemption and, 102–110

enactment of, 108–110
state passage of, 108
fox hunting under, 185
legislative costs of, 98–110
mandatory arrests under, 111–112
mandatory reporting under, 111–112
private prosecutions of, 138–144
prosecution under
  failures of, 7–8
  penalties as result of, 6
  transference of guilt as result of, 7
public popularity of, 261
race and, 166–192. *See also* Vick, Michael
  African Americans and, 168–169
  on factory farms, 188–191
  in Washington, DC, 166–169
sentencing reform under, 266–270
in South Dakota, 266
Animal Enterprise Terrorism Act, U.S. (2007), 280
animal law, 259
Animal Legal Defense Fund (ALDF), 14, 37, 57, 58–59, 75, 88
  animal cruelty and, 86–87
  funding of prosecutions by, 93–94
  Heiser and, 92, 118–119
  immigration issues and, 84–85
  private prosecutions funded by, 140–143
animal liberation, 5. *See also* animal protection movement; animal rights; criminal punishment
Animal Liberation (Singer), 31–32
animal protection movement. *See also* carceral animal law; criminal punishment
  ACLU in, 117, 280
  ALDF v. *Provimi Veal Corp.*, 20–21
  alt-right and, as short-term ally, 158–159, 164
  carceral approaches to, 6, 20. *See also* carceral animal law
    burnout and fatigue from, 21
  colorblindness in, 153–155, 275
  conflicting goals within, 3–5
  domestic violence analogy to, 111–115
  DxE, 278–279
  free speech restrictions and, 73–78
  goals of, 58–60
  history of, 19–22
  human rights as secondary in, 39, 156
    under Non-Humans First Declaration, 157
  LINK theory and, 199–205
    National Link Coalition, 199, 228
  motivated cognition as influence on, 4
  non-violent civil disobedience as strategy of, 18, 72
  in *Oregon* v. *Newcomb*, 46–48, 70–71

political paradox of, 1
public perception of, 3–4
  on criminal enforcement strategies, 8
  as single-issue movement, 151–152
racism in, 159–160
retribution angle of, 264–266
revenge angle of, 264–266
scope of, 6–7
sentencing injustices for, 2–3
U.S. v. *Stevens*, 74–78
on Vick dogfighting case, 175–183
  Heiser on, 180–181
  NAACP and, 181–182
  narrative-framing by, 176–177
  racist responses to, 181–182
  Tischler on, 180, 181–182
War on Drugs as model for, 115–126
Animal Rescue Team, 94
animal rights, 5
  carceral animal law as influence on, 260
  habeas corpus and, 152–153
  history of, 10
  as philosophy, 11
animal rights law. *See also* carceral animal law
  criminal punishment under, 12–18
    Ag-Gag laws, 15, 48
    criminal code provisions, 21
    deportation sentencing, 16
    financial costs of, 14
    immigration policy as influence on, 17
    institutional structures as impediment in, 17
  history of, 18–22
  NhRP and, 152–153
  race-based analogies in, 152–153
animal treatment programs, 253
Animal Welfare Act, U.S. (2007), 173
animal welfare movement, 4–5
  pet ownership and, 24
  scope of, 4
animal-assisted therapy, 247
animals
  in animal abuse registries, legal status of, 127
  intelligence of, 4
  moral status of, 4, 258
  used for food, 99–100
    cruelty toward, 99
    factory farms, 188–191, 251–252
anti-cruelty laws, 44–45
  expansion of, 56
  legislative history of, 54
  limitations of, 46
  reforms of, 55–62
  state support for, 58–59
Arendt, Hannah, 16

Arkow, Phil, 199, 219–220
Arluke, Arnold, 211, 222–226, 230
Ascione, Frank. R., 211, 217, 230
ASPCA. *See American Society for the Prevention of*
    Cruelty to Animals
Avirum, Hadar, 110
AVMA. *See American Veterinary Medical*
    Association

Balkin, Jack, 74
Bardot, Brigitte, 191
Baum, Dan, 117, 118
Beirne, Piers, 197, 232–233
Bekoff, Marc, 81
Bell, Derek, 249
Benavies, Arthur, 121, 122
Bennett, William, 118
Bergh, Henry, 54
Berman, Douglas, 266–267
bestiality. *See sexual abuse, of animals*
Bin Laden, Osama, 264
Black, Donald, 263–264, 267
Blackstone, William, 152
Boddie, Davon, 175
Bonilla-Silva, Eduardo, 4–5, 154
Briggs, Richard, 127
Brueck, Julia Feliz, 153–154, 157–158
Bundy, Ted, 254
Butler, Paul, 154, 165, 174–175, 192, 271

carceral animal law. *See also* reforms
    affirmative abuse under, 51
    animal cruelty provisions under, 53–54
    animal rights undermined by, 260
    anti-cruelty laws, 44–45
        expansion of, 56
        legislative history of, 54
        limitations of, 46
        reforms of, 55–62
        state support for, 58–59
    ASPCA and, 53–54
    civil death and, 31–32
    civil forfeiture laws and, 253
    under common law tradition, 31
    courthouse advocacy and, 49–53
    ethic of mutual avowal in, 165, 275
    expansion of criminal liability, 53–63
    incapacitation under, 270–272
        critique of, 271
        justifications of, 270–271
        lack of study on, 270
        legal issues with, 272
        Wattenberg's law and, 270
    incarceration under, 32–35

collateral consequences of, 30–35
    deportation after, 35
    employment restrictions as result of, 33–34
    family and community effects of, 35–39
    secondary prisonization after, 36–37
    social exclusion as result of, 34–35
    third-generation impacts of, 37
lack of alternatives to, 252–258
legal scope of, development of, 44–45
legislative development of, 53–55
LINK theory and, 193–194
    critiques of, 227–244
    incarceration under, arguments against,
        238–239
    recidivism rates and, 241–243
mens rea standards for, 57
neglect of animals under, 51–52
Oregon v. Newcomb, 46–48, 70–71
public relations campaigns for, 49–53
public support for, 44–49
racialized crimes, 183–186
racism and, 119, 153–155, 156–166, 183–192. *See*
    also Vick, Michael
    colorblindness policies, 153–155
    on factory farms, 188–191
    through unequal prosecution, 171–172
    unintended, 41
    through use of law enforcement, against per-
        sons of color, 169–171
sentencing under
    for children and minors, 61–63
    increases in, 53–63
    mandatory minimum, 44–45, 60–63
    reforms of, 266–270
Carlson, Tucker, 179, 181
Cassell, Paul, 60, 61
Cassuto, David, 75–77
Cecil the Lion, 163
Center for Constitutional Rights, 280–281
Chavez, Marco, 83–84
Cheeseboro, Anthony, 186–187
Chemerinsky, Erwin, 74, 77
Chen, Alan, 278
childhood
    animal abuse during, 213
    Children and Animals Assessment
        Instrument, 217
Children and Animals Assessment Instrument, 217
Chin, Gabriel Jack, 30–31, 41
Church of the Lukumi Babalu Aye v. *City of*
    Hialeah, 64–65, 175–176, 258
civil death, 31–32
civil forfeiture laws, 253
civil rights, mass incarceration and, 110–126

cockfighting, 184
Colb, Sherry, 7, 261
Colorado, animal cruelty laws in, 54, 71, 203–204, 256, 259–260
colorblindness, in animal protection movement, 153–155, 275
common law traditions
  carceral animal law under, 31
  criminal punishment under, 31
compassion, 246
Constitution, U.S., interpretation of
  for carceral animal law reform, 63–78
    defense options under, limitations of, 68–73
    emergency exceptions, 69–70
    under Fourth Amendment, 68–69
    through free speech restrictions, 73–78
    freedom against political targeting in, 64–68
    search and seizure rights, 68
  private prosecutions and, 144–150
Conyers, John, 27
criminal justice system
  animal cruelty prosecutions in, 258–264
  public morality influenced by, 22–24
  race and, 152–156
criminal punishment. *See also* mass incarceration
  under animal rights law, 12–18
    Ag-Gag laws, 15, 48
    criminal code provisions, 21
    deportation, 16
    financial costs of, 14
    immigration policy as influence on, 17
    institutional structures as impediment in, 17
  under common law traditions, 31
  conservative ideology as influence on, 23
  convictions as result of, 30–39
    collateral consequences of, 30–35
    deportation after, 35
    employment restrictions as result of, 33–34
    family and community effects of, 35–39
    secondary prisonization after, 36–37
    social exclusion as result of, 34–35
    third-generation impacts of, 37
  feminist theory on, 23
  historical legacy in U.S., 25–26
  human prisoners compared to animals in, 13
  as human rights issues, 26
    dehumanization as result of, 26
  racism in, 12
  stacking of additional charges and, 57–58
criminals. *See also* non-criminals
  violence among, predictions of, 213
cruelty laws. *See* animal cruelty laws; felony cruelty laws
crush videos, 74–75

Cruz, Nikolaz, 254–255, 256–258
Cummings, Scott, 278
customary farming practices, 104

Dahmer, Jeffrey, 254
Darley, John, 22, 271–272
De Waal, Frans, 81
deportation, as criminal punishment, 16
  under carceral animal law, 35
  carceral animal law reform and, 84
Deviance Generalization Hypothesis, 233, 234–235
Dilulio, John, 270
Direct Action Everywhere (DxE), 278–279
dogfighting. *See also* Vick, Michael
  as felony, 178
  as status symbol, 177–178
domestic violence
  animal protection movement and, 111–115
  criminal reforms for, 111
  mandatory arrests for, 111–115
    in Minneapolis Study, 114
    as violence prevention measure, 113, 115
  police policies for, 111
Donahue, Laura, 201
Doob, Anthony, 242–243
Downes, David, 243–244
"driving while black," 174
drug arrests, during War on Drugs, 119–120
drug prosecution and sentencing. *See War on Drugs*
drug use rates, during War on Drugs, 122–123
DxE. *See Direct Action Everywhere*

emergency exceptions, 69–70
employment restrictions, after criminal convictions, 33–34
Encompass, 159
Equal Justice Initiative, 61
Esner, Alan, 30
ethic of mutual avowal, 165, 275
ethics, for private prosecutions, 144–150
Every Twelve Seconds (Pachirat), 101–102
Ewing, Charles, 131, 133
exemptions laws, 108

factory farms, 188–191
  criminalization of, 251–252
Faeron, Joseph, 160
Fairfax, Roger, 137, 150
false positive issues, in LINK theory, 197, 223
families, after criminal convictions, 35–39
farming practices. *See customary farming practices*
felony cruelty laws
  agricultural practices exemption and, 102–110

felony cruelty laws (cont.)
    enactment of, 108–110
    state passage of, 108
Felthous, Alan
    Kellert and, 212–217
        1985 study, 212–215
        1987 study, 215–217
    with Yudowitz, 210–212
feminist theory, on criminal punishment, 23
Fetiman, Linda, 124
First Amendment. *See free speech restrictions*
Flynn, Clifton, 233
Forret, Jeff, 184
The Four Stages of Cruelty (Hogarth), 206, 235
fox hunting, 185
framing, animal protection narratives, 80, 252,
    262–263, 281
    intersectional, 159–160
    for Vick dogfighting case, 176–177
Francione, Gary, 46, 54, 65, 202
free speech restrictions
    unprotected speech, 73–78
    in *U.S. v. Stevens*, 74–78
Freeman, Andrea, 276
Freud, Sigmund, 206
Friedrich, Bruce, 185
funding, of private prosecutions, 139–144
    by Animal Legal Defense Fund, 140–143
    Memorandum of Understanding for, 141–142
    by private animal protection groups, 141–142
    by Safer Dallas Better Dallas, 140

Gaarder, Emily, 151–152, 153, 156, 169–170
Garland, David, 27
Garza, Jesus, 190
gateway drug theory, 118
Gay, Roxane, 163
Goodmark, Leigh, 112
graduation thesis, 205. *See also* LINK theory
Gray, James P., 125–126
Green, Bruce, 136, 146–147
Gruber, Aya, 6, 23, 262–263, 269
Gruen, Lori, 45–46
guardian ad litem context, 81–82

habeas corpus, 48–49
    in animal rights, 152–153
Harper, A. Breeze, 13, 40, 155, 162, 165, 181, 187–188
    on Bardot, 191
Harris, Angela, 40, 154, 161, 162
Harris-Perry, Melissa, 176
Hawaii Humane Society, 203
Hawkins, Gordon, 270
Heide, Kathleen, 217–219

Heiser, Scott, 57, 92, 115, 118–119, 126
    on Vick case, 180–181
Hensley, Christopher, 220–222
Herzog, Hal, 197
Hogarth, William, 206, 235
Holland, Jeffrey, 56–57
Holmes, Oliver Wendell, Jr., 57, 273
Holzer, Mark, 18
Homicidal Threats (Macdonald), 207
HSUS. *See Humane Society of the United States*
Huber, Nicole, 157
human rights
    in animal protection movement
        human rights as secondary in, 39, 156
        under Non-Humans First Declaration, 157
    criminal punishment and, 26
    dehumanization as result of, 26
Humane Society of the United States (HSUS), 8,
    65–66, 86–87, 279
    Animal Rescue Team and, 94
    carceral animal law reform and, 94–95
    police assistance with, 94–95

immigration policy, 17
    Animal Legal Defense Fund and, 84–85
    carceral animal law reform and, 83–85
    deportation issues, 84
incapacitation, under carceral animal law, 270–272
    critique of, 271
    justifications of, 270–271
    lack of study on, 270
    legal issues with, 272
    Wattenberg's law and, 270
incarceration. *See also* mass incarceration
    for African Americans, rates for, 41–42
    under carceral animal law, 32–35
        collateral consequences of, 30–35
        deportation after, 35
        employment restrictions as result of, 33–34
        family and community effects of, 35–39
        secondary prisonization after, 36–37
        social exclusion as result of, 34–35
        third-generation impacts of, 37
    of factory farm workers, 251–252
    rehabilitation programs after, 28–29
        RSVP, 28–29
    Vick after, public redemption of, 179–183
intelligence, of animals, 4
Interstate and Foreign Travel of Transportation in
    Aid of Racketeering Enterprises Act
    (U.S.), 173

Jamieson, Dale, 282
Jay Z, 38

Jefferson, Thomas, 283
Jim Crow, racism and, 154
Johnson, Travers, 62
Johnson, Tremayne, 62
Jones, Pattrice, 162–163, 194

Kamins, Jake, 94, 141, 142–143
Kaneshiro, Keith, 203
Kangas, Cathy, 200–201
Kant, Immanuel, 206
Kellert, Stephen, 212–217
    Felthous 1985 study with, 212–215
    Felthous 1987 study with, 215–217
Kelley, Devin, 195, 254–255
Kemerrer, Lisa, 163–164
Kennedy, Randall, 42, 155
Kerlikowske, Gil, 120
Kim, Claire Jean, 160, 161, 165, 183, 275
    ethic of mutual avowal, 165, 275
King, Martin Luther, Jr., 21, 88, 165, 261–262, 278
Kuennen, Tammy, 23
Kunstler, William, 279

LaBahn, David, 86
Last Chance for Animals, 62
Leipold, Andrew, 122
Leong, Nancy, 155
Levin, Jack, 211, 222–226, 230
LGBT rights, 277
LINK theory, animal abuse and human violence in, 193
    abusers in, 231
    in animal protection movement, 199–205
        National Link Coalition, 199, 228
    carceral animal law and, as justification for, 193–194
    critiques of, 227–244
    incarceration under, arguments against, 238–239
    recidivism rates and, 241–243
    controls in, 231
    critiques of, 225–226, 227–236, 248–250
    Deviance Generalization Hypothesis and, 233, 234–235
    false positive issues in, 197, 223
    mass shooters in, 255
    among non-criminals, 197
    origins of, 205–208
    PETA on, 201
    predictions of violence in, 197, 200, 209
        among criminals, 213
        through frequency of childhood animal cruelty, 213
        legal scholarship on, 201–204
    logical fallacy in, 219
    among non-criminals, 213
    serial killers in, 254, 255
    social science research on, 205–227
        Children and Animals Assessment Instrument in, 217
        in empirical studies, 208–227, 243. *See also specific studies*
        Macdonald Triad in, 206–208
        Mead studies in, 208
    theoretical approach to, 193–194, 196
    treatment strategies as result of, 244–248, 256–257
        through animal-assisted therapy, 247
        compassion in, 246
        through interventions, 246
        range of, 246–247
        research applications for, 245
Linzey, Andrew, 244–245
Lippe, Adam, 51
Livingston, Margit, 201, 239
Locke, John, 206
Lockwood, Randall, 13, 62, 195, 199
Lourde, Audre, 11, 283
Loury, Glen, 192
Lovvorn, Jon, 101
Lowndes, Hashim, 33
Loyd-Paige, Michelle R., 154–155
Luke, Carter, 211, 230

Macdonald, John, 206–208
Macdonald Triad, 206–208
MacKinnon, Catherine, 80, 81
Madfis, Eric, 225–226
magnetic resonance imaging (MRI), 265
mandatory arrests
    under animal cruelty laws, 111–112
    for domestic violence, 111–115
        in Minneapolis Study, 114
        as violence prevention measure, 113, 115
mandatory reporting, under animal cruelty laws, 111–112
Margalli, Jiulo, 146–147
marijuana, legalization of, 125–126
mass incarceration, in U.S., 27–30
    civil rights and, 110–126
    community-level damage from, 110
    costs of, 29–30
    demographics of, 27
    etymology of term, 27
    global incarceration rates, comparisons to, 27
    incarceration rates, increases in, 3, 29, 41
    overcrowding issues, 30
    race and, 39–43

mass incarceration, in U.S. (cont.)
    African American incarceration rates, 41–42
    rehabilitation programs and, declines in, 28–29
    RSVP, 28–29
    social change through, 110–111
    from War on Drugs, 117
mass shooters, animal abuse and, 255
McLaughlin, Sheila, 203
Mead, Margaret, 208
Meek Mill, 38
Mendell, Steve, 190
mens rea standards, for carceral animal law, 57
Mercy for Animals, 15, 16, 251
Merz-Perez, Linda, 217–219
Minneapolis Study, 114
moral status, of animals, 4, 258
MRI. *See magnetic resonance imaging*
Myers, Steve, 197

NAACP. *See National Association for the*
    Advancement of Colored People
Nagin, Daniel, 123–124
Nast, Heidi, 177–178, 183
National Association for the Advancement of
    Colored People (NAACP), 117
    animal protection movement and, 181–182
National District Attorney Association, 237
National Institute of Justice, 241
National Link Coalition, 199, 228
National Research Council, 240, 242
Navarro, Daniel Ugarte, 190
neglect, of animals, 51–52
Nejaime, Doug, 278
The New Jim Crow (Alexander), 40–41, 155, 187
NhRP. *See Non-Human Rights Project*
non-criminals, animal abuse and, 197
    predictions of violence for, 213
Non-Human Rights Project (NhRP), 152–153, 260
Non-Humans First Declaration, 157
non-public animal abuse registries, 134
non-violent civil disobedience, 18, 72
Novisky, Meghan, 114

Ofer, Udi, 90
Office of National Drug Control Policy, U.S.
    (ONDCP), 122–123
Oleske, James, 64–65
ONDCP. *See Office of National Drug Control*
    Policy
Oregon v. Newcomb, 46–48, 70–71
overcrowding, in prisons, 30

Pacelle, Wayne, 8
Pachirat, Timothy, 15, 35, 101–102, 189

Panzram, Carl, 254
Patterson-Kane, Emily, 226–227, 229–230, 234,
    254, 255
People for the Ethical Treatment of Animals
    (PETA), 14, 18
    animal abuse registries supported by, 129–130
    on LINK theory, 201
    racist campaigns of, 160–161
        African Americans compared to animals
        in, 162
People v. Eubanks, 144–145
People v. Garcia, 195
Peralta, Robert, 114
pet ownership, 24
PETA. *See People for the Ethical Treatment of*
    Animals
Pfaff, John, 120, 136
Phillips, Allie, 140, 203–204, 248–249, 250
Phillips, Scott, 124–125
Pinel, Phillipe, 206
Pinker, Steven, 277
Piper, Heather, 193, 197, 219–220, 225, 232–233, 246
police
    carceral animal law reform and, 85–96
        with HSUS, 94–95
        investigation assistance and, 94–96
        privately-funded police in, 95–96
    domestic violence policies, 111
Portugal, drug policy in, 124
Prescott, J. J., 132
prisoner's dilemma, 129
Pritikin, Martin H., 271
private animal protection groups, 141–142
private prosecutions, 135–150
    of animal cruelty, 138–144
        delegations of prosecutorial authority, 138
    constitutional issues with, 144–150
    disqualification of cases, 147
    ethical issues with, 144–150
    funding of, 139–144
        by Animal Legal Defense Fund, 140–143
        Memorandum of Understanding for, 141–142
        by private animal protection groups, 141–142
        by Safer Dallas Better Dallas, 140
    historical context of, 137
        colonial justice system and, 137
    People v. Eubanks, 144–145
    State v. Culbreath, 145–146
    in U.S., 93
    victim-funded, 139
privately-funded police, 95–96
Probus, Joi Maria, 13
professional athletes, rates of violence among, 179
progression thesis, 205. *See also* LINK theory

Project Hope, 242
prosecutors
  animal cruelty laws and
    penalties under, 6
    prosecution failures, 7–8
    transference of guilt as result of prosecution, 7
  carceral animal law reform and, 85–96
    external influences on, 85–92
    lobbying of, 90–92
    outreach for, 85–92
    payments to, 93–94
    targeted recognition of, 89–91
    training for, 86–87
  discretion of, 136
  neutrality of, 135–136
  Vick dogfighting case and, 173–174
public morality, criminal law as influence on,
    22–24
punishment-lust, 265–266

Race, Crime, and the Law (Kennedy), 42
race and racism
  animal cruelty laws and, 166–192
    African Americans under, 168–169
    on factory farms, 188–191
    in Washington, DC, 166–169
  in animal protection movement, 159–160
  under carceral animal law, 119, 153–155, 156–166,
    183–192. *See also* Vick, Michael
    colorblindness policies, 153–155
    on factory farms, 188–191
    through unequal prosecution, 171–172
    unintended racism in, 41
    through use of law enforcement, against per-
      sons of color, 169–171
  in criminal punishment, 12
  Jim Crow, 154
  mass incarceration in United States and, 39–43
    of African Americans, 41–42
  in Non-Humans First Declaration, 157
  in PETA campaigns, 160–161
  in Vick dogfighting case, 181–182
racialized crimes, 183–186
Racism without Racists (Bonilla-Silva), 154
Rattling the Cage (Wise), 10–11
recidivism rates
  animal abuse registries and, 135
  LINK theory and, 241–243
  sex offender registries and, 128–129
reforms, in carceral animal law, 63–96
  animal advocates in, 78–83
    guardian ad litem context for, 81–82
    lack of resources for, 82–83
    lack of training for, 82–83

for anti-cruelty laws, 55–62
  *Church of the Lukumi Babalu Aye v. City of
    Hialeah*, 64–65, 175–176
  under federal constitution, interpretation lim-
    itations of, 63–78
    defense options under, limitations of, 68–73
    emergency exceptions, 69–70
    under Fourth Amendment, 68–69
    through free speech restrictions, 73–78
    freedom against political targeting, 64–68
    search and seizure rights, 68
  immigration enforcement, 83–85
    deportation issues, 84
  police and, 85–96
    with HSUS, 94–95
    investigations by, assistance in, 94–96
    privately-funded, 95–96
  prosecutors and, 85–96
    external influences on, 85–92
    lobbying of, 90–92
    outreach for, 85–92
    payments to, 93–94
    targeted recognition of, 89–91
    training for, 86–87
  for sexual abuse of animals, 83
  U.S. v. Reynolds, 65
rehabilitation programs, after incarceration, 28–29
  RSVP, 28–29
Reitz, Kevin, 31, 38
Resolve to Stop the Violence Project (RSVP),
    28–29
retribution, animal protection movement and,
    264–266
revenge
  animal protection movement and, 264–266
  as dopamine response, 265
  gender responses to, 265–266
  MRI scans and, 265
  as punishment-lust, 265–266
Richardson, Jamie, 124–125
Ristroph, Alice, 38–39, 268
Robinson, Andre, 52–53, 186–187
Robinson, Matthew, 122
Robinson, Paul, 22, 271–272
Rockoff, John, 132
Rojas Loayza, Javier Victor, 190
Rosengard, David, 79, 80
RSVP. *See Resolve to Stop the Violence Project*
Rubin, Jessica, 78–79
Runkle, Nathan, 100–101, 251
Ruttenberg, Miriam, 112

Safer Dallas Better Dallas, 140
Sanchez Herrera, Rafael, 190

Schaffner, Joan, 58, 61
Scherlen, Renee, 122
search and seizure rights, 68
secondary prisonization, 36–37
sentencing
    animal protection movement and, 2–3
    under carceral animal law
        for children and minors, 61–63
        increases in, 53–63
        mandatory minimum sentencing, 44–45, 60–63
        reforms in, 266–270
    deportation as result of, 16
    of Vick, Michael, 173–174
    during War on Drugs, 120
Sentencing Project, 117
serial killers, animal abuse history among, 254, 255
sex offender registries, animal abuse registries
        compared to, 128–129
    as legislative necessity, 128
    recidivism rates in, 128–129
sexual abuse, of animals, 83
Siebert, Charles, 62
Silverman, Ira J., 217–219
Simon, Jonathan, 22
Sinclair, Upton, 188
Singer, Peter, 31–32
Sistah Vegan (Harper), 13, 40, 155, 162
Slobogin, Christopher, 244
Smith, Kimberley K., 39, 43, 66, 175, 177, 275
social change, through mass incarceration, 110–111
social exclusion, after criminal convictions, 34–35
social rejection, 264
social science research, LINK theory and, 205–227
    Children and Animals Assessment Instrument in, 217
    in empirical studies, 208–227, 243. *See also specific studies*
    Macdonald Triad in, 206–208
    Mead studies in, 208
South Dakota, animal cruelty laws in, 266
State v. Culbreath, 145–146
Stephens, James Fitzjames, 275
Stone, Geoffrey, 74
Stuntz, William, 26, 58, 269
Sunstein, Cass, 251

Tallichet, Suzanne E., 220–222
Tarankow, Paul, 166–169
Taub, Edward, 18–19
Tedisco, James, 249
Thompson, John, 199
Three-Strikes Law, 240–241

Tischler, Joyce, 19, 21, 25, 63, 72
    on Vick case, 180, 181–182
tough on crime policies, 1–2
Travel Act, U.S. (1952), 173
Trump, Donald, 151, 164

United States (US). *See also* mass incarceration; War on Drugs
    Animal Enterprise Terrorism Act, 280
    Animal Welfare Act, 173
    ASPCA, 7
    HSUS, 8, 65–66, 86–87, 279
        Animal Rescue Team and, 94
        carceral animal law reform and, 94–95
        police assistance with, 94–95
    Interstate and Foreign Travel of Transportation in Aid of Racketeering Enterprises Act, 173
    private prosecutions in, 93
    unprotected speech, 75
Urban, Diana, 79
U.S. v. Reynolds, 65
U.S. v. Stevens, 74–78

veganism, 160
Veganism in an Oppressive World (Brueck), 153–154
Vick, Michael, dogfighting case of, 172–183
    animal protection movement's response to, 175–183
        Heiser, Scott, on, 180–181
        NAACP and, 181–182
        narrative-framing by, 176–177
        racism in, 181–182
        Tischler on, 180, 181–182
    Animal Welfare Act and, 173
    charges against, 173
    Interstate and Foreign Travel of Transportation in Aid of Racketeering Enterprises Act, 173
    investigation of, 174–175
    media response to, 175–176
    moral panic around, 176
    post-incarceration redemption of, 179–183
    prosecution of, 173–174
    sentencing of, 173–174
violence, human. *See also* domestic violence; LINK theory
    predictions of, 197, 200, 209
        among criminals, 213
        through frequency of childhood animal cruelty, 213
        legal scholarship on, 201–204
        logical fallacy in, 219
        among non-criminals, 213
        among professional athletes, 179

violence graduation thesis, 205. *See also* LINK theory

War on Drugs
animal protection movement influenced by, 115–126
drug arrests as result of, 119–120
drug use rates, 122–123
escalation of, 119
failure of, 124–126
gateway drug theory in, 118
legalization of marijuana and, 125–126
mass incarceration and, 117
ONDCP and, 122–123
Portuguese drug policy compared to, 124
sentencing during, 120
Washington Humane Society, 166–167

Wattenberg's law, 270
Webster, Cheryl, 242–243
Weinstein, Harvey, 135
welfare movements. *See animal welfare movement*
Wells, Steve, 195
Wise, Steven, 10–11, 152, 153
Wolf, Stacy, 201, 228–229
Wolfson, David, 98–99
women, revenge and, 265–266

Yudowitz, Bernard, 210–212

Zacharias, Fred, 136
Zimbardo, Philip, 189
Zimring, Franklin, 270

CPSIA information can be obtained
at www.ICGtesting.com
Printed in the USA
LVHW041749180423
744640LV00007B/328